"A helpful synthesis of themes in Paul with one another and with Old Testam... .... Many of these insights will resonate with Protestant as well as Catholic exegetes, and Protestants such as myself will find these authors gracious, worthy, and willing conversation partners."

— CRAIG S. KEENER,
Asbury Theological Seminary

"The world of biblical studies and Pauline theology has been waiting a generation for this book. Covering a wide range of major issues, while engaging the wide spectrum of current perspectives, this is a major contribution to Pauline scholarship from three outstanding Catholic scholars—well worth the wait."

— SCOTT HAHN,
Franciscan University of Steubenville

"Pitre, Barber, and Kincaid persuasively argue that Paul was a new covenant Jew, an approach that proves to be a convincing way of describing the continuities between Paul and Judaism as well as the discontinuities that emerge out of Paul's explicit christological recasting of the Jewish worldview. In a deliciously ecumenical approach, their vision of Paul brings together various threads of Jewish apocalypticism, Paul's core conviction about Jesus, his account of the cross and justification, as well as new creation and communion. A genuinely fresh and insightful study of Paul that all serious students of the Bible will need to read."

— MICHAEL F. BIRD,
Ridley College

"This synthetic work is a goldmine for scholars and students alike. Drawing upon the full range of contemporary Pauline scholarship, the authors carefully and generously describe the positions that differ from their own, thereby enabling beginning students to get their bearings in the debates. At the same time, scholars will be enthralled by the nuanced, rigorous, and serene case they make for overcoming well-known polarities in Pauline studies. They present a Paul who joyfully proclaims the new covenant in Christ Jesus, with implications for sonship, faith, baptism, grace, atonement, justification, Israel, the Eucharist, and much more. Not only for biblical scholars, but also for theologians, this spectacular scholarly study is a 'must read.'"

— MATTHEW LEVERING,
Mundelein Seminary

"As the scholarly guild continues to churn out monographs on St. Paul and his writings, it is rare to read one that proposes a truly fresh perspective. Brant Pitre, Michael Barber, and John Kincaid, however, have managed to write just such a book. Their proposal that Paul is best described as a new covenant Jew (because he himself does so!) allows them to capture both points of continuity with prior Jewish traditions as well as the *novum* of Paul's gospel concerning the crucified-and-risen Jesus. Their Catholic 'both-and' approach, done with sound exegetical argumentation and wide consultation with the best of contemporary scholarship, enables them to set forth the coherence of Paul's theological vision. I highly recommend this volume and will use it in my teaching."

— THOMAS D. STEGMAN, SJ,
Boston College School of Theology and Ministry

"While a lot is published on Paul, much of it is regurgitated and mundane, a mere reshuffling of the same worn furniture—and my eyes glaze. Others, however, try so hard to push the boat out and become polemical that my eyes roll. Not many manage to negotiate the waters between Scylla and Charybdis, but you are holding one that does! It's a riveting read that presents answers to conundrums that are jarring in their economy, elegance, and power. Presented with a contagious verve and enthusiasm, these three brilliant young scholars weave cutting-edge and up-to-date scholarship into a highly readable tapestry. No stodgy, tired, overly pompous detail. No academic posturing. You are presented with fresh ideas, new proposals, and it's all delivered at just the right pace. It's a truly enjoyable read that deserves much critical meditation. So in short: the time you give to reading this book will be time very well spent. Even where questions remain, I know that I've learned much from them; I've glimpsed things that were previously hidden from me. In this presentation of Paul as a 'new covenant' Jew, the Apostle might just burst out of his letters afresh. This is Paul the pop-up book!"

— CHRIS TILLING, St. Mellitus College

Paul, a New Covenant Jew

Rethinking Pauline Theology

Brant Pitre, Michael P. Barber, and John A. Kincaid

WILLIAM B. EERDMANS PUBLISHING COMPANY
GRAND RAPIDS, MICHIGAN

Wm. B. Eerdmans Publishing Co.
4035 Park East Court SE, Grand Rapids, Michigan 49546
www.eerdmans.com

25 24 23 22 21 20 19   1 2 3 4 5 6 7

ISBN 978-0-8028-7376-7

Library of Congress Cataloging-in-Publication Data

A catalog record for this book is available from the Library of Congress.

To Elizabeth, Kimberly, and Kristen,
who continually teach us what the apostle Paul meant when he said,
"Love is patient; love is kind. . . . Love never ends" (1 Cor 13:4, 8)

CONTENTS

Foreword *by Michael J. Gorman*   ix

Acknowledgments   xiii

Abbreviations   xv

Introduction   1

1. What Kind of Jew Was Paul?   11

     A Former Jew   13

     An Eschatological Jew   20

     A Torah-Observant Jew   30

     A New Covenant Jew   38

     *In Summary: A New Covenant Approach
to Reading Paul within Judaism*   62

2. Paul and Apocalyptic   64

     This World and the New Creation   67

     The Law Ordained through Angels   73

     The Jerusalem Above   82

     The Hidden Messiah   88

     In Summary: Paul and the Apocalyptic New Covenant   93

3. Pauline Christology   95

     The Messiah Descended from David   96

     Equality with God   102

One God and One Lord   108

In Summary: Jesus Christ as the Divine Son   126

4. The Cross and Atonement   129

    Christ Gave Himself for Our Sins   131

    A Sacrifice of Atonement   140

    The Righteousness of God Revealed   155

    *In Summary: The Cross as Apocalyptic Revelation
and New Covenant Sacrifice*   160

5. New Covenant Justification through Divine Sonship   162

    The Ministry of Righteousness   164

    Conformed to the Image of His Son   186

    You Were Washed, You Were Justified   201

    In Summary: The Righteousness of Divine Sonship   207

6. The Lord's Supper and the New Creation   211

    A Resurrection Like His   212

    Participation in the Body and Blood of Christ   222

    Spiritual Food and Spiritual Drink   241

    *In Summary: Cosmic Redemption
and the Table of the Lord's Body*   247

Conclusion: Paul's Gospel of Divine Sonship   251

Bibliography   255

Index of Authors   283

Index of Subjects   289

Index of Scripture and Other Ancient Texts   299

FOREWORD

The unique book you are about to read interprets Paul within at least three significant contexts: the Jewish world of the first century, the world of ecumenical and interfaith biblical scholarship, and the world of Roman Catholic faith and practice. In a similar yet different way, these are also my worlds, even though I am a Protestant rather than a Catholic. For more than a quarter century, I have taught the New Testament, and especially the apostle Paul, at the oldest Catholic seminary in the United States and the only one in the world (as far as we know) that has an ecumenical graduate theological school within the institution: St. Mary's Ecumenical Institute. Because the authors' worlds and mine overlap, I am especially happy to introduce and commend this volume.

Each of these three worlds is important to the book's three authors: Brant Pitre, Michael Barber, and John Kincaid. In a way, however, it may be their shared Catholic faith that leads them so fully into the other two worlds. Indeed, what stands out most about this book is not so much its particular Catholic perspectives on Pauline theology—though they are present—but rather its deep immersion in the other two worlds. Allow me to explain.

For Pitre, Barber, and Kincaid, Paul is simply incomprehensible without reference to the scriptures of Israel and Second Temple Judaism. That is why the book constantly discusses Jewish thought and praxis, citing scriptural and other texts, and showing us both where Paul resonates with certain ideas and practices and where he goes his own way in light of Jesus the Messiah and Lord. In particular, Pitre, Barber, and Kincaid propose—rightly, in my view—that Paul is a "new covenant Jew." Still more specifically, they argue that Paul proclaims the "*apocalyptic* new covenant": something that is earth-shattering new while simultaneously fulfilling ancient Jewish hopes and divine promises. Again, I think this thesis is precisely correct.

This approach to Paul situates the authors solidly within the field of Pauline studies, in which everyone agrees that Paul is a Second Temple Jew and yet there is debate about what kind of Jew he was. Pitre, Barber, and Kincaid have been heavily influenced by certain scholars who have also emphasized some of the key dimensions of Paul that they stress. These scholarly siblings include, of course, some fellow Roman Catholic scholars such as Frank Matera, Joseph Fitzmyer, Scott Hahn, and Thomas Stegman. Yet the most frequently cited scholars in the book are not Catholic: E. P. Sanders, N. T. Wright, James Dunn, Richard Hays, and the present writer.

Both of these contexts for interpreting Paul, I suggest, are part of what it means for this book to offer Catholic perspectives on Pauline theology. The authors engage in careful historical study of ancient texts and times, following the precepts of all modern Catholic documents on biblical interpretation. They also often take a "both-and" approach to disputed historical and exegetical matters (such as covenant vs. apocalyptic), which is part of the ethos of a Catholic theological method. And in drawing so heavily on academic perspectives from outside the realm of Roman Catholic scholarship, they manifest a truly catholic (lowercase "c"), or universal, approach to the pursuit of knowledge.

To be sure, this book contains specific emphases one would expect from faithful Catholic interpreters of Paul. For instance, the authors find in Paul a "high" Christology. Moreover, they argue that the Lord's Supper/Eucharist, as realistic participation in Christ's sacrifice, is absolutely central to Paul the new covenant Jew. The former claim, however, is hardly unique to Catholic interpreters, while the latter is a more distinctive contribution of Catholic scholarship that the rest of us would do well to heed. It is in the Supper, they contend, that individual and corporate participation in Christ—which is so important to many interpreters of Paul today—reaches its fullest expression prior to eschatological glory.

This book is not, however, a work of Catholic apologetics, and Catholic readers will find themselves both enlightened and, occasionally, challenged. It is significant—and quite Catholic—that the authors insist on the priority of grace and on the work of the Spirit in Pauline theology, but these are themes that may surprise some readers who have particular expectations of Catholic biblical interpreters. Some readers of this book will be challenged by other themes, including the authors' rich, nuanced interpretation of justification in terms of "cardiac righteousness" that is both juridical and ethical. Yet the authors' understanding of justification as participatory and transformative can also be found among contemporary Protestant scholars, not to mention Orthodox.

There are of course aspects of this book, as with any book, with which readers (Protestant, Catholic, or other) will disagree. But this work by Brant Pitre, Michael Barber, and John Kincaid is an important study of themes in Pauline theology. It is in *certain* ways Catholic, in *many* ways catholic, and in *all* ways stimulating.

MICHAEL J. GORMAN
*Raymond E. Brown Professor of Biblical
Studies and Theology
St. Mary's Seminary & University
Baltimore, Maryland*

ACKNOWLEDGMENTS

The authors would like to extend their gratitude to those who helped make this book possible. In particular, we would like to thank Michael Thomson at Eerdmans for his invaluable support of this project and for providing us with key advice as we worked on it. We are also extremely grateful to scholars and colleagues who generously read early drafts of the manuscript and offered important feedback—specifically Ben Blackwell, Craig Keener, Chris Tilling, Gregory Tatum, OP, Pablo Gadenz, Isaac Morales, OP, Thomas Stegman, SJ, James Prothro, Matthew Levering, and Jeff Morrow. In addition, we thank the following individuals with whom we have had important conversations that shaped the argument of this book in decisive ways, including A. J. Levine, Matthew Bates, Scott Hahn, Mark Reasoner, Nathan Eubank, Greg Vall, Wendy Cotter, CSJ, Michael Bird, Leroy Huizenga, Jason Staples, John Bergsma, Bill Wright, Michael Waldstein, Reinhard Hütter, Curtis Mitch, and David Burnett. Michael Barber would also like to express gratitude to his colleagues at the Augustine Institute who offered key suggestions, including Tim Gray, Douglas Bushman, Mark Gisczcak, Chris Blum, and especially John Sehorn, who provided extensive responses and editorial assistance that considerably strengthened the book. Special thanks are also due to copyeditor Jeremy Cunningham as well as Jenny Hoffman and all those at Eerdmans who offered important feedback and editorial work in preparing the manuscript for publication. Furthermore, we would like to thank those who participated in the Paul within Antiquity Continuing Seminar of the Catholic Biblical Association at the 2017 meeting in Washington, DC, which helped focus our presentation of the issues discussed in chapters 1 and 3. Of course, the weaknesses of this volume are the result of the authors' limitations and should not be attributed to those mentioned above.

Finally, and most importantly, we wish to express our profound gratitude to our wives, who made countless sacrifices that enabled us to complete this project. We dedicate this book to them.

ABBREVIATIONS

AB	Anchor Bible
ABD	*Anchor Bible Dictionary.* Edited by D. N. Freedman. 6 vols. New York, 1992
ABRL	Anchor Bible Reference Library
AcBib	Academia Biblica
AGJU	Arbeiten zur Geschichte des antiken Judentums und des Urchristentums
AnBib	Analecta Biblica
ANTC	Abingdon New Testament Commentary
AYB	Anchor Yale Bible
AYBRL	Anchor Yale Bible Reference Library
BDAG	Bauer, W., F. W. Danker, W. F. Arndt, and F. W. Gingrich. *Greek-English Lexicon of the New Testament and Other Early Christian Literature.* 3rd ed. Chicago, 1999
BECNT	Baker Exegetical Commentary on the New Testament
BJS	Brown Judaic Studies
BNTC	Black's New Testament Commentary
BTS	Biblical Tools and Studies
BZNW	Beihefte zur Zeitschrift für die neutestamentliche Wissenschaft
CBQ	*Catholic Biblical Quarterly*
CBQMS	Catholic Biblical Quarterly Manuscript Series
CCSS	Catholic Commentary on Sacred Scripture
COQG	Christian Origins and the Question of God
DSD	*Dead Sea Discoveries*
DSSSE	García Martínez, Florentino, and Eibert J. C. Tigchelaar. *The Dead Sea Scrolls Study Edition.* 2 vols. Leiden: Brill, 1997/1998
FAT	Forschungen zum Alten Testament

FRLANT	Forschungen zur Religion und Literatur des Alten und Neuen Testaments
HNT	Handbuch zum Neuen Testamen
HTR	*Harvard Theological Review*
ICC	International Critical Commentary
JBL	*Journal of Biblical Literature*
JPSTC	JPS Torah Commentary
JSHJ	*Journal for the Study of the Historical Jesus*
JSNT	*Journal for the Study of the New Testament*
JSNTSup	Journal for the Study of the New Testament Supplement Series
JSOTSup	Journal for the Study of the Old Testament Supplement Series
JSPL	*Journal for the Study of Paul and His Letters*
JSPSS	Journal for the Study of the Pseudepigrapha Supplement Series
JTS	*Journal of Theological Studies*
LCL	Loeb Classical Library
LNTS	Library of New Testament Studies
LSJ	Liddell, H. G., R. Scott, H. S. Jones. *A Greek-English Lexicon.* 9th ed. with revised supplement. Oxford, 1996
NCBC	New Cambridge Bible Commentary
NGS	New Gospel Studies
NICNT	New International Commentary on the New Testament
NICOT	New International Commentary on the Old Testament
NIGTC	New International Greek Text Commentary
NovTSup	Supplements to Novum Testamentum
NSBT	New Studies in Biblical Theology
NTL	New Testament Library
NTS	*New Testament Studies*
OTT	Old Testament Theology
PG	Patrologia Graeca [= Patrologiae Cursus Completus: Series Graeca]. Edited by J.-P. Migne. 161 vols. Paris, 1857–86
PNTC	Pillar New Testament Commentary
RevExp	*Review and Expositor*
SBL	Studies in Biblical Literature
SBLDS	Society of Biblical Literature Dissertation Series
SBT	Studies in Biblical Theology

SJLA	Studies in Judaism in Late Antiquity
SNTSMS	Society for New Testament Studies Monograph Series
SP	Sacra Pagina
TDNT	*Theological Dictionary of the New Testament.* Edited by G. Kittel and G. Friedrich. Translated by G. W. Bromiley. 10 vols. Grand Rapids, 1964–1976
TOTC	Tyndale Old Testament Commentary
TS	*Theological Studies*
VT	*Vetus Testamentum*
VTSup	Supplements to Vetus Testamentum
WBC	Word Biblical Commentary
WTJ	*Westminster Theological Journal*
WUNT	Wissenschaftliche Untersuchungen zum Neuen Testament
ZAW	*Zeitschrift für die alttestamentliche Wissenschaft*
ZECNT	Zondervan Exegetical Commentary on the New Testament
ZNW	*Zeitschrift für die neutestamentliche Wissenschaft und die Kunde der älteren Kirche*

INTRODUCTION

Paul is the patron-saint of thought in Christianity.

—Albert Schweitzer[1]

Just as the most frequently used writings of the Old Testament in the Church are the Psalms of David . . . so the most frequently used writings of the New Testament are the epistles of Paul. . . . In each of these writings is contained almost the whole teaching of theology.

—Thomas Aquinas[2]

The Apostle Paul

From the first days of the church, the figure of the apostle Paul has been something of an enigma. For one thing, Paul's writings have proven to be both highly revered and hotly contested. Remarkably, the New Testament itself bears witness to this dynamic. Second Peter, which contains what is arguably the earliest report concerning the way Paul's letters were received by the first Christ-believers, states:

> So also our beloved brother Paul wrote to you according to the wisdom given him, speaking of this as he does in all his letters. *There are some things in them hard to understand,* which the ignorant and unstable twist to their own destruction, *as they do the other scriptures.* (2 Pet 3:15–16)[3]

---

1. Albert Schweitzer, *The Mysticism of Paul the Apostle,* trans. William Montgomery (London: A. & C. Black, 1931), 377.

2. Thomas Aquinas, *Commentary on the Letter of Saint Paul to the Romans,* trans. Fabian R. Larcher, OP (Lander, WY: Aquinas Institute, 2012), 3.

3. Unless otherwise noted, biblical translations are taken from the NRSV.

Notice here that 2 Peter identifies Paul's epistles as works to be counted among the "scriptures [*graphas*]" (2 Pet 3:15–16), while nonetheless frankly admitting that they are "hard to understand [*dysnoēta*]" (2 Pet 3:15). Although many generations have passed since these words were penned, not much has changed. Almost two millennia later, Paul's writings are no less influential—and his letters have *remained* hard to understand.

Moreover, it was not just the letters of Paul that were difficult to grasp. Since ancient times, the man *himself* has been regarded as something of a paradox. The apocryphal *Acts of Paul and Thecla* (usually dated to the late second century AD) contains a delightful story about a man named Onesiphorus, who encounters the apostle Paul for the first time:

> And he saw Paul coming, a man small in size, bald-headed, bandy-legged, of noble mien, with eyebrows meeting, rather hook-nosed, full of grace. *Sometimes he seemed like a man and sometimes he had the face of an angel.* (*Acts of Paul and Thecla* 3:3)[4]

It is unclear whether the description of Paul's physical features is intended as flattering.[5] Either way, the historical value of the report is suspect.[6] What is remarkable is that it exists. There are no comparable early accounts of what Jesus or the other apostles looked like. The fact that it is included in the story suggests that Paul had a unique "profile" in early Christian imagination. Particularly striking is the way it indicates that Paul sometimes seemed to be human and other times looked like an angel. This suggests that ancient Christians recognized that the apostle was not always easy to "make out"—that is, those who encountered him were faced with apparent contradictions.

On the one hand, the prominence of Paul should come as no surprise. Other than Jesus, no figure has exerted more influence on Christian thought. Indeed, in the Catholic tradition, Paul's stature as a theologian

---

4. Translation from J. K. Elliot, *The Apocryphal New Testament: A Collection of Apocryphal Christian Literature in an English Translation* (Oxford: Oxford University Press, 1993), 364.

5. Some view the account as depicting Paul in terms consistent with a venerable figure, while others suggest it is meant to underscore that his widespread appeal was inexplicable apart from the brilliance of his message. See James D. G. Dunn, *Neither Jew nor Greek: A Contested Identity*, Christianity in the Making 3 (Grand Rapids: Eerdmans, 2015), 164n279.

6. See Jeremy Barrier, *The Acts of Paul and Thecla: A Critical Edition and Commentary*, WUNT 2/27 (Tübingen: Mohr Siebeck, 2009).

and apostle is so great that, following early Christian writers, medieval authors such as Thomas Aquinas simply refer to him—not Peter, despite his obvious significance—as *"the* apostle."[7] Aquinas himself composed verse-by-verse commentaries on all thirteen Pauline epistles.[8] Much more recently, it has been said—and not without some truth—that "all Christian theology is merely a footnote to Paul."[9]

On the other hand, the exegetical difficulties presented by Paul's letters have had enormous consequences in the history of Christian practice and belief. Since the time of the Reformation, some of the sharpest divisions between Christians have been drawn precisely along the lines of how one interprets the apostle.[10] At the same time, the last fifty years have witnessed two major developments in Pauline scholarship:

(1) The contemporary ecumenical movement, in which discussions between Pauline interpreters from a variety of traditions (e.g., Catholic, Protestant, Orthodox, and Jewish) have taken place with more and more frequency, often leading to greater clarity about where there is real common ground and where differences remain.[11]

(2) The rise of an interpretive movement that is broadly described as the "New Perspective on Paul." This approach emerged out of scholarly reflection on E. P. Sanders's landmark book *Paul and Palestinian Judaism*, published in 1977.[12]

---

7. See, e.g., Thomas Aquinas, *Summa Theologiae*, Prologue.

8. In addition to Thomas Aquinas's commentary on Romans (cited above), see also Thomas Aquinas, *Commentary on the Letters of Saint Paul to the Corinthians*, trans. Fabian R. Larcher, OP, Beth Mortensen, and Daniel Keating (Lander, WY: Aquinas Institute, 2012); Thomas Aquinas, *Commentary on the Letters of Saint Paul to the Galatians and Ephesians*, trans. Fabian R. Larcher, OP, and Matthew L. Lamb (Lander, WY: Aquinas Institute, 2012); and Thomas Aquinas, *Commentary on the Letters of Saint Paul to the Philippians, Colossians, Thessalonians, Timothy, Titus, and Philemon*, trans. Fabian R. Larcher, OP (Lander, WY: Aquinas Institute, 2012).

9. E.g., Robert Bruce Mullin, *A Short World History of Christianity*, rev. ed. (Louisville: Westminster John Knox, 2014), 19.

10. See, e.g., Stephen J. Chester, *Reading Paul with the Reformers: Reconciling Old and New Perspectives* (Grand Rapids: Eerdmans, 2017).

11. See, e.g., David E. Aune, ed., *Rereading Paul Together: Protestant and Catholic Perspectives on Justification* (Grand Rapids: Baker Academic, 2006).

12. E. P. Sanders, *Paul and Palestinian Judaism: A Comparison of Patterns of Religion* (Minneapolis: Fortress, 1977). The term itself originated with the work of James Dunn. See James D. G. Dunn, *The New Perspective on Paul*, rev. ed. (Grand Rapids: Eerdmans, 2008).

To be sure, there is much debate about what exactly "the New Perspective on Paul" entails and which scholars can be rightly characterized as belonging to this movement.[13] Nevertheless, one thing seems indisputable: although forty years have passed since its publication, Pauline scholarship today continues to wrestle with the questions Sanders raised about Paul's message and his relationship to Judaism. A quick glance at the titles in the veritable flood of recent studies published on Paul reveals that the field is still largely consumed with understanding Paul's relationship to Judaism and to the (real or perceived) claims of the New Perspective.[14] There can be no doubt that Sanders's seminal work has reshaped ecumenical discussions about Paul. This book seeks to make a contribution within this context.

A New Covenant Jew

As Sanders's work has underscored, the gospel Paul proclaims is unintelligible apart from the Jewish world into which he was born. Nevertheless, as scholarship since Sanders has become increasingly aware, Judaism in Paul's day was far from monolithic. Put simply, there was more than one way to be "Jewish." We know, for example, that there were various groups that disagreed on matters relating to Jewish beliefs and practices. The New Testament speaks of tensions between two groups in particular, the Pharisees and Sadducees (cf. Acts 23:6–10). Sources such as the Dead Sea Scrolls reveal that there were other sects beyond these as well. All of this raises an important question: *What kind of Jew was Paul?*

As its title indicates, this book will argue that the apostle is best understood as a *new covenant Jew*. This way of describing Paul is derived from the

13. The foreword to the fortieth anniversary edition of Sanders's watershed book rejects the idea that the study should be classified among the works of the "New Perspective." See Mark Chancey, foreword to *Paul and Palestinian Judaism: A Comparison of Patterns of Religion*, by E. P. Sanders, 40th anniversary ed. (Minneapolis: Fortress, 2017), xx–xxiii.

14. See, e.g., Chester, *Reading Paul with the Reformers*, 64–105; N. T. Wright, *Paul in Fresh Perspective* (Minneapolis: Fortress, 2009); Don Garlington, *Studies in the New Perspective on Paul: Essays and Reviews* (Eugene, OR: Wipf & Stock, 2008); Francis Watson, *Paul, Judaism, and the Gentiles: Beyond the New Perspective* (Grand Rapids: Eerdmans, 2007); Dunn, *The New Perspective on Paul*; Stephen Westerholm, *Perspectives Old and New: The "Lutheran" Paul and His Critics* (Grand Rapids: Eerdmans, 2004); Seyoon Kim, *Paul and the New Perspective: Rethinking the Origin of Paul's Gospel* (Grand Rapids: Eerdmans, 2001); Peter Stuhlmacher, *Revisiting Paul's Doctrine of Justification: A Challenge to the New Perspective* (Downers Grove, IL: IVP Academic, 2001).

language the apostle himself uses to explain his identity. In 2 Corinthians 3 he refers to himself as one of the "ministers of a new covenant" (2 Cor 3:6). As commentators have long recognized, in context the apostle is alluding to the book of Jeremiah. There, through the prophet, God announces the coming of a "new covenant," which the Lord declares will "not be like the covenant" that had been established previously with the people (Jer 31:31–32). Paul's thought, then, was indisputably shaped by Israel's scriptures.

At the same time, one must affirm that Paul's essential outlook was dramatically reconfigured by his experience of Christ. This must not be minimized or downplayed. Paul did not simply attempt to use Israel's scriptures to make sense out of the person and work of Jesus of Nazareth; for the apostle, the revelation of Jesus Christ also involved coming to a new understanding of the scriptures (cf. 2 Cor 3:14–16). God's promises of old had been fulfilled in Christ but in ways that could not have been anticipated (1 Cor 2:9). While the apostle insists that God's covenant with Israel cannot be revoked (Rom 11:29), he is nevertheless influenced by Jeremiah's text, which points to the need for something beyond what was established at Mount Sinai—a "new covenant." As we will show, thinking about Paul in this way, namely, as a "new covenant Jew," has important implications that can help us rethink questions that are often asked about various aspects of his teaching.

The Focus of This Book

The book's subtitle is meant to clarify its modest and narrow focus. Before we begin, it is important to highlight several specific limitations of this study:

(1) *Pauline Theology*: this book will only focus on Paul's theology. We do not have the space to take up many of the important literary, historical, biographical, and chronological issues that often appear in more comprehensive studies on Paul.[15] Our study will not even attempt to offer a detailed analysis of all of the major themes in Pauline theology. (For ex-

---

15. For such studies, see, e.g., Michael J. Gorman, *Apostle of the Crucified Lord: A Theological Introduction to Paul and His Letters*, 2nd ed. (Grand Rapids: Eerdmans, 2016); E. P. Sanders, *Paul: The Apostle's Life, Letters, and Thought* (Minneapolis: Fortress, 2015); Gregory Tatum, OP, *New Chapters in a Life of Paul: A Relative Chronology of His Letters*, CBQMS 41 (Washington, DC: Catholic Biblical Association of America, 2006); Jerome Murphy-O'Connor, *Paul: A Critical Life* (Oxford: Oxford University Press, 1996).

ample, there are no specific chapters dedicated to Pauline pneumatology, ecclesiology, or ethics.) Instead, this treatment is a very modest attempt to contribute to a few of the major debates that have been taking place in the scholarly discussion of Pauline theology in recent decades.

(2) *Undisputed Pauline Letters*: this study will focus its attention primarily on the seven letters that virtually all scholars agree were written by Paul himself: Romans, 1–2 Corinthians, Galatians, Philippians, 1 Thessalonians, and Philemon. It will not deal with the six disputed Pauline epistles. This does not reflect a decision by the authors for or against the authenticity of the disputed Pauline letters. It is simply a methodological recognition of the fact that today's debate over Paul is concentrated on the undisputed epistles. Any contemporary study of Pauline theology requires careful interpretation of these particular letters.[16]

(3) *Contemporary Pauline Exegesis*: for the most part, this study will limit its attention to recent exegetical studies of Paul's undisputed letters. In other words, it is not the aim of this volume to trace out the history of the interpretation of Paul in the patristic, medieval, and early modern periods—a topic to which excellent contributions have been made in recent years.[17] Rather, our focus is much narrower. In this volume we intend first and foremost to make a modest contribution to current exegetical discussions of Paul. Because of this, our primary dialogue partners will be contemporary Pauline scholars.

Simply put, this book is aimed at unpacking Paul's theology as contained in his undisputed letters. Of course, it goes without saying that the apostle did not set out to write a systematic theology. His letters are occasioned by the *particular* needs of specific communities of believers in Christ. We will therefore find that Paul's thought is not always presented with static articulation. Nevertheless, we agree with Sand-

16. For recent discussion of the authorship of disputed Pauline letters, see Scot McKnight, *Colossians*, NICOT (Grand Rapids: Eerdmans, 2017), 5–18; Douglas A. Campbell, *Framing Paul: An Epistolary Biography* (Grand Rapids: Eerdmans, 2014), 190–238; N. T. Wright, *Paul and the Faithfulness of God*, 2 vols., COQG 4 (Minneapolis: Fortress, 2013), 1:56–63; Luke Timothy Johnson, *The First and Second Letters to Timothy*, AB 35A (New York: Doubleday, 2001), 55–90.

17. See, e.g., Benjamin C. Blackwell, *Christosis: Engaging Paul's Soteriology with His Patristic Interpreters* (Grand Rapids: Eerdmans, 2016); Matthew Levering, *Paul in the Summa Theologiae* (Washington, DC: Catholic University of America Press, 2014); Michael F. Bird and Joseph Dodson, eds., *Paul and the Second Century*, LNTS 412 (London: T&T Clark, 2012); Margaret M. Mitchell, *The Heavenly Trumpet: John Chrysostom and the Art of Pauline Interpretation* (Louisville: Westminster John Knox, 2002).

ers: while Paul is not a "systematic theologian," he is nevertheless a "*coherent* thinker."[18] While aspects of Paul's thought may at first seem in tension, as with any writer, to simply assume inconsistency is to obstruct attempts at sympathetic listening. Our hope is to interpret Paul *on his own terms* and to help make sense of what he actually says in his letters. In the words of Joseph Fitzmyer, "A sketch of Pauline theology must . . . ascertain first of all what Paul meant, and in this sense it must be descriptive."[19] The ultimate goal of this volume is to unpack Paul's theology in light of his original context.

We hope that this book will be useful to both students and scholars alike. In the main text we have attempted to avoid technical jargon familiar only to scholars. Furthermore, while the first chapter does seek to introduce the reader to the broad landscape of contemporary Pauline scholarship, we keep the focus on Paul himself. Moreover, we have transliterated terms from the biblical languages so as to help readers who would otherwise be unable to read them. Nevertheless, this book does hope to make a genuine contribution to the field of Pauline scholarship. Scholars will note the extensive footnotes and nuanced engagement with exegetes. Though space precludes detailed discussion of many interpretive debates, Pauline studies involves so many complexities that such qualifying statements are even common in technical academic monographs that deal with the apostle's thought. And yet that is the beauty of Paul. Even at the distance of nearly two thousand years, the depth of his teaching appears nearly inexhaustible.

A Catholic Perspective

One of the interesting things about contemporary debates over Paul is that they continue to be largely dominated by non-Catholic voices, mostly from Protestant traditions. In this context, we hope to contribute something distinctive to the discussion. All three of the authors are Roman Catholics and have been shaped by Catholic tradition. At the same time, this volume

---

18. Sanders, *Paul and Palestinian Judaism*, 433 (emphasis original). See also p. 519, where Sanders identifies Paul as "a coherent, but not systematic, thinker."

19. Joseph A. Fitzmyer, SJ, "Pauline Theology," in *The New Jerome Biblical Commentary*, ed. Raymond E. Brown, SS, Joseph A. Fitzmyer, SJ, and Roland E. Murphy, OCarm (Upper Saddle River, NJ: Prentice Hall, 1990), 1383.

represents the work of scholars who come from a generation of exegetes that grew up in the ecumenical era. The academic formation that all three of us have received has been directly influenced by Protestant and Jewish interpreters. In this book, we hope to enter into an irenic and thoughtful dialogue with scholars from whom we have learned much and with whom we are often sympathetic.

Of course, at the end of the day we will need to make interpretive decisions. Due to the fact that one can never fully divest oneself of one's presuppositions, a reading that appears in any way consistent with an author's theological tradition can appear suspect. To check our potential biases we have attempted to listen carefully to scholars from a broad array of viewpoints and to thoughtfully engage their contributions. As the reader will find, virtually all of our core interpretive conclusions are supported in the works of non-Catholic Pauline interpreters. That said, we do feel that a distinctively Catholic approach should also have a seat at the table.

Yet what exactly do we mean by "Catholic"? That is a fair question. After all, Catholicism is a rather large tent. Inside it one finds Jesuits and Carmelites, Dominicans and Franciscans, and a myriad of other distinctive spiritualities and schools of theological thought. Nevertheless, while there is variation, there remains a certain unity and continuity. As John Henry Newman wrote:

> Catholic inquiry has taken certain definite shapes, and has thrown itself into the form of a science, with a method and a phraseology of its own, under the intellectual handling of great minds, such as St. Athanasius, St. Augustine, and St. Thomas; and I feel no temptation at all to break in pieces the great legacy of thought thus committed to us for these latter days.[20]

This legacy entails reading the biblical books in a way that is informed by a tradition that, among other things, finds expression in liturgical worship. We believe this liturgical dimension of the Catholic faith helps make us attentive to features of Paul's own teaching that reflect ritual worship in the Jewish temple that are often overlooked by those who do not belong to a liturgical tradition.

---

20. John Henry Newman, *Apologia Pro Vita Sua* (New York: D. Appleton and Company, 1865), 276.

Furthermore, the Catholic tradition tends to seek integration in a way that emphasizes the harmony of reason and faith: God is recognized as both transcendent and immanent; salvation is viewed as entirely gratuitous (possible only by grace) and yet also involves human participation; the material world is both fallen and subject to decay and, at the same time, reflects the resplendent glory of God; and so on.[21] We offer an analysis of Pauline theology that is shaped by this outlook. In the words of Luke Timothy Johnson:

> The "Catholic tradition" as such . . . is both broader and deeper than a set of polemical postures, embodying the sort of "universal and inclusive" connotations suggested by the term. . . . I approach the letters of Paul as a Catholic in this older and broader tradition, defined not by any single standpoint (either in Paul or in the interpreter) but in a conversation among standpoints, trying to avoid whenever possible the sharp alternatives of "either-or" in favor of a more balanced (even when dialectical) "both-and."[22]

Specifically, we hope to show how a "both-and" approach has the potential to *integrate* seemingly disparate positions on topics such as Paul's relationship to Judaism, his apocalyptic outlook, his Christology, his theology of atonement, his view of justification, and his theology of baptism and the Lord's Supper. It is hoped that this book will help signal a launching point for further Catholic-Protestant dialogue with a focus on Pauline *exegesis* rather than later doctrinal developments.

The Structure of This Study

Before delving in, we offer a very brief overview of our study, which explains how the different aspects of this book relate to one another. As this summary should make clear, the various chapters are not stand-alone studies. The discussions in the various chapters form a coherent argument and build on one another.

---

21. See, e.g., Gerald O'Collins and Mario J. Farrugia, *The Story of Catholic Christianity*, 2nd ed. (Oxford: Oxford University Press, 2015), 397–401.

22. Luke Timothy Johnson, "The Paul of the Letters: A Catholic Perspective," in *Four Views on the Apostle Paul*, ed. Michael F. Bird (Grand Rapids: Zondervan, 2012), 65.

Since our goal is to understand Paul's theology within his original context, the opening two chapters look at the question of Paul's relationship to Judaism. Would Paul have identified himself as "former Jew," or did he see himself as still standing within Judaism? To answer this question, we will look at some key features of his thought that have been subject to intense scrutiny in recent decades, including his view of the Jewish Torah and his belief that "all Israel will be saved" (Rom 11:26). After detailing other perspectives that have been advanced, we will make our case that Paul is best viewed as a "new covenant Jew." The second chapter will consider the way the apostle's teaching appears influenced by the tradition of Jewish apocalypticism. Among other things, apocalyptic texts spoke of the in-breaking of heavenly realities. This perspective, we will show, informs Paul's particular "new covenant" outlook.

In chapter 3 we will move into the heart of Paul's gospel, namely, his teaching about Christ, whom he identifies as God's "Son." According to the apostle, Christ not only brings fulfillment to God's covenant promises but the revelation that comes through him also goes beyond anything that could have been anticipated—it even requires a new understanding of Israel's God. Chapter 4 examines what is easily the most scandalous nature of Paul's message: the cross. For Paul the cross is both the revelation of divine love and the sacrifice that establishes the new covenant. Chapter 5 discusses the controverted question of Pauline justification as it relates specifically to his "new covenant" ministry, highlighting the way it explicates his gospel message about the divine Son. Finally, chapter 6 focuses on the Lord's Supper as the new covenant sacrifice that ushers in the church's participation in the new creation.

With this road map in place, we are now ready to begin our study with the question: What kind of Jew was Paul?

CHAPTER 1

What Kind of Jew Was Paul?

Paul was and remained a Jew.

—E. P. Sanders[1]

Christianity rapidly became a new covenantal nomism.

—E. P. Sanders[2]

Over the course of the last century, New Testament scholars have come to a consensus about the historical fact that Jesus of Nazareth was a Jew, and that he cannot be properly understood apart from first-century Judaism.[3] The same conclusion has been reached by scholars who study the apostle Paul. No serious exegete disputes the notion that Paul was profoundly formed by the Judaism of his day, the period in Jewish history typically referred to as the "Second Temple" era.[4] Paul himself makes his Jewish heritage clear. For example, in Galatians, Paul writes, "We ourselves are Jews [*Ioudaioi*] by birth" (Gal 2:15). Yet when it comes to Paul's relationship with Judaism *after* his transformation from persecutor of the church

---

1. E. P. Sanders, *Comparing Judaism and Christianity: Common Judaism, Paul, and the Inner and the Outer in Ancient Religion* (Minneapolis: Fortress, 2016), 231.

2. E. P. Sanders, *Paul and Palestinian Judaism: A Comparison of Patterns of Religion* (Minneapolis: Fortress, 1977), 552.

3. See John P. Meier, *A Marginal Jew: Rethinking the Historical Jesus*, AYBRL, 5 vols. (New Haven: Yale University Press, 1991–2016); E. P. Sanders, *Jesus and Judaism* (Minneapolis: Fortress, 1985).

4. The term is used to loosely describe the period in Jewish history from the sixth century BC to the destruction of the temple built by Herod in AD 70. Of course, further distinctions can be made within this rather lengthy time frame (e.g., the Persian period, which ends in the fourth century BC, gives way to the Hellenstic era, which is marked by the rise of Alexander the Great's rule, etc.). See, e.g., Gabriele Boccaccini and Carlos A. Segovia, eds., *Paul the Jew: Rereading the Apostle as a Figure of Second Temple Judaism* (Minneapolis: Fortress, 2016).

to apostle of Christ, things are not so simple. *What kind of Jew was the apostle Paul?* On this point, scholars are divided. As Douglas Campbell rightly notes, "Debate over Paul's relationship with Judaism, and especially over his view of the law, has dominated discussion of the apostle for the last quarter century."[5]

In this chapter, we will begin our study of Pauline theology by attempting to situate it within the context of first-century Judaism. As we will see, when it comes to the question of how best to describe Paul's relationship to Judaism, contemporary scholarship can be broadly categorized according to three major approaches: (1) Paul the "former Jew"; (2) Paul the "eschatological Jew"; and (3) Paul the "torah-observant Jew." To these we will propose a fourth option: (4) Paul the "new covenant Jew." We will make the case that this category of "new covenant Jew" is the most helpful way to locate Paul within the wider and complex world of first-century Judaism.[6] As we hope to show, exploring the question "What kind of Jew was Paul?" is extremely important for understanding his overall theology. How one thinks about the apostle's relationship to Judaism will have a direct impact on how one answers other questions about his eschatology, Christology, soteriology, and so on.

A couple of caveats before we begin. First, this chapter is by no means a comprehensive account of contemporary Pauline scholarship. Nor should the various views discussed be read in terms of a chronological progression. Rather, what we offer here is a brief *taxonomy* of perspectives that will introduce the reader to a representative sampling of recent scholarly assessments of Paul and Judaism. It will also help us identify some of the fundamental difficulties involved in interpreting Paul's overall theology. We must insist, though, that the different perspectives outlined here should not be seen as hermetically sealed categories.[7] Even though some scholars may be listed as major representatives of one approach, aspects of

5. Douglas A. Campbell, *The Quest for Paul's Gospel: A Suggested Strategy* (London: T&T Clark, 2005), 132.

6. Other categories could be suggested. See Michael F. Bird, *An Anomalous Jew: Paul among Jews, Greeks, and Romans* (Grand Rapids: Eerdmans, 2016), 1–30, whose treatment inspired the idea for this chapter.

7. For example, in the "torah-observant Jew" category we have grouped Pamela Eisenbaum with other scholars with whom she both identifies with ("the same basic orientation") and also departs from "on many of the details of my reading of Paul." See Pamela Eisenbaum, *Paul Was Not a Christian: The Original Message of a Misunderstood Apostle* (San Francisco: HarperOne, 2009), 250.

their thought may cohere well or overlap with certain features of the other general outlooks mentioned.[8] For this reason, the reader should keep in mind that the taxonomy is intended for heuristic purposes and should not be understood in an overly rigid fashion. With this in mind, we begin our overview with three different common approaches to explaining Paul's relationship to Judaism. After this we will offer our own proposal, which will set the stage for our discussion of the apostle in the rest of this book.

A Former Jew

The first major approach to the question of Paul's Jewishness is one that many readers are probably familiar with: Paul as a "former" Jew. This approach tends to emphasize the discontinuity between the practices and beliefs of *Paul the Christian apostle* and the practices and beliefs of *Saul the Jewish Pharisee*. It can be associated to varying degrees with the work of scholars such as Rudolf Bultmann,[9] Ernst Käsemann,[10] Stephen Westerholm,[11] and Love Sechrest.[12] In order to clarify the basic contours of this perspective, it is helpful to focus on three aspects of Paul's relationship with Judaism: (1) his "conversion"; (2) his relationship with the Jewish "law" or "torah";[13] and (3) his views on the salvation of Israel.

8. For example, those that we have linked to the "torah-observant Jew" approach will readily acknowledge that Paul believes that the eschatological age has dawned in Christ and that this has key implications for issues such as the inclusion of gentiles.

9. Rudolf Bultmann, *Theology of the New Testament*, trans. Kendrick Grobel (New York: Charles Scribner's Sons, 1951, 1955).

10. Ernst Käsemann, *New Testament Questions of Today*, trans. W. J. Montague and Wilfred F. Bunge (Philadelphia: Fortress, 1969); Käsemann, *Perspectives on Paul*, trans. Margaret Kohl (1969; repr., London: SCM, 1971); Käsemann, *Commentary on Romans*, trans. Geoffrey W. Bromiley (Grand Rapids: Eerdmans, 1980).

11. Stephen Westerholm, *Perspectives Old and New on Paul: The Lutheran Paul and His Critics* (Grand Rapids: Eerdmans, 2003); Westerholm, *Justification Reconsidered: Rethinking a Pauline Theme* (Grand Rapids: Eerdmans, 2013).

12. Love L. Sechrest, *A Former Jew: Paul and the Dialectics of Race*, LNTS 410 (London: T&T Clark, 2009). It is worth noting that both Bultmann on one side and the heirs of Käsemann on the other emphasize radical discontinuity between Paul's former life as a Jew and his new life as a believer in Christ. Yet scholars such as Westerholm and Sechrest view Paul's life in Christ in greater continuity with Judaism while still describing him as a former Jew.

13. Throughout this book we will alternate between the terms "law" and "torah," the latter of which had the broader connotation of "teaching." The point is to try to avoid the risk of legalistic reduction. See Mark D. Nanos, "A Jewish View," in *Four Views on the Apostle*

Paul as a Convert from Judaism to Christianity

First, according to the portrait of Paul as a "former Jew," Paul is best seen as having experienced a *conversion*—a radical "turning" (Lat. *conversio*)—from the religion known as "Judaism" to the religion that would come to be known as "Christianity." In support of this perspective, scholars of this persuasion point to several important texts in Paul's letters in which he speaks of no longer being "under" the Jewish law and of his "earlier life in Judaism." These writers interpret the latter expression as indicating that Judaism was part of his "past" and not his present identity:

> To the Jews I became as a Jew, in order to win Jews. To those under the law I became as one under the law (though *I myself am not under the law*) so that I might win those under the law. (1 Cor 9:20)

> You have heard, no doubt, of *my earlier life in Judaism.* I was violently persecuting the church of God and was trying to destroy it. *I advanced in Judaism* beyond many among my people of the same age, for I was far more zealous for the traditions of my ancestors. (Gal 1:13–14)

> If anyone else has reason to be confident in the flesh, I have more: circumcised on the eighth day, a member of the people of Israel, of the tribe of Benjamin, a Hebrew born of Hebrews; as to the law, a Pharisee; as to zeal, a persecutor of the church; as to righteousness under the law, blameless. *Yet whatever gains I had, these I have come to regard as loss because of Christ.* More than that, I regard everything as loss because of the surpassing value of knowing Christ Jesus my Lord. *For his sake I have suffered the loss of all things, and I regard them as rubbish,* in order that I may gain Christ and be found in him, not having a righteousness of my own that comes from the law, but one that comes through faith in Christ, the righteousness from God based on faith. (Phil 3:4–9)

Paul's declaration that he is not himself "under the law [*hypo nomon*]" (1 Cor 9:20) is especially important for the "former Jew" approach. The statement suggests that he does not consider himself subject to the torah

---

Paul, ed. Michael F. Bird (Grand Rapids: Zondervan, 2012), 166–71; Fẹmi Adeyẹmi, *The New Covenant Torah in Jeremiah and the Law of Christ in Paul,* SBL 94 (New York: Peter Lang, 2006).

of Moses. Although first-century Judaism was extremely diverse, a solid case can be made that one thing that virtually all Jews held in common was the belief that they were bound to obey the law of Moses as contained in the Pentateuch.[14] It is hard to imagine any ordinary first-century Jew ever declaring, as Paul does, that he or she is not "under the law" (1 Cor 9:20). Notice also that Paul twice uses the language of "Judaism" (*Ioudaismos*) to refer to his *earlier* religious life (Gal 1:13, 14). This could be taken as implying that he no longer sees himself as living within Judaism. To be sure, Paul acknowledges and even boasts about the fact that he is "of the people of Israel [*ek genous Israēl*]" and "a Hebrew [*Hebraios*]" (Phil 3:5). Nevertheless, he appears to turn this immediately on its head by declaring that he has not only suffered the "loss of all things"—that is, what he had gained through righteousness under the torah—but counts them as "rubbish" (Phil 3:8). This translation dramatically softens the original (and quite crude) Greek word Paul uses, *skybala*, which literally means "crud" or "excrement."[15] One could hardly think of a more vivid way (and one could easily think of several less offensive ways) of describing a radical break with his earlier life.

Pointing to these and other such passages, various scholars do not hesitate to speak of Paul's "conversion" *from* Judaism *to* Christianity.[16] For example, the famous twentieth-century scholar Rudolf Bultmann describes Paul as having experienced a "conversion" that "brought" Paul "into the Hellenistic Church" and situated him "within Hellenistic Christianity."[17] Along similar lines, Ernst Käsemann places Paul's Jewish identity in his past: "Paul is here [in Philippians 3:4–9] setting a boundary between himself and his own past—as the past of a devout Jew."[18] More recently, certain Protestant scholars have made similar comments. For example, Stephen Westerholm argues that Paul may correctly be described as "a Christian" who had "abandoned" his Jewish way of life.[19] Likewise, Love Sechrest writes that Paul "does not see himself as a Jew in the first place" but believes instead that he and his fellow Christians "had become members of

---

14. For the idea of "common Judaism," see Wayne O. McCready and Adele Reinhartz, eds., *Common Judaism: Explorations in Second Temple Judaism* (Minneapolis: Fortress, 2008), following E. P. Sanders, *Judaism: Practice and Belief 63 BC–66 CE* (London: SCM, 1992).

15. Frederick William Danker, ed., *A Greek-English Lexicon of the New Testament and Other Early Christian Literature*, 3rd ed. (Chicago: University of Chicago Press, 2000), 932.

16. E.g., Käsemann, *New Testament Questions of Today*, 38.

17. Bultmann, *Theology of the New Testament*, 1:187–89 (emphasis added).

18. Käsemann, *New Testament Questions of Today*, 184.

19. Westerholm, *Perspectives Old and New*, 368.

a new racial identity."[20] Put differently, in the words of Rudolf Bultmann, Paul represented "a Torah-free Gentile Christianity."[21]

Paul and the Torah—Justification by Faith versus Works-Righteousness

Second, scholars who depict Paul as a "former Jew" also tend to regard Paul's doctrine of justification by faith apart from works of the law as *a*, if not *the*, central feature of his theology. According to this point of view, Paul's doctrine of justification is directed *against Jewish "legalism,"* which saw the performance of the works commanded in the Jewish torah as a means of acquiring righteousness through one's own efforts. As Ernst Käsemann once put it, "The apostle's message of justification is a fighting doctrine, directed against Judaism."[22]

In support of this view, scholars cite, for example, Paul's famous statements in Romans about justification by faith apart from works of the law:

> *For we hold that a person is justified by faith apart from works prescribed by the law.* . . . For if Abraham was justified by works, he has something to boast about, but not before God. For what does the scripture say? "Abraham believed God, and it was reckoned to him as righteousness." Now to one who works, wages are not reckoned as a gift but as something due. *But to one who without works trusts him who justifies the ungodly, such faith is reckoned as righteousness.* (Rom 3:28; 4:2–5)

> Brothers and sisters, my heart's desire and prayer to God for them is that they may be saved. I can testify that they have a zeal for God, but it is not enlightened. For, *being ignorant of the righteousness that comes from God, and seeking to establish their own,* they have not submitted to God's righteousness. *For Christ is the end of the law so that there may be righteousness for everyone who believes.* (Rom 10:1–4)

In these texts Paul articulates his doctrine that a person is "justified [*dikaiousthai*]" by "faith [*pistei*]" without "works of the law [*ergōn no-*

---

20. Sechrest, *A Former Jew*, 156, 164; we owe these quotations to Bird, *An Anomalous Jew*, 12.

21. Bultmann, *Theology of the New Testament*, 1:108.

22. Käsemann, *Perspectives on Paul*, 70.

mou]" (Rom 3:28 NRSV, adapted). According to Stephen Westerholm, "justification" here refers to sinners being "declared by God to be righteous" because of the forgiveness won by Christ on the cross.[23] "Faith" refers to the act of believing in the gift of forgiveness through the death of Christ and confessing his lordship. And "works of the law" refers to *all of the works* required by the Jewish torah: both ritual or ceremonial works (such as circumcision and Sabbath observance) and moral works (such as keeping the Ten Commandments).[24] Notice also that Paul's criticism of his Jewish contemporaries is that they sought "to establish their own" righteousness—that is, to establish themselves as righteous through their own efforts alone, rather than realizing that "no one" will be "justified" by anything other than "faith" in Christ (Gal 2:16). In other words, the performance of such works is "the attempt to achieve security before God."[25]

Because of passages in Paul such as these, many scholars have come to the conclusion that justification by faith represents the center of Paul's theology.[26] They also assert that Paul's polemic is aimed at a "Jewish legalism" that endeavors to "win God's favor by the toil of minutely fulfilling the Law's stipulations."[27] In the influential words of Rudolf Bultmann:

> In rejecting *erga* ["works"] Paul is rejecting a specific and indeed a characteristic attitude—the attitude of human self-assurance before God, or the attempt to attain it. Thus *pistis* ["faith"] as genuine *hypakoē* ["obedience"], as the basic attitude made possible by God's gracious act in Christ, stands opposed not only to the specifically Jewish attitude but also to the specifically pagan attitude of man, i.e., to the attitude of natural man generally, who fancies that he can stand before God in his own strength.[28]

Other similar statements could be given.[29] For our purposes here (see chapter 5 for more discussion on this topic), notice that Bultmann sees in

23. See Westerholm, *Perspectives Old and New*, 261–96 (here 296).

24. Käsemann, *Perspectives on Paul*, 72: "The apostle did not for a single moment detach the ritual from the ethical law."

25. Käsemann, *Romans*, 103.

26. E.g., Käsemann, *Perspectives on Paul*, 64, 65, 76.

27. Bultmann, *Theology of the New Testament*, 1:11.

28. Rudolf Bultmann, "*pisteuō, ktl.*," in *TDNT* 6:220.

29. See, e.g., Westerholm, *Perspectives Old and New*, 404; Käsemann, *Romans*, 103; Käsemann, *Perspectives on Paul*, 72.

Paul's doctrine of justification by faith a counterpoint not only to Jewish legalism but also to a kind of pagan "legalism" in which human beings would have a natural inclination to attempt to justify themselves through their own efforts before God. According to scholars of this school of thought, Paul's doctrine is thus said to anticipate the later fifth-century debates that took place between Augustine of Hippo (who claimed that we are saved by grace, through faith) and Pelagius (who claimed that human beings can be saved by good works apart from grace)[30] and, eventually, the sixteenth-century debates between Protestants and Catholics over the role of grace, faith, and works.[31]

Paul and the Salvation of Israel:
Only through Explicit Faith in Christ

Third, the portrait of Paul as a "former Jew" tends to place a heavy emphasis on the fact that for Paul there is *no salvation apart from explicit faith in Jesus Christ*. For Paul, the temporary rejection of the messiahship of Jesus by the majority of Jews is a great mystery that will be superseded only by the even greater mystery of their future conversion to faith in him.

The classic text cited in support of this position comes from Paul's complex discussion in Romans 9–11 about the salvation of Israel. Scores of books have been written on these critical chapters, and much could be said about the difficulties involved in interpreting them.[32] For our purposes here let it suffice to say that those in the "former Jew" approach often tend to emphasize the section in Romans in which Paul declares that explicit belief and confession of faith in Jesus is necessary for salvation:

> What then are we to say? Gentiles, who did not strive for righteousness, have attained it, that is, righteousness through faith; but Israel, who did

---

30. See Bultmann, *Theology of the New Testament*, 1:107.

31. See Alister E. McGrath, *Iustitia Dei: A History of the Christian Doctrine of Justification*, 3rd ed. (Cambridge: Cambridge University Press, 2007); Bruce L. McCormack, ed., *Justification in Perspective: Historical Developments and Contemporary Challenges* (Grand Rapids: Baker Academic, 2006); Thomas P. Scheck, *Origen and the History of Justification: The Legacy of Origen's Commentary on Romans* (Notre Dame, IN: University of Notre Dame Press, 2008).

32. For an in-depth engagement with the history of interpretation, see esp. Pablo T. Gadenz, *Called from the Jews and from the Gentiles: Pauline Ecclesiology in Romans 9–11*, WUNT 2/267 (Tübingen: Mohr Siebeck, 2009).

strive for the righteousness that is based on the law, did not succeed in fulfilling that law. Why not? Because they did not strive for it on the basis of faith, but as if it were based on works. . . . Brothers and sisters, *my heart's desire and prayer to God for them is that they may be saved.* I can testify that they have a zeal for God, but it is not enlightened. For, being ignorant of the righteousness that comes from God, and seeking to establish their own, they have not submitted to God's righteousness. For Christ is the end of the law so that there may be righteousness for everyone who believes. . . . *If you confess with your lips that Jesus is Lord and believe in your heart that God raised him from the dead, you will be saved.* For one believes with the heart and so is justified, and one confesses with the mouth and so is saved. The scripture says, "No one who believes in him will be put to shame." For there is no distinction between Jew and Greek; the same Lord is Lord of all and is generous to all who call on him. For, "Everyone who calls on the name of the Lord shall be saved." (Rom 9:30–32; 10:1–4, 9–13)

Those who view Paul as a convert from Judaism to Christianity point to texts such as this to show that the apostle states that salvation comes to both Jews and Greeks through the same path: explicit confession of faith in Jesus. As Ernst Käsemann affirms, "Even for Israel no other possibility of salvation exists."[33] Likewise, in the words of Stephen Westerholm:

They [the Jews] are wrongly pursuing righteousness through keeping the law's commandments (through works) rather than through faith. Paul can only pray for their salvation (10:1) and do whatever he can, however indirect (11:13–14), to promote it. But even the eventual salvation of "all Israel" [11:26]—in which Paul fervently believes—will only take place when Israel as a whole abandons its unbelief.[34]

Westerholm's last point demarcates a fault line in interpretive approaches. As we will see momentarily, some scholars will take Paul's reference to "all Israel" being "saved" (Rom 11:26) as evidence of "two ways" of salvation—one for torah-observant Jews, another for Christ-believing gentiles.

---

33. Käsemann, *Romans*, 283.

34. Westerholm, *Perspectives Old and New*, 398. For a much fuller discussion, see Stephen Westerholm, "Paul and the Law in Romans 9–11," in *Paul and the Mosaic Law*, ed. James D. G. Dunn (Grand Rapids: Eerdmans, 2001), 215–37.

Scholarly advocates of Paul as a "former Jew" emphatically reject such an interpretation. As Käsemann writes, Paul's reference to "all Israel" being "saved" does "not imply an *apokatastasis*"—the universal salvation of all human beings.[35] Instead, Paul's insistence on salvation taking place only through explicit faith in the lordship of Christ leads to an inevitable "parting of the ways" between Judaism and Christianity.[36]

An Eschatological Jew

A second major approach to characterizing Paul's relationship with Judaism emphasizes his identity as an "eschatological Jew"—one whose worldview was rooted in and transformed by Jewish expectations about the "end" (Gk. *eschaton*) of the world.[37] This perspective has been advanced in different ways by the work of scholars such as Albert Schweitzer,[38] W. D. Davies,[39] E. P. Sanders,[40] and James D. G. Dunn.[41] Of course, that Paul's thought has an important eschatological dimension is recognized by virtually all Pauline scholars. Nevertheless, for those we have placed in this approach, special emphasis is given to the way Jewish eschatology structures various aspects of his thought. In particular, these scholars make the case that Paul's teaching was heavily influenced by an emerging Jewish tradition that distinguished between "two ages" or "two worlds": (1) this

35. Käsemann, *Romans*, 313–14.

36. Cf. James D. G. Dunn, *The Parting of the Ways: Between Christianity and Judaism and Their Significance for the Character of Christianity*, 2nd ed. (London: SCM, 2006). Cf. Käsemann, *Romans*, 314.

37. It should be noted here that we have deliberately chosen the adjective "eschatological" rather than "apocalyptic," which has a much wider range of meanings in Pauline scholarship. For further discussion, see chapter 2 below.

38. Albert Schweitzer, *The Mysticism of Paul the Apostle*, trans. William Montgomery (London: Black, 1931).

39. W. D. Davies, *Paul and Rabbinic Judaism*, 5th ed. (1948; repr., Mifflintown, PA: Sigler, 1998); Davies, *Jewish and Pauline Studies* (Philadelphia: Fortress, 1984).

40. Sanders, *Paul and Palestinian Judaism*; Sanders, *Paul, the Law, and the Jewish People* (Minneapolis: Fortress, 1983); Sanders, "Paul's Jewishness," in *Paul's Jewish Matrix*, ed. Thomas G. Casey and Justin Taylor (Rome: Gregorian and Biblical Press, 2011), 51–73; Sanders, *Paul: The Apostle's Life, Letters, and Thought*.

41. James D. G. Dunn, *The Theology of Paul the Apostle* (Grand Rapids: Eerdmans, 1998); Dunn, *The New Perspective on Paul*; Dunn, *Jesus, Paul, and the Gospels* (Grand Rapids: Eerdmans, 2011).

present age/world, which the later rabbis called "this world" (Heb. *ha-ʿolam hazzeh*), and (2) the new age/world—the new creation—which the later rabbis referred to as "the world to come" (Heb. *ha-ʿolam habba'*).[42]

Like the portrait of Paul as a "former Jew," this eschatological approach takes seriously key elements of discontinuity between Paul and his Jewish contemporaries. Nevertheless, scholars who view Paul as an "eschatological Jew" contend that the discontinuous elements in Paul's thought can be best explained not by setting Paul *against* Judaism but by situating his thought *within* the context of first-century Jewish *eschatology*. While Paul shared the idea of "two ages" with his Jewish contemporaries, he also believed that the new creation had *already* been ushered in by the passion, death, and resurrection of Jesus the messiah. In other words, Paul is not less Jewish than his Jewish contemporaries; the differences between him and fellow Jews who did not believe in Jesus arose from their disagreement about whether or not the world to come had actually been inaugurated.[43] Let us take a few moments to look carefully once again at how this plays out in the three areas of Paul's conversion, his view of the torah, and the salvation of Israel.

Paul's Conversion: Becoming a "New Creation" "in Christ"

First, when it comes to the question of Paul's "conversion," the "eschatological Jew" approach holds that his transformation from persecutor to apostle should not be construed in terms of changing from one "religion" to another; this would be anachronistic. Nevertheless, these scholars contend that his transformation can legitimately be described as a "conversion" to a radically new way of life and an entry into a new sphere of reality: *being "in Christ."*

Consider, for example, the following passages, in which Paul speaks of being "in Christ" in terms reminiscent of Jewish expectations of a coming new creation (cf., e.g., Isa 65:17; 66:22):

May I never boast of anything except the cross of our Lord Jesus Christ, by which *the world has been crucified to me, and I to the world.* For nei-

---

42. See Dunn, *The Theology of Paul the Apostle*, 464–65, for a helpful diagram.
43. Cf. Schweitzer, *Mysticism of Paul*, xxv, 113.

ther circumcision nor uncircumcision is anything; but *a new creation is everything!* (Gal 6:14–15)

From now on, therefore, we regard no one from a human point of view; even though we once knew Christ from a human point of view, we know him no longer in that way. So *if anyone is in Christ, there is a new creation: everything old has passed away; see, everything has become new!* (2 Cor 5:16–17)

Several aspects of these important texts stand out. For one thing, Paul uses the language of early Jewish eschatology and its concept of "two worlds." He speaks about being "crucified" to the present age—which he calls "the world [*kosmos*]" (Gal 6:14)—and "the old [*ta archaia*]" (2 Cor 5:17). He also speaks of entering into the age to come, which he calls the "new creation [*kainē ktisis*]" (2 Cor 5:17).

Moreover, Paul ties "crucifixion" to the old creation to union with Christ in baptism. Think here of his words in Romans: "Do you not know that all of us who have been baptized into Christ Jesus were baptized into his death? . . . We know that our old self was *crucified with him*" (Rom 6:3, 6). In other words, Paul sees himself as having died to the old creation by being crucified with Christ and rising to become part of the new creation through baptism.

Finally, Paul describes the difference between his past life and present life by declaring that he is now not only part of the new creation but also "in Christ" (*en Christō*)—an expression that Paul uses (in various forms) about one hundred times in the undisputed letters.[44] In sum, when Paul describes the change that took place in his life, he uses a framework familiar to Jewish eschatology—the distinction between the old and new creation. In particular, baptism is understood against this backdrop. Those who are baptized "die" to the old creation and are "raised" to the new creation.[45]

In view of the radical new reality implied by such language, scholars who depict Paul as an eschatological Jew tend to admit that "conversion"—properly understood—is a legitimate way to define what had occurred to him as a result of becoming a believer in Christ. Thus, in the words of Sanders, Paul "thought of the church as the fulfillment of the promises to

---

44. Dunn, *Theology of Paul*, 396–97.
45. We return to the topic of Paul's baptismal theology in chapter 5.

Abraham. In that sense it was not at all a new religion."[46] Nevertheless, Sanders also maintains, "the language of dying to the old self . . . in order to live 'to God in Christ Jesus' (Rom. 6:11), is the language of conversion."[47] Along similar lines, James Dunn contends that what happened to Paul on the road to Damascus "*was* a conversion . . . a conversion *to* a better, a more correct understanding of [God's] will and purpose for Israel."[48] For Dunn, although Paul was an "Apostle to the Gentiles," he was not thereby "an *apostate* from Israel" but rather "an *apostle* of Israel."[49] Dunn even refers to Paul as an "eschatological Apostle."[50] Why? Because he, like other early Christians, believed that "in Jesus Messiah the new age had dawned—not just *a* new age, but the final age, the *eschaton* (= last)."[51]

In summary, those who view Paul as an eschatological Jew hold that there was nothing more thoroughly Jewish than his belief that God would one day fulfill his promise to usher in the new creation—that is, the "new heavens and new earth" spoken of by the Jewish scriptures (cf. Isa 64–66). On the other hand, there was nothing about Paul that set him apart from the majority of his Jewish contemporaries more than his conviction that the "new creation" had *already been inaugurated* through the death and resurrection of Jesus, and that both Jews and gentiles could now participate in this new creation through Christ.

Paul and the Torah:
Being "in Christ" versus Being "under the Law"

Second, when it comes to Paul and the torah, the "eschatological Jew" approach makes two key points that distinguish it from the "former Jew" perspective.

For one thing, it contends that when Paul talks about "works of the law," he is not polemicizing against "Jewish legalism." Following Sanders, many who emphasize Paul's role as an "eschatological Jew" argue that the

---

46. Sanders, *Paul, the Law, and the Jewish People*, 178.

47. Sanders, *Paul, the Law, and the Jewish People*, 177. See also Sanders, "Paul's Jewishness," 68; Sanders, *Paul: The Apostle's Life, Letters, and Thought*, 102; Davies, *Paul and Rabbinic Judaism*, 37, 324.

48. Dunn, *Jesus, Paul, and the Gospels*, 141 (emphasis original).

49. Dunn, *Jesus, Paul, and the Gospels*, 141 (emphasis original).

50. Dunn, *Jesus, Paul, and the Gospels*, 143.

51. Dunn, *Jesus, Paul, and the Gospels*, 143 (emphasis original).

Judaism of Paul's day has often been misconstrued as a religion of legalistic "works-righteousness." In contradistinction to that view, Sanders characterizes Jewish theology in terms of "covenantal nomism," a phrase taken from the Greek term *nomos*, meaning "law." According to Sanders, Jews viewed keeping the law—that is, doing good works—as a response to the covenant God had established with them. Sanders insists that first-century Jews believed God had elected them as a "grace." As such, they did not believe that their covenant relationship with God was itself something that had been merited by good works. To use Sanders's language, for Jews, "getting in" the covenant was by grace, but "staying in" the covenant was by obedience.[52] Sanders summarizes the "structure" of "covenantal nomism" as follows:

> (1) God has chosen Israel and (2) given the law. The law implies both (3) God's promise to maintain the election and (4) the requirement to obey. (5) God rewards obedience and punishes transgression. (6) The law provides a means of atonement, and atonement results in (7) maintenance or re-establishment of the covenantal relationship. (8) All those who are maintained in the covenant by obedience, atonement and God's mercy belong to the group which will be saved.[53]

Sanders therefore argues that the claim that Jews simply believed they earned salvation by works fails to appreciate the complexity of ancient Judaism.

Against this backdrop, Sanders maintains that Paul is not arguing against the importance of good works for those who belong to Christ. Instead, Paul is making the case that the "works of the law" that make one Jewish are not what justifies those who are in Christ. Sanders writes:

> The common misunderstanding of [Paul's] argument is greatly facilitated by the belief that by "works of law" Paul meant "good deeds." It is possible to conceive that people might try to save themselves by compiling meritorious deeds. But once one grasps that the first "work of the law" is circumcision, and that the phrase "works of the law" means simply "obeying the law," it is impossible to imagine people piling up

---

52. See Sanders, *Paul and Palestinian Judaism*, 75, 420–24, in particular.

53. Sanders, *Paul and Palestinian Judaism*, 422. For a response to critics, see Sanders, *Comparing Judaism and Christianity*, 51–83.

circumcisions or tripling the number of Sabbath days in order to observe them and accumulate merit. *We must always bear in mind that we should not confuse "works of law" with "good deeds."* . . . *These are two separate categories.* "Works of law" are those works that make people Jewish; "good deeds" are "the fruit of the Spirit," the deeds that Christianity expects.[54]

This is the aspect of the portrait of Paul as an eschatological Jew that is most frequently associated with what has come to be called "the New Perspective on Paul." This "perspective" is "new" insofar as it stands in stark contrast to older approaches that viewed Paul's theology as targeting Jewish works-righteousness. Nevertheless, Sanders insists that Paul is not a covenantal nomist himself. Instead, Sanders holds that at the heart of Paul's soteriology is the notion of real participation in Christ.

This brings us to the second major difference between the "former Jew" approach and the "eschatological Jew" perspective. Following Sanders, advocates of Paul the eschatological Jew tend to reject the contention that justification by faith apart from works of the law is the "center" of Paul's theology. Instead, these scholars often argue that the center of Paul's theology is the concept of *participation "in Christ."* It is this concept, rather than justification by faith, that provides the key for understanding how Paul can claim that both Jews and gentiles do not have to follow the Jewish law in order to be saved. In the words of Albert Schweitzer, "This 'being-in-Christ' is the prime enigma of the Pauline teaching: once grasped it gives the clue to the whole."[55]

In support of these positions, scholars in the "eschatological Jew" camp will note that in the undisputed letters Paul uses the language of "justification" by "faith" apart from "works of the law" only a handful of times in only two letters (cf. Rom 3:24–4:5; 5:1; Gal 2:16–17; 5:4).[56] In striking contrast, the phrase "in Christ" (*en Christō*) occurs some sixty-one times, and the substantially equivalent expression "in the Lord" (*en Kyriō*) occurs thirty-nine times—to say nothing of expressions that only utilize the pronoun "in/with him"![57] The following passages provide a sample of

---

54. Sanders, *Paul: The Apostle's Life, Letters, and Thought*, 681–82 (emphasis added).

55. Schweitzer, *Mysticism of Paul*, 3.

56. Davies, *Paul and Rabbinic Judaism*, 222.

57. Dunn, *Theology of Paul*, 396–97. For a detailed list of Paul's use of the expression "in Christ," see Schweitzer, *Mysticism of Paul*, 123–25.

how Paul contrasts being "in Christ" with being under or obligated to the Jewish "law":

> So you also must consider yourselves *dead to sin and alive to God in Christ Jesus*. Therefore, do not let sin exercise dominion in your mortal bodies, to make you obey their passions. No longer present your members to sin as instruments of wickedness, but present yourselves to God as those who have been brought from death to life, and present your members to God as instruments of righteousness. For sin will have no dominion over you, since *you are not under law [hypo nomon] but under grace*. (Rom 6:11–14)

> For his sake I have suffered the loss of all things, and count them as refuse, in order *that I may gain Christ* and be found *in him, not having a righteousness of my own, based on law*, but that which is through faith in Christ, the righteousness from God that depends on faith; that I may know him and the power of his resurrection, and may share his sufferings, becoming like him in his death, that if possible I may attain the resurrection from the dead. (Phil 3:8–11 RSV)

Above all, then, for Paul, once a person is "in Christ Jesus [*en Christō Iēsou*]" (Rom 6:11) he or she is, by definition, thereby no longer "under law [*hypo nomon*]" (Rom 6:14). Significantly, Romans is not the only place Paul uses such language: in Galatians, Paul likewise speaks of being no longer "under the law [*hypo nomon*]" after baptism but "in Christ Jesus [*en Christō Iēsou*]" (Gal 3:23–28). When we couple this with Paul's previous description above of his own personal transformation as moving from one sphere of reality (the "old creation") to another (the "new creation"), we can see that, according to the apostle, there are two fundamentally different modes of reality. Those who belong to the old creation are "under the law" or even "in the law [*en tō nomō*]" (Rom 3:19),[58] whereas those who belong to the new creation are "in Christ" and "under grace" (Rom 6:14).

Because of such passages, scholars who portray Paul as an eschatological Jew contend that his doctrine of "being in" or "participating in" Christ is more central than the much less frequently attested language of justification by faith. The classic expression of this goes back to the Lutheran scholar Albert Schweitzer, who famously described Paul's doctrine of justification by

---

58. See Schweitzer, *Mysticism of Paul*, 123.

faith as a "subsidiary crater" that formed within "the rim of the main crater—the mystical doctrine of redemption through *being-in-Christ*."[59] Schweitzer goes on to argue that for Paul, there are currently two overlapping spheres of reality: for those who belong to the old creation, the torah remains binding; for those who have died to the old creation, the torah is no longer valid:

> The Law is no longer valid for those who are in-Christ-Jesus. As those who have died—died with Christ!—they are liberated from the Law in the same way as the dead and risen Christ. Upon the dead and risen again it has no power. . . . Paul thus affirms the co-existence of a validity and non-validity of the Law corresponding to the difference of world-era within the sphere of being-in-Christ and outside of it.[60]

To be in the "new creation" is thus to be "in Christ"—and thereby to no longer be under the law.

In the wake of Schweitzer's work, several others went on to assert—often explicitly against the writings of figures such as Rudolf Bultmann—that participation in Christ (rather than justification by faith) was the "center" of Paul's theology and the key to understanding Paul's view of the torah.[61] Perhaps no contemporary scholar has been more influential in advocating this view than Sanders:

> What is wrong with it [Judaism] is not that it implies petty obedience and minimization of important matters, nor that it results in the tabulation of merit points before God, but that it is not worth anything in comparison with being in Christ (Phil 3.4–11). The fundamental critique of the law is that following the law does not result in being found in Christ.[62]

In other words, the reason Paul can say both positive and negative things about the torah—that is, why he can speak of it as both being given by God and as no longer required—is because he believes that "in Christ" the new

---

59. Schweitzer, *Mysticism of Paul*, 225 (emphasis added).

60. Schweitzer, *Mysticism of Paul*, 188, 189.

61. It is fascinating to note that over a decade before the terminology of "the New Perspective on Paul" was made famous by James Dunn in his 1984 essay, already in 1970 W. D. Davies described Schweitzer's emphasis on participation "in Christ" as the emergence of a "new perspective." See Davies, *Paul and Rabbinic Judaism*, xxix.

62. Sanders, *Paul and Palestinian Judaism*, 550. For more on the centrality of participation in Christ, see *Paul and Palestinian Judaism*, 453–72, 522–23.

creation has already broken into the old creation. Because the new creation has already come, the old creation—and therefore the torah—is passing away.

Paul and the Salvation of Israel:
End-Time Conversion of the Remnant

Third, when it comes to the salvation of Israel, those who take this eschatological perspective on Paul tend to interpret his declaration that "all Israel will be saved" (Rom 11:26) as referring to something other than the salvation of every individual Israelite. Rather, according to them, it refers to the *elect remnant* of Israel who accept Christ. From this point of view, what Paul expects is a great eschatological *conversion* of the full "remnant" of Israel to the belief that Jesus is the messiah.

To understand this interpretation, several key passages in Romans leading up to Paul's declaration are important to highlight:

> *For not all Israelites truly belong to Israel, and not all of Abraham's children are his true descendants*; but "It is through Isaac that descendants shall be named for you." This means that it is not the children of the flesh who are the children of God, but the children of the promise are counted as descendants. (Rom 9:6–8)

> And Isaiah cries out concerning Israel, "Though the number of the children of Israel were like the sand of the sea, *only a remnant of them will be saved*." (Rom 9:27)

> Now I am speaking to you Gentiles. Inasmuch then as I am an apostle to the Gentiles, I glorify my ministry in order *to make my own flesh jealous, and thus save some of them*. For if their rejection is the reconciliation of the world, what will their acceptance be but life from the dead! (Rom 11:13–15 NRSV, slightly adapted)

> I want you to understand this mystery: a hardening has come upon part of Israel, until the full number of the Gentiles has come in. And so all Israel will be saved. (Rom 11:25–26)

A few aspects of these passages need to be considered. For one thing, if we want to know what Paul means when he says that "all Israel [*Israēl*] will be saved [*sōthēsetai*]" (Rom 11:26), it is critical to interpret it within the broader context of Romans 9–11. Here Paul has already declared that "not all who are descended from Israel [*Israēl*] belong to Israel" (Rom 9:6 RSV). With these words, he reduces "true" Israel to "those who put their faith in Christ."[63] Moreover, Paul explicitly anchors his expectation of "Israel" being "saved" in Isaiah's prophecy that "only a remnant [*hypoleimma*] of them will be saved [*sōthēsetai*]" (Rom 9:27).[64] This strongly suggests that he does not expect every individual Israelite to be saved. Instead, Paul thinks that at some point in the future there will be a conversion of the full number of the elect remnant that will reveal that God has not rejected Israel (cf. Rom 11:1–5). Finally, Paul does seem to think that his fellow Jews need to come to faith in Christ in order to be saved. Why does he say he magnifies his ministry in order to make them "jealous" and thereby "save some of them [*sōsō tinas ex autōn*]" (Rom 11:14) if they are already saved simply by virtue of being Jews and keeping the law?[65]

With such statements from the apostle in mind, scholars who emphasize Paul's identity as an eschatological Jew stress that Paul's declaration of the salvation of "all Israel" should be understood within the context of Jewish eschatology—that is, it is not a declaration of universal salvation but rather refers to the conversion of the full number of Israelites in the "elect" remnant. Albert Schweitzer puts it this way:

> Hitherto exegesis has been at a loss as to how to deal with this redemption of all [in Rom 11:26]; and that for two reasons. First, it has overlooked the fact that by "all" is meant nothing more nor less than all the Elect. . . . Paul is not speaking here of a restoration of all the men who have ever lived upon the earth (*apokatastasis pantōn*) as a conferring of universal blessedness, which is to happen in the moment when God becomes all in all. . . . He is thinking only of the turning to belief of the whole of the Elect.[66]

---

63. Sanders, *Paul: The Apostle's Life, Letters, and Thought*, 676.
64. See Davies, *Paul and Rabbinic Judaism*, 75.
65. Cf. Schweitzer, *Mysticism of Paul*, 184.
66. Schweitzer, *Mysticism of Paul*, 185–86. Our reason for citing Schweitzer is to show that scholars who take the "eschatological view" of Paul think his statement that "all Israel" will be saved refers to something other than the notion that every individual Israelite will experience salvation.

In sum, when Paul speaks of "all Israel" being "saved" (Rom 11:26), he is not thereby endorsing "two ways" of salvation—one for Jews and another for gentiles. Instead, as Sanders observes, Paul is drawing once again on the early Jewish idea of an eschatological "remnant" of Israel: Paul must "reduce" or "redefine" the Israel that God has chosen.[67] Paul's expectation is not, therefore, that every single individual Israelite will be saved, but that there will be a miraculous end-time conversion of a remnant of Israel that believes in Christ.[68]

A Torah-Observant Jew

A third major approach to Paul and Judaism is one that builds on the eschatological portrait of Paul but goes beyond it. This view has gained considerable ground in Pauline scholarship in recent years; it emphasizes Paul's identity as a *torah-observant Jew*—as one who did not "convert" from Judaism to Christianity. According to this approach—which is sometimes called the "Paul within Judaism" perspective or the "Radical New Perspective"—even after coming to faith in Christ Paul kept the torah and followed the practices and beliefs of Judaism, all the while committing himself to bring Jewish monotheism to the gentiles.[69] This point of view can be associated with the work of Christian scholars such as Krister Stendahl,[70] Lloyd Gaston,[71] and John Gager,[72] and Jewish scholars such as Mark Nanos,[73]

---

67. Sanders, *Paul: The Apostle's Life, Letters, and Thought*, 676. See also Dunn, *Theology of Paul*, 508.

68. It is worth noting that in the Mishnah (compiled ca. AD 200), the rabbinic teaching that "all Israel will have a share in the world to come" clearly *does not* mean that every single Israelite will be saved (*m. Sanh.* 10:1). In fact, the text immediately goes on to list all of the Israelites who *will* be excluded from the world to come, such as the wilderness generation and the Babylonian exiles, as well as those who *may* be excluded, such as the Assyrian exiles.

69. See Mark D. Nanos and Magnus Zetterholm, eds., *Paul within Judaism: Restoring the First-Century Context to the Apostle* (Minneapolis: Fortress, 2015).

70. Krister Stendahl, *Paul among Jews and Gentiles* (Philadelphia: Fortress, 1976); Stendahl, *Final Account: Paul's Letter to the Romans* (Minneapolis: Fortress, 1995).

71. Lloyd Gaston, *Paul and the Torah* (Vancouver: University of British Columbia Press, 1987).

72. John G. Gager, *Reinventing Paul* (Oxford: Oxford University Press, 2000).

73. Nanos, "A Jewish View," 159–93; Nanos, *The Mystery of Romans: The Jewish Context of Paul's Letter* (Minneapolis: Fortress, 1996).

Pamela Eisenbaum,[74] and Paula Fredriksen.[75] In contrast to the portrait of Paul as a former Jew, this "Paul within Judaism" perspective emphasizes *continuity* in the three areas of (1) Paul's "conversion"; (2) his relationship to the torah; and (3) the salvation of Israelites.

Paul Is a Torah-Observant Jew— Not a "Convert" to "Christianity"

First and foremost, scholars who identify Paul as a torah-observant Jew insist that, despite the widespread assumption to the contrary, the apostle is *not* and should not be referred to as a "convert" from Judaism to Christianity. Several reasons for this are cited.

For one thing, Paul never uses the language of "Christian" (*Christianos*) to refer to himself or to any of the believers in Jesus to whom he addresses his letters. Such terminology only appears in Acts and 1 Peter (Acts 11:26; 26:28; 1 Pet 4:16).[76] As Pamela Eisenbaum insists, Paul could not have referred to himself or believers as "Christians," since such terminology "did not yet exist."[77] Whenever Paul does wax autobiographical in his letters, he always refers to himself as a Jew or Hebrew. Consider some of the following passages:

> *We ourselves are Jews by birth* and not Gentile sinners. (Gal 2:15)

> For I could wish that I myself were accursed and cut off from Christ for the sake of *my own people, my kindred according to the flesh. They are Israelites.* (Rom 9:3–4)

> I, too, have reason for confidence in the flesh. If anyone else has reason to be confident in the flesh, I have more: *circumcised on the eighth day, a*

---

74. Eisenbaum, *Paul Was Not a Christian.*

75. Paula Fredriksen, *Paul: The Pagan's Apostle* (New Haven: Yale University Press, 2017). See also Kimberly Ambrose, *Jew among Jews: Rehabilitating Paul* (Eugene, OR: Wipf & Stock, 2015).

76. Cf. Zetterholm, "Paul within Judaism: The State of the Questions," in Nanos and Zetterholm, *Paul within Judaism*, 48n36. It worth noting that most advocates of the "Paul within Judaism" approach tend to regard Acts as chronologically late (after AD 70) and historically unreliable.

77. Eisenbaum, *Paul Was Not a Christian*, 9.

*member of the people of Israel, of the tribe of Benjamin, a Hebrew born of
Hebrews*; as to the law, a Pharisee; as to zeal, a persecutor of the church;
as to righteousness under the law, blameless. (Phil 3:4–6)

Important here is the string of terms that Paul uses to describe himself:
he is a "Jew [*Ioudaios*]" by "birth" or, more literally, by "nature [*physis*]"
(Gal 2:15). Paul counts himself among the "Israelites [*Israēlitai*]." They are
his kindred "according to the flesh [*kata sarka*]" (Rom 9:3–4), and he is a
"Hebrew [born] of Hebrews [*Hebraios ex Hebraiōn*]" (Phil 3:5). He even
speaks of himself as "blameless" when it comes to keeping the torah!

Scholars who advocate the position that Paul was a torah-observant
Jew therefore emphasize that according to Paul himself he never ceased being a Jew. This emphasis goes at least as far back as 1963, when the Swedish-
American Lutheran scholar Krister Stendahl penned a famous essay in
which he argued that what Paul experienced was a "*call*" to apostleship,
not a "conversion" to a new "religion."[78] In more recent years, scholars
(several of them students of Stendahl) have taken up this interpretation,
vigorously arguing that referring to Paul as a "Christian" or to his "conversion" from Judaism to Christianity is intrinsically anachronistic. For
example, the Princeton scholar John Gager declares:

> To speak of Paul's Christianity implies that he thought of himself as
> fundamentally different from, even opposed to Jews/Israel. The term
> is not only anachronistic; it is misleading. . . . From the moment we
> begin to speak of Christianity in Paul, the conversion issue is settled.
> Paul became a Christian! And he repudiated Judaism. But if he had no
> concept of Christianity or of Christians, if there was no Christianity, this
> cannot be the case. He became something else: apostle to the Gentiles![79]

Perhaps the most striking formulation of this perspective comes from
Eisenbaum, who provocatively says:

> Paul was not a *Christian*—a word that was in any case completely un-
> known to him because it had not yet been invented. He was a Jew who
> understood himself to be on a divine mission. . . . Paul clearly identifies
> himself as a Jew in his letters. . . . It is very important to stress that Paul

78. Stendahl, *Paul among Jews and Gentiles*, 11.
79. Gager, *Reinventing Paul*, 24.

does not use the designation 'Jew' of himself as a label of his religious past. He speaks in the present tense.[80]

Other statements to similar effect could be given.[81] These should suffice to represent the basic position that Paul lived his life as a torah-observant Jew and that, as such, he remained "within Judaism" until his death.[82] According to this perspective, if we are to interpret the theology of Paul's letters properly we must always keep this in mind.

Paul and the Law: Torah Observance for Jews, but Not for Gentiles

Second, in stark contrast to the portrait of Paul as a "former Jew," those who view Paul as a "torah-observant Jew" interpret his statements about the torah in a radically different way. According to this position, Paul himself *never* abandoned the torah of Moses, nor did he ever require his fellow Jews to give up observing it. Instead, Paul merely insists—indeed, he fights tooth and nail against his opponents—that *gentiles are not obligated to keep the Jewish torah*. Hence, whenever Paul says anything negative about the law, it is always about gentiles' relationship to the law, not Jews'.[83]

In support of this hypothesis, advocates of this position contend that Paul's letters were written exclusively to *gentile audiences* and that all of his apparently negative statements about the law must always be interpreted with this in view. In the words of Pamela Eisenbaum, "Paul's audience is made up of Gentiles, so everything he says about law applies to Gentiles, unless specified otherwise."[84] For scholars who take this perspective, when Paul insists on his doctrine of justification by faith and not by "works of the law," he is *not* polemicizing against Jewish observance of the law. Instead, he is attacking the notion that the *gentiles* have to be circumcised and follow the distinctive practices of the torah.

---

80. Eisenbaum, *Paul Was Not a Christian*, 4, 6 (emphasis added).

81. See Gaston, *Paul and the Torah*, 6; Pinchas Lapide and Peter Stuhlmacher, *Paul: Rabbi and Apostle* (Minneapolis: Fortress, 1984), 47.

82. Nanos, "A Jewish View," 167, 177.

83. See Gager, *Reinventing Paul*, 48.

84. Eisenbaum, *Paul Was Not a Christian*, 216. For other scholars contending that Paul is writing only to gentiles/non-Jews, see Zetterholm, "Paul within Judaism," 48; Gager, *Reinventing Paul*, 44; Gaston, *Paul and the Torah*, 23, 77.

In support of this conclusion, scholars will often point to the first oc-
currence in Paul's letters of the doctrine of justification by faith apart from
"works of the law" (Gal 2:11–16). In context, Paul describes an incident
in which he opposed Peter ("Cephas") for withdrawing from eating with
non-Jewish Christians because of the "circumcision faction":

> But when Cephas came to Antioch, I opposed him to his face, because
> he stood self-condemned; for until certain people came from James, he
> used to eat with the Gentiles. But after they came, he drew back and
> kept himself separate for fear of the circumcision faction. And the other
> Jews joined him in this hypocrisy, so that even Barnabas was led astray
> by their hypocrisy. But when I saw that they were not acting consistently
> with the truth of the gospel, I said to Cephas before them all, *"If you,
> though a Jew, live like a Gentile and not like a Jew, how can you compel
> the Gentiles to live like Jews?"*
>
> We ourselves are Jews by birth and not Gentile sinners; yet we
> know that *a person is justified not by the works of the law but through
> faith in Jesus Christ.* And we have come to believe in Christ Jesus, so that
> we might be justified by faith in Christ, and not by doing the works of
> the law, because no one will be justified by the works of the law. (Gal
> 2:11–16)[85]

Picking up on the implications of Sanders's work and similar to those in
the New Perspective, interpreters who emphasize the apostle's identity as a
torah-observant Jew point out that *Paul's argument is not primarily directed
against the performance of good works simply speaking.*[86] Such scholars observe that there is nothing to suggest that Paul was here opposing a form
of Jewish legalism that advocated the view that salvation is simply "earned"
by one's own efforts at performing good works. In what is likely Paul's
earliest expression of justification by faith apart from works of the torah,
his teaching does not involve a polemic against Judaism per se. Though the
precise nature of the controversy is somewhat opaque, one thing seems
evident: some were insisting that "gentiles" must be compelled to "live

85. There is a debate here about how to translate the Greek phrase "faith in Christ"
(*pistis Christou*). Here we simply provide the NRSV's rendering without prejudice to this
controversy, which we will discuss in chapter 5.

86. It is worth noting that many in the eschatological Jew camp, particularly Sanders
and Dunn, would agree on this point. Indeed, the "torah-observant Jew" school is thus
frequently seen in terms of a *"Radical* New Perspective."

like Jews" (Gal 2:14).[87] By insisting on justification "apart from works of the law [*ergōn nomou*]" (Gal 2:16 NRSV, adapted), Paul is not targeting the specific notion that one is saved by one's good works. Rather, he seems to be making the case that gentiles are saved apart from keeping the specific regulations of the torah God gave to Israel. Indeed, since Peter changes his behavior due to the presence of a group which, in Greek, is simply called, "the circumcision [*ek peritomēs*]" (Gal 2:12), scholars like Nanos argue that "works of the law" in this context refer specifically to this rite.[88]

In light of such observations, proponents of the Paul within Judaism perspective contend that when Paul polemicizes against the idea of "justification" by "works of the law" (Gal 2:16), he is not arguing against *Jews* keeping the law, but against *gentiles* doing so.[89] Consider the following statements from John Gager, Pamela Eisenbaum, and Mark Nanos, who represent this position well:

The apostle to the Gentiles is writing to Gentiles who are being pressured by other apostles, within the Jesus-movement, to take on circumcision and a selective observance of the law.[90]

When Paul rails against circumcision, as he does in Galatians, it is not because circumcision is inherently bad. It is because he does not want *Gentiles* to get circumcised. There is no question he is adamantly opposed to it: "I, Paul, say to you that if you become circumcised, Christ will be of no benefit to you" (Gal 5:2). But *you* clearly means *Gentiles*, not Jews and not people in general.[91]

Proselyte conversion is the contextual contrast to "justification by faithfulness to Christ" in every case in Paul's letters where the phrase arises,

---

87. Some of the most important treatments of this episode from the "torah-observant Jew" approach can be found in Mark D. Nanos, "Reading the Antioch Incident (Gal 2:11–21) as a Subversive Banquet Narrative," *JSPL* 7.1–2 (2017): 26–52; Nanos, "How Could Paul Accuse Peter of 'Living *Ethnē*-ishly' in Antioch (Gal 2:11–21) If Peter Was Eating according to Jewish Dietary Norms?," *JSPL* 6.2 (2016): 199–223; Nanos, "What Was at Stake in Peter's 'Eating with Gentiles' at Antioch?," in *The Galatians Debate: Contemporary Issues in Rhetorical and Historical Interpretation*, ed. Mark D. Nanos (Peabody, MA: Hendrickson, 2002), 282–318; Nanos, *Mystery of Romans*, 339–40.

88. See, e.g., Nanos, "What Was at Stake," 315.

89. For an early expression of this view, see Stendahl, *Paul among Jews and Gentiles*, 9.

90. Gager, *Reinventing Paul*, 86.

91. Eisenbaum, *Paul Was Not a Christian*, 218.

rather than doing good deeds, or obeying Torah, or legalism, ethnocentrism, works-righteousness, human effort, and so on. The question is: Are non-Jews legitimately included (i.e., justified) in the family while remaining non-Jews? Paul's answer is "Yes," just as Jews are legitimately included while remaining Jews.[92]

In sum, a contextual reading of Galatians indicates that Paul's doctrine of justification by faith emerges out of his conflict with others who are insisting that gentiles be circumcised—that is, become Jews[93]—in order to be saved. Hence, for Paul, "Jews must remain Jews (or better, Israelites must remain Israelites), non-Jews must remain non-Jews (or better, members of other nations must remain members of other nations)."[94] This point is at the heart of the scholarly picture of "Paul the torah-observant Jew."

Paul and the "Two Ways" of Salvation: Law for Jews, Christ for Gentiles

Third and finally, many proponents of the Radical New Perspective also claim that Paul taught "two ways" of salvation: one for gentiles (through faith in Jesus Christ), and another for Jews (through fidelity to the Mosaic covenant). In other words, salvation is "through *Christ* for the Gentiles, through *the law* for Israel."[95]

In support of this basic contention, scholars often point to Paul's famous and mysterious declaration in Romans that, one day, "all Israel will be saved" (Rom 11:26). At the climax of a lengthy and complex argument about the people of Israel in the history of salvation, Paul writes:

> So that you may not claim to be wiser than you are, brothers and sisters, *I want you to understand this mystery*: a hardening has come upon part of Israel, until the full number of the Gentiles has come in. And so *all Israel will be saved*; as it is written, "Out of Zion will come the Deliverer; he will banish ungodliness from Jacob." "And this is my covenant with them, when I take away their sins." As regards the gospel they are

---

92. Nanos, "A Jewish View," 189. For earlier scholars, see Gager, *Reinventing Paul*, 57.
93. See Nanos, "What Was at Stake," 306–10.
94. Nanos, "A Jewish View," 187.
95. Gager, *Reinventing Paul*, 59 (emphasis original).

enemies of God for your sake; but as regards election they are beloved, for the sake of their ancestors; for *the gifts and the calling of God are irrevocable.* (Rom 11:25–29)

Notice here that Paul does not say "all Israel will *convert* to Christianity" or that "all Israel will confess Jesus as messiah." Instead, he simply says "all Israel will be saved [*pas Israēl sōthēsetai*]" (Rom 11:26).[96] When this statement is read in the context of Paul's immediately following declaration that the election of the people of Israel by God is "irrevocable," or something that "cannot be taken back [*ametameleta*]" (Rom 11:29), the passage is said to have a clear meaning: all Jews, including those who do not confess Jesus as messiah, will in fact be granted salvation. As Pamela Eisenbaum puts it, "When Paul says 'all' he means all."[97]

On the basis of such evidence, several scholars argue that Paul's letters reveal a belief in "a 'special way' for non-Jews to be included in salvation through Christ, alongside the historical Sinai covenant with Israel."[98] This is sometimes referred to as the *Sonderweg* hypothesis (German "special path"). Take, for example, the following statements from various scholars who advocate this interpretation:

Why will all Israel be saved? *Not* by individual Jews converting to faith in Christ.... Nowhere in these chapters does Paul refer to Jewish Christians as such.[99]

Paul never speaks of Israel's ultimate redemption as a conversion to Christ. In line with this, an increasing number of readers have spoken of two ways or paths to salvation—through Christ for Gentiles, through the law for Israel.[100]

---

96. Cf. Eisenbaum, *Paul Was Not a Christian*, 255. For detailed commentary on Romans 9–11 from a "Paul within Judaism" perspective, see Eisenbaum, *Paul Was Not a Christian*, 250–55; Gager, *Reinventing Paul*, 128–42; Nanos, *Mystery of Romans*, 239–88; Stendahl, *Final Account*, 33–44.

97. Eisenbaum, *Paul Was Not a Christian*, 255.

98. Mark D. Nanos, "Introduction," in Nanos and Zetterholm, *Paul within Judaism*, 3. For a full discussion, see Nanos, *Mystery of Romans*, 239–88. For an early formulation, see Stendahl, *Paul among Jews and Gentiles*, 4.

99. Gaston, *Paul and the Torah*, 148 (emphasis original).

100. Gager, *Reinventing Paul*, 59; see also p. 10: "He [Paul] did not expect Jews to find their salvation through Jesus Christ."

Once again, perhaps the most provocative formulation comes from the pen of Eisenbaum:

> The death and resurrection of Jesus has achieved reconciliation between Gentiles and God that was envisioned by Israel's prophets. *To put it boldly, Jesus saves, but he only saves Gentiles.*[101]

Thus, for a growing number of contemporary scholars, the reason Paul did not demand that his fellow Jews abandon the observance of the law of Moses is that he believed that torah-observant Jews would be saved through the Mosaic covenant. Hence, Paul's mission was primarily to bring the good news to the gentiles; he had, for all intents and purposes, no mission at all to his fellow Jews. Formulated negatively, this means that Jesus Christ did not die for the sins of Jews, but only for the sins of gentiles.[102] Formulated positively, it means for several of these scholars that Paul taught an early form of universalism, in which every human being would be saved.[103]

A New Covenant Jew

The fourth and final approach to the question "What *kind* of Jew was the apostle Paul?" is our own proposal. We follow Paul's lead and refer to him as a "minister of a new covenant" (2 Cor 3:6)—that is, as *a new covenant Jew*. Although we do not know of any scholars who have specifically argued for such terminology, it is inspired by aspects of the work done by Protestant scholars such as Michael Gorman,[104] Richard Hays,[105] N. T. Wright,[106]

---

101. Eisenbaum, *Paul Was Not a Christian*, 242 (emphasis added).

102. Eisenbaum, *Paul Was Not a Christian*, 242.

103. See Stendahl, *Final Account*, 39, and Eisenbaum, *Paul Was Not a Christian*, 254, who link their positions with the "universal salvation" envisioned by Christian theologians such as Origen, Peter Abelard, and Karl Barth.

104. See Gorman, *Apostle of the Crucified Lord*; Gorman, *The Death of the Messiah and the Birth of the New Covenant* (Eugene, OR: Cascade, 2014).

105. Richard B. Hays, *Echoes of Scripture in the Letters of Paul* (New Haven: Yale University Press, 1989), 122–53; Hays, "The Letter to the Galatians," in *New Interpreter's Bible*, 12 vols., ed. L. E. Keck (Nashville: Abingdon, 2000), 11:183–348.

106. See esp. Wright, *Paul and the Faithfulness of God*, 2:980–84. See also N. T. Wright, "The Letter to the Romans," in *New Interpreter's Bible*, 12 vols., ed. L. E. Keck (Nashville: Abingdon, 2002), 10:395–770; Wright, *The Climax of the Covenant: Christ and the Law in Pauline Theology* (Minneapolis: Fortress, 1992).

and Michael Bird,[107] as well as by Catholic scholars such as Joseph Fitzmyer,[108] Frank Matera,[109] and Scott Hahn.[110] Building on their insights, we contend that while there are valid points made by each of the three proposals outlined above—the former Jew, the eschatological Jew, and the torah-observant Jew—the best way to explain Paul is to view him as a *new covenant Jew*. To be specific: the concept of the "new covenant," taken directly from the Jewish scriptures (Jer 31:31–34), has within itself the power to account for elements of both *continuity* ("covenant") and *discontinuity* ("new") with Judaism in Paul's theology. In making a case for this proposal, we will return once again to our three topics of inquiry: Paul's conversion, his relationship to the torah, and his thoughts on the salvation of Israel.

The Conversion of Paul:
A "Minister of the New Covenant"

One of the most compelling reasons Paul is best described as a "new covenant" Jew is this: *that is the terminology he uses to describe himself.*[111] It is difficult to overestimate the importance of this fact. Helpful as the categories suggested by contemporary scholars may be, nowhere in Paul's letters does he ever refer to his present ministry as that of a "former" Jew, or a "faithful" Jew, or an "eschatological" Jew. But Paul *does* refer to himself as a new covenant Jew, insofar as he refers to himself as a "minister of the new covenant" (2 Cor 3:6). In fact, he uses this expression in the same context in which he employs the language of "turning"—that is, a conversion—to Christ (2 Cor 3:16). In 2 Corinthians, Paul writes:

---

107. Bird, *An Anomalous Jew*, 58–63.

108. Joseph A. Fitzmyer, SJ, *First Corinthians*, AYB 32 (New Haven: Yale University Press, 2008); Fitzmyer, *Romans*, AYB 33 (New Haven: Yale University Press, 1993).

109. Frank J. Matera, *God's Saving Grace: A Pauline Theology* (Grand Rapids: Eerdmans, 2012); Matera, *Romans*, Paideia (Grand Rapids: Baker Academic, 2010); Matera, *II Corinthians: A Commentary*, New Testament Library (Louisville: Westminster John Knox, 2003); Matera, *Galatians*, SP 9 (Collegeville, MN: Liturgical Press, 1992); Matera, "Philippians," in *The Paulist Commentary*, ed. José Enrique Aguilar Chiu et al. (New York: Paulist Press, 2018), 1419–28.

110. Scott W. Hahn, *Kinship by Covenant: A Canonical Approach to the Fulfillment of God's Saving Promises*, AYBRL (New Haven: Yale University Press, 2009), 238–76.

111. Matera, *God's Saving Grace*, 23.

You yourselves are our letter, written on our hearts, to be known and read by all; and you show that you are a letter of Christ, prepared by us, written not with ink but with the Spirit of the living God, not on tablets of stone but on tablets of human hearts.

Such is the confidence that we have through Christ toward God. Not that we are competent of ourselves to claim anything as coming from us; our competence is from God, who has made us competent to be *ministers of a new covenant*, not of letter but of spirit; for the letter kills, but the Spirit gives life.

Now if the ministry of death, chiseled in letters on stone tablets, came in glory so that the people of Israel could not gaze at Moses' face because of the glory of his face, a glory now set aside, how much more will the ministry of the Spirit come in glory? For if there was glory in the ministry of condemnation, much more does the ministry of justification abound in glory! Indeed, what once had glory has lost its glory because of the greater glory; for if what was set aside came through glory, much more has the permanent come in glory!

Since, then, we have such a hope, we act with great boldness, not like Moses, who put a veil over his face to keep the people of Israel from gazing at the end of the glory that was being set aside. But their minds were hardened. Indeed, to this very day, when they hear the reading of *the old covenant*, that same veil is still there, since only in Christ is it set aside. *Indeed, to this very day whenever Moses is read, a veil lies over their minds; but when one turns to the Lord, the veil is removed.* (2 Cor 3:2–16)

Several aspects of this witness to Paul's self-understanding stand out as important.

From the very opening line, with its contrast between "tablets of stone" and "tablets of the human heart" (2 Cor 3:3), Paul alludes to the prophet Jeremiah's famous oracle of the "new covenant" (Jer 31:31–33), the first and only time the expression occurs in the Jewish scriptures:[112]

The days are surely coming, says the LORD, when *I will make a new covenant* with the house of Israel and the house of Judah. *It will not be like the covenant that I made with their ancestors* when I took them by the hand to bring them out of the land of Egypt—a covenant that they broke, though I was their husband, says the LORD. But this is the cove-

112. Matera, *2 Corinthians*, 79; Hays, *Echoes*, 128.

nant that I will make with the house of Israel after those days, says the LORD: I will put my law within them, and I will write it on their hearts. (Jer 31:31–33)

In this oracle, the Lord highlights the discontinuity that will accompany the making of a "new covenant" with Israel and Judah, emphasizing that "it will *not be like* the covenant" he established with Israel at Mount Sinai (Jer 31:32). The reason: the new covenant will be written "on their hearts" (Jer 31:33). Unlike the covenant with Moses, that was summed up in the Ten Commandments and written on tablets of stone (cf. Exod 34:1–4, 28–29), the new covenant will be "enfleshed rather than inscribed."[113] Given this biblical background, we can chart the differences between the old and new covenants for Paul as follows:

New Covenant Ministry in 2 Corinthians 3[114]

The Old Covenant	*The New Covenant*
of (the) letter	of (the) Spirit
ministry of death	gives life
chiseled on stone tablets	written on tablets of human hearts
came through glory	greater glory
ministry of condemnation	ministry of justification
a glory now set aside	permanent
cf. 2 Cor 3:6, 7, 3, 9, 10–11	*cf. 2 Cor 3:6, 3, 10–11, 9, 11*

It would seem that the teaching in 2 Corinthians 3 goes a long way toward helping us understand how Paul, as a Jew, can speak of the Mosaic law as at once good and yet also affirm that it passes away (2 Cor 3:11). In the words of Michael Gorman:

> Paul is *not* denigrating the Law and the covenant it represents; rather, he is praising the new covenant because of its surpassing greatness and glory vis-à-vis the already glorious first covenant, comparing the greater with the lesser (*not* the worthless). . . . It is important, therefore, to see Paul at work *as a Jew* describing the realization of his Jewish hopes for a new

---

113. Hays, *Echoes*, 129.
114. Chart adapted from Gorman, *Apostle of the Crucified Lord*, 355.

covenant that would remake the old, a covenant that would be different from and superior in effect to the old—as the prophet Jeremiah himself had said (Jer 31:32). It would be a covenant in which the laws of God would be internalized by the presence of the Spirit and would therefore be actually observed (Jer 31:33–34; Ezek 36:26–27). *For Paul, depending especially upon on the prophets Jeremiah and Ezekiel, the old covenant was never intended to be permanent but to be renewed by a covenant involving God's Spirit,* which for Paul came into effect with the death and resurrection of the Messiah (3:11; cf. Gal 3:1–5:1; esp. 3:23–25).[115]

In other words, the notion that a "new covenant" is needed is taken *from the Jewish scriptures themselves*—particularly Jeremiah and Ezekiel.

We have already seen that Paul utilizes Jeremiah's announcement of a coming new covenant. His use of Ezekiel, however, is also important. Paul writes that believers are letters of Christ written by the Spirit "not on tablets of stone but *on tablets of hearts of flesh [kardiais sarkinais]*." The expression translated "hearts of flesh" is found in only one other place in the Greek Old Testament (the Septuagint): the book of Ezekiel. The prophet announces how God will save the people in the future age—the Lord promises both to pour out the Spirit on them and to remove their "heart of stone":

> A new heart I will give you, and *a new spirit* I will put within you; and I will remove from your body the heart of stone and give you *a heart of flesh*. I will put my spirit within you, and make you follow my statutes and be careful to observe my ordinances. (Ezek 36:26–27; cf. 11:19)

Other interpreters have recognized the influence of this passage on Paul's teaching in 2 Corinthians 3.[116] Not only does Paul employ "heart" language, but he also emphasizes the Spirit's role, saying, for example, "the letter kills, but *the Spirit gives life*" (2 Cor 3:6). Thus, the language of the "new covenant" in 2 Corinthians 3 refers to Jeremiah, but the emphasis on the connection between the *Spirit* and heart-renewal is drawn from Ezekiel. For Paul, these two ideas are inseparable—the new covenant is written on the heart by the Spirit.

---

115. Gorman, *Apostle of the Crucified Lord*, 355 (emphasis original).
116. See, e.g., Ralph P. Martin, *2 Corinthians*, 2nd ed., WBC 40 (Grand Rapids: Zondervan, 2014), 192.

With this we come to a critique of Sanders that distinguishes our "new covenant Jew" view from the "eschatological Jew" perspective. Though Sanders was absolutely correct to insist that the covenant context of the law is crucial to understand Jewish attitudes toward good works, John Barclay has offered a correction to Sanders's view. Barclay maintains that Sanders has confused matters by his use of the language of "grace." Briefly put, according to Barclay, Sanders assumes that one definition is always at work in Jewish sources, a definition that only insists on the priority of grace.[117] This creates further problems when reading Paul. In denying that Paul was a covenantal nomist, Sanders fails to explain fully why Paul teaches that good works are necessary for final justification (cf. Rom 2:1–16; 2 Cor 5:9–10).[118] Though Sanders is right to insist on the priority of grace for Paul, Barclay contends that his portrayal of what this means fails to account for a notion of circularity—that is, the way grace enables the proper human response. Barclay demonstrates that while Paul teaches that grace is given to the unworthy, the apostle also insists that it empowers believers to perform the good works required for them to be accounted "righteous" at the final judgment.[119] In short, for Paul, one does not sim-

117. See John M. G. Barclay, *Paul and the Gift* (Grand Rapids: Eerdmans, 2015), 151–58 and 318–28.

118. In addition to the texts noted above, Paul also seeks that his churches be pure and blameless for the day of Christ (1 Thess 3:13; 5:23; Phil 1:10). Moreover, there are a myriad of both OT and NT texts that speak of divine judgment being in accordance with works or one's moral character. See Ps 62:12 (61:13 LXX); Job 34:11; Isa 59:18; Jer 17:10; Hos 12:2; Sir 16:12–14; Matt 16:27; 25:34–46; John 5:29; 1 Pet 1:17; Rev 2:23; 20:12; 22:12. For more in regard to the role of works at the final judgment, see our discussion in chapter 5.

119. Aside from Barclay, *Paul and the Gift*, see also Barclay, "Grace and the Counter-cultural Reckoning of Worth: Community Construction in Galatians 5–6," in *Galatians and Christian Theology: Justification, the Gospel, and Ethics in Paul's Letter*, ed. Mark W. Elliot, Scott J. Hafemann, N. T. Wright, and John Frederick (Grand Rapids: Baker Academic, 2014), 306–17; Barclay, "Under Grace: The Christ-Gift and the Construction of a Christian *Habitus*," in *Apocalyptic Paul: Cosmos and Anthropos in Romans 5–8*, ed. Beverly Roberts Gaventa (Waco, TX: Baylor University Press, 2013), 59–76; Barclay, "Believers and the 'Last Judgment' in Paul: Rethinking Grace and Recompense," in *Eschatologie—Eschatology*, ed. Hans Joachim Eckstein, Christof Landmesser, and Hermann Lichtenberger (Tübingen: Mohr Siebeck, 2011), 195–208; Barclay, "Manna and the Circulation of Grace: A Study of 2 Corinthians 8:1–15," in *The Word Leaps the Gap: Essays on Scripture and Theology in Honor of Richard B. Hays*, ed. J. Ross Wagner, C. Kavin Rowe, and A. Katherine Grieb (Grand Rapids: Eerdmans, 2008), 409–26; Barclay, "Grace and the Transformation of Agency in Christ," in *Redefining First-Century Jewish and Christian Identities: Essays in Honor of Ed Parish Sanders*, ed. Fabian E. Udoh (Notre Dame, IN: University of Notre Dame Press, 2008),

ply "get in" to the covenant by grace, one "stays in" by it as well—grace bestows the power needed to do the works that are necessary for "staying in." New Perspective accounts that simply affirm the "get in by grace" / "stay in by works" framework might even be seen as similar to Pelagianism (i.e., the notion that salvific works can be accomplished without grace). This, we believe, fails to adequately represent Paul's gospel.

As we will later explain further, Jewish texts do not necessarily construe divine and human action in antithetical terms. This can be seen in the very passage from Ezekiel Paul alludes to in 2 Corinthians 3. For our purposes here let us simply make one important observation: Ezekiel does not see the gift of the Spirit as replacing or canceling out the need for obedience.[120] Rather, God's giving of the Spirit will *enable* Israel to keep the law: "I will put my spirit within you, and *make you follow my statutes*" (Ezek 36:27). For the prophet, the fact that Israel was given the law was not enough; a coming outpouring of the Spirit would be necessary to keep it.[121] Ezekiel is no outlier here. Later in chapter 5 we will see how Deuteronomy, Jeremiah, and other sources discuss the way God promised to address a core problem standing in the way of obedience: hard-heartedness.[122] When Paul connects Jeremiah's new covenant with Ezekiel's eschatological Spirit, it is the image of the heart that serves as a bridge between the two prophecies. In fact, the Dead Sea Scrolls bear witness to an entire Jewish community devoted to the hope of a future

---

372–89; Barclay, "'By the Grace of God I Am What I Am': Grace and Agency in Philo and Paul," in *Divine and Human Agency in Paul and His Cultural Environment*, ed. John M. G. Barclay and Simon J. Gathercole (London: T&T Clark, 2006), 140–57; Barclay, *Obeying the Truth: A Study in Paul's Ethics in Galatians* (Edinburgh: T&T Clark, 1998).

120. According to Augustine (*On the Spirit and the Letter* 8.14), the Pelagians insisted that the giving of the law *itself* entailed the gift of righteousness.

121. As various scholars have noted, the spirit/Spirit played an important role in various Second Temple texts such that the spirit/Spirit could be viewed as the "eschatological principle of obedience." See Barry D. Smith, "'Spirit of Holiness' as Eschatological Principle of Obedience," in *Christian Beginnings and the Dead Sea Scrolls*, ed. John J. Collins and Craig A. Evans (Grand Rapids: Baker Academic, 2006), 75–99. See also Rodrigo J. Morales, *The Spirit and the Restoration of Israel: New Exodus and New Creation Motifs in Galatians*, WUNT 2/282 (Tübingen: Mohr Siebeck, 2014), 58–106; Preston M. Sprinkle, *Paul and Judaism Revisited: A Study in Divine and Human Agency in Salvation* (Downers Grove, IL: IVP Academic, 2013), 95–121.

122. See Kyle B. Wells, *Grace and Agency in Paul and Second Temple Judaism: Interpreting the Transformation of the Heart*, NovTSup 157 (Leiden: Brill, 2014); Morales, *The Spirit and the Restoration of Israel*, 58–106; Sprinkle, *Paul and Judaism Revisited*, 95–121.

spiritual renewal. This community looked forward to the day these expectations would be fulfilled—hopes they also happened to link to the notion of a "new covenant."[123] To recognize, then, that the law was not sufficient to save is hardly anti-Jewish.

Paul breathes the same air as the "new covenant" community responsible for the Dead Sea Scrolls. The apostle's teaching is thoroughly Jewish. For Paul, the day of the fulfillment of God's promises was not a distant future reality but had now come in Christ, and with it had come the power to keep the law. Israel had been given the torah, but as Ezekiel pointed out, the Spirit's coming was necessary. Hays rightly notes:

> The problem with this old covenant is precisely that it is (only) written, lacking the power to effect the obedience it commands. Since it has no power to transform the readers, it can only stand as a witness to their condemnation. That is why Paul remarks aphoristically, "The script kills, but the Spirit gives life" (cf. Rom. 7:6–8:4). As Paul's earlier allusion to Ezekiel 36 and 37 indicates, the life-giving power of the Spirit shown forth precisely in the creation of the enfleshed eschatological community. That is the sense in which the Corinthians are a letter from Christ: they are a breathing instantiation of the word of God. Paul is a minister of the new covenant of the Spirit because he proclaims the message that brings this eschatological community into being.[124]

As a minister of the new covenant, Paul's message announces the dawning of the eschatological age. Yet, as Ezekiel testifies, this eschatological people of God is made capable of obedience by the Spirit. Paul, therefore, is a new covenant Jew who believes that since the eschatological age has dawned, true obedience is now possible. The promise made in Ezekiel is thus fulfilled: "I will put my spirit within you, and make you follow my statutes" (Ezek 36:27).

But the value of 2 Corinthians 3 for understanding Paul does not end here. For Paul also uses the language of Jeremiah to describe his identity

---

123. For the connection between the Spirit and the new covenant see, e.g., 1QS 3:6–10, which associates the "holy spirit of the community" and the future "covenant of an everlasting Community." Unless otherwise noted, all Dead Sea Scrolls quotations are taken from *DSSSE*. See also 1QS 9:20–22, which links the "spirit of truth" to those God has chosen "for an everlasting covenant"—namely, those to whom will belong "all the glory of Adam." Wells, *Grace and Agency*, 102–3.

124. Hays, *Echoes*, 131.

and that of other apostles: they are "ministers of a new covenant [*dia-konous kainēs diathēkēs*]" (2 Cor 3:6).[125] To be sure, this is not the only self-description used by Paul: he elsewhere refers to himself as an "apostle," a "slave" of Jesus Christ, and a "father" to his congregation.[126] None of these titles, however, clarifies Paul's understanding of his relationship with Judaism like "minister of the new covenant." This expression shows that while Paul remains firmly planted in the soil of salvation history ("covenant"), he is decidedly *not* a minister of the Sinai covenant. Much less was he the founder of a new "religion." Instead, he is a minister of the new covenant as foretold by the prophet Jeremiah. This ministry "has had the effect, through the spirit, of bringing about the 'new covenant' spoken of by Jeremiah: in other words, of redefining election."[127]

Lastly, it is in the context of identifying himself as a minister of the new covenant that *Paul also employs the language of "conversion."* This happens when he speaks of how the veil over the scriptures is removed when a person "turns [*epistrepsē*] to the Lord" (2 Cor 3:16). As other scholars have noted, this passage justifies speaking not only of Paul's "call" to be an apostle but also of his "conversion" to faith in the Lord.[128] In the words of Michael Bird, "It is probable that *Christos* as the remover of the veil in v. 14 is to be identified with the *kyrios* of v. 16, meaning that the turning (*epistrephō*) to the Lord is essentially conversion to Christ (see 2 Cor 4:3–4)."[129] We would add that it is not just a conversion to belief in Jesus's messiahship but also a conversion to a particular way of interpreting Israel's scriptures.[130] This new way of interpreting the Law and the Prophets is bound up with the belief that the "new covenant" spoken of by Jeremiah 31 has come and that, as a result, the "old covenant," albeit glorious in its own right, is in some sense passing away.[131]

---

125. See Scott J. Hafemann, *Paul, Moses, and the History of Israel: The Letter/Spirit Contrast and the Argument from Scripture in 2 Corinthians 3* (Tübingen: Mohr Siebeck, 1995), 110–19.

126. For "apostle," see Rom 1:1; 1 Cor 1:1; 2 Cor 1:1; Gal 1:1; for "slave," see Rom 1:1; Gal 1:10; Phil 1:1; for "father," see 1 Cor 4:15–16.

127. Wright, *Paul and the Faithfulness of God*, 2:982.

128. See Gorman, *Apostle of the Crucified Lord*, 72; Sanders, *Paul, the Law, and the Jewish People*, 177.

129. Bird, *An Anomalous Jew*, 61. For similar comments, see Matera, *God's Saving Grace*, 228.

130. Hays, *Echoes*, 122–25. See also Richard B. Hays, *The Conversion of the Imagination: Paul as an Interpreter of Israel's Scripture* (Grand Rapids: Eerdmans, 2005). See also Antonio Pitta, "Second Corinthians," in Chiu et al., *The Paulist Commentary*, 1353.

131. See Matera, *II Corinthians*, 85–87.

Before moving on, we should ask, How did Paul exercise his new covenant ministry?[132] Above all, by preaching "the gospel" of "the cross of Christ" (1 Cor 1:17). Indeed, the broader context in 2 Corinthians points to the proclamation and interpretation of scripture (one might even say the liturgy/ministry of "the word") as the context of Paul's use of the terminology of "ministry" of the new covenant (e.g., 2 Cor 3:14; 4:1–6). Yet we would also hasten to add that Paul's reference to ministry of the new covenant among the Corinthians likely also involved *the liturgical celebration of the new covenant* in the Lord's Supper.[133] Should there be any doubt about this, recall that Paul's most famous reference to the "new covenant" occurs in his description of the Lord's Supper:

> For I received from the Lord what I also handed on to you, that the Lord Jesus on the night when he was betrayed took a loaf of bread, and when he had given thanks, he broke it and said, "This is my body that is for you. Do this in remembrance of me." In the same way he took the cup also, after supper, saying, "This cup is *the new covenant in my blood.* Do this, as often as you drink it, in remembrance of me." *For as often as you eat this bread and drink the cup, you proclaim the Lord's death until he comes.* (1 Cor 11:23–26)

The centrality of this liturgical celebration of the new covenant in Paul's life and ministry is particularly prominent if, as seems likely, the church at Corinth gathered as a "liturgical assembly" to celebrate the Lord's Supper "on the first day of every week" (1 Cor 16:2; cf. Acts 20:7).[134] We will offer more discussion on this in chapter 6 below. For now, we simply quote Joseph Fitzmyer: "Those who partake of the cup become the new covenant community."[135] If this is correct, then we begin to see with greater precision to what Paul and his communities are "converting": to the interpretation of the Jewish scriptures in light of the new covenant, and to the celebration of the Lord's Supper as a "participation" (*koinōnia*) in the "blood" of the new covenant (1 Cor 10:14–16). Indeed, it is this practice of *the new covenant supper of the Lord* that, in the end, may constitute the starkest difference between the worship taking place in ordinary Jewish

---

132. Matera, *II Corinthians*, 82. See also Gorman, *Apostle of the Crucified Lord*, 354.

133. See chapter 6 below.

134. Fitzmyer, *First Corinthians*, 614.

135. Fitzmyer, *First Corinthians*, 443.

synagogues and the worship taking place in the churches of Jews and gentiles founded by Paul.[136]

Paul and the Law:
The Freedom of the New Covenant Jerusalem

A second reason for suggesting that Paul is best described as a new covenant Jew is that it offers a thoroughly *Jewish* explanation of Paul's otherwise puzzling self-descriptions as a "Jew" and, at the same time, as one no longer "under the law" (1 Cor 9:20).[137] The concept of a new covenant provides a coherent account of how Paul can say that the Jewish torah is both "holy and just and good" and from God (Rom 7:12) and, at the very same time, *unnecessary* for Paul or his audience to keep, insofar as they are "not under law but under grace" (Rom 6:14).

An important illustration of this new covenant logic can be found in Galatians, when Paul explicitly speaks of there being "two covenants" (Gal 4:24). Although this text is somewhat long, it is worth quoting in full, with key passages italicized:

> Tell me, you who desire to be subject to the law, will you not listen to the law? For it is written that Abraham had two sons, one by a slave woman and the other by a free woman. One, the child of the slave, was born according to the flesh; the other, the child of the free woman, was

136. Note here that the celebration of the Lord's Supper would even constitute a break of some sort with the Jewish communities reflected in the Dead Sea Scrolls (likely Essenes), who adopted the phrase "new covenant" to refer to their communities (e.g., CD 6:19; cf. 8:21; 19:33–34; 20:10–12; 1QpHab 2:4–6). Obviously, they did not see this new covenant as being realized through the death and resurrection of Jesus of Nazareth. See James C. VanderKam, "Covenant," in *Encyclopedia of the Dead Sea Scrolls*, ed. Lawrence H. Schiffman and James C. VanderKam (Oxford: Oxford University Press, 2000), 151–55; Jean Sébastien Rey, ed., *The Dead Sea Scrolls and Pauline Literature* (Leiden: Brill, 2014); Jerome Murphy-O'Connor and James H. Charlesworth, eds., *Paul and the Dead Sea Scrolls* (New York: Crossroad, 1990).

137. Here we disagree with Mark D. Nanos, "Paul's Relationship to Torah in Light of His Strategy 'to Become Everything to Everyone' (1 Corinthians 9:19–23)," in *Paul and Judaism: Crosscurrents in Pauline Exegesis and the Study of Jewish-Christian Relations*, ed. Reimund Bieringer and Didier Pollefeyt, LNTS 463 (London: T&T Clark, 2012), 106–40, who views the expression as an instance of "rhetorical adaptability" rather than "lifestyle adaptability" (p. 130). Nanos's suggestion is tantalizing, but given the passages we cover in this section, we simply cannot follow his proposal.

born through the promise. Now this is an allegory: these women are *two covenants*. One woman, in fact, is *Hagar, from Mount Sinai, bearing children for slavery*. Now Hagar is Mount Sinai in Arabia and *corresponds to the present Jerusalem, for she is in slavery with her children*. But the other woman corresponds to *the Jerusalem above; she is free, and she is our mother*. For it is written,

"Rejoice, you childless one, you who bear no children,
burst into song and shout, you who endure no birth pangs;
for the children of the desolate woman are more numerous
than the children of the one who is married."

Now you, my friends, are children of the promise, like Isaac. But just as at that time the child who was born according to the flesh persecuted the child who was born according to the Spirit, so it is now also. But what does the scripture say? "Drive out the slave and her child; for the child of the slave will not share the inheritance with the child of the free woman." *So then, friends, we are children, not of the slave but of the free woman. For freedom Christ has set us free. Stand firm, therefore, and do not submit again to a yoke of slavery.* Listen! I, Paul, am telling you that if you let yourselves be circumcised, Christ will be of no benefit to you. (Gal 4:21–5:2)

Two primary aspects of this text stand out in support of describing Paul's identity as a new covenant Jew. For one thing, he explicitly refers to "two covenants [*dyo diathēkai*]" (Gal 4:24).[138] Although Paul does not use the explicit language of a "new covenant" as in 2 Cor 3:6, Frank Matera is correct that the "covenant that is not explicitly named here" is "the new covenant."[139] Although it can seem puzzling that Paul reads the new covenant back into the life of Sarah, as Scott Hahn has argued, Paul does not conceptualize the two covenants in strictly chronological categories:

Paul (unlike many modern covenant theologians) does not explain the Old and New Covenants exclusively in temporal terms (i.e., before/after Christ). Instead, by linking the New Covenant with Abraham, and the Old Covenant with Moses, Paul shows how the new surpasses the old

138. For a discussion of "covenant" in Galatians, see Hahn, *Kinship by Covenant*, 238–45.

139. Matera, *God's Saving Grace*, 149.

precisely because it preceded it, in view of the promise and oath that God pledged to Abraham.[140]

Hahn's basic point is correct, yet further nuance is needed. We would add that what is true of Abraham and Moses is *also* true of the matriarchs Sarah and Hagar: the new covenant already exists in the promise that Sarah would bear a "son" and that God's "everlasting covenant" will be through him, not Ishmael (Gen 17:18–21; 18:9–15). By linking the new covenant with Sarah, and the old with Hagar, Paul reveals that the new surpasses the old and, in a sense, is the *older* covenant (cf. Gen 15:4).

Even more strikingly, Paul links these two matriarchal covenants with *two Jerusalems*:[141] (1) The "Hagar" covenant of "slavery" (cf. Gen 16:1–7). This covenant corresponds to "the present Jerusalem [*tē nyn Ierousalēm*]" (Gal 4:25), which in Paul's day of course operated under the covenant of Mount Sinai and everything it entailed: circumcision, Sabbath observance, and animal sacrifices.[142] (2) The "Sarah" covenant of "freedom" (cf. Gen 21:1–7). This covenant corresponds to "the Jerusalem above [*hē anō Ierousalēm*]" (Gal 4:26)—that is, the heavenly Jerusalem.[143] Here Paul is drawing directly on the prophet Isaiah's oracle of a new Jerusalem, which he said would have more children than a mysterious "desolate" woman in the days of a future "covenant" (see Isa 54:1–55:5). The implication of these words is earth-shattering: Paul declares that he (a Jew) and his audience (gentiles) are not children of the *earthly* Jerusalem, its temple, or its torah. Instead, they are children of the *heavenly* Jerusalem. This heavenly Jerusalem, like Sarah, is a "free woman" (Gal 4:31); she and her children are not "under law" (Gal 4:21 RSV). For the sake of clarity, Paul's understanding of the two covenants can be charted out as follows:

---

140. Hahn, *Kinship by Covenant*, 243.

141. Hahn, *Kinship by Covenant*, 273.

142. Matera, *Galatians*, 170.

143. For the early Jewish idea of a heavenly Jerusalem, see *4 Ezra* 7:26; 8:52; 13:36; *2 Bar.* 4:2–3; Andrew T. Lincoln, *Paradise Now and Not Yet: Studies in the Role of the Heavenly Dimension in Paul's Thought with Special Reference to His Eschatology*, SNTSMS 43 (Cambridge: Cambridge University Press, 1981), 9–32.

The "Two Covenants" in Galatians 4[144]

Covenant 1 (Old Covenant)	Covenant 2 (New Covenant)
Hagar: slave	[Sarah:] free woman
[Ishmael:] children for slavery	Isaac: children of the promise
born according to the flesh	born according to the Spirit
Mount Sinai = present Jerusalem	[Mount Zion] = the Jerusalem above
yoke of slavery = under the law	free = not under the law
(Gal 4:22, 24, 29, 24; 5:1)	(Gal 4:22, 23, 26; 5:1)

When it comes to understanding Paul's relationship to Judaism, the implications of Galatians 4 are difficult to overestimate. It shows us that *Paul, precisely as a Jew, understands himself and his audience to be children of the heavenly—not the earthly—Jerusalem.*[145] As Paul puts it elsewhere, their "citizenship is in heaven" (Phil 3:20). Because of this they are no longer "under the law" (1 Cor 9:20; cf. Gal 4:21). The reason Paul can both praise the torah as being given by God and also declare that Christ will be of "no advantage" to those who seek circumcision (Gal 5:2 RSV) is that to do so is to abandon the freedom of the new covenant Jerusalem in heaven for the slavery of the old covenant Jerusalem on earth. As Michael Gorman puts it, the result of Jesus's inauguration of the new covenant "is both shockingly new and surprisingly continuous with the prophetic promises of Scripture."[146]

Of course, all of this raises the question, How does Paul believe one *becomes* a free child of the new covenant Jerusalem, one who is no longer "under law" (Gal 4:21 RSV)? In Galatians, the answer is simple but important: through faith and baptism. As Paul writes earlier in the letter:

Now before faith came, we were imprisoned and guarded *under the law* until faith would be revealed. Therefore the law was our disciplinarian until Christ came, so that we might be *justified by faith*. But now that faith has come, we are no longer subject to a disciplinarian, for *in Christ Jesus* you are all children of God through faith. *As many of you as were*

144. Chart adapted from Gorman, *Apostle of the Crucified Lord*, 258–59.
145. Bird, *An Anomalous Jew*, 158; Hays, "The Letter to the Galatians," 11:304.
146. Michael J. Gorman, "The Apocalyptic New Covenant and the Shape of Life in the Spirit according to Galatians," in *Paul and the Apocalyptic Imagination*, ed. Ben C. Blackwell, John K. Goodrich, and Jason Maston (Minneapolis: Fortress, 2016), 319.

baptized into Christ have clothed yourselves with Christ. *There is no longer Jew or Greek*, there is no longer slave or free, there is no longer male and female; for all of you are one in Christ Jesus. And if you belong to Christ, then you are *Abraham's offspring*, heirs according to the promise. (Gal 3:23–29)

In stark contrast to some proponents of the "Paul within Judaism" perspective who insist that Paul maintained that Jews must "remain Jews," Paul seems to presuppose that *both Jews and Greeks* are called to "put on Christ" through faith *and baptism*. This is no small point. One often gets the impression that scholars aligned with the "torah-observant" view of Paul assume he did not believe Jews needed to be baptized. But Paul speaks of "faith" and being "baptized into Christ" as two ways of referring to the transfer from being "under the law" to receiving the freedom of being "sons" of God "in Christ" (see Gal 4:1–7). Paul does not speak of new covenant Jews as those who simply believe in the messiah. For Paul, members of the new covenant have been *baptized* into the messiah, and, therefore, are no longer under the Mosaic torah.[147] Through faith and baptism, one not only becomes an heir of Abraham and a son of God but also *a child of the new Jerusalem* who is no longer bound to the "slavery" of the present Jerusalem. In other words, they are free with respect to the torah of Moses.

Against this backdrop, we are in the position to take up the question of how to interpret what Paul means by the phrase "works of the law" (*ergōn nomou*). James Dunn has famously argued that "works of the law" are to be seen primarily as referring to "boundary markers" such as the torah's regulations concerning circumcision and the dietary laws, which serve to distinguish Jews from gentiles. Dunn's argument centers on various pieces of Jewish literature, and in particular, one of the Dead Sea Scrolls (4QMMT), in which the "works of the torah" seem to refer to ritual boundary markers.[148] In response, scholars across the various perspectives have objected to Dunn's account and made the case that Paul's use of the phrase "works of the law" should be seen as describing all works required by the torah, including good deeds. This debate is by no means "new." It

---

147. See Hahn, *Kinship by Covenant*, 269.

148. See Dunn, *The New Perspective on Paul*, 121–40, 315–45, in particular. He writes that "not exclusively but particularly to those requirements which bring to sharp focus the distinctiveness of Israel's identity" (130).

has roots in the writings of the early church fathers who also debated the precise meaning of this phrase in Paul's letters.[149]

Can the debate be resolved? Critics of Dunn's argument have pointed out that Paul never defines "works of the law" simply as boundary markers.[150] Furthermore, the nuances of Paul's teaching suggest the phrase includes more than such practices. For instance, in Romans 3:20 Paul insists that no one will be justified by "works of the law" (*ergōn nomou*). He goes on in chapter 4 to elaborate on this very point by referring to David, who "speaks of the blessedness of those to whom God reckons righteousness *apart from works*" (Rom 4:6). Paul then quotes Psalm 32:1–2, which speaks of how God forgives "sins." In the case of David, the "works" in view therefore include moral actions, not merely boundary markers. Furthermore, Romans 7:7 states that knowledge of sin, which Paul had identified with "works of the law" in Romans 3:20, comes through the commandment not to covet: "If it had not been for the law, I would not have *known sin*. I would not have known what it is to covet if the law had not said, '*You shall not covet*.'" Not coveting—a moral injunction—would therefore seem to be among the "works of the law." Given the nuances of the discussion in places such as Romans 4 and 7, it seems difficult to prove that the term refers only to boundary markers. For Paul, we would suggest, "the works of the law" were *quintessentially but not exclusively* circumcision and other such markers.[151]

149. Dunn's position is anticipated in the works of writers such as Origen and Jerome who interpret "works of the law" as referring to the ceremonial aspects of law, such as circumcision and the dietary regulations of the torah. On the other side of the debate were fathers such as Augustine who held that when Paul taught that one is justified "apart from works of the law," he referred to all works performed apart from the grace of faith. Despite the differences, the two sides held two things in common: (1) both sides agreed that Paul insisted that works performed apart from grace do not justify and (2) both groups held that members of the new covenant are called to do works that are empowered by grace. For more, see Matthew J. Thomas, *Paul's "Works of the Law" in the Perspective of Second Century Reception*, WUNT 2/468 (Tübingen: Mohr Siebeck, 2018); Mark Reasoner, *Romans in Full Circle: A History of Interpretation* (Louisville: Westminster John Knox, 2005); Scheck, *Origen and the History of Justification*.

150. See, e.g., Douglas A. Campbell, *The Deliverance of God: An Apocalyptic Rereading of Justification in Paul* (Grand Rapids: Eerdmans, 2009), 450.

151. In this regard it is worth noting that the story in Genesis 17 of God giving Abraham the command to be circumcised comes immediately on the heels of the patriarch's act of abandoning hope that his wife, Sarah, would give him a son. Just prior to receiving this directive, Abraham attempts to take it upon himself to fulfill God's promise to give him a son by sleeping with his maidservant. Circumcision, then, could thus be viewed as God's

As for the rather thorny question of whether Jews are required to follow the torah within the new covenant, if keeping the law was *mandatory* for Jews within the new covenant, it is hard to imagine Paul being able to say that circumcision counts for nothing (Gal 5:6; 6:15) and that he himself is not "under the law" (1 Cor 9:20).[152] While it is possible to respond that Paul is speaking to a gentile audience, it is absolutely essential to recognize that the "works of the law" do not justify, *even for Jews.*

> *We ourselves are Jews by birth* and not Gentile sinners; yet *we* know
> that a person is justified not by the works of the law but through faith
> in Jesus Christ. And *we* have come to believe in Christ Jesus, so that
> *we* might be justified by faith in Christ, and not by doing the works
> of the law, because *no one* will be justified by works of the law. (Gal
> 2:15–16)

Even if one grants that Paul is speaking to a gentile audience, he indicates that "we Jews" are not justified by works of the law but through "faith in Christ" (*pistis Christou*).[153] That is why he says "no one"—literally, "all flesh" (*pasa sarx*)—will be "justified by works of the law" (Gal 2:16). As a result, it is our contention that Jews are not *required* to observe the torah in the new covenant. This does not mean that Jews are *prohibited* to follow various dietary regulations of the torah (see Rom 14), but instead that they are *not obligated* to do so. What is more, mandatory torah observance for Jews would serve to undercut a primary aspect of the new covenant itself—namely, bringing about one new people out of both Jew and gentile.

---

response to an act performed without trust or "faith" (*pistis*). It is easy to see in this light how it might thus be seen as a rite especially representative of the problem of works performed apart from faith.

152. *Contra* Nanos, "Paul's Relationship to Torah in Light of His Strategy," 106–40; Nanos, "Was Paul a 'Liar' for the Gospel? The Case for a New Interpretation of Paul's 'Becoming Everything to Everyone' in 1 Corinthians 9:19–23," *RevExp* 110 (2013): 591–608; David J. Rudolph, *A Jew to the Jews: Jewish Contours of Pauline Flexibility in 1 Corinthians 9:19–23*, WUNT 2/304 (Tübingen: Mohr Siebeck, 2011). For further discussion see Bird, *An Anomalous Jew*, 5–6.

153. As mentioned above, there is a debate about the proper translation of this phrase. Here we simply use the NRSV translation given above. We will discuss this issue in greater detail below in chapter 5.

Paul and Salvation: "All Israel Will Be Saved" through the New Covenant

Paul's commitment to Jeremiah's new covenant promise helps clarify what he means when he says that "all Israel will be saved" (Rom 11:26). While it is certainly true that Paul articulates a remnant theology in Romans 9–11, it is equally important to point out that, when interpreted in context, Paul's statements also imply that *everyone who will be saved—whether Jew or gentile—will be saved through the new covenant*. In order to see this clearly, we need to pay close attention to his teaching in Romans 11:25–27:

> Lest you be wise in your own conceits, I want you to understand this mystery, brethren: a hardening has come upon part of Israel, until the full number of the Gentiles come in, and so *all Israel will be saved; as it is written*, "The Deliverer will come from Zion, he will banish ungodliness from Jacob"; "and *this will be my covenant with them when I take away their sins." (RSV)

Accounting for Paul's assertion that "all Israel will be saved" is required for rightly parsing Paul's gospel message vis-à-vis Judaism. Specifically, this involves answering two questions. First, what does Paul mean by "all Israel"? Second, what does he mean when he indicates that they will be "saved"?[154]

We are persuaded by the thesis of Jason Staples, Bryan Lewis, and Scott Hahn that the term "all Israel" (*pas Israēl*) refers *not* to the notion of *the salvation of every individual Israelite* but rather to the concept of *the twelve-tribe restoration of Israel*.[155] As others have shown, *Ioudaios* means "Judean" in many Old Testament and Second Temple Jewish sources, and *Israēlitēs* often refers to an "Israelite"—that is, signaling a wider concern for the twelve tribes.[156] While the two terms can be used interchangeably, the

---

154. For an in-depth engagement with the history of interpretation, see esp. Gadenz, *Called from the Jews and from the Gentiles*.

155. See Jason A. Staples, "What Do the Gentiles Have to Do with 'All Israel'? A Fresh Look at Romans 11:25–27," *JBL* 130, no. 2 (2011): 371–90; Staples, "Reconstructing Israel: Restoration Eschatology in Early Judaism and Paul's Gentile Mission" (PhD diss., University of North Carolina–Chapel Hill, 2016); Bryan E. Lewis, *Jew and Gentile Reconciled: An Exploration of the Ten Tribes in Pauline Literature* (Wilmore, KY: Glossa House, 2016); Scott Hahn, "'All Israel Will Be Saved': The Restoration of the Twelve Tribes in Romans 9–11," *Letter & Spirit* 10 (2015): 63–104.

156. For a comprehensive look at the use of the term "Israel" in the Old Testament, see

Old Testament and the wider world of Second Temple literature testify to a widespread and real distinction between the terms.[157] Indeed, the hope for the restoration of all the *twelve* tribes was far from an obscure concept. Ancient Jews knew that ten of the northern tribes—that is, those that broke away from the Davidic kingdom (cf. 1 Kgs 12; 2 Chr 10)—had largely disappeared since being carried off into exile by the Assyrians in the eighth century BC. Yet hope for their future restoration abounds in Jewish works.[158] In addition, given the fact that the last king to reign over all Israel was the son of David, it is no wonder that expectations for the twelve-tribe restoration were often linked to the notion of a coming king from the line of David.[159]

What especially strengthens the suggestion that Paul has the twelve-tribe structure of Israel in mind in Romans 11 is the fact that his specific statement about "all Israel" being saved draws directly from Jeremiah 31.[160] Strikingly,

---

James M. Scott, "And Then All Israel Will Be Saved," in *Restoration: Old Testament, Jewish, and Christian Perspectives*, ed. James M. Scott (Leiden: Brill, 2001), 500–515. See also the exhaustive overview in Staples, "Reconstructing Israel," 1–461.

157. See, e.g., John S. Bergsma, "Qumran Self-Identity: 'Israel' or 'Judah'?," *DSD* 15 (2008): 172–89.

158. See Scott, "All Israel Will Be Saved," 489–526, esp. 519n79, where he catalogues the presence of such hopes in the biblical literature (cf. Deut 30:3–4; Neh 1:9; Hos 1:11; 11:10–11; Isa 11:10–16; 14:1–2; 27:2–13; 43:4–6; 49:5–6; 66:18–21; Jer 3:11, 18; 16:14–15; 23:5–8; 31:7–14; 32:37; Ezek 11:17; 20:1–44; 34:11–16; 36:24; 37:11–14, 15–28; 47:13, 21–23; 48:1–29, 30–35; Zech 2:10; 8:13; 9:1; Amos 9:11–15) as well as other Second Temple–era texts (cf. Sir 36:10–13; 48:10; 2 Macc 1:27–29; 2:7, 17–18; Philo, *On Rewards and Punishments* 164–72; Tob 13:5, 13; 14:6–7; Bar 4:37; 5:5; *Pss. Sol.* 8:28; 11:1–9; 17:26–32; *T. Benj.* 9:2; 10:11; *1 En.* 57:1; 1Q33 [*1QWar Scroll*] 1:2–3; 2:7–8; 3:13–14; 5:1–2; 4Q373 1:16–20; 4Q448 B 3–6; 4Q504 1–2 vi 10–13; 4Q554 1 i 13–25; 11Q19 [*11QTemple*ᵃ] 18:14–16; 39:12–13; 40:11–14; 41:1–11; 57:5–6; *1 En.* 90:33; *4 Ezra* 13:12–13, 32–50; *2 Bar.* 78:1–7; *Sib. Or.* 2:170–73; *T. Jos.* 19:3–8 (Arm.); *Jub.* 1:15–17, 28; *Amidah*, 10th benediction; *m. Sanh.* 10:3; *Gen. Rab.* 98:2. For further discussion, see David C. Greenwood, "On the Jewish Hope for a Restored Northern Kingdom," *ZAW* 88 (1976): 376–85; Stephen D. Ricks, "The Prophetic Literality of Tribal Reconstruction," in *Israel's Apostasy and Restoration*, ed. A. Gileadi (Grand Rapids: Baker, 1988), 273–81; David E. Aune with Eric Stewart, "From the Idealized Past to the Imaginary Future: Eschatological Restoration in Jewish Apocalyptic Literature," in Scott, *Restoration: Old Testament, Jewish, and Christian Perspectives*, 147–78; Konrad Schmid and Odil Hannes Steck, "Restoration Expectations in the Prophetic Tradition of the Old Testament," in Scott, *Restoration: Old Testament, Jewish, and Christian Perspectives*, 52; Brant Pitre, *Jesus, the Tribulation and the End of the Exile*, WUNT 2/205 (Tübingen: Mohr Siebeck, 2005), 31–40.

159. See Isa 9:1–9; 11:1, 11–13; Jer 23:5–6; 30:1–11; Ezek 34:23–31; 37:15–19; *Pss. Sol.* 17:31.

160. The influence of this text on the passage is affirmed in the margin of the standard critical Greek text, *Novum Testamentum Graece*, Nestle-Aland, 28th ed. [NA²⁸], 505. See also,

this oracle is explicitly concerned with the reunification of the northern ("the house of Israel") and southern ("the house of Judah") tribes. The parallels between Paul's language and Jeremiah 31 can be illustrated as follows:

Romans 11:26–27	Jeremiah 31:31, 33, 34
"And so *all Israel* will be saved; as it is written . . ."	"I will make a new covenant with *the house of Israel* and *the house of Judah*" (v. 31)
"*And this is my covenant with them*"	"But *this is the covenant that I will make with the house of Israel*" (v. 33)
"*when I take away their sins*"	"*for I will forgive their iniquity, and remember their sin no more*" (v. 34)

When Paul talks about "all Israel," he therefore likely refers to the restoration of *all twelve tribes of Israel* and not to the salvation of every individual Israelite.[161]

This reading helps to explain why Paul deploys such a large number of prophetic texts in this section of his letter that specifically have the restoration of the northern tribes in view (cf., e.g., Rom 9:25 = Hos 2:23; Rom 9:26 = Hos 1:10; Rom 9:27 = Isa 10:22, 23). In fact, as one of the present authors has demonstrated, the hope of the restoration of all Israel was also directly connected to another aspect of Jewish expectations—namely, the understanding of a coming period of eschatological tribulation.[162] Though we will say more about this in chapter 6 below, it bears mentioning that immediately before taking up the topic of the salvation of Israel in Romans 9–11, Paul discusses the eschatological tribulation of the sons of God in Romans 8. He even speaks of their sufferings in terms of "labor pains"

---

e.g., Adeyẹmi, *New Covenant Torah*, 92; Wright, *Climax of the Covenant*, 250–51; Fitzmyer, *Romans*, 625; Thomas R. Schreiner, *Romans*, BECNT (Grand Rapids: Baker, 1998), 619; C. E. B. Cranfield, *A Critical Exegetical Commentary on the Epistle to the Romans*, ICC, 2 vols. (Edinburgh: T&T Clark, 1975), 2:579.

161. This is not to deny that the language in Rom 11:27 draws from other texts such as Isa 27:9 and 59:20. See the scholars listed above who usually note their influence. Here we disagree with A. Andrew Das, *Paul and the Stories of Israel: Grand Thematic Narratives in Galatians* (Minneapolis: Fortress, 2016), 86–88, who glosses over the parallels with Jer 31 and believes that an allusion to this chapter can be dismissed on the grounds that other passages account for the language.

162. See Pitre, *Jesus, the Tribulation and the End of the Exile*.

(Rom 8:22), an image Jewish sources use in connection with eschatological tribulation traditions.[163] The shape of Paul's overall discussion, which brings together the hope of the eschatological salvation of "all Israel" with tribulation imagery, fits well within a Jewish context.

But how does Paul envision the salvation of "all Israel" taking place? The exile—specifically, the Assyrian exile of the northern tribes in the eighth century BC—would seem to present a major difficulty here.[164] The northern tribes were "gentilized"—that is, dissolved among the various peoples to which they were exiled. This very problem is addressed by one of the key prophetic texts Paul alludes to: the book of Hosea. In that book, Hosea is told to name his child "Lo-ammi," which means "Not my people" (cf. Hos 1:9). In context, the child's name is a prophetic sign that indicates the coming exile of the northern tribes. The term refers to their coming scattering among the nations. Commenting on Paul's use of Hosea, Staples explains what the prophet's message would have meant: "*These Israelites have become gentiles—after all, what does 'not my people' mean if not 'gentiles'?*"[165] In other words, the northern tribes were absorbed into the nations. Yet God promised a future restoration, which Paul quotes in Romans 9: "Those who were not my people, I will call 'my people'" (Rom 9:25).

Some scholars have argued that Paul wrenches Hosea's prophecy out of context in Romans 9, claiming that he reapplies a passage that once applied to Israel to the gentiles.[166] Yet we concur with Staples and Hahn that such an explanation fails to grasp Paul's point. Paul's argument is more nuanced than is often realized. By going out to the nations, Paul understands that he will bring back the descendants of the scattered northern tribes of Israel, the ones who became "not my people." By embracing Christ, the descendants of the northern tribes are restored.[167]

163. See chapter 6 below for further discussion of this.

164. One of the present authors has pointed out that scholars who focus on the theme of exile, such as N. T. Wright, often overlook the significance of the Assyrian exile. See Pitre, *Jesus, the Tribulation, and the End of the Exile*, 35.

165. Staples, "Reconstructing Israel," 520.

166. See, e.g., E. Elizabeth Johnson, *The Function of Apocalyptic and Wisdom Traditions in Romans 9–11*, SBLDS (Atlanta: Scholars Press, 1989), 150; Wright, *Climax of the Covenant*, 250. While our "new covenant" view builds on the work of scholars like Wright, we depart from them in some key ways, such as in this instance.

167. Such a reading would also be consistent with the climax of Isa 40–66, a section of the book that Paul draws from heavily. In particular, in Isa 66:18–24 it is the nations who bring the lost sheep of Israel back to Zion in the age of a new heaven and a new earth, further validating the suggestion that for Paul the mission to the gentiles is inseparably connected to

In further support of this reading, Staples analyzes another feature of Paul's language. Paul's statement that "all Israel will be saved" is preceded by the statement "a hardening has come upon part of Israel, *until the full number of the Gentiles has come in*" (Rom 11:25). This, Staples convincingly argues, evokes Jacob's promise in Genesis 48 that Ephraim's "*seed will become the fullness of the nations*" (Gen 48:19).[168] Ephraim, of course, was the patriarch of one of the northern tribes. In alluding to this promise, Paul "has placed his cards on the table in grand style: the Gentiles now receiving the spirit are the fulfillment of Jacob's prophecy. . . . God had planned all along that Ephraim's seed would become 'the fullness of the nations,' so that when Ephraim was restored, it would result also in the redemption of the Gentiles in Abraham's seed."[169] Staples concludes, "Paul's mission to the gentiles is therefore ultimately about Israel's restoration."[170]

Turning now to what "being saved" means for "all Israel," it would seem that, contrary to the claims made by some in the torah-observant Jew camp, Paul does not envision "all Israel" being saved through a different means than that through which the gentiles will also find salvation. *All are saved in Christ through the new covenant.* Paul's use of the "olive tree" metaphor in Romans 11 further underscores this idea. The image is taken from Jeremiah, who used it as a reference for Israel (Jer 11:16–17). Warning the gentile believers not to become smug and look down on Israel for its past failures, Paul tells the Romans, "For if you have been cut from what is by nature a wild olive tree and grafted, contrary to nature, into a cultivated olive tree, how much more will these natural branches be grafted back into their own olive tree" (Rom 11:24). The implications of this should not be overlooked: gentiles are "grafted in" to *the one olive tree*—that is, they are made members of the one covenant people of God. Paul's new covenant theology is thus ultimately ecclesial in shape—but not because the church

---

the reunification of Israel. This also makes sense of Paul's teaching at the beginning of Rom 11. Paul quotes Elijah, who believed that he was alone in northern Israel in refusing to worship Baal (cf. Rom 11:2–3). The apostle recounts the way God assured Elijah that there was a righteous remnant the prophet did not know about. This could be seen as Paul indicating that while it seemed the descendants of the northern Israelites were lost and gone forever, God knew where they were and how to save them.

168. Translation from Staples, "What Do the Gentiles," 385.

169. Staples, "What Do the Gentiles," 387.

170. Staples, "Reconstructing Israel," 590. This also serves to respond to Das's argument against the presence of Jer 31 in Rom 11:26–27 on the grounds that Paul views the new covenant in 2 Corinthians as something in which the gentiles share. See Das, *Paul and the Stories of Israel*, 91.

"replaces" Israel. As Staples puts it, "Paul sees the *ekklēsia* [church] in full continuity with Israel—in fact as the righteous remnant of Israel (see Rom 9:27–29; 11:6)."[171]

For Paul, the new covenant, therefore, does not involve a "separate" arrangement for gentiles. Rather, the gentiles have been incorporated into the righteous remnant of Israel. Significantly, Paul thus moves immediately from the olive-tree image in Romans 11:24 to the climactic statement in Romans 11:25–27, which includes the allusion to Jeremiah's new covenant prophecy.

> And so all Israel will be saved; as it is written,
>   "Out of Zion will come the Deliverer;
>   he will banish ungodliness from Jacob."
>   "And this is my covenant with them,
>   when I take away their sins." (Rom 11:26–27)

In addition to the allusion to Jeremiah, we also see Paul quoting a key passage about the future deliverer or "redeemer" from Isaiah (cf. Isa 59:20–21; cf. 27:9).[172] Paul obviously identifies Jesus in these terms—as we shall explain in chapter 3, Jesus is described as the Davidic messiah (cf. Rom 1:3; 15:12). This is further consistent with Jewish hopes that, as we mentioned above, frequently tied the hope for the restoration of the twelve tribes to the notion of a future Davidic king.[173] As Paula Fredriksen notes, the bi-covenantal approach of the *Sonderweg* position, which holds that Paul believed that Jesus's work of salvation pertains to gentiles and not to Jews, fails to account for this dimension of the apostle's teaching. She writes, "Christ as the messiah son of David could never be of null import for Israel."[174]

When Paul declares that "all Israel will be saved" (Rom 11:26) and then quotes Jeremiah's prophecy of the "new covenant," which entails the for-

---

171. Staples, "What Do the Gentiles," 388.

172. Fitzmyer, *Romans*, 624. Given the importance of the heavenly Jerusalem in Paul's other discussion of the "two covenants" in Gal 4:21–5:1, it is worth noting here that when Paul says the "deliverer" will come from "Zion," he means that "Christ" will come from "the heavenly Jerusalem." So Matera, *God's Saving Grace*, 203. For more on this idea, see the next chapter.

173. As noted above, this hope is found in Isa 9:1–9; 11:1, 11–13; Jer 23:5–6; 30:1–11; Ezek 34:23–31; 37:15–19; *Pss. Sol.* 17:31.

174. Fredriksen, *Paul*, 234n64.

giveness of sins (Jer 31:33–34), he is signaling to his readers that he expects the rest of Israel to be saved in the same way that everyone else (including himself) is: through the forgiveness of "sins," brought about by the "new covenant." In the words of N. T. Wright and Joseph Fitzmyer:

> This [Rom 11:27] is not, then, an alternative "covenant," a way to salvation for Jews and Jews only, irrespective of the entire salvation history Paul has laid out in 9:6–10:21. . . . This is the same covenant renewal Paul has spoken of again and again in the letter.[175]

> The salvation of all Israel is for Paul a certainty and an act that will be brought about by God's grace. . . . The "covenant" [in Rom 11:27] is undoubtedly a reference to "the new covenant" of Jer 31:31.[176]

These scholars drive home an important point. The only way to make Paul say that Jews are saved through one covenant and gentiles through a different one is to wrench his declaration that "all Israel will be saved" completely out of context. It is precisely Paul's fidelity to the Jewish scriptures that enables him to recognize that, somehow—it is, after all, a "mystery" (Rom 11:25)—Israelites will be saved through the same covenant as the gentiles. Through this covenant will come the forgiveness of sins. In critiquing the *Sonderweg* approach, Paula Fredriksen notes this as a key problem, pointing out that "Paul states that Jews as well as gentiles are 'under sin'" (Rom 3:9–20).[177] For Paul, forgiveness comes as Jeremiah announced it would: through inclusion in the new covenant. For him, this must apply to both the Jew and the gentile since all are "under the power of sin" (cf. Rom 3:9).

In support of this, it is also important to remember that when Paul uses the language of "salvation" (*sōtēria*) or being "saved" (*sōzō*) elsewhere, it unequivocally refers to salvation in Christ (cf. Rom 10:1, 10; 1 Cor 9:22).[178] In sum, however we understand the exact identity and timing of "all Israel" being saved, a proper focus on Paul's use of the biblical prophecies answers the question of "how" it will occur: both Israel and the gentiles will be saved *through the new covenant*. The biblical intertex-

---

175. Wright, "The Letter to the Romans," 692.
176. Fitzmyer, *Romans*, 625.
177. Fredriksen, *Paul*, 234n64.
178. Fitzmyer, *Romans*, 619.

tuality of Romans 11 itself shows that Paul is a "new covenant" Jew, not a "two-covenant" Jew.

In Summary: A New Covenant Approach to Reading Paul within Judaism

The question of Paul's Jewishness is one of the most complex and most important issues in Pauline scholarship. In this chapter, we have only scratched the surface and attempted to give the reader a general sense of the wide-ranging discussion taking place in the contemporary field of Pauline studies.

All of the positions outlined above have their strengths; there is some truth in each of them. We hope to have given some sound reasons for thinking that the strengths of seeing Paul as a "former Jew," a "torah-observant Jew," and an "eschatological Jew" can be brought together into a reasonable synthesis through the lens of seeing Paul as a "new covenant Jew." As we hope to have shown, the language of the new covenant helps to explain both the continuity (covenant) and discontinuity (new) with Judaism that is undeniably present in Paul's letters. As a concept, the new covenant is not only Pauline but also has a great "capacity to integrate" the various aspects of Paul's thought.[179] Even more, it is Paul's own language: he does not describe himself as a "minister of Christianity," or a "minister of Judaism," or even as a "minister of the new creation," but he does describe himself as a "minister of the new covenant" (2 Cor 3:6). Yet in order to summarize this chapter it is helpful to ask: What does it mean that Paul is a new covenant Jew?

While our summary here of Paul as a new covenant Jew is one that we will unpack in subsequent chapters, for now we can say the following. First, Paul is a minister of the promised new covenant wherein "all Israel" is being reunited and saved *together* with the gentiles. Far from being a two-covenant arrangement wherein Jews and Greeks are saved through two different "paths," Paul's new covenant is one where both Jew and Greek are united together in the one olive tree of the people of God. This leads to the second tenet of Paul's new covenant Judaism: for Paul, the new covenant involves the Spirit's writing on the heart. In other words, in Paul's account of the new covenant, believers are empowered by grace. Because of this,

179. Wright, *Paul and the Faithfulness of God*, 2:1513.

they no longer need to be under the law and the works of the law—they are under a new covenant. This is not to in any way denigrate the torah (Mosaic covenant). Rather, it is to say that with the new covenant, the age to come has dawned, bringing with it a superior mode of obedience through the promised "eschatological principle of obedience," which Paul identifies with the Spirit.[180] The life of the new covenant is neither antinomian nor legalistic. For Paul, the new covenant involves a mode of faithful obedience that transcends that which was possible under the torah. As we shall see, through the Spirit believers will participate in the Son by dying with him and suffering with him. They will share in the eschatological suffering—the birth pangs—that usher in the new creation, suffering obediently as he did. For this reason we would even go so far as to suggest that the faith and practice preached by Paul can be fittingly described as *new covenantal nomism*—that is, as a system whereby one "gets in" to the new covenant through the grace of faith and baptism, and "stays in" by fidelity and fulfilling "the law of Christ [*ton nomon tou Christou*]" (Gal 6:2), which can also be accomplished only by grace.[181]

In order to see this complex combination of continuity and discontinuity with Judaism in Paul's writings with reference to other topics—such as his eschatology—we need to turn to another aspect of Paul's distinctive theology: its apocalyptic character.

---

180. Smith, "'Spirit of Holiness' as Eschatological Principle of Obedience," 75–99.

181. While Sanders does not believe that Paul himself is a new covenantal nomist, he nonetheless rightly points out, "Christianity rapidly became a new covenantal nomism" (*Paul and Palestinian Judaism*, 552). On our reading, however, Paul is a new covenantal nomist precisely because he holds that one "gets in" *and* "stays in" the covenant community by grace.

CHAPTER 2

Paul and Apocalyptic

Apocalyptic was the mother of all Christian theology.

—Ernst Käsemann[1]

Since the early twentieth century, New Testament scholars who focus on Paul have had a love-hate relationship with Jewish apocalyptic literature. . . . It is important to recognize that Paul developed his distinctive theology and eschatology within a Jewish apocalyptic framework.

—Karina Hogan[2]

In recent years, an increasing number of New Testament scholars have begun to describe Paul's theology as "apocalyptic."[3] In the middle of the twentieth century, the German New Testament scholar Ernst Käsemann famously described "apocalyptic" as "the mother of all Christian theology" and placed Paul as the foremost representative of this.[4] Decades later, the American scholar J. Louis Martyn reignited the discussion regarding the apocalyptic nature of Paul's thought with his massive and influential commentary on Galatians.[5] More recently, prominent interpreters such as Douglas Campbell and N. T. Wright, who disagree strongly on a host of other matters, have at least agreed on this: "an 'apocalyptic' reading of

---

1. Käsemann, *New Testament Questions of Today*, 102.

2. Karina Martin Hogan, "The Apocalyptic Eschatology of Romans: Creation, Judgment, Resurrection, and Glory," in *The Jewish Apocalyptic Tradition and the Shaping of New Testament Thought*, ed. Benjamin E. Reynolds and Loren T. Stuckenbruck (Minneapolis: Fortress, 2017), 155, 174.

3. See esp. J. P. Davies, *Paul among the Apocalypses? An Evaluation of the "Apocalyptic Paul" in the Context of Jewish and Christian Apocalyptic Literature*, LNTS 562 (London: Bloomsbury T&T Clark, 2016).

4. See Käsemann, *New Testament Questions of Today*, 102, 124–37.

5. See J. Louis Martyn, *Galatians*, AB 33A (New York: Doubleday, 1997).

Paul" has the power to "solve a lot of difficulties in the field,"[6] and "Paul's message is thoroughly 'apocalyptic.'"[7] Given this emerging consensus, a major recent study of Paul and apocalyptic could therefore conclude that "it is now almost universally affirmed that Paul had an apocalyptic worldview."[8]

At the same time, an often-heated conversation has been taking place over exactly what it *means* to say that Paul's theology is "apocalyptic." This debate, which is quite complex, involves a number of different questions— far too many to cover in this short chapter.[9] For our purposes here, one particular point of contention stands out: the debate over the continuity between Paul's teachings and the Judaism of his day. At the risk of oversimplifying the situation, the discussion essentially involves two perspectives.

On one side, many scholars who describe Paul as apocalyptic use this terminology in order to emphasize the discontinuity between Paul's teaching and his "earlier life in Judaism" (Gal 1:13). This perspective has recently been described as the "Eschatological Invasion" approach.[10] It tends to emphasize the "radical discontinuity" between the old and new ages,[11] in which the advent of Christ was an unprecedented event that caused Paul to rethink all of reality, beginning with what God had done in Christ. Rooted in the work of Ernst Käsemann mentioned above, this view is largely associated with the work of Pauline scholars such as J. Louis Martyn, Martinus de Boer, Beverly Roberts Gaventa, and Douglas Campbell.[12]

6. Campbell, *The Deliverance of God*, 191.

7. N. T. Wright, *Paul and His Recent Interpreters* (Minneapolis: Fortress, 2015), 184.

8. Ben C. Blackwell, John K. Goodrich, and Jason Maston, "Paul and the Apocalyptic Imagination: An Introduction," in Blackwell, Goodrich, and Maston, *Paul and the Apocalyptic Imagination*, 3.

9. See esp. Blackwell, Goodrich, and Maston, *Paul and the Apocalyptic Imagination*; Davies, *Paul among the Apocalypses?*, 1–38; Wright, *Paul and His Recent Interpreters*, 135–218; Wright, *The Paul Debate: Critical Questions for Understanding the Apostle* (Waco, TX: Baylor University Press, 2015), 41–64; Gaventa, *Apocalyptic Paul*; R. B. Matlock, *Unveiling the Apocalyptic Paul: Paul's Interpreters and the Rhetoric of Criticism* (Sheffield: Sheffield Academic Press, 1996).

10. See Blackwell, Goodrich, and Maston, *Paul and the Apocalyptic Imagination*, 7–12.

11. Martinus C. de Boer, *Galatians: A Commentary*, NTL (Louisville: Westminster John Knox, 2011), 93.

12. See Gaventa, *Apocalyptic Paul*; Gaventa, *Our Mother Saint Paul* (Louisville: Westminster John Knox, 2007); Douglas A. Campbell, "Apocalyptic Epistemology: The *Sine Qua Non* of Valid Pauline Interpretation," in Blackwell, Goodrich, and Maston, *Paul and the Apocalyptic Imagination*, 65–86; Campbell, *The Deliverance of God*, especially 188–91; de Boer, *Galatians*, 31–35; de Boer, *The Defeat of Death: Apocalyptic Eschatology in 1 Corinthians*

On the other side of the fence, other scholars who describe Paul as "apocalyptic" employ this terminology to emphasize the continuity between Paul's teaching and his early Jewish context. This perspective has recently been described as the "Unveiled Fulfillment" approach.[13] It tends to highlight Paul's view of Christ as the climax of the covenants between God and Israel and the consummation of Jewish salvation history. It also focuses on the indispensable role the Jewish scriptures play in Pauline theology and the close affinities between Paul's thought and early Jewish literature outside the Bible. It is commonly associated with the recent work of scholars such as N. T. Wright, Michael Gorman, Richard Hays, and J. P. Davies.[14]

In this chapter, we offer a "both-and" approach to the debate over the apocalyptic aspects of Paul's gospel. As we hope to show, Paul's thought will prove to be deeply rooted in the concepts and beliefs found in early Jewish apocalypses (continuity). At the same time, Paul will also radically transform these beliefs around the "revelation" of what God has done in Christ (discontinuity). In order to accomplish this goal, we will look briefly but carefully at four key themes: (1) eschatology: the expectation of the end of this world and the beginning of a new creation; (2) angelology: the key role played by angels and demons in salvation history; (3) cosmology: the belief in a heavenly Jerusalem; and (4) messianism: in particular, the notion of a hidden and revealed messiah.[15] As we will see, each of these themes are prominent both in early Jewish apocalypses and in the seven undisputed letters of Paul. More importantly, we contend that it is precisely by showing the continuity between Paul's teachings and early Jewish apocalyptic literature that one can offer compelling explanations for some of the more radical elements of *discontinuity* in his theology. As we will see, Paul is not just a "new covenant Jew." He is an *apocalyptic new*

---

15 and Romans 5, LNTS (Sheffield: Sheffield Academic Press, 1988); J. Louis Martyn, *Theological Issues in the Letters of Paul* (Edinburgh: T&T Clark, 1997), 85–156; Martyn, *Galatians*.

13. See Blackwell, Goodrich, and Maston, *Paul and the Apocalyptic Imagination*, 12–17.

14. See, e.g., Wright, *Paul and the Faithfulness of God*; Wright, *Climax of the Covenant*; Hays, *Conversion of the Imagination*; Hays, *Echoes*; Michael J. Gorman, *Becoming the Gospel: Paul, Participation, and Mission* (Grand Rapids: Eerdmans, 2015); Gorman, *Inhabiting the Cruciform God: Kenosis, Justification, and Theosis in Paul's Narrative Soteriology* (Grand Rapids: Eerdmans, 2009); Gorman, *Cruciformity: Paul's Narrative Spirituality of the Cross* (Grand Rapids: Eerdmans, 2001); Davies, *Paul among the Apocalypses?*

15. See Brant Pitre, "Apocalypticism, Apocalyptic Teaching," in *Dictionary of Jesus and the Gospels*, ed. Joel B. Green, Jeannine K. Brown, and Nicholas Perrin (Downers Grove, IL: IVP Academic, 2014), 23–33, for a similar discussion with reference to Jesus.

covenant Jew—that is, one who sees the new covenant through the lens of the coming of an entirely "new creation" (cf. Gal 6:15).

Before we begin, a necessary methodological point. Here and in the next chapter, we will cite various Jewish apocalypses to demonstrate points of contact between Paul's thought and first-century Judaism. Our point here is not to argue that Paul drew directly upon these extrabiblical writings. While scholars agree that books such as Daniel and portions of *1 Enoch* undoubtedly predate Paul, other apocalypses such as *4 Ezra* and *2 Baruch* are dated to the end of the first century AD. Nevertheless, these books are commonly utilized in studies of first-century Judaism as well as in Pauline studies. The reason: these apocalypses are fundamentally *Jewish* texts, and even those that are written several decades after Paul's death provide important evidence for ideas and traditions that can be traced back to the time of Paul himself. The supposition here is that Paul "breathes the same air" as these early Jewish apocalypses and represents, in some cases, an early attestation of some of the ideas found in such works.[16]

This World and the New Creation

In contemporary English, the word "apocalypse" has come to connote the cataclysmic "end of the world." In a first-century context, however, the Greek word *apokalypsis* simply meant "revelation" or "unveiling" and could be used to describe any reality that, at first hidden or unseen, has now become known.[17]

Jewish Eschatology of "Two Worlds"

Nevertheless, it remains true that ancient Jewish apocalypses are often extremely interested in the cataclysmic end of this world and the beginning of a new world.[18] For example, the book of Daniel describes "the time of

16. For a classic introduction, see John J. Collins, *The Apocalyptic Imagination: An Introduction to Jewish Apocalyptic Literature*, 3rd ed. (Grand Rapids: Eerdmans, 2016), 53–142, 220–89. For the use of Jewish apocalypses in Pauline studies, see Reynolds and Stuckenbruck, *The Jewish Apocalyptic Tradition and the Shaping of New Testament Thought*, 131–273; Davies, *Paul among the Apocalypses?*, 36–37.

17. See Danker, *Greek-English Lexicon*, 112.

18. See Edward Adams, *The Stars Will Fall from Heaven: Cosmic Catastrophe in the*

the end" as a period of unparalleled tribulation climaxing in the resurrection of the dead and their entry into "everlasting life" (literally, "the life of the age") (Dan 12:1–4). Along similar lines, *1 Enoch* portrays the time of the final judgment as a global catastrophe, in which "the earth will be wholly rent asunder, and everything on earth will perish, and there will be judgment on all" (*1 En.* 1:7).[19] Most significant for our purposes is the early Jewish concept of "two worlds" or "two ages": (1) this present world and (2) the world to come.[20] Though the roots of this schema can be found in books now contained in the Old Testament,[21] this specific framework is characteristic of the early Jewish apocalypses. According to such traditions, this present world is a place of sorrow, suffering, and evil that will eventually come to an end; it will be replaced by the world to come, a place of joy, immortality, and righteousness. The following examples are offered as illustrations:

> He proclaims peace to you in the name of *the age that is to be*. (*1 En.* 71:15)[22]

> The entrances of *this world* were made narrow and sorrowful and toilsome; they are few and evil, full of dangers and involved in great hardships. But the entrances of *that coming world* are broad and safe and yield the fruit of immortality. (*4 Ezra* 7:12–13)[23]

New Testament and Its World, LNTS 347 (London: T&T Clark, 2007); David E. Aune, *Prophecy, Apocalypticism, and Magic in Early Christianity*, WUNT 199 (Tübingen: Mohr Siebeck, 2006), 34–36.

19. All translations of *1 Enoch* herein are taken from George W. E. Nickelsburg and James C. VanderKam, *1 Enoch: The Hermeneia Translation* (Minneapolis: Fortress, 2012).

20. For a classic discussion, see Emil Schürer, *The History of the Jewish People in the Age of Jesus Christ (175 B.C.–A.D. 135)*, rev. and ed. Geza Vermes et al., 3 vols. (Edinburgh: T&T Clark, 1973, 1979, 1986, 1987), 2.495–96, 537–38. More recently, see Davies, *Paul among the Apocalypses?*, 72–112; Adams, *The Stars Will Fall from Heaven*, 52–99; Michael E. Stone, "Excursus on the Two Ages," in *4 Ezra*, Hermeneia (Minneapolis: Fortress, 1990), 92–93.

21. Richard B. Hays, *Moral Vision of the New Testament: A Contemporary Introduction to New Testament Ethics* (San Francisco: HarperSanFrancisco: 1996), 20, points out, for example, the way the vision of "a new heaven and a new earth" in Isa 65:17 seems to undergird this apocalyptic framework.

22. For compelling arguments in support of the late first century BC to early first century AD dating of the so-called *Book of Parables* (*1 Enoch* 37–71), see especially George Nickelsburg and James C. VanderKam, *1 Enoch 2*, Hermeneia (Minneapolis: Fortress, 2012), 58–63; Collins, *The Apocalyptic Imagination*, 220–21.

23. All translations of *4 Ezra* are from Stone, *4 Ezra*.

The Most High has made *not one world but two*. (*4 Ezra* 7:50)

And that period is coming which will remain forever; and there is *the new world* which does not carry back to corruption those who enter into its beginning. (*2 Bar.* 44:12)[24]

Therefore, they leave *this world* without fear and are confident of *the world which you have promised them* with an expectation full of joy. (*2 Bar.* 14:13)

For they [those who are saved] shall see *that world which is now invisible to them*, and they will see a time that is now hidden to them. (*2 Bar.* 51:8)

On the basis of such evidence, many conclude that the concept of two worlds or two ages—"this world" and "the world to come"—was the "basic presupposition of an apocalyptic-eschatological worldview."[25] John Collins even states, "The belief in another world, beyond this one, is fundamental to all the apocalypses in some form."[26]

How did the idea of two worlds come to be so widely held in early Jewish writings? The answer seems to be rooted in the Jewish scriptures themselves, especially the book of Isaiah, which gives several prophecies of the eventual coming of a "new heavens and new earth" (see Isa 64–66).

Pauline Eschatology of "Two Worlds" (Temporal Axis)

When we turn to the letters of Paul, we find that he shares the basic apocalyptic Jewish idea of two worlds or two ages.[27] For example, Paul says to

---

24. Unless otherwise noted, all translations of the Pseudepigrapha used herein are from James H. Charlesworth, ed., *The Old Testament Pseudepigrapha*, 2 vols., ABRL (New York: Doubleday, 1983, 1985).

25. Martinus C. de Boer, "Apocalyptic as God's Eschatological Activity," in Blackwell, Goodrich, and Maston, *Paul and the Apocalyptic Imagination*, 50n25.

26. Collins, *The Apocalyptic Imagination*, 253.

27. See Karina Hogan, "The Apocalyptic Eschatology of Romans: Creation, Judgment, Resurrection, and Glory," in Reynolds and Stuckenbruck, *The Jewish Apocalyptic Tradition and the Shaping of New Testament Thought*, 157–63; Wright, *Paul and the Faithfulness of God*, 2:1059–60.

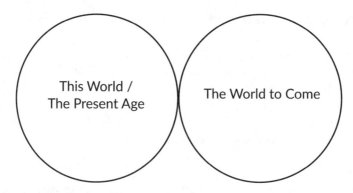

The "Two Worlds" in Early Jewish Eschatology

the Corinthians, "For the present form of this world [*tou kosmou toutou*] is passing away" (1 Cor 7:31).[28] Even more striking, Paul explicitly uses the language of "revelation" (Gk. *apokalypsis*) to describe the resurrection of the dead and the glory of the world to come:

> I consider that the sufferings of *this present time* are not worth comparing with *the glory about to be revealed* to us. For the creation waits with eager longing for the *revealing* of the children of God; for the creation was subjected to futility, not of its own will but by the will of the one who subjected it, in hope that *the creation itself will be set free from its bondage to decay and will obtain the freedom of the glory of the children of God.* We know that the whole creation has been groaning in *labor pains* until now; and not only the creation, but we ourselves, who have the first fruits of the Spirit, groan inwardly while we wait for adoption, the redemption of our bodies. (Rom 8:18–23)

> You are not lacking in any spiritual gift as you wait for the *revealing* of our Lord Jesus Christ. He will also strengthen you to the end, so that you may be blameless on the day of our Lord Jesus Christ. (1 Cor 1:7–8)

Notice here that Paul shares the Jewish idea of "two ages" when he draws a contrast between "this present time [*tou nyn kairou*]" and "the

---

28. See John M. G. Barclay, "Apocalyptic Allegiance and Disinvestment in the World," in Blackwell, Goodrich, and Maston, *Paul and the Apocalyptic Imagination*, 257–74.

impending glory [*tēn mellousan doxan*]" (Rom 8:18).[29] Moreover, just as the Jewish apocalypses did not await the irrevocable destruction of the cosmos but rather the coming of a "new heavens and new earth" (Isa 65:17; 66:22), so too Paul declares that "the whole creation" itself will somehow share in the glory of the bodily resurrection of the dead (Rom 8:18–19). Nevertheless, as we also noted above, the resurrection life of the world to come will only come in full after the eschatological tribulation of the sons of God, here described as connected to the "labor pains" of the whole creation. Finally, Paul describes both the resurrection of the dead and the final coming of Christ with the language of "revelation [*apokalyptō/apokalypsis*]" (Rom 8:18–19; 1 Cor 1:8). If passages like these are not strongly continuous with Jewish "apocalyptic," then nothing is.[30]

Yet Paul also makes statements that are strikingly discontinuous with the eschatology of the early Jewish apocalypses. For example, Paul affirms that, in some sense, the end of this world and the beginning of the new creation have *already taken place*. Some of the clearest expressions of this are from Paul's letters to the Galatians and the Corinthians:

> Grace to you and peace from God our Father and the Lord Jesus Christ, who gave himself for our sins to set us free from *the present evil age*, according to the will of our God and Father, to whom be the glory for *the age of ages*. Amen. (Gal 1:3–5 NRSV, slightly adapted)

> May I never boast of anything except the cross of our Lord Jesus Christ, by which *the world* has been crucified to me, and I to *the world*. For neither circumcision nor uncircumcision is anything; but *a new creation* is everything! (Gal 6:14–15)

> From now on, therefore, we regard no one according to the flesh; even though we once regarded Christ according to the flesh, we regard him thus no longer. Therefore, if any one is in Christ, he is *a new creation*; the old has passed away, behold, *the new has come*. (2 Cor 5:16–17 RSV, slightly adapted)

---

29. See Hogan, "The Apocalyptic Eschatology of Romans," 160; Barclay, "Apocalyptic Allegiance and Disinvestment in the World," 263.

30. See de Boer, "Apocalyptic as God's Eschatological Activity," 60.

In these passages, Paul's language reflects the common Jewish apocalyptic idea of "two worlds"—this present world, which Paul refers to as "this present evil age [*aiōnos*]" (Gal 1:4), and the world to come, which Paul calls the "new creation [*kainē ktisis*]" (Gal 6:15; 2 Cor 5:17).[31] That said, Paul radically transfigures the standard Jewish concept of the two worlds when he makes the claim that through the crucifixion of Jesus Christ, "the world [*kosmos*]" was somehow *put to death* (Gal 6:14). This means that, *for Paul, the death of Christ was, in some sense, the end of the world*. It also means that the long-awaited "world to come" is "no longer solely a future expectation."[32] Paul therefore goes on to declare that if anyone is "in Christ," he is a "new creation" (Gal 6:14; 2 Cor 5:17). As Albert Schweitzer once wrote, "The Pauline assertion that he who is in Christ is a new creature" means that "inasmuch as he has died and risen again in Christ, he belongs already to the new world."[33] With this, Paul is saying something not found in any extant Jewish apocalypse: *through the crucifixion and resurrection of the messiah, the present cosmos "passed away," so that anyone who belongs to the messiah ("in Christ") already belongs to the world to come.*

It is difficult to overestimate the significance of Paul's declaration that anyone who is in Christ already is a "new creation" (Gal 6:14; 2 Cor 5:17) for his overall eschatology. For one thing, it goes a long way toward explaining why Paul is constantly contrasting the realities of "this world"—the flesh, sin, death, the torah, and so on—with the realities of the "new creation"—the Spirit, righteousness, everlasting life, freedom, and so on.[34] These are not vestiges of a Hellenistic "dualism" in which the visible material world is evil while the invisible spiritual world is good. Rather, they are deeply Jewish, apocalyptically based expressions of the belief that this present world is *fallen* but will one day be *transformed* into a new creation.[35]

Moreover—and this is critical—the concept of the "two ages" also points to a major difference between Paul and the eschatology of the Jewish apocalypses. In the Jewish apocalypses, the two worlds are successive realities; the new creation only comes after the old world is destroyed or

---

31. Martyn, *Galatians*, 565. Indeed, the future world is expressly referred to as the "new creation" in several major early Jewish apocalypses (e.g., *Jub.* 4:26; *1 En.* 72:1, 4; *4 Ezra* 7:75; *2 Bar.* 32:6).

32. De Boer, "Apocalyptic as God's Eschatological Activity," 52.

33. Schweitzer, *Mysticism of Paul*, 15.

34. For examples of this, see especially Rom 6–8; 1 Cor 1–2; Gal 5–6.

35. Wright, *Paul and the Faithfulness of God*, 2:1059.

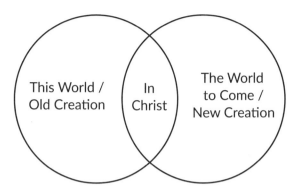

The "Two Worlds" in Pauline Eschatology

dissolved. But for Paul, the old and new creations are *overlapping spheres of reality* that find their meeting point *in Christ*.[36]

Through the passion, death, resurrection, and exaltation of Christ, the old world was put to death and the new world began. Because of this, believers who are "in Christ" live in a kind of "in-between" realm, where the old and new creations "intermingle" with one another.[37] On the one hand, they continue to live and suffer in this world of sin and death; yet, as we will see momentarily, in several very profound ways they already share in the glory of the life of the new creation.

The Law Ordained through Angels

Another prominent feature of early Jewish apocalyptic literature is a heightened focus on the reality of invisible spirits commonly known as "angels" and "demons."[38] For our purposes, two aspects of this early Jewish angelology and demonology stand out as important.

36. Wright, *Paul and the Faithfulness of God*, 1:477–500; 2:1101.

37. See Dunn, *Theology of Paul*, 464, which contains a helpful diagram of this overlap.

38. For discussions of angels and demons in apocalyptic literature, see Angela Kim Harkins, Kelley Coblentz Bautch, and John C. Endres, SJ, eds., *The Watchers in Jewish and Christian Tradition* (Minneapolis: Fortress, 2014); K. P. Sullivan, *Wrestling with Angels: A Study of the Relationship between Angels and Humans in Ancient Jewish Literature and the New Testament*, AGJU 55 (Leiden: Brill, 2004); Christopher Rowland, *The Open Heaven: A Study of Apocalyptic in Judaism and Early Christianity* (New York: Crossroad, 1982), 78–123; D. S. Russell, *The Method and Message of Jewish Apocalyptic* (Philadelphia: Westminster, 1964), 235–62.

Early Jewish Angelology

First, in early Jewish apocalypses, angels are frequently depicted as *mediators of divine revelation*.[39] For example, in the book of Daniel, an unnamed angel gives Daniel the proper interpretation of his startling vision of the four beasts and the coming of "one like a son of man" on the "clouds of heaven" (Dan 7:1–27 RSV). Similarly, the angel "Gabriel" later helps Daniel to understand the vision of the ram, the he-goat, and the little horn (Dan 8:1–27). Along similar lines, in *1 Enoch* the wicked angels reveal such things as the arts of weaponry, sorcery, spells, and astrology (*1 En.* 8), while good angels reveal things such as the coming of the great flood (*1 En.* 10). Finally, in *4 Ezra* the angel "Uriel" is sent to Ezra repeatedly in order to help him comprehend the various supernatural visions that he sees about salvation history and the future of Israel (*4 Ezra* 3–12).

Second, although the point is often overlooked, in early Jewish apocalyptic literature, the angels are depicted as *invisibly governing the kingdoms of the world*.[40] For example, in the book of Daniel, the people of Israel are governed by the archangel "Michael, one of the chief princes," while an unnamed evil angel is described as "the prince of the kingdom of Persia" (Dan 10:13). Along similar lines, *1 Enoch* depicts "seventy" angelic "shepherds" as ruling over (and even abusing) the seventy pagan nations of the world (*1 En.* 89:59).[41] Perhaps most explicit of all is the book of *Jubilees*, which says of the nations, "*Over all of them he caused spirits to rule* so that they might lead them astray from following him" (*Jub.* 15:31).[42] This Jewish belief that the various nations of the world are under the power and guidance of angelic beings, both good and evil, was extremely significant to ancient Jewish sources, and its relevance should not go unnoticed. From a Jewish apocalyptic perspective, the invisible spirits are the most impor-

39. See David P. Melvin, *The Interpreting Angel Motif in Prophetic and Apocalyptic Literature* (Minneapolis: Fortress, 2013).

40. See John J. Collins, *Daniel*, Hermeneia (Minneapolis: Fortress, 1993), 374–75, who traces the belief back to Deut 32:8 (4QDeut^j; LXX), which reads: "When the Most High gave to the nations their inheritance, when he separated the sons of men, he fixed the boundaries of the peoples *according to the number of the sons of God*." (The later Hebrew Masoretic Text [MT] reads instead, "sons of Israel.") See also Archie T. Wright, "Angels," in *The Eerdmans Dictionary of Early Judaism*, ed. John J. Collins and Daniel C. Harlow (Grand Rapids: Eerdmans, 2010), 329.

41. George W. E. Nickelsburg, *1 Enoch 1*, Hermeneia (Minneapolis: Fortress, 2001), 390–91.

42. Charlesworth, *Old Testament Pseudepigrapha*, 2:87.

tant players on the world stage. The unseen powers operate directly in the lives of individual human beings as well as in the conflicts of nations. This applied both to the people of Israel and to the pagan empires. According to the Jewish apocalyptic mind-set, the angels are everywhere.

Third and finally, and perhaps most important of all, in Jewish apocalyptic literature, the angels are also identified with *the heavenly bodies that govern the visible universe*, such as the stars. Here we can simply offer a few examples:

> I [Enoch] traveled to . . . a chaotic and terrible place. And there I saw *seven of the stars of heaven*, bound and cast in it together . . . and burning in fire. Then I said, "For what reason have they been bound, and for what reason have they been cast here?" . . . And he said, "This place is *a prison for the angels*. Here they will be confined forever." (*1 En.* 21:1–4, 10)

> Again, I glorified God . . . and I commanded another *demon* to appear before me. There came *seven spirits* bound up together hand and foot, fair of form and graceful. When I, Solomon, saw them, I was amazed and asked them, "Who are you?" They replied, "We are *heavenly bodies* [*stoicheia*], *rulers of this world of darkness*. . . . *Our stars in heaven* look small, but we are named like gods." (*T. Sol.* 8:1–2, 4)[43]

> For on the first day he created the heavens, which are above, and the earth, and the waters and all of the spirits which minister before him: the angels of the presence, and the angels of sanctification, and *the angels of the spirit of fire*, and *the angels of the spirit of the winds*, and *the angels of the spirit of the clouds and darkness and snow and hail and frost, and the angels of resoundings and thunder and lightning*, and *the angels of the spirits of cold and heat and winter and springtime and harvest and summer*, and all of the spirits of his creatures which are in heaven and on earth. (*Jub.* 2:2)[44]

A few things to note about these passages. Chapter 21 is not the only place in *1 Enoch* where angels and the stars are identified with one another. The entire so-called *Book of the Luminaries* (*1 En.* 72–82) depicts

---

43. Charlesworth, *Old Testament Pseudepigrapha*, 2:162.
44. Charlesworth, *Old Testament Pseudepigrapha*, 2:55.

the angel Uriel as the leader of the "stars." Significantly, these angels govern the time and seasons (e.g., day and night, *1 En.* 82:7), as well as the liturgical calendar of Israel (*1 En.* 82:8). Thus, when the book goes on to speak of "the stars which set in their places seasons, festivals, and months" (*1 En.* 82:9–11), it is surely the case that angels like Uriel and the angelic "leaders" and "captains" are in view—the book even provides their names (*1 En.* 82:10–20). Second, the quote from *Jubilees* offers another illustration of the Jewish tradition that holds that the material elements of the cosmos are governed by angels. Finally, as for the *Testament of Solomon*, although its specific date continues to be debated, there is "general agreement" that it largely reflects first-century Judaism.[45] However one dates it, it bears witness to the ancient Jewish idea that the language of "elemental spirits" (*stoicheia*) could be utilized to describe not only the four basic elements (fire, earth, wind, and water) but also the "heavenly bodies" that were personified as angelic powers and even "worshiped as deities" by the pagans.[46]

Pauline Angelology

When we turn back to the letters of Paul, we can immediately find evidence that he stands in strong continuity with apocalyptic Jewish angelology. For one thing, angels and demons play a very prominent role in his letters. In some cases, Paul explicitly uses the word "angel" (*angelos*) or "demon" (*daimonion*), such as when he declares that neither "angels" nor "powers" (*dynameis*) can separate believers from the love of God in Christ (Rom 8:38);[47] that "Satan disguises himself as an angel of light" (2 Cor 11:14); that women should wear veils during worship "because of the angels" (1 Cor 11:10); and that "what pagans sacrifice, they offer to demons and not to God" (1 Cor 10:20 NRSV, slightly adapted).[48] In other cases, it is somewhat more difficult to catch Paul's references to the angelic powers,

45. Dennis C. Duling, "The Testament of Solomon," in Charlesworth, *Old Testament Pseudepigrapha*, 1:942.

46. Duling, "Testament of Solomon," in Charlesworth, *Old Testament Pseudepigrapha*, 1:970. For a full discussion, see Gerhard Dellin, "*stoicheion*," in *TDNT* 7:670–87.

47. The term likely refers to spiritual powers—e.g., angelic forces. See Robert Jewett, *Romans*, Hermeneia (Minneapolis: Fortress, 2007), 552.

48. In his undisputed letters, Paul uses the word "angel" (*angelos*) some ten times and the word "demon" (*daimonion*) four times (1 Cor 10:20 [2x], 21 [2x]).

because he uses other terms to speak about angelic beings, both good and evil—terms such as "principalities [*archai*]," "powers [*dynameis*]," "authorities [*exousiai*]," and "elemental spirits of the world [*stoicheia tou kosmou*]" (Rom 8:38; 1 Cor 15:24; Gal 4:3, 9). Moreover, Paul shares the widespread apocalyptic Jewish idea of the angels as mediators of revelation. An illustration of this is his warning to the Galatians: "Even if we, or an angel from heaven, should preach to you a gospel contrary to that which we preached to you, let him be accursed" (Gal 1:8 RSV). When it comes to the basics of his angelology and demonology, Paul is very much in line with Jewish apocalyptic literature.

On the other hand, Paul also makes claims that are strikingly discontinuous with early Jewish practice and belief. In fact, it is specifically in his comments about the angels that we find some of the most striking divergences from typical Jewish thought and practice attested in his letters. Paul declares that *anyone who is "in Christ" is no longer under the angels, and therefore no longer under the torah of Moses*. In order to fully account for this teaching, we must look carefully at Paul's argument for why the Galatians do not need to be circumcised or keep the torah in order to be saved. Although the passage is long, it is worth quoting in full:

> Why then the *law*? It was added because of transgressions, until the offspring would come to whom the promise had been made; and *it was ordained through angels* by a mediator. Now a mediator involves more than one party; but God is one. . . .
>
> Now before faith came, we were imprisoned and guarded under the law until faith would be revealed. Therefore the law was our disciplinarian until Christ came, so that we might be justified by faith. But now that faith has come, we are no longer subject to a disciplinarian, for in Christ Jesus you are all children of God through faith. As many of you as were baptized into Christ have clothed yourselves with Christ. There is no longer Jew or Greek, there is no longer slave or free, there is no longer male and female; for all of you are one in Christ Jesus. And if you belong to Christ, then you are Abraham's offspring, heirs according to the promise.
>
> My point is this: heirs, as long as they are minors, are no better than slaves, though they are the owners of all the property; but they remain under guardians and trustees until the date set by the father. *So with us; while we were minors, we were enslaved to the elemental spirits of the world.* But when the fullness of time had come, God sent his Son,

born of a woman, born under the law, in order to redeem those who were under the law, so that we might receive adoption as children. And because you are children, God has sent the Spirit of his Son into our hearts, crying, "Abba! Father!" So you are no longer a slave but a child, and if a child then also an heir, through God.

Formerly, when you did not know God, you were enslaved to beings that by nature are not gods. Now, however, that you have come to know God, or rather to be known by God, *how can you turn back again to the weak and beggarly elemental spirits? How can you want to be enslaved to them again? You are observing special days, and months, and seasons, and years.* I am afraid that my work for you may have been wasted. (Gal 3:19–20, 23–29; 4:1–11)

For our purposes here, four observations are necessary.

First, Paul declares that "the law" was "ordained through angels" (*diatageis di' angelōn*) by the hand of a "mediator" (Gal 3:19). With these words, Paul reflects a first-century Jewish belief that the law of Moses was given by angels.[49] For example, the Jewish historian Josephus states matter-of-factly, "We have learned the noblest of our doctrines and the holiest of our laws from the angels [*angelōn*] of God" (*Antiquities* 15.136).[50] According to this tradition, although the torah was given to Israel by God, it was given *through the angels*. For Paul, therefore, during the time of the torah given by "angels" (Gal 3:19), the people of Israel were also under the power of the angels.[51]

Second, Paul declares that before "faith" came, people were not just "under the law," they were "slaves" to the "elemental spirits of the world [*stoicheia tou kosmou*]" (Gal 4:3, 9). While many think Paul is simply speaking about the material elements of the world, a more likely reading is that Paul is conflating such elements with the angelic powers who were seen as governing them.[52] As E. P. Sanders explains, in this verse the *stoichea*

---

49. See Martyn, *Galatians*, 357n208, citing Deut 33:2 (LXX); Ps 68:17 (LXX); *Jub.* 1:27–29; Philo, *On Dreams* 1.140–44; *Life of Adam and Eve* 1. See also Acts 7:38, 53; Heb 2:2. Cf. Wright, *Paul and the Faithfulness of God*, 2:871n273, who admits "the tradition of good angels being involved in the divine giving of Torah" but seems strangely reluctant to give it any prominence.

50. Flavius Josephus, *Jewish Antiquities, Books XV–XVII*, trans. Ralph Marcus and Allen Wikgren, LCL (Cambridge: Harvard University Press, 1963), 67 (slightly adapted).

51. Schweitzer, *Mysticism of Paul*, 68–69.

52. See esp. Robert Ewusie Moses, *Practices of Power: Revisiting the Principalities and*

"more likely include supernatural beings such as the gods that govern the stars."[53] In his recent full-length study of the angelic powers in the Pauline letters, Robert Moses writes:

> Paul has in essence argued [in Galatians] that being under the Law is in some way equivalent to being under the *stoicheia*! Another way to restate Paul's argument is that prior to Christ, the condition of all humanity (both Jews and gentiles) was enslavement to the elements. But Christ has come to redeem all (both Jews and gentiles) who are under the Law. . . . Paul sets up an equation where *hypo ta stoicheia tou kosmou* ["under the elemental spirits of the world"] is equivalent to *hypo nomou* ["under the law"].[54]

As we just saw above, in early Jewish texts the heavenly bodies were identified with the angels, the ones who governed the nations of the world, the seasons, and the liturgical calendar.[55] In a similar way, Paul personifies the "elemental spirits of the world" and describes the Galatians' return to keeping the Jewish torah as a return to "slavery under the *stoicheia*."[56] As Richard Hays rightly asks, "How could Law-observant worship of the God of Israel possibly be categorized as slavery to the principalities and powers?"[57] The answer is quite simple: *if Paul is referring to the angelic powers through whom the Mosaic torah was given*, then his words make perfect

---

Powers in the Pauline Letters (Minneapolis: Fortress, 2014); Guy Williams, *The Spirit World in the Letters of Paul the Apostle: A Critical Examination of the Role of Spiritual Beings in the Authentic Pauline Epistles*, FRLANT 231 (Göttingen: Vandenhoeck & Ruprecht, 2009), 136–37. For similar conclusions, see Clinton E. Arnold, *Powers of Darkness: Principalities and Powers in Paul's Letters* (Downers Grove, IL: IVP Academic, 1992); G. B. Caird, *Principalities and Powers: A Study in Pauline Theology* (Oxford: Oxford University Press, 1956). Almost a century ago and well ahead of his time, Albert Schweitzer had already grasped the relationship between the law and the angelic powers. See Schweitzer, *Mysticism of Paul*, 70–71.

53. Sanders, *Paul: The Apostle's Life, Letters, and Thought*, 540.

54. Moses, *Practices of Power*, 131.

55. See Wright, "Angels," 330, citing *1 En.* 14:19–23; 40:1–7; 60:2–6; 61:9–13; *4 Ezra* 8:21–22; *Apoc. Ab.* 10:9; 18:11–14.

56. Hays, "Galatians," 282. See also de Boer, *Galatians*, 252–61. De Boer's emphasis on the calendar is correct but needs to be filled out by the fact that if the angels gave the Mosaic torah, they also gave the Jewish liturgical calendar, whose oversight they governed in a direct way through their "liturgical roles" in the heavenly temple.

57. Hays, "Galatians," 282.

sense.[58] Before the coming of Christ, everyone—Jews and Greeks—were "slaves" to the angels.

Third, now that faith has come, anyone who is "in Christ Jesus" is *no longer "under the torah,"* precisely *because* he or she is no longer a "slave" to the "elemental spirits" of the world (Gal 4:9).[59] They are no longer slaves, but rather "children of God" (Gal 3:26). As Paul states elsewhere, "Do you not know that we are to judge angels?" (1 Cor 6:3). In other words, with the death and resurrection of Christ, the order of creation has been turned upside down. In the old creation the angels ruled over human beings, both Jew and gentile alike. In the new creation those who are "in Christ" have been exalted above the angels, precisely because they now belong to the "new creation" (cf. Gal 6:15).[60] According to Paul's logic, to seek salvation through the torah of Moses is nothing less than to prefer slavery to angels over divine adoption.

Fourth and finally, how does this radical deliverance from angelic bondage come about? What could possibly transform a person from being a slave to the angels into a son of God? What could possibly have the power to deliver a person from being bound by the entire law of Moses? The answer: faith and baptism.[61] As Paul states, "In Christ Jesus you are all children of God *through faith.* As many of you as were *baptized into Christ* have clothed yourselves with Christ" (Gal 3:26–27). According to Paul, by dying to the old creation through baptism, a person is freed from the angelic rulers of the old creation and therefore freed from the torah given at Sinai. This is what Paul means when elsewhere in Galatians he declares, "I have been *crucified* with Christ; and it is no longer I who live, but it is Christ who lives in me" (Gal 2:19–20). Expanding on this statement, he later affirms, "The world has been crucified to me, and I to the world." He also insists that circumcision counts for nothing since all that matters is a "new creation" (Gal 6:14–15).

---

58. See Martyn, *Galatians*, 393–406. Here we might add that while it was Israel that was under the law, nonetheless Paul associated being under the law with being under the principalities and powers—namely, angels (Gal 3:19; 4:3). Notably, he goes on to explain that the gentiles were under these same powers (Gal 4:8) and that by returning to the observance of the law, they will in effect place themselves under them once again (Gal 4:9–10).

59. Schweitzer, *Mysticism of Paul*, 70–73.

60. See Hays, "Galatians," 283.

61. Wright, *Paul and the Faithfulness of God*, 2:1103: "Paul believed that in baptism one entered a new reality, a new family, a new version of the human race, in which all sorts of things were possible that previously had not been."

The "Two Worlds" in Pauline Angelology

When was Paul crucified with Christ? *When he was baptized.* Paul explicitly includes himself among the baptized in various places, such as in Romans 6: "Do you not know that all of us who have been baptized into Christ Jesus were baptized into his death? *We were buried therefore with him by baptism into death,* so that as Christ was raised from the dead by the glory of the Father, we too might walk in newness of life" (Rom 6:3–4 RSV; cf. 1 Cor 12:13). For Paul, then, baptism itself is, to use the language of Michael Gorman, a kind of "co-crucifixion" and "co-resurrection" with Jesus.[62] And by rising to new life through baptism, Paul, and every person who is "in Christ," no longer belongs to this world ruled by the angels, but to the new creation, which is ruled by Jesus Christ, the Son of God. This is depicted in the diagram above.

If this interpretation is correct, then Paul's teaching on angels and demons has important implications for the question we looked at in chapter 1: his relationship to the Mosaic torah. How can Paul the Jew, who says the torah is "holy" and "good" (Rom 7:12–13), at the same time declare in no uncertain terms that circumcision, which is expressly required by the torah (Gen 17:9–14), is no longer "anything" (Gal 6:15: *oute gar peritomē ti estin*; cf. Gal 5:1–12)? Is this caprice on Paul's part? Is it part of an evangelistic strategy, devised to make the gospel more palatable to the gentiles? The answer is a resounding no. As we can see from the argument made in Galatians, the rationale for Paul's new covenant soteriology regarding circumcision and the torah derives directly from Paul's deeply Jewish es-

---

62. See Gorman, *Inhabiting the Cruciform God*, 63–79.

chatology and his equally Jewish angelology. By placing Paul squarely in his apocalyptic Jewish context, we are able to explain how it is that Paul the Jew could argue that the torah was both given by God and, at the same time, no longer binding on the baptized. The answer: because those who belong to the new creation are no longer under the power of angels who rule the old creation.[63]

The Jerusalem Above

A third feature of early Jewish apocalypses that is important for understanding the theology of Paul is the existence and importance of *a heavenly realm*. In addition to revelations about the unknown future (the "temporal axis"), these books also contain visions of the unseen world "above" (the "spatial axis").[64] In other words, in early Jewish apocalypses, cosmology is just as important as eschatology. For our purposes here, two aspects of Jewish apocalyptic cosmology stand out as important.

Early Jewish Cosmology (Spatial Axis)

First, in early Jewish apocalypses, the seer or visionary is frequently given a vision or tour of "heaven" or "Paradise." For example, the prophet Daniel has a "vision by night" in which he sees the throne of God in heaven and the mysterious one like a "son of man" coming with "the clouds of heaven" to receive an everlasting kingdom (Dan 7:1–14 RSV). In *1 Enoch*, Enoch ascends into heaven and sees God seated on his throne (*1 En.* 14:1–22); on another occasion, he is taken by the angels to the mountain of God and the tree of life (*1 En.* 24:1–25:7).[65] Along similar lines, one apocalypse describes

63. Notice here that there is nothing "anti-Jewish" about Paul's position regarding freedom from the angels and the law in the new covenant. Paul's problem with the law is *not* a problem with "Judaism" as such. Rather, the problem is with "the old creation," to which the law of Moses and slavery to the angels—to say nothing of sin, suffering, and death—belong. Baptized believers in Christ have been set free from the torah quite simply because they no longer belong to "this world" but have already become members of the "new creation" in Christ.

64. See Collins, *Apocalyptic Imagination*, 5. For a classic study of the importance of the heavenly dimension of apocalyptic literature, see Rowland, *The Open Heaven*.

65. See Nickelsburg, *1 Enoch 1*, 313: the "garden" of Eden and "heaven" are two names for the realm of the righteous dead (see *1 En.* 60:7, 23; 61:12; 70:1–4).

Abraham as being taken up "in the body" by the archangel Michael to be shown the two gates through which the "souls" of the dead enter, either to everlasting "life" or "destruction" (*T. Ab. B* 8:2–16). Finally, in *2 Enoch*, Enoch is "brought up" by angels into the third heaven, and thus to Paradise itself: "And the men [angels] took me [Enoch] from there. *They brought me up to the third heaven. And they placed me in the midst of Paradise.* . . . And the tree of life was in that place, under which the LORD takes a rest and when the LORD takes a walk in Paradise" (*2 En.* 8:1, 3).[66] For early Jewish apocalyptic literature, revelations about the transcendent heavenly world above were just as important as revelations about the future world.[67]

Second, this transcendent realm is often depicted as *a heavenly Jerusalem*—an invisible city of God that is currently hidden but that will be revealed in the future.[68] The notion of a heavenly Jerusalem is directly rooted in the Jewish scriptures, which speak of a future Jerusalem that will be far more glorious than the present-day city (see Isa 2:1–5; 65:17; 66:22).[69] Over time and in various texts, this future or ideal Jerusalem becomes "indisputably heavenly."[70] Consider the following examples:

> For behold, the time will come, when . . . *the city which now is not seen shall appear*, and the land which now is hidden shall be disclosed. (*4 Ezra* 7:26–27)

> It is for you [Ezra] that Paradise is opened, the tree of life is planted, *the age to come is prepared*, plenty is provided, *a city is built*, rest is appointed. (*4 Ezra* 8:52)

> And when these things come to pass and the signs occur which I showed you before, then my Son will be revealed. . . . He will stand on the top

66. In favor of a first-century date for *2 Enoch*, see Collins, *Apocalyptic Imagination*, 301–10.

67. See, e.g., John J. Collins, *Apocalypse, Prophecy, and Pseudepigraphy: On Jewish Apocalyptic Literature* (Grand Rapids: Eerdmans, 2015), 178–97; Daniel C. Harlow, "Ascent to Heaven," in Collins and Harlow, *The Eerdmans Dictionary of Early Judaism*, 387–90; Martha Himmelfarb, *Ascent to Heaven in Jewish and Christian Apocalypses* (Oxford: Oxford University Press, 1993); Rowland, *The Open Heaven*, 78–135.

68. See, e.g., Lorenzo DiTomasso, "Jerusalem, New," in Collins and Harlow, *The Eerdmans Dictionary of Early Judaism*, 797–99; Aune, *Prophecy, Apocalypticism, and Magic in Early Christianity*, 26–31; Russell, *Method and Message of Jewish Apocalyptic*, 283–84, 295–97.

69. Cf. Isa 52:1; 54:11–12; 60:10–11; Ezek 40–48; Zech 2:5–9.

70. DiTomasso, "Jerusalem, New," 797.

of Mount Zion. *And Zion will come and be made manifest to all people, prepared and built,* as you saw the mountain carved out without hands. (*4 Ezra* 13:32–36)

The Lord said to me: . . . Do you think that this is *the city* of which I said: On the palms of my hands I have carved you? [Isa 49:16] *It is not this building that is in your midst now; it is that which will be revealed,* with me, that was already prepared from the moment that I decided to create Paradise. (*2 Bar.* 4:2–3)

Notice here that the idea of the heavenly Jerusalem is tied in both apocalypses to the idea we discussed above regarding the two worlds—that is, "this world" and "the world to come." It is also important to recognize that for both of these apocalyptic works the ideal Jerusalem is a "heavenly, preexistent city," which will be manifested on earth in the age to come.[71] In other words, it is a present reality that has been kept hidden by God in heaven since the beginning of time. Finally, for both these Jewish apocalypses—and this is crucial—*the heavenly Jerusalem is not the earthly Jerusalem restored.* Instead, the earthly city of Jerusalem will be "replaced by the new Jerusalem," which will come down from God out of heaven.[72]

Pauline Cosmology (Spatial Axis)

When we turn from early Jewish apocalypses to the letters of Paul, this emphasis on the heavenly realm is equally prominent.[73] Nevertheless, in stark contrast to interest in Paul's future eschatology, the heavenly dimension of Paul's apocalyptic thought is widely neglected, if not rejected.[74] But Paul stands squarely within the context of Jewish apocalyptic cosmology in at least two ways.

71. DiTomasso, "Jerusalem, New," 798.
72. Russell, *Method and Message of Jewish Apocalyptic,* 284.
73. See Lincoln, *Paradise Now and Not Yet.*
74. Important exceptions to this tendency can be found in Edith M. Humphrey, "Apocalyptic as Theoria in the Letters of Paul," in Blackwell, Goodrich, and Maston, *Paul and the Apocalyptic Imagination,* 87–110; and Markus Bockmuehl, "Did Paul Go to Heaven When He Died?," in *Jesus, Paul, and the People of God: A Theological Dialogue with N. T. Wright,* ed. Nicholas Perrin and Richard Hays (Downers Grove, IL: IVP Academic, 2011), 211–30.

First, like the visionaries and seers of the apocalypses, Paul thinks the heavenly world exists and is important. He even records his own experience of a heavenly vision in which he was "caught up" into Paradise itself:

> It is necessary to boast; nothing is to be gained by it, but I will go on to visions and *revelations* of the Lord. *I know a person in Christ who fourteen years ago was caught up to the third heaven*—whether in the body or out of the body I do not know; God knows. And I know that such a person—whether in the body or out of the body I do not know; God knows—*was caught up into Paradise and heard things that are not to be told, that no mortal is permitted to repeat.* On behalf of such a one I will boast, but on my own behalf I will not boast, except of my weaknesses. (2 Cor 12:1–5)

As commentators agree, although Paul is speaking in the third person here, he is most likely referring to a vision that he himself experienced.[75] He even uses the Greek word *apokalypsis* to describe the "revelation" he received (2 Cor 12:1). Of course, Paul's reticence about what he saw and heard is somewhat different from the detailed descriptions of the "heavenly tours" found in early Jewish apocalypses. Nevertheless, his basic claim of having been caught up into the "third heaven" (1 Cor 12:2) and into "Paradise [*paradeison*]" (2 Cor 12:4) fits quite nicely into the context of early Jewish apocalypses, in which figures such as Adam, Enoch, Moses, and Abraham were likewise "taken up" into the heavenly world or Paradise.[76]

Second, in keeping with the imagery found in Jewish apocalyptic books, Paul also asserts the existence of a heavenly city of Jerusalem, and even declares that those who are in Christ have their "citizenship" in the heavenly realm, and, hence, not primarily on earth:

> Now this is an allegory: these women are two covenants. One woman, in fact, is Hagar, from Mount Sinai, bearing children for slavery. Now Hagar is Mount Sinai in Arabia and corresponds to *the present Jerusalem,*

75. See Matthew Goff, "The Mystery of God's Wisdom, the Parousia of a Messiah, and Visions of Heavenly Paradise: 1 and 2 Corinthians in the Context of Jewish Apocalypticism," in Reynolds and Stuckenbruck, *The Jewish Apocalyptic Tradition and the Shaping of New Testament Thought*, 188–92; Martin, *2 Corinthians*, 577–620; Paula R. Gooder, *Only the Third Heaven? 2 Corinthians 12.1–10 and Heavenly Ascent*, LNTS 313 (London: Bloomsbury T&T Clark, 2006).

76. Martin, *2 Corinthians*, 598.

for she is in slavery with her children. But the other woman corresponds to *the Jerusalem above*; she is free, and *she is our mother.* (Gal 4:24–26)

For many live as enemies of the cross of Christ; I have often told you of them, and now I tell you even with tears. Their end is destruction; their god is the belly; and their glory is in their shame; their minds are set on earthly things. But *our citizenship is in heaven,* and it is from there that we are expecting a Savior, the Lord Jesus Christ. (Phil 3:18–20)

Four points are essential to draw out of these passages.

First, Paul seems to assume his readers share his belief in a heavenly Jerusalem.[77] He also indicates that the ideal city spoken of by Isaiah (see Isa 54:1) is in reality "the Jerusalem above [*hē anō Ierousalēm*]" (Gal 4:26).[78] Thus, here Paul does *not* identify the earthly city of Jerusalem with the eschatological hopes of the biblical prophets. To the contrary, he refers to "this present Jerusalem" (*tē nyn Ierousalēm*) as a place of "slavery" that belongs to the realm of "the flesh" (Gal 4:21–25). For Paul, the biblical prophecies of the new Jerusalem have indeed been "translated" into the heavenly realm.[79]

Second, for Paul, *those who are in Christ already belong to the heavenly Jerusalem.* They are citizens of the celestial city, children of the heavenly metropolis. That is what Paul means when he says that "our citizenship [*politeuma*]" is "in heaven [*en ouranois*]" (Phil 3:20). As Andrew Lincoln writes, "The Christian's commonwealth and government is *en ouranois* because that is where his or her Lord is."[80] That is also what Paul means when he declares that the "Jerusalem above" is "our mother [*mētēr*]" (Gal 4:26). This striking affirmation seems to be rooted in the Greek version of Psalm 87, which describes gentiles being "begotten" or "born" of "Mother Zion [*mētēr Siōn*]" (Ps 86:4–5 LXX).[81] In any case, it means that those who are in Christ are in a familial relationship with the personified heavenly mother city. She, and not the earthly Jerusalem, defines their life in Christ. As Jewish scholar Shaye J. D. Cohen states, "Paul understands the

77. Humphrey, "Apocalyptic as Theoria in the Letters of Paul," 99.

78. James D. G. Dunn, *The Epistle to the Galatians,* BNTC (1993; repr., Grand Rapids: Baker Academic, 2011), 253.

79. *Pace* Wright, *Paul and the Faithfulness of God,* 2:1250.

80. Lincoln, *Paradise Now and Not Yet,* 101.

81. Of course, the numeration of the psalms in the Septuagint differs slightly from the Hebrew text, called the Masoretic Text (MT).

relationship between the earthly and heavenly Jerusalem to be not complementary but adversarial."[82]

Third, in light of the fact that the members of the new covenant already share in the life of the heavenly Jerusalem, it would seem to follow that *the return from exile of "all Israel" mentioned in chapter 1 has the Jerusalem above rather than the earthly Jerusalem as its final destination.* In seeking the salvation of "all Israel," Paul seeks to bring a reunited Israel back from exile to the heavenly Jerusalem. This helps to explain why Paul does not seem especially interested in getting the gentiles to travel to the earthly Jerusalem in order to fulfill the biblical prophecies of the ingathering of the gentiles to Mount Zion (cf. Mic 4–5; Isa 2; 56; Zech 8–10; etc.).[83] While Paul was interested in taking up a collection to support believers living there (cf. Rom 15:25–26; 1 Cor 16:3), we do not any have evidence that he expected gentiles to make a pilgrimage there themselves. From his apocalyptic point of view, such an earthly pilgrimage would simply bring them to *the wrong city.* It also makes sense of why Paul does not seem all that interested in getting his congregations to go up to Jerusalem to keep the covenant by sacrificing in the Jerusalem temple. If "the Jerusalem above" is their "mother," then those who are "in Christ" are not under the Mosaic "covenant" and do not primarily belong to earthly Jerusalem. Rather, they are under the new covenant and the Jerusalem above is their mother (Gal 4:22).[84]

Fourth and finally, *because those who are in Christ belong to the heavenly Jerusalem, they are "free" from the earthly Jerusalem and its torah.* Paul's emphatic repetition of "freedom" (Gal 4:26, 31; 5:1) means freedom from the angelic powers, and therefore freedom from the torah of Moses.[85] Citizens of the earthly Jerusalem are still "slaves" to the angels (Gal 4:9 RSV) and therefore "bound" by the torah of Moses, which was "ordained by angels" (Gal 3:19 RSV). Circumcision obliges them to keep "the whole law" (Gal 5:1–3 RSV). But the citizens of the heavenly Jerusalem are not slaves to the angels or the torah; instead, they are "children of promise" (Gal 4:28 RSV), children "of the free woman" (Gal 4:31), and "born according to the Spirit" (Gal 4:29). As such they are free from the angelic powers who

82. See Shaye J. D. Cohen, "Galatians," in *The Jewish Annotated New Testament*, ed. Amy-Jill Levine and Marc Zvi Brettler, 2nd ed. (Oxford: Oxford University Press, 2017), 384.

83. Wright, *Paul and the Faithfulness of God*, 2:1250.

84. See Craig S. Keener, *Galatians*, NCBC (Cambridge: Cambridge University Press, 2018), 220–21.

85. Dunn, *Galatians*, 254.

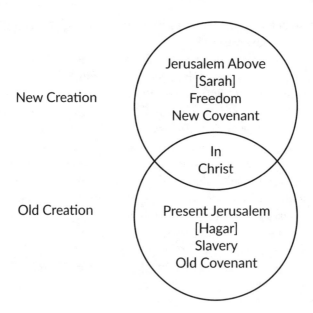

New Creation

Jerusalem Above
[Sarah]
Freedom
New Covenant

In
Christ

Old Creation

Present Jerusalem
[Hagar]
Slavery
Old Covenant

The "Two Worlds" in Pauline Cosmology

govern this world and the present Jerusalem and therefore free from the law of circumcision given by angels.

In short, a proper focus on the heavenly world demonstrates that for Paul, those who are in Christ not only live in the overlapping *time* between the present world and the future new creation (temporal axis); they also live "in between" the visible and invisible realms (spatial axis). As Edith Humphrey puts it, "The Galatian Christians are to see themselves as inhabiting two realms, *both earth and heaven.*"[86]

The Hidden Messiah

The fourth and final aspect of early Jewish apocalyptic literature that is important for understanding Paul is the notion of *a preexistent, hidden messiah.*[87] In his famous work *Jesus the Jew*, the Jewish scholar Geza Vermes

86. Humphrey, "Apocalyptic as Theoria," 101 (emphasis added).
87. See Nickelsburg and VanderKam, *1 Enoch 2*, 170–71, 263–64; Sigmund Mowinckel, "The Hidden Messiah," in *He That Cometh: The Messiah Concept in the Old Testament and*

spoke of this as the Jewish tradition of "the hidden and revealed Messiah."[88] Although this tradition is well known in studies of Jewish apocalyptic literature, it does not seem to have had as much impact on recent studies of the apocalyptic Paul as one might expect.[89] Nevertheless, it is highly relevant for understanding Paul's apocalyptic Christology.

Early Jewish Christology: The Hidden Messiah

According to certain early Jewish apocalypses, the long-awaited messiah would be "hidden" so that God would have to reveal his identity to the elect. Consider the following examples:

> And in that hour, that *son of man* was named in the presence of the Lord of Spirits; and his name, before the Head of Days. Even before the sun and the constellations were created, before the stars of heaven were made, his name was named before the Lord of Spirits. He will be a staff for the righteous, that they may lean on him and not fall; he will be the light of the nations, and he will be a hope for those who grieve in their hearts. All who dwell on the earth will fall down and worship before him, and they will glorify and bless and sing hymns to the name of the Lord of Spirits. *For this (reason) he was chosen and hidden in his presence before the world was created and forever.* And the wisdom of the Lord of Spirits has *revealed him* to the holy and the righteous. (*1 En.* 48:2–7)

> Pain will seize them when they see that Son of Man sitting on the throne of his glory. And the kings and the mighty and all who possess the land will bless and glorify and exalt him who rules over all, *who was hidden. For from the beginning the Son of Man was hidden,* and the Most High preserved him in the presence of his might, and he *revealed him* to the chosen. (*1 En.* 62:5–7)

Later Judaism, trans. G. W. Anderson (1954; repr., Grand Rapids: Eerdmans, 2005), 304–8; Russell, *Method and Message of Jewish Apocalyptic,* 329–40.

88. Geza Vermes, *Jesus the Jew* (Philadelphia: Fortress, 1973), 137–39.

89. For example, in his otherwise excellent book, Davies, *Paul among the Apocalypses?,* discusses Paul's epistemology, eschatology, cosmology, and soteriology but has no chapter on Paul's apocalyptic Christology.

"As for your seeing a man come up from the heart of the sea, this is *he whom the Most High has been keeping for many ages*, through whom he will deliver his creation. . . . And when these things come to pass and the signs occur which I showed you before, *then my son will be revealed*." . . . I said, "O sovereign Lord, explain this to me: Why did I see the man coming up from the heart of the sea?" He said to me, "Just as no one can explore or know what is in the depths of the sea, *so no one on earth can see my servant* or those who are with him, except in the time of his day." (*4 Ezra* 13:25–26, 32, 51–52)

Three points need to be kept in mind about these important texts.

First, although the passages quoted above do not use the word "messiah," elsewhere in both apocalypses, the "Son of Man" and the "servant" are explicitly identified as the "Anointed One" or "Messiah" (cf. *1 En.* 48:10; 52:4; *4 Ezra* 13:51).[90] Therefore, we can speak quite properly of a "hidden messiah" tradition in both *1 Enoch* and *4 Ezra*.

Second, in both cases, the idea of the hidden messiah seems to derive from a messianic interpretation of Isaiah's "servant" figure.[91] As John Collins writes, "the portrait of the Son of Man" is modeled on "the hidden servant of the Lord (Isa 49:2)."[92] For example, in one passage, the Servant in Isaiah declares:

The LORD called me from the womb,
   from the body of my mother he named my name.
He made my mouth like a sharp sword,
   in the shadow of his hand *he hid me*;
he made me a polished arrow,
   in his quiver *he hid me away*.
And he said to me, "*You are my servant*." (Isa 49:1–3 RSV)

---

90. See Nickelsburg and VanderKam, *1 Enoch 2*, 113–20; Stone, *4 Ezra*, 401.

91. See Nickelsburg and VanderKam, *1 Enoch 2*, 258–59, 263; Stone, *4 Ezra*, 207–13 (esp. 209). See also James C. VanderKam, "Righteous One, Messiah, Chosen One, and Son of Man in *1 Enoch* 37–71," in *The Messiah: Developments in Earliest Judaism and Christianity*, ed. James H. Charlesworth (Minneapolis: Fortress, 1992), 189: "The related idea in the Similitudes that the Lord has hidden the son of man (48:6; 62:7) reminds one of verses such as Isa 49:2 and 51:16."

92. John J. Collins, *The Scepter and the Star: Messianism in Light of the Dead Sea Scrolls*, 2nd ed. (Grand Rapids: Eerdmans, 2010), 182.

Along similar lines, when the servant is finally revealed, the kings and princes of the earth will "see" that which "has not been told them" and "understand" that which "they have not heard," so that they fall prostrate before him (Isa 49:7 RSV; cf. 52:13–16). This is precisely what happens when, at the final judgment, the kings and rulers "fall on their faces" in the presence of the Son of Man and worship him (*1 En.* 62:7–9). Likewise, the messiah is repeatedly called "My servant messiah" or just the "servant" (*4 Ezra* 7:28–29; 13:32, 37, 52; 14:9).

Third, as experts in Jewish apocalyptic literature agree, in both texts the messiah is not just hidden; he is also a *"preexistent" or heavenly being.*[93] That is what it means when they say that he was "hidden in his [God's] presence before the world was created" (*1 En.* 48:6) or that he was "hidden" in God's presence "for many ages" (*4 Ezra* 13:26), only later to be "revealed" (*4 Ezra* 7:28–29). The idea of messianic preexistence may derive from a messianic interpretation of the mysterious "son of man" figure in Daniel (cf. Dan 7:13–14 RSV), whose coming on the clouds of heaven, in the words of John Collins, "could easily suggest preexistence."[94] It is worth pointing out that both apocalypses unmistakably depict the messiah as the Danielic "son of man" (*1 En.* 62:3–7; *4 Ezra* 13:1–52). In sum: the identity of the messiah is a heavenly mystery that must be revealed to the elect and the righteous. Eventually, the entire world, even the pagan kings and princes, will see him. But for now, he remains hidden, known only to the righteous.

Paul's Apocalyptic Christology

With this apocalyptic tradition of a hidden and revealed messiah in mind, we now turn to the letters of Paul. In two key passages, Paul shows a striking affinity with the apocalyptic idea of a "hidden and revealed messiah":

> For I want you to know, brothers and sisters, that *the gospel that was proclaimed by me is not of human origin*; for I did not receive it from a

---

93. See Nickelsburg and VanderKam, *1 Enoch 2*, 170; Stone, *4 Ezra*, 401; 209; Russell, *Method and Message of Jewish Apocalyptic*, 328. See also Joseph A. Fitzmyer, SJ, *The One Who Is to Come* (Grand Rapids: Eerdmans, 2007), 121, who speaks of "a transcendent hidden (= preexistent?) figure" in *4 Ezra* 13. See also *1 En.* 48:2–3, 6; 62:7; *4 Ezra* 13:26, 52; 14:9; *2 Bar.* 29:3; 30:1 (implied).

94. Collins, *Scepter and the Star*, 204.

human source, nor was I taught it, but *I received it through a revelation [apokalypsis] of Jesus Christ.*

You have heard, no doubt, of my earlier life in Judaism. I was violently persecuting the church of God and was trying to destroy it. I advanced in Judaism beyond many among my people of the same age, for I was far more zealous for the traditions of my ancestors. But when God, who had set me apart before I was born and called me through his grace, was pleased *to reveal [apokalypsai] his Son to me,* so that I might proclaim him among the Gentiles, I did not confer with any human being, nor did I go up to Jerusalem to those who were already apostles before me, but I went away at once into Arabia, and afterwards I returned to Damascus. (Gal 1:11–17)

Yet among the mature we do impart wisdom, although it is not a wisdom of this age or of the rulers of this age, who are doomed to pass away. But we impart *a secret and hidden wisdom of God,* which God decreed before the ages for our glorification. *None of the rulers of this age understood this; for if they had, they would not have crucified the Lord of glory.* But, as it is written,

"What no eye has seen, nor ear heard,

nor the heart of man conceived,

what God has prepared for those who love him,"

God has *revealed [apekalypsen]* to us through the Spirit. (1 Cor 2:6–10 RSV)

With these words, Paul describes his "gospel" message in explicitly "apocalyptic" terms: it is not a gospel "of human origin," nor was Paul taught it, but it came to him directly through a "revelation [*apokalypsis*]" (Gal 1:12).[95] And what was revealed? That Jesus of Nazareth, whose followers he had persecuted and tried to destroy, was in fact the "Christ" (*christos*)" (Gal 1:12), the messiah.[96] This very notion of Christ being "revealed" to Paul presupposes that the messiah's true identity was previously *hidden* from him.

Moreover, should there be any doubt about the importance of the hidden messiah motif for Paul, notice that in 1 Corinthians, he applies the language of "revelation" not only to Jesus's personal identity but also to

95. Martyn, *Galatians,* 98–99.
96. De Boer, *Galatians,* 82.

the event of the crucifixion. Here Paul insists that the truth about Jesus was so "secret" and "hidden" that it was even concealed from the "rulers of this age"—a phrase that may refer to human rulers, or angels, or both.[97] As a result, they unknowingly crucified "the Lord of glory [*ton kyrion tēs doxēs*]" (1 Cor 2:8).[98] Nevertheless, according to the apostle, the truth has been "revealed" (*apekalypsen*) to those who believe through the power of the Spirit (1 Cor 2:10). With this evidence in hand, it seems safe to conclude that Paul's Christology can (and should) be described as "apocalyptic."[99]

In Summary: Paul and the Apocalyptic New Covenant

What then are we to make of the "apocalyptic Paul" debate? Are Paul's apocalyptic teachings more continuous or discontinuous with the Judaism of his day?

On the one hand, as we have seen, there is indisputable continuity between early Jewish apocalyptic thought and Paul's eschatology, angelology, cosmology, and even his Christology. Paul's beliefs about the "two ages," the end of this world, the coming of the new creation, the resurrection of the dead, the role of angels and demons, the importance of the

---

97. See John K. Goodrich, "After Destroying Every Rule, Authority, and Power: Paul, Apocalyptic, and Politics in 1 Corinthians," in Blackwell, Goodrich, and Mason, *Paul and the Apocalyptic Imagination*, 279–85.

98. See Fitzmyer, *First Corinthians*, 177: "In applying glory to the risen Christ, Paul implicitly is putting him on the same level as YHWH (see Ps 29:3; quoted in Acts 7:2)." See also Gordon Fee, *Pauline Christology* (Grand Rapids: Baker Academic, 2007), 136; Chris Tilling, *Paul's Divine Christology* (Grand Rapids: Eerdmans, 2015), 225–27, who recognizes that the expression "Lord of glory" in 1 Cor 2:8 is used in *1 Enoch* for the divine creator, "the Lord of Spirits." When taken together, 1 Cor 2 and Phil 2 cast serious doubt on the claim that Paul thought Jesus only "became" the divine Son of God after his resurrection and ascension. Cf., e.g., Bart Ehrman, *How Jesus Became God: The Exaltation of a Jewish Preacher from Galilee* (San Francisco: HarperOne, 2014), 211–45. Significantly, Ehrman completely ignores Paul's statement that Jesus was already "the Lord of glory" when he was "crucified" (1 Cor 2:8).

99. In the next chapter we will look at another key christological passage in Paul—namely, Phil 2:5–8, which scholars have seen as relating to the hidden messiah traditions as well. See, e.g., Adela Yarbro Collins and John J. Collins, *King and Messiah as Son of God: Divine, Human, and Angelic Messianic Figures in Biblical and Related Literature* (Grand Rapids: Eerdmans, 2008), 208.

heavenly Jerusalem, the notion of a hidden and revealed messiah—all of these are only fully intelligible within his first-century Jewish context.

On the other hand, it is precisely these apocalyptic beliefs that enable Paul to make claims that are radically (but nevertheless explicably) discontinuous with the Judaism of his day. Paul claims that, through the passion, death, resurrection, and exaltation of Jesus Christ, the old creation has been "crucified" and the "new creation" already begun. Because of this, those who are in Christ are no longer under the power of angels and therefore no longer under the torah of Moses. They are citizens of the celestial city, for "all Israel" and the gentiles together are children of the heavenly Jerusalem and not the earthly Jerusalem. Most striking of all, Jesus of Nazareth, who was crucified on Calvary, is none other than the long-awaited messiah and the "Son of God." This is the great *apokalypsis* for Paul—the divine sonship of Jesus Christ. Paul is not just a "new covenant Jew"; his ministry centers on what Michael Gorman helpfully calls an "apocalyptic new covenant,"[100] which consists of the in-breaking of *heavenly* realities.

In the next chapter we will look at the way the very heart of Paul's message—the person of Jesus Christ—builds on these apocalyptic themes. For now, let us simply concur with Ernst Käsemann: "Apocalyptic" was indeed the "mother of all Christian theology." But not just Christian theology in general; it was the mother of *Pauline* theology in particular. In the words of Paul himself, "The Jerusalem above . . . *she is our mother*" (Gal 4:26).

---

100. Gorman, "Apocalyptic New Covenant," 317–37. Indeed, the "new covenant" prophecy of Jeremiah was often featured in apocalyptic literature, showing us that the two categories were easily connected by other ancient Jewish thinkers. See Wells, *Grace and Agency in Paul and Second Temple Judaism*, 102–3; T. J. Deidun, IC, *New Covenant Morality in Paul*, AnBib 89 (Rome: Editrice Pontificio Instituto Biblico, 1981), 35n118.

CHAPTER 3

Pauline Christology

> Paul's Gospel . . . was centered wholly on Jesus Christ. . . . Christ became the key to understanding God's purpose for mankind, and indeed God himself.
>
> —James D. G. Dunn[1]

> Paul's theology is predominantly a christology.
>
> —Joseph Fitzmyer[2]

If there is any word that is essential for understanding Pauline theology, it is the word "Christ" (*christos*). As Douglas Campbell rightly points out, "Christ himself (in some sense) . . . is at the centre of Paul."[3] And yet it is precisely Paul's theological understanding of Christ—that is, Paul's Christology—which is at the focal point of a complex debate.

In recent decades, Pauline scholars have written thousands of pages discussing key questions in Pauline Christology.[4] For our purposes here, three in particular stand out: (1) What does Paul mean when he speaks of Jesus as the "Christ"? Is he using the term more as a "personal name" for Jesus, or is it a royal title for the Jewish "messiah"? (2) What exactly does Paul mean when he refers to Jesus as the "Son of God"? Does Paul

---

1. Dunn, *The Theology of Paul the Apostle*, 181.
2. Fitzmyer, "Pauline Theology," 1388.
3. Campbell, *Quest for Paul's Gospel*, 32.
4. See, e.g., Tilling, *Paul's Divine Christology*; Wright, *Paul and the Faithfulness of God*; Richard Bauckham, *Jesus and the God of Israel: God Crucified and Other Studies on the New Testament's Christology of Divine Identity* (Grand Rapids: Eerdmans, 2008), 182–232; Fee, *Pauline Christology* (itself over 700 pages!); Larry Hurtado, *Lord Jesus Christ: Devotion to Jesus in Early Christianity* (Grand Rapids: Eerdmans, 2003), 79–154; Frank J. Matera, *New Testament Christology* (Louisville: Westminster John Knox, 1999), 83–134; Dunn, *The Theology of Paul the Apostle*, 163–316.

think of Jesus's divine sonship as something bestowed on him only after his resurrection from the dead? Or is this divine sonship something possessed by Jesus from the very beginning of his human life, or even *prior* to becoming human? (3) How does Paul reconcile his identification of Jesus as "the Lord" (*kyrios*) with his Jewish confession of "one God" (1 Cor 8:6)? Does he think Jesus was a human being who was later exalted and made divine? Or does Paul believe that Jesus is something more even than that? As we will see, most exegetes agree that Paul describes Jesus as "divine." A thornier question involves fully explaining what Paul *means* when he uses relational language about God with reference to Jesus.

In this chapter we will briefly explore Paul's view of (1) Jesus's identity as "messiah" or "Christ"; (2) Jesus's identity as God's "Son" sent into the world; and (3) the relationship between Jesus and the "one God." Building on our analysis in chapters 1 and 2, we will contend that Paul's Christology is deeply *rooted* in first-century Judaism and—at the same time—goes *beyond* other early Jewish sources in his messianic claims. As we will see, for Paul the apocalyptic revelation of Christ seems to have reshaped the way he thought about *everything*, even the one God.

The Messiah Descended from David

The question that needs to be asked is this: In a first-century Jewish context, what would it have meant to identify someone as the "messiah" or "Christ" (*christos*)? And what does Paul mean when he uses this terminology repeatedly with reference to Jesus of Nazareth?

Entire books have been written just on the concept of the messiah in early Judaism.[5] For our purposes here, it is important to point out that while first-century Jewish sources often disagree about exactly how God would ultimately save the people, there was a "dominant notion" that God

---

5. Two of the most recent and important studies, which are characterized by important methodological nuances, are Matthew V. Novenson, *The Grammar of Messianism: An Ancient Jewish Political Idiom and Its Users* (Oxford: Oxford University, 2017); Novenson, *Christ among the Messiahs: Christ Language in Paul and Messiah Language in Ancient Judaism* (Oxford: Oxford University Press, 2012). See also, e.g., Collins, *The Scepter and the Star*; Collins and Collins, *King and Messiah as Son of God*; Fitzmyer, *The One Who Is to Come*; Gerbern S. Oegema, *The Anointed and His People: Messianic Expectations from the Maccabees to Bar Kochba*, JSPSS 27 (Sheffield: Sheffield Academic Press, 1998).

would send a royal deliverer from the line of King David.[6] On multiple occasions, the scriptures of Israel attest that the Lord God had sworn that David's kingdom would endure "forever" (2 Sam 7:13–16; 1 Chr 17:11–14; Ps 89:3–4, 35–37).[7] By the time of Paul in the first century AD, even though it had been centuries since a Davidic king sat on the throne and ruled, the hope for the restoration of the Davidic kingdom endured. As a result, Jewish texts written in and around the time of Paul express expectations of a coming "anointed one"—"messiah" (*mashiyach*) in Hebrew, *christos* in Greek—from the line of David.[8]

The relevance of such hopes for understanding Paul, however, has been a source of debate. Over and over again, Paul refers to Jesus as "Christ." In the undisputed letters alone, the frequency of this word is remarkable, occurring around 270 times.[9] This repetitive usage is simply unprecedented; as far as we can tell, no early Jewish author spoke of the "messiah" or *christos* with this kind of regularity. Due in part to this disparity, a number of scholars have come to the conclusion that in the Pauline epistles the term has a different meaning than it does in other Jewish texts. Instead of evoking "messianic hopes," these interpreters contend that in Paul's writings *christos* simply functions as a personal name for Jesus.[10]

On the other hand, a growing number of exegetes from various perspectives are now challenging this approach.[11] One substantial problem with the "non-messianic" interpretation of *christos* in Paul is that it ignores the obvious implications of Paul's language. Pointing out that Jesus is specifically called "messiah" (= *christos*) about 270 times in the Pauline corpus, John Collins concludes, "If this is not ample testimony that Paul regarded Jesus as the messiah, then words have no meaning."[12] Furthermore, this hypothesis also overlooks the fact that Paul explicitly uses the term *chris-*

---

6. Collins, *The Scepter and the Star*, 209.

7. See also Pss 110:4; 132:11; Isa 9:7; 11:1; 16:5; Jer 23:5; 30:9; 33:25; Ezek 34:23–24; 37:24; Amos 9:11.

8. See, e.g., CDᵃ (*Damascus Documentᵃ*) 7:18–21; 4Q174 (*4QFlorilegium*) 1 i 21, 2:10–13; 4Q252 (*4QCommentary on Genesis A*) 5:1–5; 4Q285 (*4QSefer ha-Milhamah*) 5:2–3; *Pss. Sol.* 17:4–10, 21; *4 Ezra* 12:31–32.

9. See Novenson, *Christ among the Messiahs*, 64.

10. See Novenson, *Christ among the Messiahs*, 12–33, 64–67, citing F. C. Baur, *Paul the Apostle: His Life and Works, Epistles and Teachings*, trans. Allan Menzies, 2 vols. (1873–1875; repr., Peabody, MA: Hendrickson, 2003), 1:370–37, as an example.

11. See Novenson, *Christ among the Messiahs*; Fredriksen, *Paul*, 133–45; Wright, *Climax of the Covenant*, 18–55.

12. Collins, *Scepter and the Star*, 2.

tos as a generic reference to the "messiah" when he says that "from them [Israel], according to the flesh, comes *the messiah*" (Rom 9:5).[13] Finally, the non-messianic interpretation assumes an overly simplistic approach to personal names and titles. In the ancient world in general and the first century in particular, honorifics could be combined to function with personal names. Think here of the obvious example of "Caesar Augustus."[14] Having therefore weighed all of this evidence, Matthew Novenson concludes, "*christos* in Paul is best conceived neither as a sense-less proper name nor as a title of office but rather as an honorific, a word that can function as a stand-in for a personal name but part of whose function is to retain its supernominal associations."[15]

When we turn to the undisputed letters, Paul specifically identifies Jesus with the Davidic royal family only in Romans, yet there is no mistaking its significance there. The letter itself opens with a programmatic passage:

> Paul, a servant of *Jesus Christ*, called to be an apostle, set apart for the gospel of God, which he promised beforehand through his prophets in the holy scriptures, the gospel concerning his Son, who was *descended from David according to the flesh* and was declared to be Son of God with power according to the spirit of holiness by resurrection from the dead, Jesus Christ our Lord, through whom we have received grace and apostleship to bring about *the obedience of faith among all the Gentiles for the sake of his name*, including yourselves who are called to belong to Jesus Christ,
>
> To all God's beloved in Rome, who are called to be saints: Grace to you and peace from God our Father and the Lord Jesus Christ. (Rom 1:1–7)

Though much could be said about this passage,[16] three aspects of Paul's Christology in this passage should be addressed: the connections between (1) Jesus's identity as God's Son and his identity as the Davidic messiah;

---

13. NRSV adapted. See Fredriksen, *Paul*, 135; Andrew Chester, *Messiah and Exaltation: Jewish Messianic and Visionary Traditions and New Testament Christology*, WUNT 207 (Tübingen: Mohr Siebeck, 2007), 383.

14. See Novenson, *Christ among the Messiahs*, 64–97.

15. Novenson, *Christ among the Messiahs*, 138.

16. See Matthew W. Bates, "A Christology of Incarnation and Enthronement: Romans 1:3–4 as Unified, Nonadoptionist, and Nonconciliatory," *CBQ* 77 (2015): 107–27; Matera, *Romans*, 29–31.

(2) Jesus's messianic role and the Spirit; and (3) Jesus's messianic sonship and the resurrection.

First, for Paul, Jesus's identity as "Son of God" appears closely bound up with his role as *the Davidic messiah.* For one thing, Paul moves immediately from speaking of how Jesus "was descended from David according to the flesh" to speaking of his being "declared to be Son of God" (Rom 1:3–4).[17] As is well known, language of divine sonship was frequently associated with the royal son of David (2 Sam 7:14; Pss 2:7; 89:27).[18] In addition, Paul also stresses Jesus's Davidic identity at the end of Romans. Quoting a prophecy from Isaiah regarding a coming descendant of "Jesse," David's father (cf. 1 Sam 16:1–23), Paul writes:

> Again Isaiah says,
>   "*The root of Jesse shall come,*
>   the one who rises to rule the Gentiles;
>   in him the Gentiles shall hope." (Rom 15:12)

This passage constitutes incontrovertible evidence that Paul identified Jesus as a descendant of David.[19] As Aquila Lee states in his recent study of messianism in Paul, "No interpreter of Paul would deny that he believed Jesus to be Israel's Messiah, the long promised one from the line of David."[20] As we saw in chapter 1, this belief coheres well also with Paul's expectation of the restoration of all twelve tribes of Israel, an expectation that was frequently connected to Davidic traditions.

Second, Jesus's status as the messianic Son of God is inseparably tied to *the Spirit.* For one thing, notice how all three ideas—Son of God, Spirit, and messiah ("Christ")—occur together: Jesus was "declared to be *Son of God* [*huiou theou*] with power according to the *Spirit* [*pneuma*] of holiness by resurrection from the dead, Jesus *Christ* [*Christou*] our Lord" (Rom 1:4). Paul's identification of Jesus as the "messiah" with the Spirit has deep roots

---

17. See Novenson, *Christ among the Messiahs,* 167–72; Bates, "Christology of Incarnation and Enthronement," 114–17.

18. Among the Dead Sea Scrolls, see also 4Q252 5:3–4; 4Q174 1 i 21, 2; 1Q28a 2:11–12; 4Q369. See Collins, *Scepter and the Star,* 162; Vermes, *Jesus the Jew,* 194–95.

19. *Contra* Baur, *Paul the Apostle,* 1:370–72. To get around the implications of this passage, Baur implausibly contends that it represents a later textual corruption.

20. Aquila H. I. Lee, "Messianism and Messiah in Paul," in *God and the Faithfulness of Paul,* ed. Christoph Heilig, J. Thomas Hewitt, and Michael F. Bird (Minneapolis: Fortress, 2017), 375, cf. n. 1.

in biblical tradition, which linked the practice of "anointing" key figures to their reception of the Spirit. To mention just a couple of biblical examples, see the following passages from 1 Samuel and Isaiah:

> Then Samuel took the horn of oil, and *anointed him* in the midst of his brothers; and *the Spirit of the* LORD came mightily upon *David* from that day forward. (1 Sam 16:13 RSV)

> The *Spirit* of the Lord GOD is upon me,
> because the LORD has *anointed* me. (Isa 61:1 RSV)

Paul himself thus went on to link Christ's status as "anointed one" to the Spirit:

> It is God who establishes us with you into the *anointed one* ["Christ"] and *anointed* ["christened"] us, who moreover sealed us and gave us the collateral of the *Spirit* in our hearts. (2 Cor 1:21)[21]

In Paul's day, the one "anointed" by God's Spirit in Isaiah 61 was read as a prophecy about the messiah.[22] The connection was a natural one since, as we mentioned, "messiah" literally means "anointed one." Therefore, as Martin Hengel points out, it is no surprise that Paul uses the word "anoint" (*chriō*) "to show the connection between those 'anointed' with God's Spirit and him who is the 'Christos,' that is, the Anointed *par excellence.*"[23]

Third, Jesus's messianic identity is closely associated with *his resurrection from the dead.* As Paul puts it: he was "declared to be [*horisthentos*] Son of God with power according to the spirit of holiness by resurrection from the dead [*ex anastaseōs nekrōn*]" (Rom 1:4).[24] Some have read this as indicating that Jesus received his divine sonship only at the resurrection.

---

21. Adapted from the translation by Novenson, *Christ among the Messiahs*, 147.

22. See, e.g., the use of Isa 61 in 11Q13 in John Sietze Bergsma, *The Jubilee from Leviticus to Qumran: A History of Interpretation*, VTSup 115 (Leiden: Brill, 2007), 282–91.

23. Martin Hengel, *Studies in Early Christology* (Edinburgh: T&T Clark, 1995), 6. We owe the quotation to Novenson, *Christ among the Messiahs*, 147.

24. In the Greek, "his" is not present. In this Paul seems to point to the way he views Jesus's resurrection as the "first fruits" of the final resurrection (cf. 1 Cor 15:23). Fredriksen, *Paul*, 142, makes too much of this by suggesting that Paul holds that Jesus will *only* be appointed at the future resurrection. Since Paul sees Jesus's resurrection as the "first fruits," it is more likely that the majority opinion is correct—namely, that Paul has *Jesus's* resurrection in view here.

While this reading is possible at the level of grammar alone, the larger context rules out such an interpretation. Later on in Romans Paul will explicitly state that "we were reconciled to God through the death of his Son" (Rom 5:10)—a statement that necessarily implies that Christ was God's Son *when he died.* This is precisely why God's love is revealed through the cross—God gave up the divine Son.[25] Paul repeats the point later in the epistle when he writes, "He who did not spare *his own Son* but gave him up for us all, will he not also give us all things with him?" (Rom 8:32 RSV). Consequently, it makes far better sense to conclude that when Paul says Jesus was "declared to be Son of God . . . by resurrection from the dead" (Rom 1:4) he means that the resurrection establishes Christ with a new kind of existence. In the words of Frank Matera:

> Paul is not saying that Jesus became the Son of God at his resurrection but that God appointed or enthroned Jesus as Son of God with full power at his resurrection. . . . It was only at the resurrection, by the power of God's Spirit, that Jesus was enthroned with the full power that rightly belonged to him as God's Son.[26]

According to Paul, it is in the resurrection that Jesus becomes the source of righteousness for others (cf. Rom 4:25). Nevertheless, he does not teach that Jesus simply *became* God's Son when he rose from the dead, since he holds that he was already God's Son when he was given over to be crucified.

There should be little doubt, then, that Paul understood Jesus to be the Davidic messiah. Moreover, Jesus's divine sonship is surely related to his identity as the son of David. Nevertheless, Jesus's identity as the divine Son is not entirely explicable in light of his connection to the king of Israel. For Paul, Jesus is "Son of God" in ways that appear to go beyond what was true of the human kings of the past. As Aquila Lee puts it, "In Paul Jesus's messiahship is inseparable from his eternal sonship. . . . While Paul's Christology may have begun with the [Old Testament] narrative of God's dealings with Israel, it in fact goes beyond its historical messianic understanding."[27] We now turn our attention to this aspect of his teaching.

---

25. See Fitzmyer, *Romans*, 235–37; Wright, *Paul and the Faithfulness of God*, 2:700–701.

26. Matera, *Romans*, 30. See also Bates, "A Christology of Incarnation and Enthronement," 124–26; Fitzmyer, *Romans*, 235.

27. Lee, "Messianism and Messiah in Paul," 389.

Equality with God

Moving on from the question of Jesus's Davidic role, the second key question that any study of Paul's Christology has to wrestle with is this: What does Paul mean when he refers to Jesus as the "Son of God"? As James Dunn rightly points out, Paul's gospel is, in its essence, "the gospel concerning [God's] Son" (Rom 1:3).[28] What kind of divine sonship does Paul have in mind when he speaks of Jesus?

God Sent His "Son" in "the Likeness of Sinful Flesh"

In order to answer these questions, we need to look carefully at three important passages that, taken together, strongly suggest that Paul sees Jesus as *more* than just a human messiah. Specifically, these passages provide compelling evidence that Paul believed in Jesus's *preexistent divine sonship*—that is, that Jesus was the Son of God not only during his earthly life but even *before* he was conceived and born. Consider the following:

> Have this mind among yourselves, which is yours in Christ Jesus, who, though he was *in the form of God*, did not count *equality with God* a thing to be *grasped*, but *emptied himself*, taking the form of a servant, *being born in the likeness of men*. And *being found in human form* he humbled himself and became obedient unto death, even death on a cross. Therefore God has highly exalted him and bestowed on him the name which is above every name, that at the name of Jesus every knee should bow, in heaven and on earth and under the earth, and every tongue confess that Jesus Christ is Lord, to the glory of God the Father. (Phil 2:5–11 RSV)

> But when the fullness of time had come, *God sent his Son, born of a woman*, born under the law, in order to redeem those who were under the law, so that we might receive adoption as children. (Gal 4:4–5)

> God has done what the law, weakened by the flesh, could not do: by *sending his own Son in the likeness of sinful flesh*. (Rom 8:3)

28. See James D. G. Dunn, *Beginning from Jerusalem*, Christianity in the Making 2 (Grand Rapids: Eerdmans, 2009), 574.

There can be little doubt that these verses present us with an exalted view of Jesus.[29] Nor can anyone dispute the christological significance of the text in Philippians 2, which, because of its poetic style, is often referred to as the "Christ hymn." James Dunn rightly observes that its "importance can hardly be overestimated."[30] With that said, the precise nature of the divine sonship envisioned by Paul has been the topic of considerable debate.[31] Nevertheless, several observations tip the balance in favor of seeing the notion of preexistence in the sending passages of Galatians 4:4 and Romans 8:3 as well as in the famous text of Philippians 2.

He Was in "the Form of God"

First, Paul clearly says that Christ was in "the form of God" *before* his human birth (Phil 2:6). As E. P. Sanders rightly notes, with these words Paul is affirming that "Christ existed before he appeared as a human."[32]

Furthermore, though the terminology of "form of God" (*morphē theou*) has various semantic possibilities (Phil 2:6), as Frank Matera points out, in context the meaning that makes the most sense is "'nature' or 'status.'"[33] Should there be any doubt about this, Paul goes on to use *the same term* for Jesus's human nature or status, telling us that in addition to being in the "form [*morphē*] of God," Jesus also took the "form [*morphē*]" of a servant when he was "born[34] in the likeness of men." As Michael Gorman

---

29. The passage from Philippians is widely seen as a pre-Pauline composition. See, e.g., G. F. Hawthorne, *Philippians*, WBC 43 (Waco, TX: Word, 1983), 99–104. This hypothesis in no way undercuts the passage's relevance for understanding Paul's thought, as he gives no indication that he somehow finds it incompatible with his teaching. To the contrary, he uses it as the basis for explaining proper Christian behavior (cf. Phil 2:12). Whether the passage is best seen as a "hymn" or "poem" is debated. Here we simply follow the conventional language of hymn without prejudice to such debates.

30. Dunn, *Theology of Paul*, 281.

31. For an overview of the discussion, see esp. John Reumann, *Philippians*, AYB 33B (New Haven: Yale University Press, 2008), 333–83 (with bibliography); Fee, *Pauline Christology*, 370–400.

32. Sanders, *Paul: The Apostle's Life, Letters, and Thought*, 603.

33. Matera, *New Testament Christology*, 128. See also Andrew Ter Ern Loke, *The Origin of Divine Christology*, SNTSMS 169 (Cambridge: Cambridge University Press, 2017), 13–17; Moisés Silva, *Philippians*, 2nd ed., BECNT (Grand Rapids: Baker Academic, 2005), 98–116.

34. The Greek term *genomenos* need not necessarily be translated "born" and could simply be rendered "to become." Given, however, that Paul elsewhere uses the exact same

writes, "The parallel phrases 'form of God' and 'form of a slave' mean that to the extent that this one really took on the form of a slave, he also really was in the form of God—and vice versa."[35] In other words, the divine "form" or status that Jesus possessed before he was born is just as real as the human "form" or status that he possessed during his earthly life and death.

Additional support for this reading of Philippians 2 can be found in the fact that the language used there echoes that which is employed to describe the "birth" and "sending" of God's Son in Galatians and Romans:

Philippians 2:7	Galatians 4:4
"emptied himself . . . being born [*genomenos*] in the likeness of men"	"God sent his Son born [*genomenon*] of a woman"

Philippians 2:7	Romans 8:3
"emptied himself . . . being born in the likeness of men" (*en homoiōmati anthrōpōn*)	"sending his own Son in the likeness of sinful flesh" (*en homoiōmati sarkos hamartias*)

In both of these passages from Galatians and Romans, Paul seems to imply that Jesus existed before his human birth. As Frank Matera puts it, "Although the preexistence of Christ is not explicitly stated here [in Galatians 4:4], it is probably implied."[36] Matera is correct to say, "In a word, Paul affirms that the preexistent Son, whom the Father 'sent' into the world [Romans 8:3], possessed the very 'form,' 'image,' and 'likeness' that defines the human condition."[37]

Given these parallels, the Christ hymn in Philippians 2 is best read as suggesting Jesus has some sort of preexistent "divine" status. In the words of Adela Collins and John Collins:

Paul sometimes speaks of Jesus as preexistent. . . . The clearest example of the portrayal of Christ as preexistent in the letters of Paul is the prose

---

term to speak of Jesus being "*born* of a woman" (Gal 4:4) it seems unnecessary to alter the translation in Phil 2:7.

35. Gorman, *Inhabiting the Cruciform God*, 22.

36. Matera, *Galatians*, 150.

37. Matera, *Romans*, 192.

hymn in Phil 2:6–11. The political rhetoric of the hymn suggests that the description of Christ as "in the form of God" (*en morphē theou*) signifies that he is . . . *the preexistent heavenly messiah.*[38]

Remarkably, even Bart Ehrman, a scholar who disputes the notion of Jesus's preexistence in other New Testament works, acknowledges that Philippians 2 contains what he calls an "incarnational Christology," since it "portrays Jesus as a preexistent divine being who becomes human."[39]

"Equality with God" Before His Birth

Second, Paul also implies that Christ possessed "equality with God" *before* he was born. We say "implies" because Paul's words about Christ not counting "equality with God" (*to einai isa theō*) something to be "grasped" (*harpagmos*) is admittedly ambiguous and can be taken in different ways (Phil 2:6).[40] Some scholars, such as James Dunn, take an "Adamic" interpretation. According to this reading, when Paul says Christ did not deem "equality with God" as something to be "grasped" (the RSV's rendering), the language indicates that Christ did not have equality with God but that it was something to be "reached for" or "desired."[41] From this point of view, Paul's language of Jesus being in the "form [*morphē*] of God" is synonymous with the description of Adam's status as the "image [*eikōn*] of God" in Genesis 1:26–27. This analysis coheres with other passages in Paul that compare Jesus to Adam (Rom 5:12–19; 1 Cor 15:22, 45–49). Therefore, Dunn reads Paul's statements about Christ having "emptied himself" not in terms of moving from divine preexistence to human birth but as referring to a movement away from "the mythic stage of pre-history."[42]

While having some explanatory power, this Adamic interpretation of Philippians 2 is ultimately unconvincing. Aquila Lee highlights three major

---

38. Collins and Collins, *King and Messiah as Son of God*, 208 (emphasis added).

39. Ehrman, *How Jesus Became God*, 266. Cf. Bates, "Christology of Incarnation and Enthronement," 114–17, who suggests that the odd use of *ginomai* (rather than the more natural *gennaō*) in Phil 2:7; Rom 1:3; and Gal 4:4 points in a similar direction. As we will see momentarily, Ehrman thinks of this preexistence as angelic rather than divine.

40. Sanders, *Paul: The Apostle's Life, Letters, and Thought*, 602.

41. See, e.g., A. A. T. Ehrhardt, "Jesus Christ and Alexander the Great," *JTS* 46 (1945): 45–51.

42. Dunn, *Theology of Paul*, 287.

problems with Dunn's approach. First, it is doubtful that "form" (*morphē*) should be read as synonymous with "image" (*eikōn*).[43] Second, Dunn's reading seems extremely unlikely given that there is no evidence to support the idea that ancient Jews drew sharp distinctions between history and "pre-history" in the Genesis narrative.[44] Third, if Jesus had never been anything other than human, it is hard to account for the description of his "being born in the likeness of men" (Phil 2:7 RSV). In the words of Lee:

> The Adam-Christ parallel does not do justice to the force of the recapitulary phrase . . . "and being found in form as man" (v. 7), which is very odd if it refers to a person who had never been anything else but a man.[45]

Fourth and finally, a strong case can be made that the language of "equality with God" defines what being in the "form of God" means.[46] This point is important because it clarifies the fact that, before his birth, Christ was not just an angel or heavenly being of some kind, but "equal with God" (cf. Phil 2:6).[47] Matera helpfully writes:

> Although the English word "form" gives the impression of Christ being like but not truly God, the Greek word has a fuller meaning: the form is the outward manifestation of the inner reality. This is made clear by the next phrase, which describes Christ as possessing "equality with God."[48]

For these and other reasons, the majority of interpreters have come to read the expression "grasped [*harpagmos*]" (Phil 2:6 RSV) as indicating "not whether one possesses something, but whether or not one chooses to exploit

43. So too Collins and Collins, *King and Messiah as Son of God*, 208n8.

44. For example, Josephus, *Antiquities of the Jews* 1.27–36, bears no evidence of such a transition.

45. Aquila H. I. Lee, *From Messiah to Preexistent Son: Jesus' Self-Consciousness and Early Exegesis of Messianic Psalms*, WUNT 2/192 (Tübingen: Mohr Siebeck, 2005), 306.

46. Numerous scholars agree on this point. See, e.g., Wright, *Climax of the Covenant*, 83; Gerald F. Hawthorne, "In the Form of God," in *Where Christology Began: Essays on Philippians 2*, ed. R. P. Martin and B. J. Dodd (London: Westminster John Knox, 1998), 104.

47. *Pace* Ehrman, *How Jesus Became God*, 263, who unconvincingly argues that Paul thinks of Christ as "existing before his birth as an angelic being . . . but not as God Almighty." In flat contradiction to Paul's own language, Ehrman asserts that Christ "is not—most definitely not—'equal' with God before he becomes human."

48. Frank J. Matera, "Philippians," in Chiu et al., *The Paulist Commentary*, 1424.

something."[49] In short, Jesus's "equality with God" is best seen as a divine status that he possesses prior to "emptying himself" and taking human form.[50]

The "Exaltation" of the Son

Third, when Paul says that God "exalted" Christ, *he does not mean that Jesus was given a "higher" status than that which he possessed before he was born.* After all, what could be higher than "equality with God"? Moreover, if Christ did not in some way possess this equality with God, then how can Paul say that he voluntarily "emptied himself [*ekenōsen*]" of it (Phil 2:7)? How can a person voluntarily empty oneself of something one does not actually possess? Rather, what happens after the resurrection is that God exalts the "human form" (*schēmati . . . hōs anthrōpos*) that Christ voluntarily assumed in his birth and which was put to death on the cross (Phil 2:7). That is what Paul means when he says that God "has highly exalted [*hyperypsōsen*]" Christ (Phil 2:9 RSV). In contrast to the humiliation of Christ that took place during his earthly life and crucifixion, his exaltation will result in "every knee" bending to him and "every tongue" confessing that he "is Lord [*kyrios*]" (Phil 2:10–11).

Yet this reading is contested. Some have read the description of the exaltation of Jesus in the passage as describing the divinization of a merely human figure.[51] In support of this interpretation, adherents of this view point to early Jewish texts that speak of mere human beings experiencing glorious transformations. For example, Philo of Alexandria (first century AD) talks about how the Jewish high priest was glorified when he ministered in the inner sanctum of the Jerusalem temple such that he became "a being whose nature is midway between (man and) God, less than God, superior to man."[52] Moreover, in the Greco-Roman world, deification was

---

49. See Hawthorne, "In the Form of God," 102, following Roy W. Hoover, "The Harpagmos Enigma: A Philological Solution," *HTR* 64 (1971): 118. See also Loke, *Origin of Divine Christology*, 37.

50. For these and other critiques of Dunn's approach, see Lee, *From Messiah to Preexistent Son*, 306.

51. See Chester, *Messiah and Exaltation*, 392; cf. *1 En.* 71.

52. Philo, *On Dreams* 2.188–89 (Colson and Whitaker, LCL). See also Philo, *On Dreams* 2.231–32. For a discussion of other examples of this kind of deification in Sirach and the Dead Sea Scrolls, see Michael P. Barber and John A. Kincaid, "Cultic Theosis in Paul and Second Temple Judaism," *JSPL* 5, no. 2 (2015): 243–47.

often attributed to royal figures (e.g., Caesar)—and Paul, as we have seen, views Jesus as the royal messiah. Bart Ehrman therefore insists that Jesus is given a "higher" status after his resurrection than he possessed before it, suggesting he has a lower divine status in the first half of the Christ hymn than in the second.[53] Yet Paul's text does not necessitate this conclusion. As Andrew Ter Ern Loke writes:

> While Ehrman . . . has asked if Christ was equal in ontological status with God the Father why was there a need to exalt him (Phil 2:9), the answer is evident from the context: because Christ (even though already truly divine) was said to have humbled himself on the cross.[54]

This should be kept in mind when it comes to other passages that suggest that Jesus receives authority or might be seen as in some way subordinate to God (1 Cor 3:23; 11:3; 15:24–28). For Paul, Christ *voluntarily chooses* to become subordinate insofar as he takes a "human form" and is willingly crucified. This does not, however, necessarily mean that he somehow *ceased* being in the "form of God."

To summarize, then, we can say the following: the christological hymn in Philippians 2 is best read as indicating both that Jesus was preexistent and that his preexistent state involved being "in the form of God" and possessing "equality with God." In multiple places—Philippians, Galatians, and Romans—Paul's language seems to indicate that, in some sense, Jesus possessed this equality with God prior to becoming human. Contrary to what some have recently argued, Paul cannot simply think that Christ was a preexistent angel, since, from an ancient Jewish perspective, angels are not equal with the one God. In becoming human, the preexistent Christ voluntarily accepted a "human form." Thus, for Paul, Jesus's divine sonship was not something bestowed upon him only at his resurrection.

One God and One Lord

With these conclusions regarding Jesus's human and Davidic messiahship and his preexistent sonship in mind, we can now ask: How does one rec-

---

53. Erhman, *How Jesus Became God*, 263.
54. Loke, *Origin of Divine Christology*, 39.

oncile Paul's identification of Jesus as an "incarnate divine being"[55] with his affirmation that "there is no God but one" (1 Cor 8:4)? In other words, how do we reconcile Paul's Christology with his identity as a Jew who professed that Israel had "one LORD" (Deut 6:4 RSV)?

Jewish "Monotheism" and the Question of "Divinity"

Determining what Paul means when he speaks of Jesus as if he is equal with God is complicated by a number of factors. While Christian theology has come to reserve the language of "divinity" for the triune God, within Paul's ancient context "divinity" could have several different meanings. Greco-Roman culture recognized various gradations of divinity; not only was there a hierarchy of sorts among the gods[56] but humans, such as rulers, could also be "deified." For instance, Gaius Caligula is recognized as "Jupiter" in Roman documents.[57] To speak of someone as "divine" did not necessarily mean that person was an all-powerful deity. It could simply indicate that they had "suprahuman" qualities. It is no surprise, then, that Pauline scholarship has had a long history of appealing to Hellenistic contexts to explain the emergence of the apostle's Christology.[58]

More recently, however, following the pioneering work of Richard Bauckham[59] and Larry Hurtado,[60] Paul's Christology has been put directly in conversation with the Jewish confession of the "one God." This belief is formulated most famously in the Jewish prayer known as the *Shema'* ("Hear"), which is taken from Deuteronomy 6: "Hear, O Israel: *The LORD our God is one LORD*; and you shall love the LORD your God with all your

55. Ehrman, *How Jesus Became God*, 269.

56. See M. David Litwa, *We Are Being Transformed: Deification in Paul's Soteriology*, BZNW 187 (Berlin: De Gruyter, 2012), 241.

57. Dio Cassius, *Roman History* 59.28.8; 59.30.1. See M. David Litwa, *Iesus Deus: The Early Christian Depiction of Jesus as a Mediterranean God* (Minneapolis: Fortress, 2014), 181–212.

58. The classic study is Wilhelm Bousset, *Kyrios Christos: A History of the Belief in Christ from the Beginnings of Christianity to Irenaeus*, trans. John E. Steeley (1913; repr., Waco, TX: Baylor University Press, 2013).

59. See esp. Bauckham, *Jesus and the God of Israel*; Bauckham, *God Crucified: Monotheism and Christology in the New Testament* (Grand Rapids: Eerdmans, 1999).

60. Larry Hurtado, *One God, One Lord: Early Christian Devotion and Ancient Jewish Monotheism* (Philadelphia: Fortress, 1988); Hurtado, *Lord Jesus Christ*; Hurtado, *How on Earth Did Jesus Become a God? Historical Questions about Earliest Devotion to Jesus* (Grand Rapids: Eerdmans, 2005).

heart, and with all your soul, and with all your might" (Deut 6:4–5 RSV). While this confession has often been seen as "monotheistic," interpreters increasingly recognize that such language needs to be carefully parsed out. Jews of Paul's day did not use the word "monotheism." The term itself is rather recent, appearing for the first time in the seventeenth century, when it was coined by the Platonist Henry More.[61] If we give the term the same meaning More originally assigned to it—that is, belief in the existence of only one God—difficulties emerge. For one thing, the Hebrew word translated "God" (*elohim*) is actually plural in form, and there are instances in Israel's scriptures where it refers to gods other than Israel's (e.g., Exod 15:11; Ps 89:6–7). These deities are not simply identified as cultic objects (e.g., statues) but are recognized as heavenly beings, sometimes being called "angels"[62] and "demons" (see, e.g., Deut 32:17). Some texts identify Israel's God as the "Most High"—that is, the divine ruler who is over a council of heavenly figures (e.g., Ps 82:1, 6). Philo, an Alexandrian Jew, even spoke of the divine Word as a "second god."[63] In addition, the term "god" is also applied to humans, such as Moses (Exod 7:1), as well as to the future Davidic king ("Mighty God," Isa 9:6). Other figures are also depicted in terms associated with divinity, such as the "son of man" figure in Daniel 7, who rides on clouds,[64] or the high priest, who is associated with divine glory imagery.[65]

As David Litwa explains, it is important to recognize that there are strong similarities between conceptions of "divinity" in first-century Jewish sources and Hellenistic writers.[66] While bright lines are often drawn to demarcate Judaism from Hellenism, Martin Hengel demonstrated several decades ago that this fails to come to grips with the profound way first-century Judaism had been impacted by Hellenization.[67] Jewish theological

61. Nathan MacDonald, "The Origin of 'Monotheism,'" in *Early Jewish and Christian Monotheism*, ed. Loren T. Stuckenbruck and Wendy E. S. North, JSNTSup 263 (London: T&T Clark, 2004), 205.

62. For example, the Septuagint translates *elohim* as "his angels" (Ps 97:7).

63. Philo, *Questions and Answers on Genesis* 2.62; *Allegorical Interpretation* 3.207–8; *Dreams* 1.229–30.

64. Cloud-riding has divine associations elsewhere. See Deut 33:26; Pss 68:4; 104:3.

65. Compare the depiction of the priest in Sir 50:7 with that of the God of Israel in Ezek 1:28. For more examples, see Barber and Kincaid, "Cultic Theosis in Paul and Second Temple Judaism," 243–47.

66. See Litwa, *We Are Being Transformed*, 86–97.

67. Martin Hengel, *Judaism and Hellenism: Studies in Their Encounter in Palestine during the Early Hellenistic Period*, 2 vols. (Philadelphia: Fortress, 1974).

expressions were not immune to such influence. Litwa thus argues that just as gradations of divinity are found in Greco-Roman culture, a similar dynamic should be recognized in Judaism as well.[68] Nevertheless, it would be historically irresponsible to insist that Israelite religion lacked distinctive features.[69] The question, then, remains: What distinguishes the God of Israel from other "gods"? Three features of Jewish beliefs have often been highlighted.

The "One God" of Israel

First, Israel's God has *a name*: YHWH. The confession "The LORD our God is one LORD" (Deut 6:4 RSV) represented a defining characteristic of early Judaism. Of course, this formula recognizes Israel's God by a specific name. This name—referred to as the *tetragrammaton* (the four letters)—was understood to be so holy that it was treated with special reverence.[70] Ancient Jews would avoid pronouncing it.[71] In the great Isaiah scroll found among the Dead Sea Scrolls, the Hebrew term for "Lord" is written above the divine name (Isa 28:16; 30:15; 65:15), which suggests that "Lord" was vocalized instead of YHWH.[72] Similarly, in the works of the Greek writer Philo, an Alexandrian Jew, the divine name is replaced with *kyrios*, the Greek word for "Lord." This is a tradition that continues on in English Bible translations to this day, which typically render "YHWH" as "LORD" (usually in all uppercase letters). In sum, the name of God was handled in a special way because the one God of the *Shemaʿ* was understood to be "God" like no other. Because of this, despite the difficulties involved with the language, to abandon the terminology of monotheism altogether would fail the test of "sympathetic historiogra-

---

68. See Litwa, *Iesus Deus*, 6–8.

69. Litwa, *Iesus Deus*, 31–32.

70. See David B. Capes, "YHWH Texts and Monotheism in Paul's Christology," in Stuckenbruck and North, *Early Jewish and Christian Monotheism*, 120–24; Capes, *The Divine Christ: Paul, the Lord Jesus, and the Scriptures of Israel* (Grand Rapids: Baker Academic, 2018), 1–19.

71. See Josephus, *Antiquities* 2.275–76; Philo, *Moses* 2.114; *m. Sotah* 7:5–6; Capes, *The Divine Christ*, 19.

72. The divine name appears in Aramaic though the rest of the text appears in Hebrew. In other places in the same scroll four dots appear instead of the tetragrammaton. Capes, *The Divine Christ*, 14.

phy" since "without the confession of the one God, the community of Israel . . . would not be Israel."[73]

Second, Israel's God is *the Creator* of all things. This point is driven home in the Pentateuch when Moses states: "To the LORD your God belong heaven and the heaven of heavens, the earth with all that is in it" (Deut 10:14 RSV). Perhaps the most well-known expression of this identification of the one God as Creator is found in the book of Isaiah:

> I am the LORD, *who made all things,*
>   who *alone* stretched out the heavens,
>   who *by myself* spread out the earth. (Isa 44:24)

> For thus says the LORD,
> *who created the heavens*
>   (he is God!),
> *who formed the earth and made it*
>   (*he established it*;
> he did not create it a chaos,
>   *he formed it* to be inhabited!):
> I am the LORD, and *there is no other.* (Isa 45:18)

Other Jewish sources likewise insist that all things owe their existence to the God of Israel.[74] As Litwa says, YHWH's "power to create undoubtedly proves the superiority of his divinity."[75] Moreover, with the exception of Philo's qualification that God employed assistants in the creation of humanity,[76] virtually all Jewish sources from Paul's day emphasize the same point Isaiah insists upon, namely, that "God had no helper, assistant, or servant to assist or to implement his work of creation."[77] God is thus

---

73. Litwa, *We Are Being Transformed,* 237–38.

74. See Bauckham, *Jesus and the God of Israel,* 9, who cites Isa 40:26, 28; 42:5; 44:24; 45:12, 18; 48:13; 51:16; Neh 9:6; Hos 13:4 LXX; 2 Macc 1:24; Sir 43:33; Bel 5; *Jub.* 12:3–5; *Sib. Or.* 3:20–35; 8:375–76; *Sib. Or.* frg. 1:5–6; *Sib. Or.* frag. 3; *Sib. Or.* frag. 5; 2 *En.* 47:3–4; 66:4; *Apoc. Ab.* 7:10; Ps-Sophocles; *Jos. Asen.* 12:1–2; *T. Job* 2:4.

75. Litwa, *We Are Being Transformed,* 271.

76. Philo, *On the Creation of the World* 72–75; *On the Confusion of Tongues* 179.

77. Bauckham, *God Crucified,* 10, citing 2 *En.* 33:4; 4 *Ezra* 3:4; Josephus, *Against Apion* 2.192. As Loke notes (*Origin of Divine Christology,* 16n16), the objection from Philo's interpretation of Gen 1:26 is a bit misleading since the argument refers to the initial creation of the cosmos, as in Isa 44:24.

called the "Eternal One."[78] While the work of creation is also sometimes associated with God's "wisdom"[79] or "word,"[80] even there the cosmos is ultimately the work of the God of Israel, not competitive deities. In short, YHWH, the "Lord," is the Creator God.

Third, Israel's God is the *Sovereign Ruler* of all the cosmos. Since the world belongs to the God of Israel, all things are ultimately subject to YHWH. For example, the psalmist declares, "The sea is his, for he made it" (Ps 95:5). Israel's God is also judge of the world: "Rise up, O God, judge the earth; for all the nations belong to you!" (Ps 82:8). In Deuteronomy, the God of Israel declares that "there is none that can deliver out of my hand" (Deut 32:39 RSV). Likewise, the book of Daniel proclaims that Israel's God is "God of gods and Lord of kings" (Dan 2:47). Thus, in the scriptures of Israel, the other gods are, in the final analysis, ineffective—the God of Israel has supreme power. As David Litwa puts it, "God as creator is God as owner of the cosmos."[81]

The Exclusive Worship of the "One God"

With all of this in mind, it is important to add that recent scholarship has also shown that Israel's "monotheism" cannot simply be construed in terms of propositions about God. In his recent study of the subject, Nathan MacDonald argues that "the primary significance of the *Shemaʿ* is the *relationship* between YHWH and Israel. YHWH is to be Israel's one and only."[82] This means that God's transcendent "oneness" is expressed not simply in creedal formulas but in terms of a particular kind of devotion and relational dynamic.[83]

78. See Bauckham, *Jesus and the God of Israel*, 10, who cites Tob 13:1; Sir 18:1; 2 Macc 1:25; *T. Mos.* 10:7; *1 En.* 5:1.

79. See Bauckham, *Jesus and the God of Israel*, 16, who cites Jer 10:12; 51:15; Ps 104:24; Prov 3:19; 8:30; Sir 24:3; Wis 7:22; 8:4–6; 9:2; 1 QHᵃ 9:7, 14, 19–20.

80. See Bauckham, *Jesus and the God of Israel*, 16, who cites Ps 33:6; Sir 42:15; *Jub.* 12:4; *Sib. Or.* 3:20; *2 Bar* 14:17; 21:4; 48:9; *4 Ezra* 6:38; *T. Ab. A* 9:6; Wis 9:1.

81. Litwa, *We Are Being Transformed*, 271.

82. Nathan MacDonald, *Deuteronomy and the Meaning of "Monotheism,"* 2nd ed., FAT 2/1 (Tübingen: Mohr Siebeck, 2012), 151 (emphasis added). See Tilling, *Paul's Divine Christology*, 84–86.

83. See the critique of MacDonald in Richard Bauckham, "Biblical Theology and the Problems of Monotheism," in *Out of Egypt: Biblical Theology and Biblical Interpretation*, ed. Craig Bartholomew, Mary Healy, Karl Möller, and Robin Perry, Scripture and Hermeneutics 5 (Grand Rapids: Zondervan, 2004), 188–96.

Among other things, this involves offering God *exclusive worship*. As Litwa explains, "What is distinctive in Israel are the prohibitions of worshipping other Gods."[84] Intriguingly, in the Septuagint, the word *latreuō* (commonly translated as "serve") is a term used specifically for the worship of God or in denouncing that which is incorrectly given to "false gods."[85] Another term, *proskyneō* (commonly translated as "worship" or "homage"), can be used for the homage given to both God and other figures worthy of honor, though the dynamics of this appear differently in various texts. Recognizing the linguistic and cultic complexities involved here, some hesitate to identify cultic worship as a distinguishing feature of Jewish monotheism.

Nevertheless, it seems that there was agreement on one major point: the offering of *sacrifice* belongs to the exclusive worship given to the God of Israel.[86] A remarkable example is found in the book of Chronicles:

> Then David said to all the assembly, "Bless the LORD your God." And all the assembly blessed the LORD, the God of their fathers, and bowed their heads and *paid homage to the LORD and to the king*. And they offered sacrifices to the LORD, and on the next day offered burnt offerings to the LORD, 1,000 bulls, 1,000 rams, and 1,000 lambs, with their drink offerings, and sacrifices in abundance for all Israel. And they ate and drank before the LORD on that day with great gladness. (1 Chr 29:20–22 ESV)

Here we read that the people "paid homage" (Heb. *shachah*; Gk. *proskyneō*) both to God *and* the king (1 Chr 29:20). Strikingly, both figures are depicted as objects of the same verb.[87] Nevertheless, in the very next verse we learn that sacrifices are made *only to the God of Israel*. When we turn

---

84. Litwa, *We Are Being Transformed*, 245.

85. See Roland Thomas Bentley, "'Worship God Alone': The Emerging Christian Tradition of *Latreia*" (PhD diss., University of Virginia, 2009), 20–58.

86. On the connection between sacrificial worship and recognition of divinity in antiquity, see J. Lionel North, "Jesus and Worship, God and Sacrifice," in Stuckenbruck and North, *Early Jewish and Christian Monotheism*, 186–202.

87. The RSV and NRSV translators clearly had difficulty with this and therefore added another verb in English, which does not appear in the original texts, rendering the text with different terms: "[The people] worshiped the LORD, and *did obeisance to the king*" (RSV).

to other Jewish texts, it seems that not even angelic beings could be the recipient of worship involving sacrifice. Loren Stuckenbruck's detailed analysis of relevant texts leads him to conclude, "Honorific and worship *language* could, on occasion, be ascribed to angelic beings, but to have sacrificed to them would have gone too far."[88] Thus, while certain issues remain, the basic notion at the heart of the "first commandment" was seen as a constitutive principle of Judaism; sacrificial worship is to be given in a special way to YHWH alone (Exod 20:1–4).

Significantly, the rationale for this exclusivity involves more than a mere arbitrary preference; Israel's God is said to be due special worship *as Creator*. The precise problem with those who worship "other gods" is that they mistakenly ignore the Creator and turn to those things that have been "made," crying out to idols that cannot hear them (Isa 46:6–7). The author of Wisdom of Solomon thus condemns those who worship even celestial realities like stars:

> For all people who were ignorant of God were foolish by nature;
> and they were *unable from the good things that are seen to know the one*
> *who exists,*
> *nor did they recognize the artisan while paying heed to his works*;
> but *they supposed that either fire or wind or swift air,*
> *or the circle of the stars, or turbulent water,*
> *or the luminaries of heaven were the gods that rule the world.*
> If through delight in the beauty of these things people assumed them
> to be gods,
> *let them know how much better than these is their Lord,*
> *for the author of beauty created them.*
> And if people were amazed at their power and working,
> let them perceive from them
> *how much more powerful is the one who formed them.*
> For from the greatness and beauty of created things
> comes a corresponding perception of their Creator. (Wis 13:1–5)

Those who worship heavenly bodies or other aspects of creation are guilty of committing a major category error; the one true God is not a creature.

---

88. Loren Stuckenbruck, "'Angels' and 'God': Exploring the Limits of Early Jewish Monotheism," in Stuckenbruck and North, *Early Jewish and Christian Monotheism*, 69 (emphasis original).

Remarkably, even Philo, who speaks of the divine Word as a "second god," insists that worship is to be directed only to the one God.[89] There is also no evidence to suggest that worship involving sacrifice was ever rendered to God's word or wisdom. These were likely viewed as part of the divine identity of YHWH.[90]

To sum up then, we can answer the question "What distinguishes Israel's God from others?" as follows: the God of Israel (1) is the one God known as YHWH; (2) is the Creator and origin of all things; (3) is the Sovereign Ruler and Judge of the cosmos; and (4) has a unique relationship with the covenant people, which is expressed by receiving an exclusive sort of worship from them.

Paul Identifies Christ as the "One Lord" of the Shema‘

With all of this background regarding Jewish monotheism in mind, we can now turn our attention to another crucial text for Pauline Christology. In this passage, Paul not only speaks of Jesus as if he is in some sense divine, but does so precisely in the context of affirming Jewish monotheism and alluding to the *Shema‘*:

> Indeed, even though there may be so-called gods in heaven or on earth—as in fact there are many gods and many lords—yet *for us there is one God, the Father*, from whom are all things and for whom we exist, *and one Lord, Jesus Christ*, through whom are all things and through whom we exist. (1 Cor 8:5–6)

Notice here that Paul does not deny that there are other "gods" and "lords"—that is, other heavenly beings. Yet, according to him, these "so-called gods" are not "God" and "Lord" in the same way that the one God is.[91] With this in mind, we might therefore speak of the way Paul distinguishes the "one God" from the "many gods." He does this in a number of ways.[92]

---

89. Philo, *On the Decalogue* 65.

90. Hurtado, *One God, One Lord*, 38; Hurtado, *Lord Jesus Christ*, 36.

91. Paul elsewhere identifies his God as the "living and true God [*theō zōnti kai alēthinō*]" (1 Thess 1:9).

92. See, e.g., Bauckham, *Jesus and the God of Israel*, 27–28, 97–104, 210–18. Not all have agreed with Bauckham, however. See Loke, *Origin of Divine Christology*, 26–29.

First, the "one God" spoken of by Paul is clearly *YHWH of the Shema'* (1 Cor 8:6; cf. Deut 6:4–6).[93] As others have shown, the passage in 1 Corinthians 8 seems, at least in part, to be a reworking of the text at the heart of the *Shema'* (Deut 6:4–5). In the words of Richard Bauckham, "Paul has rearranged the words in such a way as to produce an affirmation of both one God, the Father, and one Lord, Jesus Christ."[94] What is particularly striking, however, is the way *Paul includes Christ in the Shema'*. As Bauckham points out, Paul creatively splits the passage so that the Father is identified as the "one God" and Jesus as the "one Lord." James McGrath has disputed this reading, insisting that Jesus's lordship is simply inserted *alongside* the confession of "one God."[95] This reading is unlikely. As Bauckham argues, "Paul is not adding to the one God of the *Shema'* a 'Lord' the *Shema'* does not mention. He is identifying Jesus as the 'Lord' whom the *Shema'* affirms to be one. . . . The unique identity of the one God *consists of* the one God, the Father, *and* the one Lord, his Messiah."[96] In other words, the torah insists that "the LORD our God is one LORD" and Paul asserts that *this* Lord—not an additional one, but the Lord of the *Shema'—is Jesus Christ*.

This conclusion is further buttressed by another Pauline text. Strikingly, 1 Corinthians 8 is not the only time Paul appears to identify Jesus as the "one LORD" of the *Shema'*. The same thing seems to take place in the Christ hymn in Philippians 2, which concludes by proclaiming:

> Therefore God has highly exalted him and bestowed on him *the name which is above every name*, that *at the name of Jesus every knee should bow*, in heaven and on earth and under the earth, and every tongue confess that *Jesus Christ is Lord*, to the glory of God the Father. (Phil 2:9–11 RSV)

Many Pauline scholars have recognized here the use of language from the very section of the book of Isaiah that emphasizes the Jewish belief that the Lord God is above all other gods.[97] With the ending of Paul's Christ hymn in mind, consider the following:

---

93. Fitzmyer, *First Corinthians*, 342.

94. Bauckham, *Jesus and the God of Israel*, 27.

95. James F. McGrath, *The Only True God: Early Christian Monotheism in Its Jewish Context* (Urbana: University of Illinois Press, 2009), 40–41.

96. Bauckham, *Jesus and the God of Israel*, 28 (emphasis original).

97. See, e.g., Sanders, *Paul: The Apostle's Life, Letters, and Thought*, 603–4; Wright, *Paul and the Faithfulness of God*, 2:664–66; Bauckham, *Jesus and the God of Israel*, 210–18; Fee, *Pauline Christology*, 89–94.

> Turn to me and be saved,
>> all the ends of the earth!
>> For I am God, and there is no other.
> By myself I have sworn,
>> from my mouth has gone forth in righteousness
>> a word that shall not return:
> *"To me every knee shall bow,*
>> *every tongue shall swear."*
> *Only in the* Lord, it shall be said of me,
>> are righteousness and strength;
> all who were incensed against him
>> shall come to him and be ashamed. (Isa 45:22–24)

In Isaiah 45, the divine name of God—YHWH—is recognized as the sole source of salvation. In the future all will recognize that it is YHWH, the "Lord," who possesses universal sovereign authority. In Philippians 2 Paul applies this passage to *Jesus*—he is the one with sovereign authority over all and whose name is above all others. In the words of Dennis Hamm, "That Paul can take this absolute declaration of monotheism [in Isaiah 45] and apply it to Jesus of Nazareth would have been astounding in the context of the Judaism of his day."[98]

Although some argue that Jesus has only been given a title—"Lord"—that is above every other name,[99] this reading is not convincing. The name that is specifically in view in Isaiah is the divine name, YHWH. It is stunning, then, that the name which Paul says is exalted above *all others* and to which "every knee shall bow" is *"Jesus."*[100] Paul indicates there is no name higher than Jesus's! The natural reading of all of this is not that Jesus somehow simply "functions" as YHWH but, rather, that *YHWH is Jesus.* This is supported by the fact that though Paul often interprets scripture passages referring to YHWH as God (Rom 4:7–8; 9:27, 29; 11:34; 15:9, 11; 1 Cor 3:20; 2 Cor 6:18), he also

98. Dennis Hamm, SJ, *Philippians, Colossians, Philemon,* CCSS (Grand Rapids: Baker Academic, 2013), 104.

99. James D. G. Dunn, *Did the First Christians Worship Jesus? The New Testament Evidence* (London: SPCK, 2010), 107n34.

100. Wesley Hill, "The God of Israel—Crucified?," in *The Crucified Apostle,* ed. Todd A. Wilson and Paul R. House, WUNT 2/450 (Tübingen: Mohr Siebeck, 2017), 266: "At [Jesus's] name . . . the action of bending knees and confessing tongues is transferred from Israel's God to Jesus."

applies texts about YHWH to Jesus himself (e.g., Rom 10:13; 1 Cor 1:31; 2:16; 10:17).[101]

Jesus Is on the "Creator" Side of the Creator-Creature Divide

Second, although elsewhere Paul differentiates his God from others by identifying him as the Creator, in 1 Corinthians 8, he also places Jesus on the "Creator" side of the Creator-creature divide.

It is not difficult to find passages in which Paul makes a clear distinction between the Creator and creatures. Think here of his insistence at the beginning of Romans that pagan idolaters erred, "because they exchanged the truth about God for a lie and worshiped and served the creature rather than the Creator" (Rom 1:25). With this in mind, look again at Paul's words in 1 Corinthians 8. Pay attention to the parallelism between the creative activity of the one God and Jesus:

> For us there is *one God*, the Father,
> *from whom are all things* and *for whom we exist*,
> and *one Lord*, Jesus Christ,
> *through whom are all things* and *through whom we exist*. (1 Cor 8:6)

Notice here the direct parallel between the "one God" the Father "from [*ex*] whom are all things [*ta panta*] and for [*eis*] whom we exist" (1 Cor 8:6) and the "one Lord" Jesus "through [*di'*] whom are all things [*ta panta*] and through [*di'*] whom we exist" (1 Cor 8:6). The obvious implication is that, when it comes to the act of creation, Jesus is not on the same side as "all" other created things. He is somehow on the Creator side of the dividing line. In the words of Joseph Fitzmyer, Jesus is here depicted by Paul as "the preexistent mediator of creation."[102]

Some will claim that Jesus's role as divine Creator is somehow less than the Father's because Paul uses different language for this creative activity;

---

101. See Capes, "YHWH Texts and Monotheism in Paul's Christology," 120–37; Capes, *Old Testament Yahweh Texts in Paul's Christology*, WUNT 2/47 (Tübingen: Mohr Siebeck, 1992); Capes, *The Divine Christ*; Bauckham, *Jesus and the God of Israel*, 186–218. To be sure, some will insist this "overreads" Paul. See, e.g., McGrath, *The Only True God*, 38–43. This, however, seems unlikely given what we argue below.

102. Fitzmyer, *First Corinthians*, 343, following Andreas Lindemann, *Der Erste Korintherbrief*, HNT 9/1 (Tübingen: Mohr Siebeck, 2000), 193.

but this fails to notice the way the language used by Paul here for Christ compares with passages in his other letters. For example, what Paul has just said about Jesus as the "one Lord" in 1 Corinthians mirrors what he affirms in Romans about God the Creator:

> O the depth of the riches and wisdom and knowledge of God! How unsearchable are his judgments and how inscrutable his ways! . . . For from him and *through him* [*di' autou*] and to him are *all things* [*ta panta*]. (Rom 11:33, 36)

In these verses Paul uses almost the exact same language for *God* that he uses in reference to Christ in 1 Corinthians 8. The formula is found in other Jewish writings to describe the one Creator.[103] As Andrew Ter Ern Loke observes, the formula "expresses the Jewish monotheistic concern that *God used no other entity to carry out his work of creation, but accomplished it alone*."[104] Moreover, "the mentioning of Christ as the mediator through whom all things come is already sufficient to imply that Paul does not regard Christ as part of 'all things.'"[105] Put another way, all created things exist through Christ, which once again puts Christ on the Creator side of the ontological divide. Jesus takes on one specific role "creatures" do not participate in, namely, creating "all things."[106]

James Dunn raises an objection to this reading. Instead of insisting that Paul necessarily identifies Jesus as YHWH, Dunn makes the case that Christ's creative role can be understood in terms of his being "Wisdom" personified (cf. 1 Cor 1:24).[107] First Corinthians 8 could thus be read as drawing on imagery from sapiential texts in which God's Wisdom is said to participate in the Lord's creative work (cf. Prov 8:22–31; Wis 9:1–2). The difficulty with all of this is that in 1 Corinthians 8, Paul does not identify

---

103. See Josephus, *Jewish War* 5.218; Philo, *On the Cherubim* 127; cf. Heb 2:10.

104. Loke, *Origin of Divine Christology*, 28.

105. Loke, *Origin of Divine Christology*, 29. The suggestion by Collins and Collins, *King and Messiah as Son of God*, 112, that the "new creation" is in view fails to account fully for the import of the *Shemaʿ* imagery. See Loke, *Origin of Divine Christology*, 27–28.

106. Some will make the observation that Philo concludes from Gen 1:26 that angels were involved in the creation of man. In response, as mentioned above, Loke notes (*Origin of Divine Christology*, 16n16) that this claim not a real objection since the claim in 1 Cor 8:6 is not that Jesus simply created man—he is the origin of "all things"—i.e., responsible for the initial creation of the cosmos, as in Isa 44:24.

107. See Dunn, *The Theology of Paul the Apostle*, 272–75.

Jesus as "Divine Wisdom." He is specifically identified as the "Lord"—that is, the subject of the *Shema'* (Deut 6:4–5).[108] To read Wisdom imagery *into* 1 Corinthians 8 is simply not necessary to explain its meaning. It becomes necessary only if one is uncomfortable with what Paul *does* say there. Although Paul identifies Christ as Divine Wisdom elsewhere in his letters, this does not necessarily exclude the possibility that he also recognizes him as YHWH.

Does Paul Have an "Angel" Christology?

Before moving into our final section, it is worth mentioning here that some scholars, such as Bart Ehrman, believe Christ is "divine" for Paul in the sense of being *a heavenly being or angel.*[109] We might refer to this view as an "angel Christology." Advocates of this position point to the fact that Paul appears to apply the word "angel" to Jesus (Gal 4:14). This, they argue, further supports the notion that Paul believed Jesus was an angelic being. Since Paul also refers to Jesus as the "Son of God," a notion that is also applied to the angels (cf. Job 1:6 RSV), these scholars insist that Christ is best viewed as an angelic being. All of this leads scholars like Ehrman to conclude that while Christ is preexistent and "divine" in Pauline theology, he is, nonetheless, not God in the same sense that YHWH is.

This view, however, suffers from having to minimize important aspects of Paul's teaching. For one thing, though a given Jewish writer (such as Philo) might nuance his distinction between God and creation, for *Paul* there is a well-defined line drawn between Creator and creature, between God and "all things [*ta panta*]" (Rom 11:36). As we have just seen, Paul places Jesus on the Creator side of that dividing line. To be sure, angels were responsible for the *governance* of the cosmos, but the apostle never describes them as *creators* of "all things" as he does Christ. In addition, viewing Christ as an "angel" faces another significant problem: as we pointed out in chapter 2, Paul identifies the torah of Moses as that which was ordained by "angels" (cf. Gal 3:19), and then contrasts it with the new "covenant" of Christ (Gal 4:21–5:1). This would seem to indicate that Christ must be *greater* than an angel. Moreover, at one point, Paul even says (somewhat matter-of-factly) that believers themselves will judge the angels:

108. See Loke, *Origin of Divine Christology*, 31–32.
109. See, e.g., Erhman, *How Jesus Became God*, 252–69.

> Do you not know that the saints will judge the world? And if the world
> is to be judged by you, are you incompetent to try trivial cases? *Do you*
> *not know that we are to judge angels*—to say nothing of ordinary matters?
> (1 Cor 6:2–3)

Here Paul makes no distinction between those angels believers will judge
and those they will not.[110] Yet he also teaches that *Christ* will be his judge
(1 Cor 4:4–5; 11:32). Now, *if Paul thinks Christ is one of the angels, does Paul*
believe he will be judged by Christ and then turn around and judge Jesus?
Such a position is contrary to the whole thrust of his argument. Lastly,
though scholars like Ehrman seem to think it highly significant that Paul
calls Christ an angel, they seem to overstate the implications of this. The
term *angelos* is *also* used in biblical and nonbiblical sources to describe *hu-*
mans who are "sent" as "messengers."[111] It would seem like special pleading
to insist that Paul's reference to Christ as an *angelos* therefore necessarily
reveals that he believes Christ is an angelic being. In sum, this peg of a
supposedly "angelic Christology" in Paul simply cannot bear the weight
of the argument.

Christ Devotion and the Language of God-Relation in Paul

In order to bring this chapter to a close, we would like to end with one final
aspect of Pauline Christology that reinforces the conclusion that Jesus is
something *more* for Paul than an agent or angel who merely represents or
functions as YHWH. In a landmark study, Chris Tilling has shown that the
case for a "divine Christology" in Paul can be demonstrated not merely by
examining specific passages such as the Christ hymn (Phil 2:5–8) but also
by examining the *overarching pattern* of how Paul's depiction of Christ's
relationship with believers consistently maps onto Jewish conceptions of
God-relation.[112] Instead of simply focusing on particular Pauline texts and
their potential christological implications, Tilling looks at larger patterns
in Paul's thought, analyzing how they conform to the way Jews spoke about
God's unique relationship with Israel. As we saw above, in Jewish writings

---

110. Fitzmyer, *First Corinthians*, 252.

111. See, e.g., LXX Gen 32:4, 7; Jdt 1:11; 3:1; 1 Macc 1:44; 7:10; Luke 7:27; Josephus,
Jewish Antiquities 14.451.

112. See Tilling, *Paul's Divine Christology*.

God's transcendent "oneness" was understood as expressed not simply by propositional formulas but relationally: Israel's relationship with God is utterly unique.

Tilling takes this idea and begins his study by showing that something astounding happens in 1 Corinthians 8–10: *Paul includes Christ himself within the dynamic of believers' relationship with God.*[113] For example, somewhat strikingly, Paul describes sin not simply as an offense against God—which would be expected in any ancient Jewish work—but, remarkably, as a sin "against Christ" (1 Cor 8:12). Similarly, Paul speaks of the Israelites who tested God in the wilderness and declares that believers who now partake in idolatry likewise test the "Lord [*kyrios*]" (1 Cor 10:9 RSV).[114] In context, the term "Lord" here is best seen as a reference to Christ, since Paul has just insisted that Jesus is the "one Lord" (1 Cor 8:6).[115] In all of this, Paul brings Christ into the unique dynamic of Israel's relationship with its "one Lord." Finally, when it comes to Paul's reworking of the *Shemaʿ* that we studied above (1 Cor 8:5–6), Tilling notes that as remarkable as the identification of Jesus's name with YHWH is, the surrounding context is even more significant:

> Precisely in a context that contrasts the monotheistic "knowledge" of the Corinthians with the relational "necessary" monotheistic knowing of love for God, Paul includes Christ directly in this relational dynamic, and does so by employing a text in Deuteronomy that was central to the daily prayer life of Jews and to the relationship between YHWH and Israel.[116]

In other words, Paul explicates Christ's relationship with believers in terms that Jewish readers would have associated exclusively with the one God of the *Shemaʿ* (Deut 6:4–6).

Furthermore, after having established Paul's use of God-relation language for Christ via an inductive study of 1 Corinthians 8–10, Tilling then goes on to demonstrate how this dynamic is present throughout the seven

---

113. See Tilling, *Paul's Divine Christology*, 75–104.

114. Some ancient manuscripts read "Christ" instead of "Lord." For a discussion that favors "Christ" as the preferred rendering, see B. J. Oropeza, *Paul and Apostasy: Eschatology, Perseverance, and Falling Away in the Corinthian Congregation*, WUNT 2/115 (Tübingen: Mohr Siebeck, 2000), 153–55.

115. See Tilling, *Paul's Divine Christology*, 99.

116. Tilling, *Paul's Divine Christology*, 91.

undisputed letters of Paul.[117] The following represents an overview of Tilling's research;[118] compare how Paul consistently uses the language of God-relation for the believers' relations with Christ:

God-Relation in Paul	Christ-Relation in Paul
Communication: Believers Pray to God "My heart's desire and *prayer to God* for them is that they may be saved." (Rom 10:1)	*Communication: Believers Pray to Christ* "Three times *I besought the Lord* about this . . . but he said to me, 'My grace is sufficient for you, for my power is made perfect in weakness.'" (2 Cor 12:8–9 RSV)
God: Present and Active "God chose what is low and despised in the world . . . so that no one might boast *in the presence of God.*" (1 Cor 1:28–29) "For it is God who is at work *in you,* enabling you both to will and to work for his good pleasure." (Phil 2:13)	*Christ: Present and Active* "What I have forgiven, if I have forgiven anything, has been for your sake *in the presence of Christ.*" (2 Cor 2:10) "But if Christ is *in you* . . . your spirits are alive because of righteousness." (Rom 8:10 RSV)
God: Present and Active by the Spirit "May the God of hope fill you with all joy and peace in believing, so that you may abound in hope *by the power of the Holy Spirit.*" (Rom 15:13) "Do you not know that you are God's temple and that *God's Spirit dwells in you?*" (1 Cor 3:16)	*Christ: Present and Active by the Spirit* "For I will not venture to speak of anything except what Christ has wrought through me to win obedience from the Gentiles . . . *by the power of the Holy Spirit.*" (Rom 15:18–19 RSV) "But you are not in the flesh, you are in the Spirit, if in fact *the Spirit of God dwells in you.* Any one who does not have *the Spirit of Christ* does not belong to him." (Rom 8:9 RSV)
God in Heaven / Presence Unrealized "For the wrath of God is revealed *from heaven.*" (Rom 1:18)	*Christ in Heaven / Presence Unrealized* "To wait for his Son *from heaven.*" (1 Thess 1:10)

117. See Tilling, *Paul's Divine Christology,* 105–80.

118. We thank Chris Tilling for his personal correspondence, which has helped further shape the presentation here.

Devotion to God	*Devotion to Christ*
contrast with idolatry (Rom 1:25)	contrast with idolatry (1 Cor 10:14–22)
"know [*oida*]" (1 Thess 4:5)	"know [*oida*]" (1 Cor 2:2)
"please [*areskō*]" (Rom 8:8)	"please [*areskō*]" (1 Cor 7:32)
"fear [*phobos*]" (2 Cor 7:1)	"fear [*phobos*]" (2 Cor 5:11)
"believe in [*pisteuō*]" (Rom 4:17)	"believe in [*pisteuō*]" (Gal 2:16)
"alive to [*zaō*]" (Rom 6:11)	"live to [*zaō*]" (Rom 14:8)

God Character-in-Relation	*Christ Character-in-Relation*
merciful (Rom 11:32)	merciful (1 Cor 7:25)
loving (1 Thess 1:4)	loving (Gal 2:20)
righteous (Rom 1:17)	righteous (1 Cor 1:30)

This remarkable series of parallels is of crucial import for understanding the shape of Pauline Christology. By rooting his approach within Paul's own epistles, Tilling makes a very distinctive exegetical move. Unlike others who have attempted to argue that Paul makes certain predications of Christ that Jews reserved for God alone, Tilling shows that throughout the Pauline corpus, the relational dynamic between the believer and Christ is taken up into the pattern of God-talk used to express the transcendent uniqueness of the God of Israel.[119] Jesus is thus subtly but inescapably identified as the one God of Israel.[120]

---

119. In the foreword to Tilling's book, Douglas Campbell writes, "[Tilling's] case for divine Christology is, at bottom, fundamentally different in its approach [from Bauckham, et al.] and in a manner that seems to avoid their vulnerabilities" (*Paul's Divine Christology*, xv).

120. It is worth noting here that while some scholars such as Bart Ehrman have attempted to explain Paul's Christology by placing Jesus on the same level as certain *divine agents* in early Jewish texts such as Sir 44–50, *1 En.* 37–71, and the *Life of Adam and Eve*, Tilling shows that such arguments are ultimately unconvincing. In each case, Tilling observes that the parallels with the divine agents in such sources pale in comparison to the overwhelming similarities between their depiction of God-relation and Christ-relation in Paul. See Tilling, *Paul's Divine Christology*, 196–233. For example, while the author of Sirach composes a hymn praising the righteous ancestors of Israel's past and depicts the high priest as a sort of embodiment of divine wisdom, these figures are not depicted as speaking back. Nowhere is "serving" or "pleasing" the fathers a priority in a way that compares credibly with Paul's language of Christ-devotion. Likewise, while the Enochic Son of Man bears certain similarities to Christ in Paul, Tilling points out important qualifications need to be made here as well. For example, though the Son of Man is "worshipped" (48:4–6; 62:9), this

In Summary: Jesus Christ as the Divine Son

Discussions of Pauline theology often begin with Jewish monotheism and then move on to consider how Paul sought to "fit" his view of Christ into it. Yet this fails to fully reckon with the significance of the Christ-event for Paul. As we have seen in chapter 2, the revelation of Christ caused Paul to rethink certain aspects of Jewish apocalyptic traditions. It seems wrong-headed, then, to insist that Paul simply had to find a way to work Christ into a static conception of the Lord God. In fact, he does not seem to have done that. Paul's teaching about Christ is therefore both in some ways consistent with and in other ways a departure from early Jewish writings of his day.

On the one hand, Paul's teaching about Jesus is similar to what is found in other Jewish sources. Paul recognizes Jesus as the Davidic messiah promised in the scriptures. Jesus is portrayed as a very *human* figure. He was "born in human likeness" (Phil 2:7), was "born of a woman" (Gal 4:4), and, notably, was "descended from David according to the flesh" (Rom 1:3). Moreover, such hopes seem to have been closely linked to the idea of a new or eschatological covenant (e.g., Isa 55:3; Ezek 34:23–25; 37:25–27; Zech 9:9–11). Significantly, in the very same context where Jeremiah speaks of a new covenant (Jer 31:31), the prophet also announces the coming of a future Davidic ruler (Jer 30:9; 33:15–26).[121] Thus, Paul views Christ in terms evocative of apocalyptic hopes for a messianic figure, in ways that fit in perfectly with our portrait of Paul as a "new covenant" Jew.

---

takes place only on earth, whereas Paul says that "at the name of Jesus every knee should bend, *in heaven* and on earth and *under the earth*" (Phil 2:10). In addition, the Enochic Son of Man is not somehow dynamically present on earth while also being in heaven, as Christ is for Paul. Nor do believers invoke the Son of Man figure directly as Paul speaks to and is spoken to by Christ. Rather, Tilling makes the case that the relational dynamic involving the Lord of the Spirits is *more* like Christ than the Son of Man figure in *1 Enoch*. Strikingly, Paul even calls Christ "the Lord of glory" (1 Cor 2:8), the same term *1 Enoch* uses for "the Lord of the Spirits"—that is, God (cf. *1 En.* 40:3; cf. *1 En.* 22:14; 25:3; 27:3, 5). In short, if one were pressed to compare Paul's teaching to what is found in *1 Enoch*, one would have to admit that his understanding of Christ-relation has far more in common with the Lord of the Spirits than with the Enochic Son of Man.

121. The connection between hopes for a new covenant relationship with God and the arrival of future Davidide is likely rooted in the biblical narratives of the monarchy where covenant renewal is particularly linked with Davidic kings Hezekiah (2 Chr 29:10) and Josiah (2 Kgs 23:21–23; cf. 2 Chr 34:31–32).

That said, in the light of Christ, Paul's new covenant hopes take on a distinctive shape. Rather than choosing between a human *or* a heavenly messiah, for Paul, Christ is somehow *both*. Prior to being in human form, the apostle tells us Jesus was in "the form of God," having "equality with God" (Phil 2:6). This divine status cannot simply be understood in terms of his being an angel since the new covenant that comes through him is contrasted with that which had previously been administered by angels (cf. Gal 3:19). Nor is it possible to identify Jesus as simply an exalted human. Paul places Jesus on the Creator side of the Creator-creature divide (cf. 1 Cor 8:6). When he speaks of how "all things" were made "through" Christ, the apostle does more than simply suggest that Jesus is the embodiment of "divine wisdom" (cf. 1 Cor 1:24). In Philippians 2 and 1 Corinthians 8, Paul depicts Christ as YHWH, that is, the one "Lord" (*kyrios*) of the Jewish *Shema'*. With that said, it is important to emphasize that Paul does *not* identify Jesus as "the Father." On this point Bart Ehrman is correct: "Paul clearly thought Jesus was God in a certain sense—but he does not think that he was the father."[122] Yet, as we have seen, to think Paul viewed Jesus as an angel creates its own problems. Instead, for the apostle, YHWH, it seems, has a second "self." The Lord God is somehow *both* Father and Son, and Jesus is the Son.

Since Paul's teaching is explicitly shaped by appeals to Jewish scriptures, it makes sense to try to account for his language in Jewish terms. Yet rather than insisting that his language of Jesus as YHWH is best understood by finding some Jewish parallel and attempting to ignore differences between it and Paul, we agree with Wesley Hill that what seems to have happened is that the Christ-event has *reconfigured the apostle's understanding of God*:

> One can take the distinction of Jesus from God and the mediatorial instrumentality of Jesus with full seriousness without thereby qualifying in any way the identification of Jesus with God by means of the *Shema*. To specify Jesus Christ as [Lord] and as the agent of God the Father's creative initiative ["from whom"] does not lessen or remove his full sharing of the divine identity acclaimed in Deut 6:4. Rather, in a non-competitive and mutually complementary way, affirming God the Father and Jesus together *as* the "one God" of Deut 6:5 and affirming their irreducible distinction from one another as unique agents

---

122. Ehrman, *How Jesus Became God*, 269.

or "persons" is to do justice to both of those elements as present in 1 Cor 8:6.[123]

In short, the one YHWH, the God of Israel, can somehow now be understood as "Father" and "Son." Of course, Paul himself never works out the implications of this reality; the trinitarian terminology of Nicaea is still three centuries away. Yet the notion of some sort of plurality *within* the one God of the *Shema'* can be seen as having its origins in Paul, whose Christology is truly "apocalyptic"—that is, a revelation of a heavenly mystery which never could have been understood apart from rereading the scriptures in light of the "revelation" (*apokalypsis*) of God's "Son" (cf. Gal 1:16).

123. Wesley Hill, *Paul and the Trinity: Persons, Relations, and the Pauline Letters* (Grand Rapids: Eerdmans, 2015), 119–20.

CHAPTER 4

The Cross and Atonement

The recognition that God is offering up his Son to save humanity in a costly act of atonement reveals God's fundamental posture toward humanity. . . . God's act of atonement through Christ, the very act that reveals his compassion, contains implicitly the solution to the pressing problem of human sinfulness, and an effective ethic as well.

—Douglas Campbell[1]

The point of the Messiah's death . . . is that it demonstrates, in action, the faithfulness of God to his covenant plan.

—N. T. Wright[2]

For almost two thousand years, Paul's teaching about the cross has baffled "the wise" (1 Cor 1:20–25). Paul's creed-like declaration that "Christ died for our sins" (1 Cor 15:3) stands at the very heart of his gospel. But why did Christ die? And what precisely did Paul think Christ's death accomplished with regard to sin? Interpreters have long struggled with how to answer these questions and to account for how the atoning death of Christ fits into the larger picture of Paul's thought.

On one hand, Paul is emphatic that salvation is a grace (*charis*)—that is, a "gift." From this point of view, it seems evident that Paul did not think Jesus's death was due to any kind of strict divine necessity. Rather, the apostle indicates the cross was the result of a divine gratuity through which God showed his "love" (*agapē*) for humanity (Rom 5:8). On the

---

1. Campbell, *The Deliverance of God*, 606.
2. N. T. Wright, "God Put Jesus Forth: Reflections on Romans 3:24–26," in *In the Fullness of Time: Essays on Christology, Creation, and Eschatology*, ed. Daniel M. Gurtner, Grant Macaskill, and Jonathan Pennington (Grand Rapids: Eerdmans, 2016), 153 (the original quote is entirely in italics).

other hand, Paul holds that the cross is the means by which salvation is accomplished. Specifically, he views it as a "sacrifice of atonement [*hilastērion*]" (Rom 3:25), using the language of "ransom" or "redemption [*apolytrōsis*]" (Rom 3:24; 1 Cor 1:30). As we shall see, such terminology carries financial connotations. This raises difficult questions. What "price" is "paid" by Jesus's death? Does not such language weigh against the notion of God's mercy? Why must there be a price associated with divine forgiveness?[3]

In this chapter we propose a "both-and" approach to the atonement, which integrates two aspects of Paul's teaching—namely, (1) his insistence that salvation occurs through a divine *gift* of love and (2) his description of Jesus's death as a sacrifice of "atonement" or "redemption." Put another way, we propose that for Paul, the cross of Christ is both an *apocalyptic revelation* of God's gratuitous love and the *new covenant sacrifice of redemption*. We will contend that these two ideas are inseparable for the apostle. Although the cross is an act of atonement and redemption, it is not an act of divine obligation or the result of strict necessity. In fact, we will make the case that when the cross is understood in terms of the "apocalyptic new covenant," we can better account for its place in Paul's theology.

As we shall see, covenantal logic is crucial for understanding the apostle's discussion of the cross. Among other things, by associating Jesus's death with covenant imagery Paul underscores the gratuitous nature of the cross—it entails a *gift of self that definitively expresses God's love*. Yet this is also closely connected to the apostle's apocalyptic message. As we shall explain, according to Paul, in giving himself on the cross Jesus reveals what it means to be God. Moreover, the cross manifests what God empowers believers to do by the gift of grace, namely, they are enabled to love as Christ did. Finally, for Paul the cross demonstrates the astonishing profundity of God's love in that the death of the divine Son is shown to have been part of the divine plan all along. God anticipates what Jesus will do in asking Abraham to offer his own beloved son; yet, unlike Isaac, Jesus is actually sacrificed. God enters into a covenant with Israel knowing that it will be broken but also with full awareness of how redemption will be

---

3. For a brilliant overview of the history of atonement doctrine from a Catholic perspective, see Philippe de la Trinité, *What Is Redemption?*, trans. Anthony Armstrong (New York: Hawthorn Books, 1961), 13–37. For discussions that reflect a Protestant perspective, see Simon Gathercole, *Defending Substitution: An Essay on Atonement in Paul* (Grand Rapids: Baker Academic, 2015), 1–54; Charles E. Hill and Frank A. James III, eds., *The Glory of the Atonement* (Downers Grove, IL: InterVarsity Press, 2004).

accomplished: the Father will give his Son to bear the curse of covenant infidelity. The cross therefore reveals that God is willing to reach into the deepest darkness of sin's ghastly consequences in order to save humanity from them.

Christ Gave Himself for Our Sins

For many contemporary readers of the New Testament, the term "atonement" conjures up images of God the Father pouring out his wrath on the Son, who dies on the cross to assuage divine anger so that believers can enjoy the love of God. In some approaches, the Father and the Son are set in opposition to each other. The image of a vengeful God thus dominates all other portraits. Such notions of the atonement are not limited to Protestant circles. For example, Alphonse Gratry, a nineteenth-century French Catholic, characterized Christ's atoning work this way:

> It seems to the Son of God that God also is against him. He, who comes to unite men among themselves and with God, in order to bring back even the most abandoned of them, undergoes the trial of absolute separation from men and from God. And so it is that the Son of man truly bore for us the *pain of hell!*[4]

Whatever one wishes to say about this perspective, it is not how Paul himself describes the cross. Nowhere, for instance, does Paul suggest that the Son believes the Father is opposed to him or speak of Christ's "absolute separation" from God.[5] Instead, Paul's theology of the atoning death of Christ consistently presents it in terms of Christ's voluntary gift to the Father.

---

4. Alphonse Gratry, *Commentaires sur l'Evangile selon Saint Matthieu* (Paris: Téqui, 1909), translation from Trinité, *What Is Redemption?*, 29. Trinité demonstrates how such interpretations appear discontinuous with patristic approaches as well as the more mature thought of Thomas Aquinas.

5. Typically, the idea of abandonment is associated with the Synoptic Gospels' accounts of Jesus's cry of dereliction, taken from Ps 22. Yet the psalm climaxes with vindication (cf. Ps 22:19–31), an observation that weighs against the view that Jesus's prayer only expresses a sense of abandonment. See Joel Marcus, *The Way of the Lord: Christological Exegesis of the Old Testament in the Gospel of Mark* (London: T&T Clark, 1992), 180–86.

The New Covenant Sacrifice and Christ's Gift of Himself

Paul insists that Jesus went to his death *willingly*. This is particularly evident in his account in 1 Corinthians 11 of Jesus's words and actions at the Last Supper:

> For I received from the Lord what I also handed on to you, that the Lord Jesus on the night when he was betrayed took a loaf of bread, and when he had *given thanks*, he broke it and said, "*This is my body that is for you. Do this in remembrance of me.*" In the same way he took the cup also, after supper, saying, "*This cup is the new covenant in my blood. Do this, as often as you drink it, in remembrance of me.*" For as often as you eat this bread and drink the cup, you proclaim the Lord's death until he comes. (1 Cor 11:23–26)

Two features of this account indicate that, according to Paul, Jesus's life is not taken from him against his will. For one thing, Jesus's announcement that his "body" is given "for you" (*hyper hymōn*) underscores the *voluntary* nature of his death (1 Cor 11:24). This reading is reinforced when one looks at the context of his declaration. Immediately prior to speaking of how his body will be given over, Jesus "gives thanks [*eucharistēsas*]" (1 Cor 11:24 NRSV, adapted). Yet thanksgiving is not the posture of one who is dragged to his death unwillingly. In short, in his account of the establishment of the new covenant sacrifice, Paul stresses the notion that Christ *freely* gave his life.

The voluntary character of Jesus's death is further emphasized by the cup saying, which underscores its *covenantal* character. As interpreters have long noted, Jesus refers to his death as a sacrifice when he says, "This cup is the new covenant in my blood" (1 Cor 11:25).[6] In the scriptures of Israel, covenants were typically established through ritual sacrifice. This understanding is illustrated in Psalm 50 when God states, "Gather to me my faithful ones, *who made a covenant with me by sacrifice!*" (Ps 50:5).[7] Even more, the juxtaposition of "blood" and "covenant" in Jesus's words is likely intended to evoke the establishment of the Mosaic covenant at Mount Sinai:[8]

---

6. See Fitzmyer, *First Corinthians*, 443.

7. See D. J. Wiseman, "The Vassal-Treaties of Esarhaddon," *Iraq* 20 (1958): 1–99; Hahn, *Kinship by Covenant*, 59.

8. Fitzmyer, *First Corinthians*, 443.

Moses took half of the blood and put it in basins, and half of the blood he dashed against the altar. Then he took the book of the covenant, and read it in the hearing of the people; and they said, "All that the LORD has spoken we will do, and we will be obedient." Moses took the blood and dashed it on the people, and said, "See *the blood of the covenant* that the LORD has made with you in accordance with all these words." (Exod 24:6–8)

By means of this echo, Paul depicts Christ's death as a sacrificial act that establishes a covenant.[9] Jesus's words over the cup also include an allusion to another text: Jeremiah's new covenant oracle. As has long been recognized, when Jesus speaks of the cup as "the new covenant in my blood" (1 Cor 11:25) he alludes to Jeremiah's famous prophecy announcing a "new covenant" (Jer 31:31).[10] By bringing together these two texts—the sacrificial covenant ratification ceremony of Exodus 24 and the new covenant prophecy of Jeremiah 31—Paul's meaning is obvious. Just as the blood of sacrifice ratified the Mosaic covenant, so Jesus's death now serves as the sacrificial offering that establishes the new covenant.[11]

By presenting Jesus's death as a *covenant* sacrifice, Paul underscores its *gratuitous* nature. In his letter to the Romans, the apostle maintains that God entered into a covenant with Israel out of sheer graciousness. At the climax of the argument in Romans 9–11, Paul declares, "The gifts [*charismata*] and the calling of God are irrevocable" (Rom 11:29). As virtually all commentators recognize, the "gifts" referred to here are best connected to the blessings enumerated earlier in Romans 9, which include "the adoption, the glory, the *covenants*" (Rom 9:4).[12] For our purposes here, the crucial point is this: according to Paul, God's "covenants" are "gifts." Paul affirms that when it comes to the covenant with Israel, God did not call Jacob instead of Esau because of anything Jacob had done. Instead, the covenant was a gift:

9. A. Andrew Das (*Paul and the Stories of Israel: Grand Thematic Narratives in Galatians* [Minneapolis: Fortress, 2016], 84) ignores the significance of this echo when he claims, "Paul describes Christ's death as a sacrifice but never as a *covenant* sacrifice."

10. Fitzmyer, *First Corinthians*, 443.

11. See, e.g., Gorman, *Death of the Messiah*, 53; Richard Horsley, *1 Corinthians*, ANTC (Nashville: Abingdon, 1988), 161; Isaac W. Oliver, "Baptism and Eucharist," in Levine and Brettler, *The Jewish Annotated New Testament*, 676–77.

12. See, e.g., Jewett, *Romans*, 708; Matera, *Romans*, 274; James D. G. Dunn, *Romans*, 2 vols., WBC 38A–B (Nashville: Thomas Nelson, 1988), 2:686.

> *Though they were not yet born and had done nothing either good or bad,* in order that God's purpose of election might continue, not because of works but because of his call, she [Rebekah] was told, "The elder will serve the younger." (Rom 9:11–12 RSV)

In a similar way, by highlighting the death of Jesus as a covenant-making sacrifice, Paul thereby shows that it was not due to strict divine necessity. In other words, it was not "owed" to humanity but is ultimately revelatory of divine gratuity.

Paul and the "Gift"

Because of its origin in divine graciousness, the cross is inseparable from the concept of "grace." To appreciate this more fully, it is helpful to return to John Barclay's work on the concept of "grace" in Paul. Barclay emphasizes a point that is often overlooked: the Greek term translated "grace," *charis*, originally had the connotation of "gift."[13] Paul also uses *charis* synonymously with other words linked to gift-giving.[14] Barclay shows, therefore, that the apostle's teaching about "grace" (*charis*) must be interpreted against the backdrop of ancient gift-giving; otherwise, it will be easily misconstrued. As Barclay explains, this is no hypothetical interpretive danger. Modern readers have often misunderstood the apostle's message due to a lack of familiarity with gift-giving in the ancient world. For example, many interpreters assume all gifts were conferred with "no strings attached"— that is, without expectations of reciprocity. Barclay demonstrates that such a perspective is peculiarly modern, influenced especially by Martin Luther:

> [Luther's] distinctive construal of grace constituted a significant break with the Augustinian and medieval tradition, and contributed to the emergence of a new perfection of gift—as "pure altruism"—that has become widely influential in the modern era.[15]

---

13. See Barclay, *Paul and the Gift*, 59–76. See also Barclay, "Under Grace: The Christ-Gift and the Construction of a Christian *Habitus*," in Gaventa, *Apocalyptic Paul*, 59–76; Barclay, "Grace and the Transformation of Agency in Christ," in Udoh, *Redefining First-Century Jewish and Christian Identities*, 384.

14. See, e.g., Rom 5: *charis* in 5:15, 17, 21; *charisma*, 5:15, 16; *dōrea*, 5:15; *dōrēma*, 5:16.

15. See Barclay, *Paul and the Gift*, 97. See also, Barclay, "Under Grace," 60–61.

The truth is, Paul's original audience would not have assumed that gift-giving was motivated by "pure altruism." While ancient gifts were bestowed freely, it was also understood that they were imparted with certain *expectations.* Barclay explains, "It was extremely common in antiquity for recipients of gifts to feel themselves obliged to their donors; in fact this is so much taken for granted that it forms the subject of delicate negotiation from both sides (see Seneca, *De beneficiis* passim)."[16] As we shall see, this has important implications for unpacking Paul's teaching about grace and clarifies his view of the cross.

One important illustration of this connection between the death of Christ and the language of gift-giving/grace can be found in two key passages from Galatians:

> Paul an apostle—sent neither by human commission nor from human authorities, but through Jesus Christ and God the Father, who raised him from the dead—and all the members of God's family who are with me,
>> To the churches of Galatia:
>> *Grace to you* and peace from God our Father and the Lord Jesus Christ, *who gave himself* for our sins to set us free from the present evil age, according to the will of our God and Father, to whom be the glory forever and ever. Amen. (Gal 1:1–5)

> I have *been crucified with Christ*; and it is no longer I who live, but it is Christ who lives in me. And the life I now live in the flesh I live by faith in the Son of God, *who loved me* and *gave himself for me.* (Gal 2:19–20)

Notice in the first passage that the "grace" (*charis*) believers receive in Christ (Gal 1:3) is "identified as a gift-event, focalized in the specific story of Jesus's death and resurrection."[17] Christ gives himself to believers not only on the cross but through grace, through which he lives with believers ("it is Christ who lives in me"). Even more striking is the way Paul

16. See Barclay, "Under Grace," 63. On gift-giving in antiquity, Barclay also cites F. W. Danker, *Benefactor: Epigraphic Study of a Graeco-Roman Semantic Field* (St. Louis: Clayton, 1982); James R. Harrison, *Paul's Language of Grace in Its Graeco-Roman Context*, WUNT 2/172 (Tübingen: Mohr Siebeck, 2003); Marcel Mauss, *The Gift*, trans. W. D. Halls (London: Routledge, 1990).

17. Barclay, *Paul and the Gift*, 352.

speaks in the second text: Jesus's death is characterized as *self-giving*. When Paul says, Christ "loved [*agapēsantos*] me" and "gave himself [*paradontos heauton*] for me" (Gal 2:20), he describes what Jesus does on the cross not only as a gift of love but also as a gift of *self*.[18] At the same time, Paul also indicates that Christ's gift involves an expectation of reciprocity; believers are now to live a different kind of life: "The life I now live in the flesh I live by faith" (Gal 2:20).[19] Among other things, Paul tells believers, "Live by the Spirit . . . and do not gratify the desires of the flesh" (Gal 5:16). This is because "those who belong to Christ Jesus have crucified the flesh with its passions and desires" (Gal 5:24). Consistent with ancient gift-giving, Christ's gift—"grace"—also comes with expectations; in particular, it entails participation in the self-giving of Christ (which, as we shall see, grace also makes available).[20]

Galatians is not the only place Paul speaks of the cross in this way. The cross is also described as an expression of love in Romans:

> For while we were still weak, at the right time Christ died for the ungodly. Indeed, rarely will anyone die for a righteous person—though perhaps for a good person someone might actually dare to die. *But God proves his love for us in that while we still were sinners Christ died for us.* Much more surely then, now that we have been justified by his blood, will we be saved through him from the wrath of God. For if while we were enemies, *we were reconciled to God through the death of his Son*, much more surely, having been reconciled, will we be saved by his life. (Rom 5:6–10)

When we inspect this text closely, we discover that, according to Paul, the "love of God" is actually revealed in Jesus's death in two significant ways.[21]

First, divine love is associated with God, who reconciles the world "through the death of his Son" (Rom 5:10). This love is both spontaneous and gratuitous. Joseph Fitzmyer puts it well: "There is no *quid pro quo* in the love manifested: divine love is spontaneously demonstrated toward

---

18. See Martyn, *Galatians*, 259; Campbell, *The Deliverance of God*, 847; Wright, *Paul and the Faithfulness of God*, 2:856, who argue from the context that Jesus's death on the cross is in view.

19. Other passages could also be mentioned here. See, e.g., 1 Cor 6:20: "You were bought with a price; therefore glorify God in your body."

20. For more on the relationship between grace/gift and works, see chapter 5 below.

21. See Fitzmyer, *Romans*, 400–401.

sinners *without a hint that it is repaying a love already shown.*"[22] For Paul, then, the cross demonstrates God the Father's love.

Second, the Father's love is also made known through *Jesus's action*. Paul focuses on the fact that Jesus did something unheard of—he died for those who were "sinners" (Rom 5:6–8, 10). From this we see that, according to Paul, God's love is therefore not simply revealed in the Father's act of giving us his Son. God's love is also displayed in Jesus's act of giving *himself* for sinners. In the words of Fitzmyer, "The death of Christ is for us, sinners, precisely the proof of God's love for us."[23] In other words, the cross is a kind of "revelation," or *apokalypsis*, of *divine love*.

The Cross as an Apocalyptic Revelation of Jesus's Divinity

This "apocalyptic" dimension of the cross is further underscored in the work of Michael Gorman on the Christ hymn of Philippians 2.[24] Although we examined this passage in chapter 3 with reference to Paul's Christology, we need to look at it again here, this time focusing on what it reveals about Paul's theology of the cross:

> Have this mind among yourselves, which is yours in Christ Jesus, who, though he was in the form of God, did not count equality with God a thing to be grasped, but *emptied himself*, taking the form of a servant, being born in the likeness of men. And being found in human form *he humbled himself and became obedient unto death, even death on a cross.* Therefore God has highly exalted him and bestowed on him the name which is above every name, that at the name of Jesus every knee should bow, in heaven and on earth and under the earth, and every tongue confess that Jesus Christ is Lord, to the glory of God the Father. (Phil 2:5–11 RSV)

Drawing on the work of Joseph Hellerman, Gorman makes the case that the passage's narrative pattern indicates a *continuous* downward descent, which contrasts Jesus's example with the Roman *cursus honorum*—that is,

---

22. Fitzmyer, *Romans*, 400 (emphasis added).
23. Fitzmyer, *Romans*, 400.
24. See Gorman, *Inhabiting the Cruciform God*, 16–39.

"the elite's upward-bound race for honors."[25] Most importantly, Gorman argues that the downward movement within the passage has its origins in Jesus's preexistent form. What Christ does in the "form of a slave" (Phil 2:7), namely, humbling himself and accepting crucifixion, parallels what he does in the "form of God" (Phil 2:6), that is, emptying himself and being born in the likeness of men.[26] Or, to put it differently, *what Jesus does in his humanity is an expression of what he does in his divinity*. Jesus's act of obedience on the cross can be seen as the culmination of the self-giving love he expressed in becoming man. For this reason, rather than rendering the passage "though he was in the form of God . . . he emptied himself," Gorman argues the passage is better translated as "*because* he was in the form of God, he . . . emptied himself."[27] Gorman's insight here is of immense significance, for it makes far better sense of the way the narrative highlights Christ's continuous descent.

Read in this way, Philippians 2 helps to illuminate the depths of Paul's understanding of Christ's death. For Paul, when Jesus embraces the cross, he acts in a way that is not *contrary* to his divine character but that is actually *expressive* of it. Specifically, the cross reveals that God manifests himself *via* Jesus's gift of self. In order to grasp this firmly, it is important to realize that the apostle does not draw a parallel between Jesus's death per se and his act of emptying himself.[28] Rather, the true counterpart of his self-emptying is his *obedience* by which he *voluntarily* surrenders his life to the Father. *Paul sees Jesus's act of giving himself on the cross as providing us with a kind of historical expression of what he does in his divinity.*[29] In this way, the cross itself becomes *apocalyptic* because it entails a revelatory in-breaking of God into history. The cross reveals the truth about Christ's divinity (i.e., his being in the "form of God"), which is made known

---

25. Gorman, *Inhabiting the Cruciform God*, 16. Here he is following the work of Joseph H. Hellerman, *Reconstructing Honor in Roman Philippi:* Carmen Christi *as* Cursus Pudorum, SNTSMS 132 (Cambridge: Cambridge University Press, 2005).

26. As Gorman notes, "The phrase 'emptied himself' in 2:7 should not be read as a reference to the divestiture of something (whether divinity itself or some divine attribute), or even as self-limitation regarding the use of divine attributes." Gorman, *Inhabiting the Cruciform God*, 21.

27. Gorman, *Inhabiting the Cruciform God*, 22–25.

28. Recall here that death per se is actually associated with *sin* in Paul's thought: "The wages of sin is death" (Rom 6:23).

29. See Norbert Hoffman, "Atonement and the Ontological Coherence between the Trinity and the Cross," in *Towards a Civilization of Love*, trans. E. Leiva-Merikakis (San Francisco: Ignatius Press, 1985), 213–66.

through what Jesus does in his humanity (i.e., in the "form of a servant"). Furthermore, Paul goes on to link what happens on the cross directly to the resurrection: "Therefore God has highly exalted him" (Phil 2:9 RSV). This helps reinforce the point made above: Christ's *willingness to die*—not death itself—is what corresponds to what he does in his divinity. The resurrection points to the way that Christ's self-giving is ultimately related to glory. Christ was "in the form of God," descended in becoming human, and gave himself in death. But the story climaxes in exaltation. Christ is now glorified after having taken the form of a slave.

Though He Was Rich He Became Poor

In support of our reading of Philippians 2, it is worth noting that Paul engages in a remarkably similar description of the "self-emptying," or *kenōsis*, of Christ in 2 Corinthians. There he writes, "For you know the grace of our Lord Jesus Christ, that *though he was rich*, yet *for your sake he became poor*, so that by his poverty you might become rich" (2 Cor 8:9 RSV). When was Jesus "rich"? And exactly when did he become "poor"? Given what we have seen so far, the reference to Christ's original state—his "wealth"—is most likely a reference to his preexistent divine status. To quote Frank Matera, "In saying that Christ became poor, Paul implies a prior condition of 'being rich' that most exegetes interpret in light of the incarnation: the preexistent Son of God who took on the poverty of humankind."[30] If this is correct, then Christ is made "poor" through humbling himself *both* in becoming human *and* in dying the humiliating death of crucifixion. In the words of N. T. Wright, "The path to the cross begins with the becoming human of the one whom from all eternity was 'equal with God.'"[31] All this was done so that believers in Christ might somehow share in the state he enjoyed even before he emptied himself of his wealth. They too will be made "rich" (2 Cor 8:9) and, in some sense, share in his divine life.[32]

---

30. Matera, *II Corinthians*, 191. See similarly Wright, *Paul and the Faithfulness of God*, 2:688; Thomas D. Stegman, SJ, *Second Corinthians*, CCSS (Grand Rapids: Baker Academic, 2009), 197; Margaret Thrall, *The Second Epistle to the Corinthians*, 2 vols., ICC (London: T&T Clark, 1994, 2000), 532–34. *Contra* James D. G. Dunn, *Christology in the Making: A New Testament Inquiry* (Grand Rapids: Eerdmans, 1980), 121–23.

31. Wright, *Paul and the Faithfulness of God*, 2:689.

32. More will be said about this in chapter 5.

Unexpected as it may be, Christ's death as the covenant sacrifice is entirely coherent with Paul's overall gospel message. By reporting Jesus's depiction of his death as the new covenant sacrifice at the Last Supper (1 Cor 11:23–24), Paul underscores the gratuitous nature of the cross. Moreover, understanding how ancient gift-giving worked helps us recognize what Jesus's self-gift is ordered to accomplish. As Barclay has shown, the recipient of Christ's gift is more than a mere "taker." The beneficiary is empowered to become a giver by the power of Christ's gift. The cross, therefore, initiates a communion of self-giving love. Moreover, the cross reveals how this aim reflects the very divinity of God. Christ's death is a divine act of self-*gift*. Christ voluntarily empties himself in love and thereby reveals what it means to be "*in the form of God*" (Phil 2:6). This gift is the source of grace, whereby Christ gives himself to believers. The cross, then, reveals what is expected of those who receive the gift of grace (*charis*): *self-giving*. Grace itself is empowerment *for self-giving*: "For it is God who is at work in you, enabling you both to will and to work for his good pleasure" (Phil 2:13). With all of this in mind, we can now turn to the second dimension of Paul's theology of the cross that demands our attention: the cross as an act of redemption, one that God had long planned to accomplish.

A Sacrifice of Atonement

As we have seen, according to Paul the cross involves something unexpected: the one who was in the "form of God" was willing to take the "form of a servant" in order to save us. Yet Paul insists that the gospel was preached "beforehand to Abraham" (Gal 3:8) and that Jesus's death was "in accordance with the scriptures" (1 Cor 15:3). Thus, while the cross reflects divine graciousness, Paul does not believe it was unforeseen—at least, it was not unforeseen by God. Christ somehow reveals the meaning of the Torah and the Prophets. His death is thus associated with terminology ancient Jews would have known from these sources: redemption, covenant sacrifice, and atonement. Yet how do these ideas cohere with his teaching that Christ's death also represents a "gift"? The concepts associated with Christ's death actually seem to be in tension with such an idea. For instance, redemption imagery, as we shall see, seems to evoke the language of a *financial* transaction. What "price" is paid, and, perhaps more importantly, *why* is such payment made? If God loves humanity, why the cross?

Why not simply "forgive" humanity without all the horror of Calvary? In this section, we hope to show how Paul would answer these questions.

Sin, Sacrifice, and the Consequences of the Covenant

As we have seen, Paul tells us that at the Last Supper Jesus himself interpreted his death as the fulfillment of Jeremiah's new covenant prophecy: "This cup is the new covenant in my blood" (1 Cor 11:25). Notably, Jeremiah explicitly explains *why* a new covenant would be needed.

> *It will not be like the covenant that I made with their ancestors* when I took them by the hand to bring them out of the land of Egypt—*a covenant that they broke.* . . . But this is the covenant that I will make with the house of Israel after those days, says the LORD: I will put my law within them, and I will write it on their hearts; and I will be their God, and they shall be my people. No longer shall they teach one another, or say to each other, "Know the LORD," for they shall all know me, from the least of them to the greatest, says the LORD; for I will forgive their iniquity, and remember their sin no more. (Jer 31:32–34)

The promise of a new covenant is predicated in some way on the notion that the former one was in some sense *broken*.[33] This broken covenant is, in the text of Jeremiah's prophecy, closely associated with the notion of "sin." In other words, ruptured covenant relations are understood in terms of "sin." The new covenant is thus identified as the solution to this problem—it will bring about forgiveness of sins and thereby restore covenant relations. Why is this so important? Because until this happens the people cannot fully "know the LORD." Sin prevents God's people from truly "knowing" the Lord, that is, it keeps them from entering into the fullness of the relationship God wants to establish with them.

Specifically, the broken covenant is identified with Sinai. As we have seen, Paul's account of the Last Supper explicitly joins together "blood" and "covenant," evoking the scene in which the Sinai covenant is established (Exod 24:3–8). Yet by alluding to Jeremiah's prophecy, the Last

---

33. See Jack R. Lundbom, *Jeremiah*, 3 vols., AB 21A–C (New York: Doubleday, 1999, 2004), 2:466–67; Gerhard von Rad, *Old Testament Theology*, 2 vols. (New York: Harper & Row, 1965), 2:212–13.

Supper tradition also implicitly draws attention to what happened next in the story. After the people enter into a covenantal bond with God, they commit the sin of idolatry. In response to this, Moses smashes the tablets of the Ten Commandments—the very symbol of "the covenant" (cf. Exod 32:19)—signifying the *breaking* of the covenant.[34] In the aftermath, Moses intercedes for Israel, whose sins trigger the penalty for covenant infidelity, which is death. Although the pentateuchal narrative assumes the reader will grasp that this consequence is the foregone conclusion of Israel's covenant-breaking conduct, modern audiences often fail to appreciate the logic involved. Here it is helpful to explain briefly the rationale involved, which, as it turns out, undergirds the imagery involved in the covenant ceremony at Sinai.[35]

Ancient covenants were typically ratified by sacrifice. Recall Psalm 50, which we quoted above: God says the people *"made a covenant with me by sacrifice!"* (Ps 50:5).[36] Such cultic acts were typically bound up with oath-swearing. The parties entering into the covenant swore oaths to deities affirming their commitment to the covenant obligations.[37] Oaths were so important to covenant-making that the Hebrew terms for "covenant" (*bĕrît*) and "oath-swearing" (*šĕbûʿâ, ʾālâ*) are frequently used interchangeably.[38] In connection with these oaths, the sacrifices offered were understood as symbolizing the consequences of breaking the cove-

---

34. Nahum M. Sarna, *Exodus*, JPSTC (Philadelphia: The Jewish Publication Society, 1991), 207.

35. See Isabelle C. Torrance, "Ways to Give Oaths Extra Sanctity," in *Oaths and Swearing in Ancient Greece* (Berlin: Walter de Gruyter, 2014), 132–55.

36. For the close connection between covenant-making and sacrifice in antiquity see, e.g., Wiseman, "The Vassal-Treaties of Esarhaddon," 1–99; Dennis J. McCarthy, *Treaty and Covenant* (Rome: Biblical Institute Press, 1981), 91–92; Walter Burkert, *Greek Religion: Archaic and Classical* (Cambridge: Harvard University Press, 1985), 250–304.

37. See D. J. McCarthy, "Twenty-Five Years of Pentateuchal Study," in *The Biblical Heritage in Modern Catholic Scholarship*, ed. J. J. Collins and J. D. Crossan (Wilmington, DE: Michael Glazier, 1986), 49: "*Covenant* in its most fundamental meaning is probably an especially strong oath binding one to something because he has tied himself to it under God." In addition, G. M. Tucker ("Covenant Forms and Contract Forms," *VT* 15 [1965]: 487–503) writes: "The oath also may be understood as calling upon God to witness a statement or a promise, on the assumption that God will hold the swearer responsible for what he has said (cf. Ju. xi 10, Jer. xlii 5, Micah i 2)" (491).

38. See Gordon P. Hugenberger, *Marriage as Covenant: A Study of Biblical Law and Ethics Governing Marriage, Developed from the Perspective of Malachi*, VTSup 52 (Leiden: Brill, 1994), 183–84; Jacob Milgrom, *Leviticus*, 3 vols., AB 3–3B (New York: Doubleday, 1991, 2000, 2001), 1:300.

nant oath; the death of the animal indicated the mortal consequences of covenant infidelity.[39] The two parties would then often symbolize their newly established covenant-bond by sharing together in a meal in which the sacrificial victims were consumed.[40] Finally, since sacrifice was related to the establishment of a covenant, it was also linked to the concept of covenant renewal; one renewed the covenant by repeating the cultic act that first ratified it.[41]

The account of the ceremony that took place at Mount Sinai in Exodus 24 coheres well with these aspects of ancient covenant-making. First, Israel offers sacrifice to YHWH (Exod 24:4-6). Second, the people pledge to keep God's commandments: "All that the LORD has spoken we will do, and we will be obedient" (Exod 24:7). Following this, Moses throws the blood of the sacrificial victims on the people (Exod 24:8). As numerous specialists have observed, in this the people ritually accept the consequences of breaking the covenant: death. The slaughter of the sacrificial animals bears witness to what will happen to the people if they fail to abide by their covenant obligations.[42] Third, the covenant is sealed with a meal (Exod 24:9-11).[43]

When Israel commits idolatry in Exodus 32 and thereby breaks the covenant, the reader is expected to understand what is at stake; by such covenant infidelity, Israel has triggered the penalty of death. For our discussion, what is especially worth highlighting is that it is precisely within this context—the concern about the deadly consequences of Israel's covenant-infidelity—that the concept of "atonement" emerges:

On the next day Moses said to the people, "You have sinned a great sin. But now I will go up to the LORD; perhaps I can *make atonement for your sin.*" So Moses returned to the LORD and said, "Alas, this people

39. See especially Jer 34:18; Hahn, *Kinship by Covenant*, 55–56.

40. See F. H. Polak, "The Covenant at Mount Sinai in the Light of Texts from Mari," in *Sefer Moshe: The Moshe Weinfeld Jubilee Volume*, ed. Chaim Cohen, Avi M. Hurvitz, and Shalom M. Paul (Winona Lake, IN: Eisenbrauns, 2004), 119–34; Paul Kalluveettil, *Declaration and Covenant*, AnBib 88 (Rome: Pontifical Biblical Institute, 1982), 11.

41. See Jon D. Levenson, *Sinai and Zion: An Entry into the Jewish Bible* (San Francisco: Harper & Row, 1985), 80–81; D. J. McCarthy, "Covenant and Law in Chronicles-Nehemiah," *CBQ* 44 (1982): 3.

42. See Polak, "Covenant at Mount Sinai," 119–34; Kalluveettil, *Declaration and Covenant*, 11.

43. See, e.g., John Davies, *A Royal Priesthood: Literary and Intertextual Perspectives on an Image of Israel in Exodus 19:6*, JSOTSup 395 (London: T&T Clark, 2004), 129–37.

has sinned a great sin; they have made for themselves gods of gold. But now, if you will only *forgive their sin*—but if not, blot me out of the book that you have written." But the LORD said to Moses, "*Whoever has sinned against me I will blot out of my book.* But now go, lead the people to the place about which I have spoken to you; see, my angel shall go in front of you. Nevertheless, when the day comes for punishment, I will punish them for their sin." (Exod 32:30–34)

Within the narrative setting, "sin" means one thing in particular: covenant infraction. Moreover, the penalty for this is described as *death*. When Moses seeks to make "atonement" (MT: *kapar*; LXX: *exilaskomai*), the meaning is unambiguous. In this context, atonement entails addressing the consequence of the people's sin. Specifically, then, Moses asks the Lord to "forgive" (*nāśā'*) them. In essence, by doing this he petitions God "not to execute the penalty which their sin deserved."[44] If the Lord will not forgive, Moses asks, "Blot me out of the book that you have written"—a phrase that is widely recognized as a reference to death.[45] Interpreters disagree about the significance of this prayer.[46] Some, such as Bernard Renaud, view it as merely expressing solidarity with the people. In this reading Moses rejects the suggestion that God will start over with him (cf. Exod 32:10).[47] Others, such as the Jewish scholar Benno Jacob, view it as indicating Moses's willingness to bear the punishment due to the people as their representative.[48] Yet the Lord insists that he will "punish them for their sin" (Exod 32:34), an allusion to a deadly plague that befalls the people in the next verse. Whatever one makes of Moses's request, *atonement* stands in opposition to *death*. Here, as in other places, sin is *either* atoned for and forgiven *or* the sinner "bears" his own sin, an

44. Jay Sklar, *Sin, Impurity, Sacrifice, and Atonement: The Priestly Conceptions*, Hebrew Bible Monographs 2 (Sheffield: Sheffield Phoenix Press, 2005), 92.

45. Others disagree, suggesting, for example, that Moses's request expresses frustration. See, e.g., Victor P. Hamilton, *Exodus: An Exegetical Commentary* (Grand Rapids: Baker Academic, 2011), 555.

46. See Michael Widmer, *Moses, God, and the Dynamics of Intercessory Prayer: A Study of Exodus 32–34 and Numbers 13–14*, FAT 2/8 (Tübingen: Mohr Siebeck, 2004), 131–33.

47. See, e.g., Bernard Renaud, *L'alliance un mystère de miséricorde: une lecture de Exode 32–34* (Paris: Cerf, 1998), 159–60.

48. Benno Jacob, *Das Buch Exodus* (Stuttgart: Calver Verlag, 1997), 43. See also John Durham, *Exodus*, WBC 3 (Waco, TX: Word, 1987), 432; Jarvis Williams, *Maccabean Martyr Traditions in Paul's Theology of Atonement: Did Martyr Theology Shape Paul's Conception of Jesus' Death?* (Eugene, OR: Wipf & Stock, 2010), 69.

expression that has the connotation of suffering punishment (cf., e.g., Lev 20:17–21; 24:15–16; Num 9:13).[49]

"Atonement" in Jewish Scripture: Forgiveness and Ransom

Interpreting atonement texts requires exegetical caution. As those familiar with the study of the sacrificial code in Leviticus know, the precise rationale behind Israel's atonement rituals is hotly debated.[50] Still, it is safe to say that at least three ideas are attached to "atonement."

First, the Hebrew term "to make atonement," *kipper*, involves "purification"/"cleansing" (e.g., Lev 12:8; 14:52; 16:30), a point stressed by Jacob Milgrom, perhaps the world's foremost expert on Leviticus.[51] Second, "atonement" is also connected to forgiveness. Although Milgrom himself downplays this aspect of atonement, it is undeniably present in Leviticus 4, where the one who offers the atoning sacrifice is said to be "forgiven" (Lev 4:26, 31, 35; 5:5, 10, 13, 16).[52] Since "sin" is understood in the torah as an impurity (e.g., adultery in Num 5:19),[53] these first two meanings appear closely related. Finally, the language of atonement had a third connotation: "ransom."[54] This is evident, for example, in the case of the census money (Exod 30:16; cf. Num 31:50) and the homicide law (Num 35:31–33):

> When you take the census of the people of Israel, then each shall give a *ransom* for himself to the LORD. . . . And you shall take *the atonement money* from the people of Israel, and shall appoint it for the service of the

49. See Sklar, *Sin, Impurity, Sacrifice, and Atonement*, 1–43, 67–72.

50. See Sklar, *Sin, Impurity, Sacrifice, and Atonement*, 44–79.

51. See, e.g., Baruch Levine, *In the Presence of the Lord: A Study of Cult and Some Cultic Terms in Ancient Israel*, SJLA 5 (Leiden: Brill, 1974), 56–61; Milgrom, *Leviticus*, 1:1040, 1080–82.

52. See the exchange between Milgrom and Gane, of which Gane seems to have come out ahead: Jacob Milgrom, "The Preposition *min* in the *ḥaṭṭā't* Pericopes," *JBL* 126 (2007): 161–63; Roy E. Gane, "Privative Preposition *min* in Purification Offering Pericopes and the Changing Face of 'Dorian Gray,'" *JBL* 127, no. 2 (2008): 209–22. Significantly, Josephus says that the Day of Atonement sacrifices are offered for sins (cf. *Jewish Antiquities* 3.240). In addition, see Roy Gane, *Cult and Character: Purification Offerings, Day of Atonement and Theodicy* (Winona Lake, IL: Eisenbrauns, 2005), 69, 106–30.

53. See the comprehensive discussion of sin as impurity in Jonathan Klawans, *Impurity and Sin in Ancient Judaism* (Oxford: Oxford University Press, 2000).

54. See Milgrom, *Leviticus*, 1:6.

tent of meeting; that it may bring the people of Israel to remembrance before the LORD, so as *to make atonement* for your lives. (Exod 30:12, 16 RSV, slightly adapted)

Moreover you shall accept no *ransom for the life* of a murderer, who is guilty of death; but he shall be put to death. And you shall accept no *ransom* for him who has fled to his city of refuge, that he may return to dwell in the land before the death of the high priest . . . for blood pollutes the land, and no *atonement* can be made for the land, for the blood that is shed in it, except by the blood of him who shed it. (Num 35:31–33 RSV, slightly adapted)

In these biblical texts, making an "atonement" (MT: *kapar*; LXX: *exilaskomai*) for the lives of the people and paying a "ransom" (MT: *kōper*; LXX: *lytra*) for the life of the condemned are almost two ways of saying the same thing (Exod 30:12, 16; Num 35:31, cf. 33). In such cases, making an "atonement" refers *to delivering the guilty from death.*[55]

Considering such evidence, there is no reason to set up a false choice between either forgiveness or ransom. As Jay Sklar has convincingly argued, atoning sacrifices appear to do both of these things *simultaneously.*[56] Atonement would therefore seem to have connotations of purity, forgiveness, *and* ransom. Building on this argument, we would like to apply this "both-and" approach to Pauline theology. To do that, however, we need to understand how "sin" itself was conceived in first-century Judaism.

The Debt of Sin, Atonement, and Redemption

As others have carefully explained, in Jewish sources sin is not only portrayed as impurity but also understood in economic terms; sin is a "debt."[57]

---

55. Milgrom, *Leviticus*, 1:1082.

56. Jay Sklar, *Leviticus*, TOTC 3 (Downers Grove, IL: IVP Academic, 2014), 53. See also Sklar, *Sin, Impurity, Sacrifice, and Atonement*; Sklar, "Sin and Impurity: Atoned or Purified? Yes!," in *Perspectives on Purity and Purification in the Bible*, ed. Baruch J. Schwartz et al. (London: T&T Clark, 2008), 18–31.

57. See, e.g., Martin McNamara, *Targum and Testament* (Grand Rapids: Eerdmans, 1972), 120; Matthew Black, *An Aramaic Approach to the Gospels and Acts* (Oxford: Clarendon Press, 1967), 140; Joachim Jeremias, *New Testament Theology*, trans. John Bowden (New York: Charles Scribner's Sons, 1971), 6n15, 196.

The best-known expression of this tradition is found in the Lord's Prayer: "And forgive us *our debts* [*ta opheilēmata hēmōn*], as we also have forgiven *our debtors* [*tois opheiletais hēmōn*]" (Matt 6:12). As Gary Anderson and Nathan Eubank have demonstrated, this "economic" perspective permeates the texts of ancient Judaism and early Christianity.[58] It was also uniquely Semitic. Anderson writes, "In contemporary Greek the words 'remit' (*aphiemi*) and 'debt' (*opheilema*) did not have the secondary meaning of 'forgive' and 'sin.' Matthew's version of the Our Father makes sense only if we assume that the wording reflects an underlying Semitic idiom."[59] Paul, therefore, reveals himself to be a thoroughly Jewish thinker when he says, "The *wages* [*opsōnia*] of sin is death" (Rom 6:23). Likewise, he speaks of Christ's work of redemption in terms of economic imagery: "You were bought with a price; do not become slaves of human masters" (1 Cor 7:23). The economic and slavery language seem interrelated.

Atonement/ransom/redemption should be seen as functioning within a broader economic conceptual matrix in which debt and slavery are related. The English words "redemption" and "ransom" are two ways of translating the same Greek term, *lytron*. Some have asserted that *lytron* can be used with no associations of payment, carrying the generic sense of "deliverance."[60] Nevertheless, as Nathan Eubank points out, there is no support for such claims in the standard Greek lexicons: "*Lytron* ["ransom"] is never used in the LXX, Josephus, Philo . . . to mean simply 'rescue' or 'deliver.' . . . It always refers to some price or exchange."[61] The word *lytron* is thus used in cases involving paying the price to release someone from debt, from slavery, or from imprisonment. In all likelihood, "release" could be used to describe more than one of these things simultaneously since slavery and imprisonment were both consequences of defaulting on a debt. To pay off a debt was to be released from its consequences.[62]

---

58. See Gary Anderson, *Sin: A History* (New Haven: Yale University Press, 2009); Anderson, "From Israel's Burden to Israel's Debt: Towards a Theology of Sin in Biblical and Early Second Temple Sources," in *Reworking the Bible: Apocryphal and Related Texts at Qumran*, ed. E. G. Chazon, D. Dimant, and R. Clements (Leiden: Brill, 2005), 1–30; Nathan Eubank, *Wages of Cross-Bearing and Debt of Sin: The Economy of Heaven in Matthew's Gospel*, BZNW 196 (Berlin: De Gruyter, 2013).

59. Anderson, *Sin: A History*, 32.

60. Many have been influenced by the earlier work of David Hill, *Greek Words and Hebrew Meaning: Studies in the Semantics of Soteriological Terms* (Cambridge: Cambridge University Press, 1967), 81.

61. Eubank, *Wages of Cross-Bearing*, 150.

62. See Eubank, *Wages of Cross-Bearing*, 59.

The interrelation of debt, sin, and slavery is also highlighted in the biblical description of the Jubilee Year (see Lev 25).[63] According to the Pentateuch, the Jubilee is to be celebrated every fifty years. It specifically addresses the economic plight of the destitute. Significantly, it entails the return of forfeited ancestral lands (Lev 25:10, 13) and the freeing of slaves (Lev 25:39–43). In this, the Jubilee legislation takes up the consequences of unresolvable debt. Unable to pay off a creditor, a debtor would be forced either to sell off land and/or be forced into debt-servitude.[64] In fact, regulations for the Jubilee Year parallel law codes from other ancient civilizations, which also dealt with the cancellation of debts.[65] Indeed, the Dead Sea Scrolls show us that by Paul's day debt-remission was understood to be a feature of the Jubilee (cf. 1Q22 3:1–12; 11Q13 2:4–6).[66] Notably, the Jubilee Year is to be proclaimed on the Day of *Atonement* (cf. Lev 25:8–10), a day also associated with forgiveness of sin (cf., e.g., Lev 16:30).

All of these themes are brought together in *11QMelchizedek* (11Q13), a text discovered among the Dead Sea Scrolls. In this fragmentary document, the Day of Atonement is explicitly connected to the eschatological Jubilee and is said to include "release" from the "debt" of "iniquity." John Bergsma concludes:

> A shift occurs in Second Temple literature concerning the type of debt the jubilee addresses. While the original legislation was clearly concerned with *monetary debt*, the later texts apply the jubilee to *moral-spiritual debt*, i.e. sin. This is implicit in many documents (cf. Dan 9:24; *T. Levi* 17:10–11; 18:9) but is made explicit in 11QMelchizedek.[67]

In short, by the first century AD, there was in Jewish circles a conceptual connection between the *release* from debt, *forgiveness* of sins, and "atonement."

It is important to see how all of these strands come together in the soteriology of the scriptures of Israel, the primary quarry for Paul's thought. Because of Israel's debt of sin, God's people stood in need of redemption. According to the biblical story that the apostle knew, disobedience cost

63. See the excellent study by Bergsma, *The Jubilee from Leviticus to Qumran*.

64. See, e.g., P. A. Barker, "Jubilee," in *Dictionary of the Pentateuch* (Downers Grove, IL: IVP Academic, 2003), 704.

65. See Milgrom, *Leviticus*, 3:2241.

66. See Bergsma, *The Jubilee from Leviticus to Qumran*, 256–57.

67. See Bergsma, *The Jubilee from Leviticus to Qumran*, 304 (emphasis added).

Israel its land and led the people to be taken off into exile as slaves. Not surprisingly, then, their deliverance from captivity is described as "redemption." This is true for both the original exodus (e.g., Exod 6:6) and for the future "ingathering of God's people, depicted as a new exodus (cf. Isa 43:1; 52:3)."[68] The captivity of exile occurred because of sin, yet the prophets announced that God would deliver them. For instance, in the lead-up to his "new covenant" prophecy, Jeremiah states, "The LORD has *ransomed* [*elytrōsato*] Jacob, and has *redeemed* [*exeilato*] him from hands too strong for him" (Jer 31:11; LXX Jer 38:11). Not surprisingly, this "redemption" is associated with remission of sins (Jer 31:34). In short, from an ancient Jewish perspective, *Israel was in the "debt" of sin and awaited God to "ransom" them from it and its consequences.*

A "Sacrifice of Atonement" by His Blood

The Jewish association of sin with debt and the Torah's presentation of cultic atonement as ransom/redemption provide us with crucial insight into Paul's overall theology of the cross. The apostle views "redemption" from sin in terms of sacrificial "atonement" in Romans 3:

> Since all have sinned and fall short of the glory of God; they are now justified by his grace as a *gift*, through the *redemption* that is in Christ Jesus, whom God put forward as *a sacrifice of atonement* by his blood, effective through faith. (Rom 3:23–25)

Interpreters have long debated how to render the Greek term that the NRSV renders as "a sacrifice of atonement [*hilastērion*]" (Rom 3:25).[69] The debate is reflected in the different English Bible translations. Some think the language is best understood in terms of "expiation" (RSV, NABRE), which emphasizes the notion of "cleansing" or "purification" of sin.[70] Others find here the notion of "propitiation" (ESV), a sacrifice that averts divine judgment.[71]

---

68. See Pitre, *Jesus, the Tribulation, and the End of the Exile*, 139.

69. See Jewett, *Romans*, 283–90; Fitzmyer, *Romans*, 349–50.

70. E.g., C. H. Dodd, "*ΙΛΑΣΚΕΣΘΑΙ*, Its Cognates, Derivatives, and Synonyms in the Septuagint," *JTS* 32 (1930–31): 352–60.

71. E.g., Leon L. Morris, *The Apostolic Preaching of the Cross* (London: Tyndale, 1955), 125–85; Morris, "The Meaning of *hilastērion* in Romans 3:25," *NTS* 2 (1955–56): 33–43.

Either way, Paul's language evokes Israel's sacrificial cult (cf. NRSV: "sacrifice of atonement"). Whatever associations the language conjures up, one cannot ignore the fact that the Septuagint, the Greek translation of Israel's scriptures—which dominates Paul's thinking—primarily uses *hilastērion* in reference to the ark of the covenant, the "mercy seat," the object at the center of the Day of Atonement liturgy:[72]

> You shall put *the mercy seat* [LXX *to hilastērion*] on the top of the ark; and in the ark you shall put the covenant that I shall give you. There I will meet with you, and from above *the mercy seat* [LXX *tou hilastēriou*], from between the two cherubim that are on the ark of the covenant. (Exod 25:21–22)

The Septuagint consistently translates these references to the "mercy seat" as a "propitiatory" or "place of atonement" (*hilastērion*) (Exod 25:21, 22 LXX).[73] Some have seen martyrdom traditions in the background of Paul's teaching, appealing to 4 Maccabees 17:21–22, where the death of the righteous is said to be a *hilastērion*. Yet, as Douglas Campbell points out, the imagery in 4 Maccabees is in fact predicated on an Israelite understanding of the Day of Atonement, so an allusion to Israel's cultic rites seems inescapable.[74] Some even make the case that, in calling Christ himself a *hilastērion*, the apostle portrays Jesus as the ark of the covenant for a new cult.[75] While such a reading is possible, what seems indisputable is that Paul believed *that Christ's death had atoning significance and that it addressed the problem of sin in a way analogous to the sacrifices of the Day of Atonement.*

Christ and the "Sin Offering"

In support of this point, it is important to look at another passage in which Paul applies the terminology of Israel's atonement sacrifices to Jesus's

---

72. See Daniel Stökl Ben Ezra, *The Impact of Yom Kippur on Early Christianity: The Day of Atonement from Second Temple Judaism to the Fifth Century*, WUNT 163 (Tübingen: Mohr Siebeck, 2003), 198–200.

73. See Albert Pietersma and Benjamin G. Wright, *A New English Translation of the Septuagint* (Oxford: Oxford University Press, 2007), 69.

74. Campbell, *The Deliverance of God*, 650.

75. See Stephen Finlan, *The Background and Content of Paul's Cultic Metaphors*, AcBib 19 (Atlanta: Society of Biblical Literature, 2004), 229.

death: "For God has done what the law, weakened by the flesh, could not do: by *sending his own Son* in the likeness of sinful flesh, and *to deal with sin*, he condemned sin in the flesh" (Rom 8:3). Here Paul affirms that Jesus was sent "to deal with sin [*peri hamartias*]." But what exactly does this mean? While the Greek phrase *peri hamartias* can be translated as "to deal with sin" (NRSV) or, more woodenly, as "for sin" (RSV), both of these translations fail to appreciate the way the language would have carried resonances from Israel's scriptures. The exact phrase *peri hamartias* is used repeatedly in the Septuagint to mean "as a sin offering" (cf., e.g., Lev 5:8; 14:31; Num 6:10 LXX).[76] Consider but one such text:

> The LORD spoke to Moses, saying, Speak to the people of Israel, saying: When anyone sins unintentionally in any of the LORD's commandments about things not to be done, and does any one of them: If it is the anointed priest who sins, thus bringing guilt on the people, he shall offer for the sin that he has committed a bull of the herd without blemish as *a sin offering* to the LORD. (Lev 4:1–3)

Although English translations like this one typically add the word "offering" for sake of clarification, in the original Hebrew, the sacrifice is simply a "sin [*chatta'th*]" (Lev 4:3 MT). Likewise, the Septuagint says the sacrifice is offered "for his sin [*peri tēs hamartias*]" (Lev 4:3 LXX). When Paul speaks of Jesus being sent *peri hamartias*, it is extremely difficult to imagine that he would have simply forgotten that the language was typically used with a sacrificial connotation in the scriptures. Instead, it seems reasonable to conclude that he means that "God sent his own son . . . as a sin offering."[77] Granted, *peri hamartias* can have a different meaning; yet given its common usage and the fact that Paul has already described Jesus's death as a *hilastērion* in Romans 3:25, it seems strange to insist a reference to the biblical sin offering is not intended in Romans 8:3.[78] This reading of Romans

---

76. See, e.g., Blackwell, *Christosis*, 128n58; Leander E. Keck, *Romans*, ANTC (Nashville: Abingdon, 2005), 199; Colin G. Kruse, *Paul's Letter to the Romans*, PNTC (Grand Rapids: Eerdmans, 2012), 327. Against some interpreters who have rejected this reading (e.g., Cranfield, *Romans*, 1:382), see Jarvis Williams, *One New Man: The Cross and Racial Reconciliation in Pauline Theology* (Nashville: B&H Academic, 2010), 82n86; Schreiner, *Romans*, 403.

77. See, e.g., Wright, *Paul and the Faithfulness of God*, 2:897; Dunn, *Romans*, 1:422; Käsemann, *Romans*, 216.

78. Cf. Fredriksen, *Paul*, 245n53. The preponderance of cultic imagery in Romans also

8 also helps us better understand 2 Corinthians 5:21, which explains that God made Christ *"to be sin [hamartian]* who knew no sin." Paul's point in this verse is not that Christ is *literally* somehow a "sin," but that he serves as the "sin offering" *(hamartia)*.[79] In other words: Christ gave his life as a sacrificial offering for the sins of others (cf. 1 Cor 11:23–26). Finally, similar imagery may also be signaled when Paul says that Jesus was "put to death for our trespasses" (Rom 4:25 RSV), an expression many see as an allusion to the Suffering Servant passage of Isaiah 53:10–12.[80] There Isaiah identifies the Servant as an atoning sacrifice.[81]

In sum: in the scriptures of Israel, redemption/ransom imagery was conceptually related to "atonement." It is therefore no surprise that in Romans Paul employs *both* concepts to describe Christ's death. His sacrifice serves to "redeem" others from the bondage due to the debt of sin.

Christ, "Redemption," and the Covenant "Curse"

Paul also speaks of redemption in Galatians: "Christ redeemed us from the curse of the law by becoming a curse for us" (Gal 3:13). What does Paul mean when he speaks of Christ "redeeming" us from "the curse of the law"? Scholars such as Barclay identify the curse terminology here in terms of the "covenant curse."[82] To understand the rationale of Paul's teaching, we need to look at it within its larger context.

At the outset of Galatians, we discover the purpose of the epistle: Paul is concerned that believers are being led astray by "another gospel" (Gal 1:7), which likely includes the notion that gentiles must be circumcised. Against those who would use the torah to insist that gentiles must undergo the rite, Paul deploys a carefully constructed argument rooted in the Genesis narrative:

> Just as Abraham "believed God, and it was reckoned to him as righteousness" [Gen 15:6], so, you see, those who believe are the descendants of

---

reinforces a cultic reading here. See Nijay Gupta, *Worship That Makes Sense to Paul: A New Approach to the Theology and Ethics of Paul's Cultic Metaphors*, BNZW 175 (Berlin: De Gruyter, 2010), 107–35.

79. Cf. Thrall, *Second Epistle to the Corinthians*, 1:440–41.

80. See Jewett, *Romans*, 342–43.

81. See Finlan, *Background and Content of Paul's Cultic Metaphors*, 226.

82. Barclay, *Paul and the Gift*, 405.

Abraham. And the scripture, foreseeing that God would justify the Gentiles by faith, declared the gospel beforehand to Abraham, saying, "All the Gentiles shall be blessed in you" [Gen 12:3; 22:18]. For this reason, those who believe are blessed with Abraham who believed. (Gal 3:6–9)

In these verses, Paul first cites a passage from Genesis 15, in which God reckons Abraham righteous. This episode occurs *prior* to the institution of circumcision in Genesis 17. This effectively shows that Abraham was "reckoned" righteous *apart from circumcision* (cf. Rom 4:10–11). The apostle then combines two passages, Genesis 12:3 and 22:18, in which God promises that all nations will be blessed through Abraham.[83]

With this in place, Paul turns to make a point we focused on in our discussion above: failure to keep the covenant's demands results in triggering its curses.

For all who rely on the works of the law are under a curse; for it is written, "*Cursed is everyone who does not observe and obey all the things written in the book of the law*" [Deut 27:26]. Now it is evident that no one is justified before God by the law; for "The one who is righteous will live by faith" [Hab 2:4]. But the law does not rest on faith; on the contrary, "Whoever does the works of the law will live by them" [Lev 18:5]. (Gal 3:10–12)

In speaking of those who rely on "works of the law," Paul seems to refer in particular to circumcision.[84] But why are those who rely on such works under a "curse"? He goes on to strategically target Deuteronomy 27, which lays out the blessings and curses of the covenant.[85] The citation from Leviticus 18:5 that follows is meant to remind the reader that salvation according to the torah is only possible through fulfilling its requirements. The close reader will remember that Moses not only warned that failure to abide by the covenant law would result in triggering the covenant curse; he also predicted at the end of the book that Israel would end up in exile due to their covenant infidelity (cf. Deut 30:1). This, of course, is what happened.

---

83. Hahn, *Kinship by Covenant*, 246.

84. See, e.g., Barclay, *Paul and the Gift*, 373–74.

85. See Hays, *Echoes*, 43. For arguments in favor of the view that Paul has the entire section of Deut 27–30 in mind, see Morales, *The Spirit and the Restoration of Israel*, 93.

With the background of the covenant curse in place, Paul cites another passage from the Torah that employs curse imagery: Deuteronomy's curse upon anyone who "hangs on a tree" (Deut 21:23). We know from other Jewish writings that this expression came to be associated with crucifixion.[86] For Paul, this passage is of crucial significance for understanding Jesus's death.

> Christ *redeemed* us from the curse of the law by becoming a curse for us—for it is written, "Cursed is everyone who hangs on a tree" [Deut 21:23]—in order that in Christ Jesus the blessing of Abraham might come to the Gentiles, so that we might receive the promise of the Spirit through faith. (Gal 3:13–14)

According to Paul, Christ bore the covenant curse *redemptively* by being crucified. Christ is not, therefore, "cursed" in the sense of being "damned." Rather, by being "hung on a tree," Christ dies a death that renders him "accursed" according to the Mosaic torah. In this, Christ bore the curse that Israel had triggered by covenant infidelity. N. T. Wright sums up the argument this way: Christ is "taking on himself the curse which hung over Israel and which on the one hand prevented her from enjoying full membership in Abraham's family and thereby on the other hand prevented the blessing of Abraham from flowing out to the Gentiles."[87] In this way, Christ's death can be described as having taken place "according to the scriptures," because he takes upon himself the curse sin had triggered. And he does this freely, as an expression of love.

What we are driving at here is this: *atonement, ransom/redemption, forgiveness of sins, and covenant curse all form a coherent conceptual matrix.* In support of this point, look once again at how all of these themes converge in one of the Dead Sea Scrolls:

> And liberty will be proclaimed for them, to free them from [the debt of] all their iniquities. And this [wil]l [happen] in the first week of the jubilee which follows the ni[ne] jubilees. And the *d[ay of aton]ement* is the e[nd of] the tenth [ju]bilee in which *atonement* shall be made for all the sons of [light and] for the men [of] the lot of Mel[chi]zedek. (*11QMelchizedek* [11Q13] II, 6–8)[88]

---

86. Cf. 4Q169 3–4 i 8; Philo, *On the Special Laws* 3.151–52; cf. also *Tg. Ps.-J.* on Num 25:15.
87. Wright, *Climax of the Covenant*, 151.
88. *DSSSE*, 2:1207.

This passage goes on to envision the coming of an anointed one—that is, a "messiah" (11Q13 2:18). In addition, it further describes how the righteous of the messianic era will "establish the covenant" (11Q13 2:24), which specialists recognize as an allusion to the "new covenant."[89] In sum, Paul's understanding of Christ's work, though by no means identical to that of the Dead Sea community, draws together similar traditions: the deliverer will come, he will atone for sin by addressing the debt it entails, and all of this is associated with the hope for a new covenant.

The Righteousness of God Revealed

With all of this in mind, it must nevertheless be emphasized here that there is no sense in which Paul suggests God somehow got "painted into a corner." The cross is not "imposed" upon God. For Paul, the Lord is not coerced into handing over the Son. To the contrary: Paul's presentation indicates that God knew what would happen all along. As N. T. Wright puts it, *"The point of the Messiah's death . . . is that it demonstrates, in action, the faithfulness of God to his covenant plan."*[90] Here we take a few moments to explain how this unfolds in Paul's thought.

The Cross and the "Blessing" of God

Consider once again the apostle's words to the Galatians, this time focusing on the ultimate aim of the cross: "Christ redeemed us from the curse of the law . . . *in order that in Christ Jesus the blessing of Abraham might come to the Gentiles*, so that we might receive the promise of the Spirit through faith" (Gal 3:13–14). Resonating softly but perceptively in the background of Paul's teaching here are echoes of the famous account of Abraham being told to sacrifice his beloved son Isaac (Gen 22:1–19).[91] In the story, Isaac is "bound" (Gen 22:9), leading it to be known by later Jewish interpreters

89. Harold Attridge, "How the Scrolls Impacted Scholarship on Hebrews," in *The Bible and the Dead Sea Scrolls*, ed. James H. Charlesworth, 3 vols. (Waco, TX: Baylor University Press, 2006), 3:219, 223.

90. N. T. Wright, "God Put Jesus Forth: Reflections on Romans 3:24–26," in Gurtner, Macaskill, and Pennington, *In the Fullness of Time*, 153 (emphasis original).

91. See Jon D. Levenson, *The Death and Resurrection of the Beloved Son* (New Haven: Yale University Press, 1993), 211–13; Matera, *Galatians*, 120.

as the *Aqedah* or "Binding" of Isaac. According to Jewish tradition, by allowing himself to be bound by his elderly father, Isaac makes himself a willing victim, an interpretation attested in various sources from the late Second Temple period.[92] Paul seems to highlight this story's importance for understanding the cross elsewhere in his epistles (e.g., Rom 8:32),[93] including in the immediate context of Galatians 3 (e.g., Gal 3:8). It should not be seen as merely coincidental that, as many commentators note, the language of Galatians 3:14a so closely mirrors God's words to Abraham in Genesis 22:18a: "All the nations will be blessed in [you] [*eneulogēthēsontai ... panta ta ethnē*]" (LXX).[94] In Genesis 22, God had sworn an oath to bless all nations through Abraham's descendants. Israel's covenant infidelity prevented that from taking place. Christ therefore takes upon *himself* the curse, simultaneously fulfilling *both* God's oath to Abraham and bearing the consequences of the broken Mosaic covenant. In Paul's eyes, it seems, this was all part of the divine plan. Genesis 22 was, in the light of Christ, a prefiguration of what would come.

For, Paul, therefore, the cross is a revelation of God's (new covenant) justice and mercy. Humanity had not gotten God "over a barrel," so to speak. Nothing *required* God to enter into a covenant with Abraham or Israel; the covenant relationship is the result of God's initiative. As we saw at the beginning of this chapter, it is pure gift. Yet, having entered into this arrangement, God remains faithful to the covenant—even when humanity is not. God knew full well how things would play out and so anticipated in Genesis 22 the act of deliverance that would be necessary. The plan of salvation thus underscores God's love (*agapē*) and righteousness (*dikaiosynē*).

The Cross as a "Revelation" of God's "Righteousness"

Paul's teaching of the cross as the revelation of God's righteousness has been a particular emphasis in the recent work of Douglas Campbell, who

---

92. See Jdt 8:26; Josephus, *Antiquities* 1:232; 4 Macc 7:12–14; 13:12; 16:20; *L. A. B.*, 32:2–3.

93. Paul's statement in Rom 8:32 (RSV) that God "did not spare" his Son (*epheisato*) parallels the terminology of Gen 22:12, 16 (*epheisō*). Dunn, *Romans*, 501, correctly observes, "A Jew as familiar with the OT language as was Paul could hardly have been unaware that he was echoing Gen 22:16." See also Hays, *Echoes*, 61; Jewett, *Romans*, 537–38; Francis Watson, *Paul and the Hermeneutics of Faith*, 2nd ed. (London: Bloomsbury T&T Clark, 2016), 215n22.

94. See Hahn, *Kinship by Covenant*, 255–56.

has written extensively on this theme in Romans.[95] In the very first chapter of the epistle, the apostle explains that in the gospel, "the righteousness of God [*dikaiosynē theou*] is revealed" (Rom 1:17). As has long been noted by scholars, Paul picks up this language again later in Romans 3, where he closely connects it with the cross:

> But now, apart from the law, *the righteousness of God has been disclosed*, and is attested by the law and the prophets, the righteousness of God through faith in Jesus Christ for all who believe. For there is no distinction, since all have sinned and fall short of the glory of God; they are now justified by his grace as a gift, through the *redemption* that is in Christ Jesus, whom God put forward as a sacrifice of *atonement* by his blood, effective through faith. *He did this to show his righteousness*, because in his divine forbearance he had passed over the sins previously committed; *it was to prove at the present time that he himself is righteous* and that he justifies the one who has faith in Jesus. (Rom 3:21–26)

This is a complex passage and aspects of this translation have been contested.[96] What is indisputable is that Paul holds that the cross is inseparably united to the demonstration of God's "righteousness [*dikaiosynē*]" (Rom 3:21), one of the crucial motifs of Romans.

The precise meaning of the "righteousness of God"—in Greek, *dikaiosynē theou*—has been intensely debated. Some insist that it refers to an attribute of God—for example, God is "just" (i.e., God's own righteousness).[97] Others maintain that the terminology should be construed as describing something God *gives*—for example, the way God "sets things right" (i.e., righteousness from God).[98] Yet the two ideas need not be seen as mutually exclusive. As James Dunn shows, such debates—often shaped by post-Reformation theological disputes—have neglected the way the terminology would have been understood within ancient Judaism. He contends that, since the "righteousness of God" was inextricably relational for ancient readers, the terminology would have evoked the notion of the covenant.[99] As

---

95. See Campbell, *The Deliverance of God*, 639–76.

96. For a fuller discussion, see Jewett, *Romans*, 269–93; Fitzmyer, *Romans*, 341–58.

97. See, e.g., S. K. Williams, "The 'Righteousness of God' in Romans," *JBL* 99 (1980): 241–90.

98. See, e.g., Cranfield, *Romans*, 1:98.

99. See James D. G. Dunn, "The Justice of God: A Renewed Perspective on Justification

Richard Hays explains, the covenant was the principal manifestation and norm of God's righteousness.[100]

This covenantal reading of *dikaiosynē theou*, however, has been disputed.[101] For instance, Douglas Campbell rightly points out that while the "righteousness/justice of God" *could* be related to covenant, there are contexts where this is not the case.[102] He argues that the language was more frequently directly linked to divine kingship, a notion that is unmistakably emphasized in Romans, specifically in Jesus's role as the messianic son of David (e.g., Rom 1:3; 15:12).[103] Campbell's insight has received further support from the recent work of Joshua Jipp, who looks at various ancient texts in which the righteousness of divine kingship is often manifested by the rescue of the righteous, particularly, a righteous king—a dynamic clearly present in Paul.[104] Jipp explains how Paul translates such traditions: "God's justice is on display, then, in God's extension of the Messiah's righteousness, namely, the Messiah's justification and deliverance from death, to those who belong to the Messiah."[105] The revelation of the "righteousness of God" in Romans 1:17 thus, according to Campbell, means "'the deliverance of God,' or something closely equivalent."[106]

Campbell is undoubtedly correct but seems to push a bit too far when he writes:

---

by Faith," *JTS* 43 (1992): 16–17; see also Ernst Käsemann, "The Righteousness of God in Paul," in *New Testament Questions of Today*, 172.

100. See, e.g., Richard B. Hays, "Justification," *ABD* 3:1129–31, who explains, "'Righteousness' characterizes faithful adherence to the covenant relationship" (1129). See also Wright, *Paul and the Faithfulness of God*, 2:795–804. In addition, see the nuanced response to critics of this view in Michael F. Bird, *The Saving Righteousness of God: Studies on Paul, Justification, and the New Perspective*, Paternoster Biblical Monographs (Eugene, OR: Wipf & Stock, 2007), 35–39.

101. See, e.g., Campbell, *The Deliverance of God*, 700–701; D. A. Carson, "Atonement in Romans 3:21–26: 'God Presented Him as a Propitiation,'" in *The Glory of the Atonement*, ed. C. E. Hill and F. A. James III (Downers Grove, IL: InterVarsity Press, 2004), 124–25; Mark Seifrid, "Righteousness Language in the Hebrew Scriptures and Early Judaism," in *Justification and Variegated Nomism*, vol. 1, *The Complexities of Second Temple Judaism*, ed. D. A. Carson, Peter T. O'Brien, and Mark A. Seifried (Tübingen: Mohr Siebeck, 2001), 415–42.

102. Campbell, *The Deliverance of God*, 700.

103. Campbell, *The Deliverance of God*, 692–98.

104. Joshua Jipp, *Christ Is King: Paul's Royal Ideology* (Minneapolis: Fortress, 2015), 211–71.

105. Jipp, *Christ Is King*, 271.

106. Campbell, *The Deliverance of God*, 699.

> [Paul] is not speaking of something overtly and fundamentally cov-
> enantal and hence rooted in the past and in a certain conception of
> history. He is discussing a liberative and eschatological act of God in
> Christ—a fundamentally present and future event rooted in the resur-
> recting God.... In sum, it seems that—on internal grounds—*dikaiosynē
> theou* in Paul denotes a singular, saving, liberating, life-giving, eschato-
> logical act of God in Christ.[107]

This insists upon a false antithesis; one need not pit eschatological royal
liberation against a covenantal connection.[108] True, one should be careful
not to overstate the connection between "righteousness" and "covenant"
in Judaism. Moreover, we must not overlook the way the *dikaiosynē* of God
is bound up with Paul's messianism. Yet when Campbell discusses "the
eschatological act of God in Christ," he simply highlights the resurrection
and fails to mention the *cross*. This is puzzling, since Campbell is specifically treating Romans 3:21–26, where it is precisely Christ's *death* (i.e., his
"blood") that is associated with the manifestation of God's righteousness.
Moreover, as we have seen, in 1 Corinthians 11 Paul identifies Jesus's death
as the means by which the new covenant is established (1 Cor 11:25). According to Paul, the redemptive act through which God's righteousness is
revealed is, contrary to Campbell's insistence, actually "overtly and fundamentally covenantal."

Moreover, the concept of the "righteousness" of God does not seem
at all unrelated to the new covenant for Paul. In the next chapter we
will look at 2 Corinthians 3, where Paul explicitly describes the new
covenant in terms of the dispensation of "righteousness [*dikaiosynē*]"
(2 Cor 3:9 RSV). Furthermore, it seems probable that this aspect of Paul's
thought is informed by a passage that undergirds much of the teaching in
2 Corinthians 3: Jeremiah's new covenant prophecy itself. In that oracle,
the prophet relays God's promise to "forgive their iniquity" (Jer 31:34).
Significantly, the Greek translation of Jeremiah translates "iniquity" as
"injustices" (*adikiais*). Insofar as the Greek prefix "a-" is essentially a
negation (as in "in-justice" or "un-righteous"), Jeremiah's reference to
iniquity as "injustices" (*adikiais*) functions essentially as an antonym for
the word "just" or "right" (*dikaios*). In sum, since Jeremiah announced
that in the new covenant God would address the problem of "injustice"

---

107. Campbell, *The Deliverance of God*, 702.
108. Cf. Campbell, *The Deliverance of God*, 700.

or "unrighteousness," it is no surprise that Paul speaks of the new covenant ushering in "righteousness."

In Summary: The Cross as Apocalyptic Revelation and New Covenant Sacrifice

For Paul, the cross is both *apocalyptic revelation* and *new covenant redemption*. These two ideas are inseparable for the apostle. For him, the death of Christ is not due to some sort of divine obligation or necessity. Paul nowhere suggests that the cross was, simply speaking, required of God. The Father is not compelled to send the Son, and the Son does not suffer against his will; instead the Son *gives* his life to reveal his love in a way that we might say is "fitting" but not absolutely "necessary." Instead, the voluntary sacrifice of Christ is what inaugurates the new covenant, which God had announced would be the response to the broken covenant (Jer 31:31–34). The previous covenant relationship was also expressive of this gift. Paul understood that gifts come with expectations. God was faithful to the gift, but Israel was not—this constituted the basis for the need for a new covenant. Hence, Jesus's act of salvation is a gift but one that did not simply come out of nowhere—it was the fulfillment of God's promise of a "new covenant" (1 Cor 11:23–24; cf. Jer 31:31–33). What is more, it seems that Paul thought God entered into the covenant knowing from the start that it would involve his future giving his Son—in establishing his covenant with Abraham he already foreshadows this through the offering of Isaac.

Indeed, Paul's conceptual framework for understanding the death of Christ is explicitly and repeatedly anchored in the Jewish scriptures in general and the language of cultic sacrifice in particular. When Paul speaks of the cross as a "sacrifice of atonement" (Rom 3:25) or as taking place "as a sin offering" (Rom 8:3), he is consciously and deliberately alluding to the cultic sacrifices tied to the Day of Atonement in Israel's scriptures. According to Paul, when Jesus makes the sacrificial gift of himself on the cross, the act is expressive of Christ's core identity: it is what it means that he is "in the form of God" (Phil 2:6). *For Paul, then, Jesus is not divine despite giving himself; his self-giving reveals what it means to God—it reveals God's righteousness and God's love.*

According to Paul, all of this highlights the plight of humanity, which is under the power of sin, from which liberation is needed. The cross shows that God recognizes the gravity of sin—it is nothing less than death. True life is union with God in Christ; anything less than this is death. Sin thus equals death. Nevertheless, God enters into the darkness of death himself to save humanity from it. In addition, Christ's act of liberation—his gift of self—is ultimately ordered toward empowering humanity to become "sons" like him. In this, they will be saved; in other words, they are freed from sin and thus are enabled to know God. Ultimately, this constitutes the meaning of new covenant righteousness in Paul, the topic we turn to next.

CHAPTER 5

New Covenant Justification through Divine Sonship

"Mere imputation" is not Paul's view of Christian righteousness. He believed that those who died with Christ were *really changed* and no longer lived in sin. One of Luther's slogans was *simul justus et peccator*, "at the same time justified and sinner." That was not Paul's view: he believed in transformation.

—E. P. Sanders[1]

It is this final point, the *simul justus et peccator*, which has proved the most difficult to overcome in ecumenical dialogue. Differing judgments of this summary statement reveal differing understandings of the human being, which turn out to be the heart of the matter. If with Roman Catholic theology we presuppose that there is some sort of "remainder" within the human creature which is not comprehended by our being sinners, we must necessarily conceive of salvation as our healing or transformation.

—Mark Seifrid[2]

Nothing that precedes justification, neither faith nor works, would merit the grace of justification; for "if it is by grace, it is no longer on the basis of works; otherwise grace would no longer be grace" (Rom 11:6).

—Council of Trent[3]

In the previous chapter, we examined the way Paul describes Jesus's self-giving death as an embodied manifestation of his divine identity. In the

1. Sanders, *Paul: The Apostle's Life, Letters, and Thought*, 457.
2. Mark Seifrid, *Christ, Our Righteousness: Paul's Theology of Justification*, NSBT 9 (Downers Grove, IL: InterVarsity Press, 2000), 185.
3. Translation in Norman P. Tanner, SJ, *Decrees of the Ecumenical Councils*, 2 vols. (Washington, DC: Georgetown University Press, 1990), 2:674.

apostle's teaching, the cross reveals the love of God, who, in Christ, takes upon himself the curse of covenant infidelity. In so doing, Jesus redeems humanity from sin and inaugurates the new covenant. This fulfills Jeremiah's new covenant promise, which, among other things, announced that God would one day deal with *adikia*, "un-righteousness" (Jer 31:34 [=Jer 38:34 LXX]). We now turn to consider how Paul views the *effects* of Christ's work on the cross. As we will show, according to the apostle, salvation is much more than mere "fire insurance"—getting out of "hell." It is also more than forgiveness of sin. For Paul, believers are destined for nothing less than being "*conformed to the image of [God's] Son*" (Rom 8:29). This is perhaps why one of Paul's favorite terms for believers is "saints" or "holy ones" (Gk. *hagioi*), which highlights the truly transformative dimension of his account of salvation.[4]

This brings us to the highly controverted issue of how the believer is not simply a "saint" but also "just" or "righteous"—in Greek, *dikaios*. When Paul teaches that God "justifies" the sinner, the Greek verb he uses is *dikaioō*. The nouns he uses are *dikaiosynē*, "righteousness," and *dikaiōsis*, "justification." He also uses the adjective *dikaios*, "righteous." How to properly understand Paul's use of these terms has remained at the center of Christian theological debate since the Reformation.

In this chapter, we will zero in on the question that stands at the heart of the controversy: Does Paul teach that justification brings about a change in character or a change in "legal" status? For some closely aligned with the Protestant "old perspective," Pauline justification is about a change in the believer's legal standing. According to this view, rather than indicating a change in the believer's character through the granting of moral righteousness, justification for Paul involves God "imputing" to believers Christ's righteousness "as if" it was their own.[5] While advocates of this position will

---

4. Paul uses the term "saints" in Rom 1:7; 8:27; 12:13; 15:25, 26, 31; 16:2, 15; 1 Cor 6:1, 2; 14:33; 16:1, 15; 2 Cor 1:1; 8:4; 9:1, 12; 13:12; Phil 1:1; 4:21, 22; 1 Thess 3:13; Phlm 5.

5. For a more standard expression of the old perspective account of imputation, see Thomas R. Schreiner, *Paul, Apostle of God's Glory in Christ: A Pauline Theology* (Downers Grove, IL: IVP Academic, 2001), 189–217; D. A. Carson, "The Vindication of Imputation: On Fields of Discourse and Semantic Fields," in *Justification: What's at Stake in the Current Debates?*, ed. Mark Husbands and Daniel J. Treier (Downers Grove, IL: InterVarsity Press, 2004), 46–78. For two more recent and sophisticated accounts that still lead to an extrinsic imputation of Christ's righteousness in justification, see Constantine R. Campbell, *Paul and Union with Christ: An Exegetical and Theological Study* (Grand Rapids: Zondervan, 2012), esp. 388–405; Jonathan A. Linebaugh, *God, Grace, and Righteousness in Wisdom of Solomon and Paul's Letter to the Romans: Texts in Conversation*, NovTSup152 (Leiden: Brill, 2013).

readily acknowledge that the apostle believes the "justified" must ultimately undergo a moral change, they nonetheless insist that moral transformation is not part of justification properly speaking.[6] In fact, advocates of this position will often argue that Paul does employ righteousness language to signify moral conduct. Nevertheless, for these interpreters the righteousness that justifies is not about a moral change in the believer.[7] Instead, pointing to passages such as Romans 4:3–5, where Paul states that God justifies the ungodly by accrediting faith as righteousness, such scholars hold that justification is merely juridical. From this point of view, those who are justified receive the legal status of Christ's righteousness before God; they are simply "acquitted" or merely "declared" to be righteous.[8] According to this account, righteousness itself remains exclusively "alien" to believers—that is, saving righteousness remains exclusively outside the believer.

All of this leads to a number of questions: How does Paul himself speak about justification? Is justification only legal or is it also moral? This chapter will examine the nature of Pauline justification and argue for a properly "new covenant" account of the apostle's teaching. To do this, we begin once again with one of the passages that has been central to the argument in this book: 2 Corinthians 3:1–9.

The Ministry of Righteousness

Righteousness under the New Covenant

In order to firmly grasp how Paul conceives of the saving righteousness of Christ, it is important to examine the stark contrast he posits between the "ministries" of the old and new covenants:

6. See Campbell, *Paul and Union with Christ*, 394–95.

7. J. A. Ziesler famously suggests that Paul uses *dikaiosynē* in a double-sided manner—namely, juridical (theological) and moral. Ziesler argues that while the juridical and the moral are distinct, "they are not really alternatives, for the chronological priority does not arise.... What matters is that God's saving righteousness does two things for men and does them inseparably: it restores their relationship with God, and it makes them new, ethical beings." See J. A. Ziesler, *The Meaning of Righteousness in Paul: A Linguistic and Theological Inquiry*, SNTSMS 20 (Cambridge: Cambridge University Press, 1972), 189.

8. Cf. Wright, *Paul and the Faithfulness of God*, 2:956–59, who seems to come close to this position. Yet due to Wright's rather robust account of both Pauline "faith" and the final judgment according to works, it would be inaccurate to suggest that his position is merely forensic.

Are we beginning to commend ourselves again? Surely we do not need, as some do, letters of recommendation to you or from you, do we? You yourselves are our letter, written on our hearts, to be known and read by all; and you show that you are a letter of Christ, prepared by us, written not with ink but with the Spirit of the living God, not on tablets of stone but on tablets of human hearts.

Such is the confidence that we have through Christ toward God. Not that we are competent of ourselves to claim anything as coming from us; our competence is from God, who has made us competent to be *ministers of a new covenant*, not of letter but of spirit; for the letter kills, but the Spirit gives life.

Now if the *ministry of death*, chiseled in letters on stone tablets, came in glory so that the people of Israel could not gaze at Moses' face because of the glory of his face, a glory now set aside, how much more will the ministry of the Spirit come in glory? For if there was glory in the *ministry of condemnation*, much more does the *ministry of righteousness* abound in glory! (2 Cor 3:1–9 NRSV, slightly adapted)

As we noted in chapter 1, in this passage Paul contrasts the torah with the new covenant by alluding to the prophecies of Jeremiah and Ezekiel, which (1) address the law's ineffectiveness to deal with Israel's corporate heart problem and (2) promise that God would solve Israel's heart problem in a *future* covenantal action (cf. Jer 31:31–34; Ezek 36:26–27). In addition, it is worth returning to a chart we shared in chapter 1, which summarizes the contents of this chapter:

New Covenant Ministry in 2 Corinthians 3[9]

The Old Covenant	*The New Covenant*
of (the) letter	of (the) Spirit
ministry of death	gives life
chiseled on stone tablets	written on tablets of human hearts
came through glory	greater glory
ministry of condemnation	ministry of righteousness
a glory now set aside	permanent
cf. 2 Cor 3:6, 7, 3, 9, 10–11	*cf. 2 Cor 3:6, 3, 10–11, 9, 11*

9. Chart adapted from Gorman, *Apostle of the Crucified Lord*, 355.

On the one side is the torah, here described as the ministry of death, which is associated with condemnation.[10] On the other side is the new covenant, here described as bringing life and "righteousness." It is particularly important to look at both sides of this contrast. First, why does the law bring "condemnation"? Second, what does Paul mean when he says that his new covenant ministry is the ministry of "righteousness"? Is this righteousness only juridical? Does it also involve a change in the believer's character? In order to fully grasp the comparison Paul is making in 2 Corinthians 3, it is worth looking at other places where Paul offers a similar contrast between the law and grace.

The Torah's Ineffectiveness versus the Grace of Christ ("Christ-Gift")

It is critical to state upfront that Paul explicitly includes the torah among the divine "gifts" (*charismata*) given to Israel (cf. Rom 9:4; 11:29). He is adamant that the torah is "holy" and "spiritual" (Rom 7:12, 14). He even insists that knowledge of sin is not completely possible apart from the torah: "If it had not been for the law, I would not have known sin" (Rom 7:7, slightly modified). Yet, according to the apostle, with the arrival of the torah the stranglehold of sin on humanity only tightened: "But law came in, with the result that the trespass multiplied" (Rom 5:20). The real source of sin, then, is not found in the torah itself. Paul maintains that the power of sin and death entered the world through Adam (Rom 5:12–13), which, of course, took place long before the torah was given to Moses. The problem with the torah is not that it is evil. The problem Paul finds with the torah is that it is incapable of bringing about obedience.[11] As he goes on to show, however, what the Mosaic torah was not capable of accomplishing, grace is. As he says in Romans:

> But the law came in, with the result that the trespass multiplied; but where sin increased, grace abounded all the more, so that, just as sin exercised dominion in death, so grace might also exercise dominion

---

10. Sanders, *Paul: The Apostle's Life, Letters, and Thought*, 607. See Gaston, *Paul and the Torah*, 157–58, who disputes that the Mosaic torah is in view in 2 Cor 3:9. Yet the allusion to the stone tablets (*lithois*) confirms that the Sinai covenant is in focus. See Adeyẹmi, *The New Covenant*, 58–59.

11. Craig S. Keener, *Romans*, NCCS (Eugene: Cascade, 2009), 77–78.

through justification leading to eternal life through Jesus Christ our Lord. (Rom 5:20–21)

A similar note is sounded in Galatians: "You who want to be justified by the law have cut yourselves off from Christ; you have fallen away from grace" (Gal 5:4).

Here we can return to John Barclay's important contribution to the study of grace as "gift" (*charis*).[12] As his analysis demonstrates, grace is nothing less than "the Christ-gift"—that is, *Christ's indwelling in the believer*.[13] This aspect of Paul's teaching is especially evident in the climax of Paul's important teaching about "righteousness" in Galatians 2:

> I have been crucified with Christ; it is no longer I who live, but *Christ who lives in me*; and the life I now live in the flesh I live by faith in the Son of God, who loved me and *gave* himself for me. I do not nullify the *grace* of God; for if *righteousness* were through the law, *then Christ died to no purpose*. (Gal 2:20–21 RSV, slightly adapted)

Notice here that Paul connects "grace" (*charis*) and "righteousness" (*dikaiosynē*) to the reality of "Christ . . . in me" (Gal 2:20–21). This means something more than having a new perspective on the world; it involves "a change of 'self.'"[14] Because Paul now has Christ within him, he lives in a new way—that is, he "lives by faith." Faith is thus enabled by the Christ-gift. This contrast between the law and grace could not be clearer; since Paul surely does *not* believe "Christ died to no purpose" (Gal 2:21), he obviously must think that saving righteousness is not available through the torah.

Such evidence leads Barclay to explain that grace for Paul is best understood as "empowerment"[15] or "energism."[16] In support of this conclusion, notice how in Romans Paul also speaks rather strongly of what the power of God's grace has accomplished in him:

---

12. Barclay, *Paul and the Gift*.

13. See Barclay, "Under Grace," 63, who draws on Käsemann, *New Testament Questions of Today*, 174: "The gift which is being bestowed here [in salvation] is never at any time separable from its Giver."

14. Barclay, *Paul and the Gift*, 386.

15. Barclay, "Grace and the Transformation of Agency in Christ," 384. See also John Nolland, "Grace as Power," *NovT* 28, no. 1 (1986): 26–31.

16. Barclay, "Grace and the Transformation of Agency," 388n38.

> Nevertheless on some points I have written to you rather boldly by way of reminder, because of the *grace* given me by God to be a minister of Christ Jesus to the Gentiles in the priestly service of the gospel of God, so that the offering of the Gentiles may be acceptable, sanctified by the Holy Spirit. *In Christ Jesus*, then, I have reason to boast of my work for God. For I will not venture to speak of anything except what Christ has accomplished through me to win obedience from the Gentiles, by word and deed. (Rom 15:15–18)

Paul believes that "grace" (*charis*) is what makes his ministry effective. This is the same theological concept that stands behind the apostle's famous account of the word of the Lord to him: "My grace is sufficient for you, for power is made perfect in weakness" (2 Cor 12:9). In this verse we can detect a parallelism between "grace" (*charis*) and "power" (*dynamis*).

Since Paul views grace in terms of divine empowerment, he can speak of the way it makes the believer *a "co-worker" with God*: "Working together with him, then, we entreat you not to accept the grace of God in vain" (2 Cor 6:1 RSV). Though not using the specific language of "grace," Philippians 2 speaks of this dynamic precisely: "Work out your own salvation with fear and trembling; for it is God who is at work in you" (Phil 2:12–13). For Paul, God's grace *causes* obedience. If this purpose is thwarted, grace is "in vain."[17] Nor does this mean that God and believers simply form a sort of fifty-fifty partnership. God does not do "some" of the work, leaving believers to "make up the rest." It would be a mistake to conclude that the apostle holds that God gives the believer the power to act obediently and then leaves them to act autonomously. Rather, all acts are both fully the result of the gift of grace and fully performed by believers.[18]

It must be conceded, though, that Paul's way of explaining this dynamic can be frustrating for those who wish he had been more systematic. Barclay observes that the apostle's articulation is not "set," or always expressed with the same formulation.[19] At times, Paul even seems somewhat self-conscious about his language, aware that it could be misunderstood. For example, when Paul says, "It is no longer I who live, but it is Christ

---

17. See Barclay, "Grace and the Transformation of Agency," 377.

18. For an account of how Augustine develops this, see John A. Kincaid, "New Covenant Justification by Cardiac Righteousness: An Augustinian Perspective on Pauline Justification," *Letter and Spirit* 12 (2017): 37–58.

19. Barclay, "Grace and the Transformation of Agency in Christ," 383.

who lives in me," he quickly adds, "And the life I now live in the flesh I live by faith in the Son of God" (Gal 2:20). The reader might be forgiven for asking, "So, Paul, do *you* live or not? You say that you 'no longer live' but you also claim, 'I live by faith.'" The answer is that Paul *has* died but lives anew. Nevertheless, he wants to insist that *he is not the source of this new life*. To live by faith "in the Son of God" is to say the indwelling of Christ is the principle of this new life. At the same time, this does not mean Paul is no longer an acting subject. Christ has not canceled out the believer's role. Paul, therefore, can truly say, "*I* live by faith." Along similar lines, when Paul writes, "I have reason to boast of my work for God," he quickly adds, "For I will not venture to speak of anything except what Christ has accomplished through me" (Rom 15:17–18). Paul himself is working and his work is effective, but *only* because Christ is working within him.

In sum, Barclay shows that Paul avoids viewing the divine and human actors as somehow in competition with one another. Instead, the apostle believes God is doing nothing less than *transforming human agency*. The works believers perform are now truly *Christ's* works—but they are not *only* Christ's works since believers are "co-workers" with him by grace. Barclay depicts this in terms of "the intertwining of agencies," going on to highlight many other passages where this dynamic appears evident (cf., e.g., 1 Thess 1:3; 3:10; 4:10; 5:23–24).[20] This analysis leads Barclay to a startling conclusion:

> Grace does not just invite "response" but itself effects the human participation in grace, such that "every good work" can be viewed as the fruit of divine power as much as the product of believers themselves. From this perspective, the old conundrum of justification by grace and judgment by works is perhaps less problematic than is commonly claimed. *The works for which believers are accountable at the judgment seat of Christ are themselves the product of the grace that has transformed their agents and empowered their performance.*[21]

This is an extremely profound insight and helps to properly situate Paul's contrast between the torah and the new covenant in 2 Corinthians 3:1–9. The reason that the new covenant must empower obedience is Israel's corporate "heart problem," a problem that the law alone could not solve.

---

20. See Barclay, "Grace and the Transformation of Agency in Christ," 383–84.
21. Barclay, "Grace and the Transformation of Agency in Christ," 385 (emphasis added).

Israel's Heart Problem and the New Covenant

While the Mosaic law is unable to solve Israel's heart problem, the promised new covenant is. This new covenant is administered through Paul and his associates: "[God] has made us competent to be *ministers of a new covenant*" (2 Cor 3:6). He tells the Corinthians, "You show that you are a letter from Christ delivered by us, written not with ink but with the Spirit of the living God, not on tablets of stone but on tablets of human hearts" (2 Cor 3:3 RSV). This verse echoes Jeremiah's new covenant oracle:

Jeremiah 31:33	2 Corinthians 3:3
"I will put my law within them, and *I will write it on their hearts.*"	"You are a letter from Christ delivered by us, *written not with ink but with the Spirit of the living God, not on tablets of stone but on tablets of human hearts*" (RSV).

For Paul, the new covenant brings about a profoundly realistic change of *the heart.*

In biblical literature, the "heart" (Heb. *lēb*; Gk. *kardia*) is understood as constituting the inner core of the person, the source of obedience or rebellion.[22] Not surprisingly, then, it has a prominent place in the scriptures of Israel. The heart is a particularly important leitmotiv in Deuteronomy:

> Hear, O Israel: The LORD our God is one LORD; and you shall love the LORD your God *with all your heart,* and with all your soul, and with all your might. (Deut 6:4–5 RSV)

> So now, O Israel, what does the LORD your God require of you? Only to fear the LORD your God, to walk in all his ways, to love him, to serve the LORD your God *with all your heart.* (Deut 10:12)

> *Circumcise, then, the foreskin of your heart,* and do not be stubborn any longer. (Deut 10:16)[23]

---

22. See BDAG 508–9; LSJ 877; Johannes Behm, *kardia, TDNT* 3:608–14; Wells, *Grace and Agency in Paul and Second Temple Judaism*, especially 232.

23. For more on the importance of this text, see Wells, *Grace and Agency in Paul*, 25–40; Adeyẹmi, *New Covenant Torah*, 58–59; Sprinkle, *Paul and Judaism Revisited*, 46–47.

Israel will only be capable of showing God the love required of them if their hearts are properly ordered to God. Yet a careful reading of the book suggests this is not something Israel can achieve on its own. By Deuteronomy 30, Moses explains that Israel will end up in exile due to its sin and disobedience. How will Israel's heart problem finally be solved? God will intervene:

> *The* LORD *your God will circumcise your heart and the heart of your descendants*, so that you will love the LORD your God with all your *heart* and with all your soul, in order that you may live. . . . Then you shall again obey the LORD, observing all his commandments that I am commanding you today. (Deut 30:6, 8)

A divine intervention will be necessary to remedy Israel's spiritual heart disease; *God* must cure Israel's heart.

This background from the torah illuminates Jeremiah's prophecy, which announces that the "new covenant" would involve God addressing Israel's "unrighteousness" (*adikia*).[24] By putting the torah on Israel's *heart*, God enables the people to do what they previously could not—act obediently. As we have seen, Ezekiel envisions a similar future:[25]

> A *new heart* I will give you, and a *new spirit* I will put within you; and I will remove from your body the heart of stone and give you a heart of flesh. *I will put my spirit within you*, and *make you follow my statutes* and be careful to observe my ordinances. (Ezek 36:26–27)

Ezekiel announces that God, the divine surgeon, will address the people's heart problem. Yet Ezekiel specifies how this will occur; God attributes this action to "my spirit." According to the prophet, the Spirit of God will even *cause* the people to walk in obedience.[26] Intriguingly, this prophecy of a new heart occurs in a section of the book where the future era of restoration includes the notion of God establishing a "covenant of peace"

---

24. See, e.g., Wells, *Grace and Agency in Paul*, 51–53; Robert C. Olson, *The Gospel as the Revelation of God's Righteousness: Paul's Use of Isaiah in Romans 1:1–3:26*, WUNT 2/428 (Tübingen: Mohr Siebeck, 2016), 240; John Goldingay, *Israel's Gospel*, OTT 1 (Downers Grove, IL: InterVarsity Press, 2003), 714.

25. See Wells, *Grace and Agency*, 53–60.

26. See also Ezek 11:19–20; Jacqueline E. Lapsley, *Can These Bones Live? The Problem of the Moral Self in the Book of Ezekiel* (Berlin: Walter de Gruyter, 2000), 166.

(Ezek 34:25; 37:26), spoken of as an "everlasting covenant" (Ezek 37:26). While the exact term "new covenant" is not present, it is easy to see how Ezekiel's promises could be read alongside Jeremiah's prophecy of a new covenant.[27] In 2 Corinthians 3:1–9, Paul connects the imagery used by both prophets in speaking of his new covenant ministry, which he provocatively calls a "ministry of righteousness." This leads to the inevitable question: In what way is Paul using the term "righteousness"? Is this righteousness juridical, moral, or both?

The "Cardiac Righteousness" of the New Covenant[28]

In order to determine the sense in which Paul is using the term "righteousness" in 2 Corinthians 3:9, it is important to read it in context. As for the most proximate context, in 2 Corinthians 3:7–11 Paul offers a series of three contrasts between the torah and the new covenant:

Mosaic Torah	New Covenant
"death" (*thanatos*)	"Spirit" (*pneuma*)
"condemnation" (*katakrisis*)	"righteousness" (*dikaiosynē*)
"what is disappearing" (*to katargoumenon*)	"what is remaining" (*to menon*)
cf. 2 Cor 3:7, 9, 11	cf. 2 Cor 3:8, 9, 11[29]

In light of Paul's use of the term "condemnation" (*katakrisis*) in the first part of 3:9, it seems right to suggest that there is a juridical dimension to Paul's use of righteousness in the second part of the verse. The reason for this centers on the meaning of *katakrisis*, which means "a judicial verdict involving a penalty, *condemnation*."[30] This basic definition appears confirmed by 2 Corinthians 7:3, where Paul tells the Corinthians that his appeal is made not "to condemn [*katakrisin*] you."

Furthermore, it is crucial to note the contrast Paul draws in 2 Corinthians 3:9: Paul's new covenant ministry is a "ministry of righteousness," while the Mosaic torah is spoken of as "the ministry of death" (2 Cor 3:7).

---

27. See Deidun, *New Covenant Morality in Paul*, 35n118; Wells, *Grace and Agency in Paul*, 102–3.

28. See Kincaid, "New Covenant Justification," 37–58.

29. Chart taken from Martin, *2 Corinthians*, 201.

30. See BDAG, κατάκρισις, 519. Moreover, Paul employs a very similar term, *katakrima*, in Rom 5:16 and 8:1 in much the same manner.

The new covenant serves to rectify the old covenant. But how? The apostle explains that the Mosaic torah is not only associated with "death" and "condemnation" but is "now set aside [*tēn katargoumenēn*]" (2 Cor 3:7). He goes on to affirm, "Indeed, what once had glory has lost its glory because of the greater glory; for if what was set aside came through glory, much more has the permanent come in glory!" (2 Cor 3:10–11). As Hays explains, the reason the law brings death and condemnation is that "it is (only) written, lacking the power to effect the obedience it commands. Since it has no power to transform the readers, it can only stand as a witness to their condemnation."[31] The reason the torah constitutes a "ministry of condemnation" can be seen from our analysis in the previous section: *since Israel has a heart problem, they lack the ability to obey the law written only on tablets of stone.*

This appears confirmed by the wider context of 2 Corinthians 3. As we have seen, Paul contrasts the manner in which the two covenants are written—while the torah is written on tablets of stone, the new covenant is written on tablets of human hearts (2 Cor 3:3). As a result, the ministry of condemnation is one that operates on the basis of a "juridical realism." The legal condemnation Paul speaks of is aligned with the reality of Israel's heart problem. When Paul speaks of the torah as a "ministry of condemnation," he is employing the word *katakrisis* (condemnation) with *both* juridical and moral implications—the legal decree of condemnation is inextricably bound up with *actual* disobedience.

The implications of this should not be glossed over. For the "ministry of condemnation" to be overcome, the new covenant "ministry of righteousness"—mentioned in the same verse—must also be *both* juridical *and* concerned with the moral character of the believer. If the ministry of righteousness is only juridical and not moral, then it suffers from the very same problem as the ministry of condemnation, namely, it is *only extrinsic*. If this is so, the problem that the new covenant is meant to rectify is not solved because the heart remains unchanged. But Paul maintains that his new covenant ministry is one that is written "on tablets of human hearts" (2 Cor 3:3) and, as a result, is able to accomplish what "the ministry of condemnation" could not. It seems safe to conclude, therefore, that Paul's ministry of righteousness involves this heart-writing effected by the Spirit such that new covenant justification can rightly be said to be by "cardiac righteousness." This cardiac righteousness must therefore be both juridical and moral at the same time.

31. Hays, *Echoes*, 131.

This approach, which views "the ministry of righteousness" as having both a juridical and moral dimension, aligns well with the way terms relating to "righteousness" are used in the scriptures of Israel. As Stephen Westerholm rightly notes, righteousness language is there indisputably connected to a person's character. The Hebrew term for "righteous" (*tzaddiq*) is used for the person "who does what he or she is morally bound to do." Westerholm goes on to point out that the deeds performed by such a person are specifically spoken of as "righteousness" (*tzedeqah*).[32] Moreover, in the description of the faithful person, the term "righteous" (*tzaddiq*) is used in parallel with the notions of being "blameless" (Gen 6:9; Job 12:4), "innocent" (Job 22:19; Ps 94:21), and, notably for our discussion above, *"upright in heart"* (Pss 32:11; 64:10 [MT 64:11]; 97:11). The opposite of being "righteous" is being "wicked" (Gen 18:25; Ps 1:6). Westerholm thus says, *"The first thing to be said about these words* [i.e., terms relating to "righteousness"] *is that they are perhaps the most basic terms in the ethical vocabulary of the Hebrew language."*[33]

Of course, the Greek term Paul uses for righteousness is *dikaiosynē*. In support of our argument, it is important to note that ancient writers commonly used it to signify the moral quality or "virtue" of justice. For example, Aristotle indicates that "everybody" took it as a reference to virtue.[34] The Septuagint, the Greek translation of Israel's scriptures, mirrors this understanding of the word. For example, in Genesis 18:19 the Lord states that Abraham will teach his sons to keep his ways, which is described as "doing righteousness" (*dikaiosynē*). Two chapters later, Abimelech defends his moral rectitude by saying he acted with both a "pure heart" (*kardia*) and "righteousness [*dikaiosynē*] of hands" (Gen 20:5 LXX). Numerous other examples could be piled up.[35] Therefore, if Paul used the term "righteousness" to signify only juridical right standing, he would have been using it in an unexpected way—even in a way that contradicted its meaning in the scriptures of Israel. This leads nicely to the question of the final judgment, to which we now turn.

---

32. For the following, see Stephen Westerholm, "Righteousness, Cosmic and Microcosmic," in Gaventa, *Apocalyptic Paul*, 21–38.

33. Westerholm, "Righteousness, Cosmic and Microcosmic," 27 (emphasis added).

34. Aristotle, *Nicomachean Ethics* 5.1.3; For similar accounts of "righteousness" (*dikaiosynē*), see Plato, *Republic*, Book IV; 4 Macc 1:4, 6, 18; 2:6; 5:24.

35. In the LXX, see Gen 21:23; 24:27, 49; 30:33; 32:11; Josh 24:14; 1 Kgdms 2:10; 2 Kgdms 22:21, 25; 3 Kgdms 3:6; Tob 1:3; 2:14; 4:5, 7; 12:8, 9; 13:7; 14:7, 11; 1 Macc 2:52; 4 Macc 1:4, 6, 18; 2:6; 5:24; Pss 7:9; 10:7; 14:2; 16:1, 15; 17:21, 25; 22:3; 37:21; 51:5; 57:2. Notably, in Deut 9:5 *dikaiosynē* is linked to the notion of "holiness of heart."

Final Judgment of the Heart

In seeking to account for Paul's teaching regarding the final judgment, it is helpful to begin with Romans 2. After a ringing indictment of the sinfulness of humanity, Paul tells the Romans:

> Do you imagine, whoever you are, that when you judge those who do such things and yet do them yourself, you will escape the judgment of God? Or do you despise the riches of his kindness and forbearance and patience? Do you not realize that God's kindness is meant to lead you to repentance? But by your hard and impenitent heart you are storing up wrath for yourself on the day of wrath, when God's righteous judgment will be revealed. For he will repay according to each one's deeds: to those who by patiently doing good seek for glory and honor and immortality, he will give eternal life; while for those who are self-seeking and who obey not the truth but wickedness, there will be wrath and fury. There will be anguish and distress for everyone who does evil, the Jew first and also the Greek, but glory and honor and peace for everyone who does good, the Jew first and also the Greek. For God shows no partiality.
>
> All who have sinned apart from the law will also perish apart from the law, and all who have sinned under the law will be judged by the law. For it is not the hearers of the law who are righteous in God's sight, but the doers of the law who will be justified. (Rom 2:3–13)

The mention of the coming day of wrath is an unmistakable allusion to the day of final judgment. Those who are judged rightly on that day are described as "justified." The apostle insists that it will be "the doers of the law who will be justified" (Rom 2:13). Yet with this statement Paul seems to contradict what he says in the next chapter: "'No human being will be justified in his sight' by deeds prescribed by the law, for through the law comes the knowledge of sin" (Rom 3:20). How can Paul insist that one is not justified by "deeds prescribed by the law" in Romans 3 after emphatically insisting that God "will repay according to each one's deeds" (Rom 2:6)?

Because of this difficulty some suggest that Paul only describes a "hypothetical" judgment by works in Romans 2.[36] In support of viewing

---

36. For an overview and critique of this position, see Bird, *Saving Righteousness*, 159–60.

Romans 2 as merely a rhetorical ploy, some point out that in his other letters Paul frequently teaches that one is justified apart from works. For example, in Galatians Paul not only states that "a person is justified not by the works of law" (Gal 2:16), he goes even further and proclaims that those who rely on the works of the law are under a curse (Gal 3:10). Yet the position that the final judgment according to works is *merely* a rhetorical move ignores the way the apostle explicitly teaches elsewhere that God will judge humanity on the basis of what they have done in the body: "For all of us must appear before the judgment seat of Christ, *so that each may receive recompense for what has been done in the body, whether good or evil*" (2 Cor 5:10). Furthermore, Paul is adamant in admonishing both the Thessalonians (1 Thess 3:13; 5:23) and the Philippians (Phil 1:10) about their need to be "pure and blameless" on the day of Christ. To suggest that Romans 2 envisions a *merely* hypothetical judgment by works rather than *also* teaching that there will be a real final judgment according to works is improbable. Instead, Paul's argument in Romans 2:1–16 is best read as exposing humanity's need for the saving righteousness of God—a saving righteousness that allows one to escape the fate of those who fail to be judged righteous: "For it is not the hearers of the law who are *righteous* in God's sight, but the doers of the law who will be *justified*" (Rom 2:13). To be declared truly "righteous" at the final judgment, one must become a "doer" of the law.

But what does this kind of righteousness required at the final judgment entail? Paul provides the answer at the beginning of the chapter. Once again, let us take a careful look at his teaching:

> But by your hard and impenitent *heart* you are storing up wrath for yourself on the day of wrath, when God's righteous judgment will be revealed. For he will repay according to each one's deeds. (Rom 2:5–6)

After previously stating that God gave humanity over to "the lusts of their hearts" (Rom 1:24), Paul here reveals the consequence of this heart problem: condemnation at the final judgment. To flip the argument around, Paul is saying that one needs an upright heart—what we call "cardiac righteousness"—in order to do the kinds of works that would allow one to be found just at the final judgment.

This reading finds validation from a close examination of the whole of Romans 2. After stating that God will "justify" those who do the law (Rom 2:13), Paul states:

When Gentiles, who do not possess the law, do instinctively what the law requires, these, though not having the law, are a law to themselves. They show that what the law requires is written on their *hearts*, to which their own conscience bears witness; and their conflicting thoughts will accuse or perhaps excuse them on the day when, according to my gospel, God, through Jesus Christ, will judge the secret thoughts of all. (Rom 2:14–16)

In other words, in the final analysis, being regarded as just concerns *the condition of the heart*. How do gentiles have the law "written on the heart"? As others have noted, the language evokes the new covenant oracle of Jeremiah.[37] This reading is further corroborated by what the apostle goes on to say in the concluding verses of the chapter.

Paul insists that to be a true Jew is to be circumcised of heart.

Circumcision indeed is of value if you obey the law; but if you break the law, your circumcision has become uncircumcision. So, if those who are uncircumcised keep the requirements of the law, will not their uncircumcision be regarded as circumcision? Then those who are physically uncircumcised but keep the law will condemn you that have the written code and circumcision but break the law. For a person is not a Jew who is one outwardly, nor is true circumcision something external and physical. Rather, a person is a Jew who is one inwardly, and *real circumcision is a matter of the heart—it is spiritual and not literal*. Such a person receives *praise not from others but from God*. (Rom 2:25–29)

Again, what is true for gentiles is also true for Jews—what matters is the heart. This reading is confirmed by Paul's own teaching in 1 Corinthians 4:

But with me it is a very small thing that I should be judged by you or by any human court. I do not even judge myself. I am not aware of anything against myself, but I am not thereby *justified* [*dikaioō*]. It is the Lord who judges me. Therefore do not pronounce judgment before the Lord comes, who will bring to light the things now hidden in darkness and will disclose the purposes of the *heart*. Then each one will receive *praise from God*. (1 Cor 4:3–5 NRSV, slightly adapted)

---

37. See, e.g., Matera, *Romans*, 66.

In short, Paul states that he will be justified when God reveals the heart, and this will bring "praise" from God. This passage is remarkably similar to Romans 2:

1 Corinthians 4	Romans 2
"I do not even judge myself"	The problem of humans passing judgment
"I am not justified"	The "doers" are "justified"
At the final judgment God will reveal "the *purposes of the heart*"	Gentiles are judged righteous because *"what the law requires is written on their hearts"* "Real circumcision is a matter of the heart"
"Each one will receive praise from God"	"A person receives praise not from others but from God"
cf. 1 Cor 4:3, 4, 5	*cf. Rom 2:1, 13, 15, 28–29*

To connect the teaching in 1 Corinthians 4 to Romans 2, if Paul is justified when the purposes of his heart are revealed, his praise will come from God. This is not only true for Paul. According to him, at the final judgment God will judge all of humanity by revealing the purposes of the heart.

In looking to rightly determine Paul's account of justification, it is hard to overestimate the importance of these passages, which indicate that both condemnation and justification are directly connected to one's heart condition—it is the heart itself that will be judged at the final judgment. Moreover, as other interpreters note, since Paul holds that justification is ordered to the final judgment, his teaching about justification in the life of the believer can be understood as "the eschatological declaration of righteousness brought into the present time."[38] As a result, if the final judgment is an evaluation of the heart, then it would seem not just plausible but also necessary for new covenant justification to be by cardiac righteousness. This suggestion is confirmed by Paul himself in Romans 10:10, where he teaches, "For one believes in the heart *resulting in righteousness* [*eis dikaiosynēs*]."[39] It is therefore our contention

---

38. See Campbell, *Paul and Union with Christ*, 410–11. See also, e.g., Wright, *Paul and the Faithfulness of God*, 2:948–49.

39. Translation taken and slightly modified from the Lexham English Bible.

that the saving righteousness of God in justification is a singular righteousness that concerns *both* legal standing *and* the interior quality of the believer. What is more, this account of Pauline righteousness broadly aligns with the manner in which the term was used in antiquity. As David deSilva rightly notes, "The common and most natural sense" of the term "righteousness" (*dikaiosynē*) is "the moral quality manifested in a particular set of commitments and practices (that will, incidentally, be recognized as 'just' at the Last Judgment)."[40]

Some interpreters would object to this reading by highlighting passages in which Paul teaches that believers are justified by simply receiving Christ's righteousness through "imputation"—that is, merely through a legal decree.[41] Such scholars claim that Paul affirms that saving righteousness remains exclusively outside of believers. In other words, believers are legally "declared" righteous without actually "becoming" inwardly righteous. We now turn to consider the evidence for this position.

New Covenant Righteousness as Merely Extrinsic Righteousness?

Those who argue that Paul's righteousness language refers only to one's legal state draw on various pieces of evidence—in particular, four passages that occur in four of Paul's letters: Philippians, 1 Corinthians, 2 Corinthians, and Romans. Let us begin with the passage from Philippians, which reads:

> For his sake I have suffered the loss of all things, and I regard them as rubbish, in order that I may gain Christ and be found in him, *not having a righteousness of my own* that comes from the torah, but one that comes through faith in Christ, the righteousness from God based on faith. *I want to know Christ and the power of his resurrection and the sharing of his sufferings by becoming like him in his death*, if somehow I may attain the resurrection from the dead. (Phil 3:8–11, slightly modified)

In these lines Paul indicates that new covenant righteousness has its origin in Christ and not the believer. Paul thus denies "having a righteousness of my own [*emēn dikaiosynēn*]" (Phil 3:9). Paul is here contrasting his own righteousness with that which comes through Christ. From this, some

---

40. David A. deSilva, *Transformation: The Heart of Paul's Gospel* (Bellingham, WA: Lexham, 2014), 29n30.

41. See, e.g., note 5 for examples.

conclude that the saving "righteousness of God" must not refer to Paul's moral character itself.[42]

Such a reading, however, seems to miss the apostle's point. When Paul rejects having a "righteousness of my own," he is specifically contrasting that which is based on the torah with that which comes through Christ. Paul insists that he did not "gain Christ" because of his own righteousness (Phil 3:8). Paul receives righteousness as a "gift," and not because he is worthy of it. Nevertheless, this does not mean that in receiving righteousness from Christ it remains purely external to him. Jean-Noël Aletti is right on the mark when he writes, "In Phil 3:9, the believer's justice is not exterior to himself, *only its origin*, which may be either the Law or God."[43]

According to Paul, the righteousness of God that depends upon faith in Christ is given so that believers might become "like him in his death" (Phil 3:10).[44] Paul affirms that saving righteousness is not *from* (*ek*) himself—it comes *only* through Christ. Yet this does not necessarily mean that receiving such a gift does not also entail a real change in himself. As E. P. Sanders explains:

> Having righteousness by faith is the same as sharing the death and resurrection of Christ. The meaning of these conjoined formulations cannot be "a juridical decision that imputes righteousness to human beings although they are not in fact righteous." The meaning is born by the terminology of the mystical participation of the believer in Christ.[45]

Likewise, in response to interpreters who claim that Paul's righteousness-language here denotes only a change in the believer's legal status, Thomas Stegman correctly observes that, in context, the focus is on "being conformed [*symmorphizomenos*]" (Phil 3:10),[46] "which is another way of

---

42. See, e.g., John Piper, *Counted Righteous in Christ: Should We Abandon the Imputation of Christ's Righteousness?* (Wheaton, IL: Crossway, 2002), 62–63; Peter Thomas O'Brien, *The Epistle to the Philippians: A Commentary on the Greek Text*, NIGTC (Grand Rapids: Eerdmans, 1991), 392.

43. Jean-Noël Aletti, *Justification by Faith in the Letters of Saint Paul: Keys to Interpretation*, trans. Peggy Manning Meyer, AnBib 5 (Rome: Gregorian & Biblical Press, 2015), 184n43.

44. *Pace* Silva, *Philippians*, 160–61, who arbitrarily insists that Phil 3:8–9 relates to justification and Phil 3:10 turns to the topic of "sanctification."

45. Sanders, *Paul: The Apostle's Life, Letters, and Thought*, 612–13.

46. For more on the connection between justification and being conformed to Christ, see below under "Conformed to the Image of His Son."

talking about transformation. . . . Paul uses *dikaio-* terminology for more than God's forensic declaration of a status; it also connotes transformation after the likeness of Christ."[47] In sum, to appeal to this teaching in Philippians 3 as evidence that Paul believes that the saving righteousness of Christ remains purely external is ultimately unpersuasive.

The second passage cited as evidence that Paul holds that saving righteousness remains extrinsic to the believer is 1 Corinthians 1:30: "He [God] is the source of your life in Christ Jesus, who became for us wisdom from God, and righteousness and sanctification and redemption." Just as in Philippians, Paul here maintains that the source of the believer's righteousness is Christ. Yet does this necessarily mean that the righteousness that comes from Christ *remains* only extrinsic to the believer? In context, nothing necessitates that conclusion. If one were to conclude that the righteousness given to believers must be exclusively extrinsic, then it would seem to follow that sanctification must also be exclusively extrinsic for the very same reason, since Christ is also said to be the source of believers' "sanctification." As N. T. Wright correctly notes, if 1 Corinthians 1:30 is forced to teach imputed righteousness, then "we should then also have to speak, presumably of 'imputed wisdom,' 'imputed sanctification' and 'imputed redemption,'"[48] a reading for which there is no support.

The third passage used to argue for a purely extrinsic account of saving righteousness in Paul is found in 2 Corinthians 5: "For our sake he [God] made him [Christ] to be sin who knew no sin, so that in him [Christ] we might become the righteousness of God" (2 Cor 5:21). Some believe this verse is the best evidence for the classical Reformed doctrine of imputation. Specifically, since Christ is said to have been "made sin" though he himself was not a "sinner," it is thought to follow that Paul must hold that sinners are therefore "considered" righteous without actually "being" righteous.[49] Still, a number of considerations weigh against this conclusion. For one thing, as we explained in the last chapter, "God made him to be sin" is best read as indicating that Jesus became an atoning sacrifice; in saying Christ was made to be "sin [*hamartia*]" (2 Cor 5:21), Paul is em-

---

47. Thomas D. Stegman, SJ, "Paul's Use of *dikaio-* Terminology: Moving beyond N. T. Wright's Forensic Interpretation," *TS* 72 (2011): 511.

48. N. T. Wright, *Justification: God's Plan and Paul's Vision* (Downers Grove, IL: IVP Academic, 2009), 157.

49. See, e.g., D. A. Carson, "The Vindication of Imputation: On Fields of Discourse and Semantic Fields," in Husbands and Treier, *Justification: What's at Stake in the Current Debates?*, 69–71.

ploying the language used in Israel's scriptures, where a "sin offering" can simply be called "sin [*hamartia*]" (Lev 4:33 LXX).[50] In addition, though Christ does not become a sinner, Paul believes that Jesus *actually* bears the consequences of sin redemptively. Christ is not simply "considered" an atoning sacrifice, he actually offers himself as such a sacrifice. As a result, it is difficult to conclude from this verse that the righteousness believers receive is *merely* juridical. If Christ actually bears the consequences of sin, then why insist believers do not actually become righteous?

The point becomes especially sharp when we recall that in context Paul has just declared that believers are a "new creation" (2 Cor 5:17). When he insists a few lines later that they also "become the righteousness of God" (2 Cor 5:21), it is hard to imagine he is thinking *only* in terms of a change in their legal standing before God. To insist that this statement necessarily excludes any sense of believers *becoming* righteous is to put a muzzle on the text.[51] Consider the words of three major Protestant Pauline exegetes: Günther Bornkamm, N. T. Wright, and Richard Hays.

God both pronounces and performs this justification of the sinner. His word accomplishes his pronouncement. *There is no place here for a legal fiction, an "as if."*[52]

The little word *genōmetha* in 2 Corinthians 5:21b—"that we might *become* God's righteousness in him"—does not sit comfortably with the normal interpretation, according to which God's righteousness is "imputed" or "reckoned" to believers. If that was what Paul meant, with the overtones of "extraneous righteousness" that normally come with that theory, the one thing he ought not to have said is that we "become" that righteousness. Surely that leans far too much toward a Roman Catholic notion of *infused* righteousness?[53]

---

50. See Craig Keener, *1–2 Corinthians*, NCBC (Cambridge: Cambridge University Press, 2005), 187; Stegman, *Second Corinthians*, 143–44; cf. LEH 1:23.

51. See, e.g., Daniel G. Powers, *Salvation through Participation: An Examination of the Notion of the Believers' Corporate Unity with Christ in Early Christian Soteriology* (Leuven: Peeters, 2001), 81, who makes the case that a reading that interprets this passage as merely an exchange of Christ's legal status for believers' would mean "that Christ became sin *instead* of us so that we become the righteousness of God *instead* of Christ."

52. Günther Bornkamm, *Paul*, trans. D. M. G. Stalker (1969; repr., Minneapolis: Fortress, 1995), 138 (emphasis added).

53. Wright, *Justification*, 165. Nevertheless, Wright insists this only applies to the apos-

[Paul] does not say "that we might know about the righteousness of God," nor "that we might believe in the righteousness of God," nor even "that we might receive the righteousness of God." Instead, the church is to become the righteousness of God: where the church embodies in its life together the world-reconciling love of Jesus Christ, the new creation is manifest. The church incarnates the righteousness of God.[54]

Suffice it to say, this passage makes it very difficult to think Paul teaches that one "becomes the righteousness of God" exclusively in the sense of a change in legal status.

Fourth and finally, the last of the passages claimed for the traditional Protestant view of imputation is also the most difficult to rightly interpret. The text is found in Romans 4 and reads as follows:

What then are we to say was gained by Abraham, our ancestor according to the flesh? For if Abraham was justified by works, he has something to boast about, but not before God. For what does the scripture say? "Abraham believed God, and it was reckoned to him as righteousness." Now to one who works, wages are not reckoned as a gift but as something due. But to one who without works trusts him who justifies the ungodly, such faith is reckoned as righteousness. (Rom 4:1–5)

Those who believe Paul views justification as involving nothing more than a change in legal status observe that Abraham is said to be *reckoned* righteous (cf. Gen 15:6; Gal 3:6–9). The quotation from Genesis 15 employs a term that some have seen as supporting an exclusively legal interpretation of Pauline justification: "Abraham believed God, and it was *reckoned* [*elogisthē*] to him as righteousness" (Rom 4:3 citing Gen 15:6; cf. Gal 3:6). In addition, in Romans 4:5 Paul uses the verb "to justify" (*dikaioō*) in order to speak of Abraham's justification, a term taken to mean "consider or declare righteous." Therefore, since Paul says that Abraham's faith was "reckoned" or "counted as"

---

tles, a conclusion we think is unwarranted. As Gorman notes, "Unless we want to posit a new version of limited atonement—Christ died only for Paul and other ministers—then we must conclude that some of the 'we' texts in Second Corinthians clearly and deliberately refer to all believers." Gorman, *Death of the Messiah*, 61n24. See also A. Katherine Grieb, "'So That in Him We Might Become the Righteousness of God' (2 Cor 5:21): Some Theological Reflections on the Church Becoming Justice," *Ex Auditu* 22 (2006): 58–80.

54. Hays, *Moral Vision*, 24. See also Stegman, "Paul's Use of *dikaio-* Terminology," 500–504.

righteousness, and since Paul says God thus "considered" the "ungodly" to be "righteous" (Rom 4:5), some conclude that the apostle must mean that Abraham was not *actually* righteous.[55] To adequately respond to this reading, it is necessary to understand two of the key terms involved—namely, the term translated "to justify" (*dikaioō*) and the word rendered as "faith" (*pistis*).

The term "to justify," *dikaioō*, is frequently used in the Greek Old Testament to signify a positive action or decision in someone's favor, particularly within legal contexts. As James Prothro rightly states, "*dikaioō* always indicates an action in favor of a personal object, and does so especially in judicial settings."[56] This certainly seems to be the sense in which Paul uses the word in Romans 2:13 and 1 Corinthians 4:5 when he speaks of the final judgment. Nevertheless, as we have shown, in both of those texts the legal dimension of this terminology also relates to the moral quality of a person's character; in each case one is "justified" on the basis of having an upright heart—that is, cardiac righteousness. Yet Paul routinely uses the verb "to justify" (e.g., Rom 3:24–26; 4:5; Gal 2:15–21; 3:23–26) to refer to the one who believes. This usage is obvious in Romans 4, where *Abraham* is justified because of his "faith." Therefore, in order to determine whether or not justification can be said to be by extrinsic righteousness alone in passages such as Romans 4:5, it is necessary to determine what it means for such a person to have "faith" (*pistis*).

As Teresa Morgan has demonstrated in a recent study, ancient Greek writers used *pistis* to signify more than simply an intellectual assent to propositions or mere trust in persons. Morgan shows that *pistis* is used to signify belief, trust, and faithfulness in a wide range of interpersonal contexts, ranging from familial to political and cultic settings.[57] On the whole, Morgan is able to conclude that *pistis* is never employed "purely in instrumental terms. It is always a virtue: an intrinsic good; an end as well as a means."[58]

It is particularly important to note that the ancient Greek translation of the Old Testament, the Septuagint, uses *pistis* in much the same way. For instance, in 1 Samuel (1 Kingdoms) 26:23, David tells Saul that God will give to

---

55. See O. P. Robertson, "Genesis 15:6: New Covenant Exposition of an Old Covenant Text," *WTJ* 42 (1980): 265–66; Douglas J. Moo, *The Epistle to the Romans*, NICNT (Grand Rapids: Eerdmans, 1996), 261–66.

56. James B. Prothro, "The Strange Case of Δικαιόω in the Septuagint and in Paul: The Origins and Oddity of Paul's Talk of Justification," *ZNW* 107 (2016): 48–69, at 56. For example, see also Exod 23:7; Deut 25:1; 2 Kgdms (2 Sam) 15:4.

57. See Teresa Morgan, *Roman Faith and Christian Faith: Pistis and Fides in the Early Roman Empire and Early Churches* (Oxford: Oxford University Press, 2015), 36–175.

58. Morgan, *Roman Faith and Christian Faith*, 76.

each according to "his righteous deeds [*dikaiosynē*] and his faith [*pistis*]."[59] Likewise, in 1 Maccabees 14:35 the people see the faith of Simon and make him high priest as a result of the "righteousness and faith" (*dikaiosynē* and *pistis*) that he fostered in Israel. It is striking that in these two passages there is a close link between righteousness and faith. In this we find significant continuity between the Greek Old Testament and Paul. While Paul does employ *pistis* to signify belief in particular propositions as well as trust, he also employs the term to signify true faithfulness or fidelity.[60] In Galatians 3:23–26, Paul speaks about the coming of Christ and the revealing of faith almost interchangeably such that the person of Christ is not only the object of faith but also the revelation of what faithfulness constitutes.[61] This broader meaning is also evident when Paul speaks of "the faithfulness of God [*tēn pistin tou theou*]" (Rom 3:3). Paul's point is not that God "believes" in some specific datum but that he is "faithful." As we shall see below, Paul tells the Galatians that living by faith in Christ defines the believer's entire existence (Gal 2:20–21)—anything that does not come from faith is a sin (Rom 14:23). *Pauline "faith," then, is a radical, all-encompassing virtue.*[62] Many scholars agree that the word has this fuller sense for Paul.[63] Matthew Bates uses the helpful language of "embodied fidelity."[64]

Therefore, we suggest that when Paul states that Abraham's faith was accredited as righteousness, it is Abraham's faith(fulness) that provides the basis for the reckoning to be realistic rather than merely imputed. Just verses before Paul says that God "justifies" Abraham (Rom 4:5), he indicates that faith(fulness) upholds rather than nullifies the law (Rom 3:31). The reason Abraham is righteous is his faith(fulness). Because of this, when Paul states that God "justifies" Abraham in Romans 4:5, it is *realistic rather than counterfactual*—Abraham's *faithfulness* is not a substitute for

---

59. Translation taken from Pietersma and Wright, *A New English Translation of the Septuagint.*

60. 1 Thess 1:3, 8–10; 3:2–10; 5:8; Gal 5:6; Rom 1:5 (=16:26); 3:31.

61. For more on Paul's identification of Christ with faith(fulness), see our discussion below. In addition, see Richard B. Hays, *The Faith of Jesus Christ: The Narrative Substructure of Galatians 3:1–4:11* (Grand Rapids: Eerdmans, 2002), especially, 200–204.

62. Fitzmyer even goes on to say that in the Pauline corpus, *pistis* "far transcends the OT idea of fidelity." See Joseph A. Fitzmyer, SJ, *Paul and His Theology: A Brief Sketch* (Englewood Cliffs, NJ: Prentice Hall, 1987), 84–85.

63. See Schreiner, *Paul, Apostle of God's Glory in Christ,* 211; Campbell, *Quest for Paul's Gospel,* 186; Matthew Bates, *Salvation by Allegiance Alone* (Grand Rapids: Baker Academic, 2017), 20–22, 98–99.

64. Bates, *Salvation by Allegiance Alone,* 98–99.

righteousness; it *is righteousness*. This account of Pauline faith allows for a realistic account of Paul's use of the term "to justify" (*dikaioō*), since whether it is employed in reference to faith(fulness)[65] or in reference to the works that reveal one's heart, Paul's uses it in a *realistic* sense. To return to our previous suggestion that new covenant justification is by cardiac righteousness, we are now in the position to connect Paul's use of the verb *dikaioō* to cardiac righteousness and suggest that Paul employs *dikaioō* to signify the divine confirmation or creation of cardiac righteousness by the grace of faith(fulness).[66] In the remainder of this chapter we will attempt to further demonstrate the rationale for such an account by arguing that Pauline justification is ultimately defined by conformity to the image of the Son.

Conformed to the Image of His Son

Justification by Christ-Empowered "Faith(fulness)"

To fully appreciate the way justification for Paul is ultimately christocentric in shape, it is important to recognize the way he ties justification to the notion of faith itself. In a passage that is characteristic of his teaching elsewhere, the apostle states the following:

> A person is *justified* not by the works of the law but through *faith* in Jesus Christ. And we have come to believe in Christ Jesus, so that we might be *justified by faith* in Christ, and not by doing the works of the law, because no one will be justified by the works of the law. (Gal 2:16)

---

65. See Rom 3:26 (24–26); Rom 4:5 (3–5); 5:1; Gal 2:16 (15–21).

66. Prothro argues that Paul employs the verb "to justify" (*dikaioō*) in order to signify that the contention between God and the sinner has ended with an eschatological trajectory. Moreover, Prothro astutely notes the connection between "to justify," faith, and baptism, leading him to argue for a robust account of justifying faith. See James B. Prothro, *Both Judge and Justifier: Biblical Legal Language and the Act of Justifying in Paul*, WUNT 2/461 (Tübingen: Mohr Siebeck, 2018). Building on Prothro's analysis, we contend that Paul's use of the verb translated "to justify" is not counterfactual but realistic due to the nature of graced faith. Nevertheless, our account goes beyond Prothro in also suggesting that the verb meaning "to justify" can also be employed in a causative manner, namely, to signify that God has made righteous the believer by grace. For more along these lines, see Kincaid, "New Covenant Justification by Cardiac Righteousness," 55–57 in particular.

The main point of this passage is that justification comes through "faith" (*pisteōs*). As we have highlighted above, "faith" involves more than mere intellectual assent. Yet, just as we saw in regard to righteousness, justifying "faith" has its source in Christ. In the apostle's letters, *faith has its origin in the divine Son, Jesus*. To return now to Galatians 3:23–26, Paul speaks of the "coming of Christ" in terms of the "coming of faith":

> Now *before faith came*, we were imprisoned and guarded under the law *until faith would be revealed*. Therefore the law was our disciplinarian *until Christ came*, so that we might be justified by faith. But *now that faith has come*, we are no longer subject to a disciplinarian, for in Christ Jesus you are all children of God through faith. (Gal 3:23–26)

The structure of the passage inescapably leads the reader to the conclusion that the coming of faith is realized with the apocalyptic coming of Christ. Other aspects of Galatians reinforce this point. For example, Paul speaks of "faith" being "revealed [*apokalyphthēnai*]" (Gal 3:23); this has a parallel in his teaching that the gospel came "through a *revelation* [*apokalypseōs*] of Jesus Christ" (Gal 1:12). Likewise, Paul speaks of the way God "was pleased to reveal [*apokalypsai*] his Son" (Gal 1:15–16). "Faith" and "Christ" could thus be used interchangeably in Galatians 3:23–26. Hence, in Pauline theology, "justifying faith" is essentially christological.

This leads us to a fiercely contested issue regarding Paul's language. When Paul speaks of justification, he says that it occurs through *pistis Christou* (see, e.g., Gal 2:16; Rom 3:22). This Greek expression could be translated two different ways: (1) "*faith(fulness) in* Christ" or (2) "*faithfulness of* Christ." The first option has long been favored and represents the reading found in most contemporary English Bibles. According to this translation, *pistis Christou* indicates that believers are justified by *their* "faith in Christ." In terms of Greek grammar, this would be an "objective genitive"; that is, it refers to the *object* of faith—namely, Christ. The second approach has been gaining traction more recently, finding its most influential advocate in Richard Hays.[67] This reading takes *pistis Christou* as referring to the "faithful-

---

67. See Hays, *Faith of Jesus Christ*. Though more persuasive than his predecessors, Hays was not the first to advocate this reading. For an older discussion and critique, see Ferdinand Prat, *The Theology of St. Paul*, trans. John L. Stoddard, 2 vols. (Westminster, MD: The Newman Press, 1950), 2:454–55.

ness of Christ," emphasizing Jesus's obedience as the source of salvation.[68] Which reading is correct? The truth is, both can be seen as consistent with Paul's overall message. On the one hand, Paul holds that Christians must put their "faith" in Jesus (e.g., Rom 10:10–13). On the other hand, as we have seen, Paul can also use "Jesus" interchangeably with "faith" itself (e.g., Gal 3:23–25). This makes sense since, according to Paul, the grace of Christ *enables* faith. Moreover, viewing Jesus as "faithful" coheres with Paul's divine Christology—the apostle speaks elsewhere of "the faithfulness of God [*tēn pistin tou theou*]" (Rom 3:3). In addition, the Greek word *pistis* can also have the connotation of "obedience" (cf. Rom 1:5), of which Paul views Jesus as the exemplar: Jesus was "obedient unto death" (Phil 2:8 RSV). As Douglas Campbell puts it, "Faithfulness in their present life *is actually also evidence of this participation in the life of Christ*, who was himself 'faithful unto death.'"[69] Given the evidence, we think it possible that Paul deliberately chose the expression *pistis Christou* because, at least in some places, he may have intended *both* connotations. In other words, he seems to insist that believers are saved by the "faithfulness of Christ," which is the source of their own faith(fulness), which remains available only "in Christ."[70]

Justification as "Co-Crucifixion"

Paul's teaching on justification in Galatians 2 corroborates this view. As Scott Schauf and Michael Gorman have perceptively pointed out, Paul's teaching about justification here climaxes with an account of "co-crucifixion" in Christ.[71] The whole section is worth reading carefully:

> A person is *justified* not by the works of the law but through *faith in Jesus Christ.* And we have come to believe in Christ Jesus, so that we

---

68. See, e.g., Hays, *Faith of Jesus Christ*, 293.

69. See Campbell, *Quest for Paul's Gospel*, 205.

70. For a similar suggestion, see Marion L. Soards and Darrell J. Pursiful, *Galatians* (Macon: GA: Smyth and Helwys, 2015), 94. For similar suggestions, see Adolf Deissmann, *Paulus, Eine Kultur- und Religionsgeschichtliche Skizze* (Tübingen: J. C. B. Mohr, 1911); Deissmann, *Paul: A Study in Social and Religious History*, trans. W. E. Wilson (New York: Harper Torchbooks, 1957), 162–83; Morna D. Hooker, *From Adam to Christ: Essays on Paul* (Cambridge: Cambridge University Press, 1990), 165–86.

71. See Scott Schauf, "Galatians 2:20 in Context," *NTS* 52 (2006): 86–101; Gorman, *Inhabiting the Cruciform God*, 64–72.

might be *justified by faith in Christ,* and not by doing the works of the law, because no one will be *justified* by the works of the law. But if, in our effort to be *justified* in Christ, we ourselves have been found to be sinners, is Christ then a servant of sin? Certainly not! But if I build up again the very things that I once tore down, then I demonstrate that I am a transgressor. For through the law I died to the law, so that I might live to God. I have been crucified with Christ; and it is no longer I who live, but it is Christ who lives in me. And the life I now live in the flesh I live by faith in the Son of God, who loved me and gave himself for me. I do not nullify the grace of God; for if *righteousness* comes through the law, then Christ died for nothing. (Gal 2:16–21 NRSV, slightly adapted)

This passage is often seen as treating two different ideas: (1) justification (Gal 2:15–18) and (2) spiritual co-crucifixion (Gal 2:19–20). This division, however, ignores the concluding verse, where the language of righteousness resurfaces: "If righteousness [*dikaiosynē*] comes through the law, then Christ died for nothing" (Gal 2:21). The motif of "righteousness" does not appear out of nowhere; it is connected with the topic at hand, namely, "justification [*dikaioō*]" (Gal 2:16).

Therefore, instead of viewing the teaching about co-crucifixion in Galatians 2:19–20 as unrelated to what precedes it, Gorman makes the case that here Paul reveals what justifying faith is—it is *nothing less than co-crucifixion with Christ.* Gorman admits that "Paul does not specifically say 'justification' is by co-crucifixion"; nevertheless, the larger structure of Paul's argument makes this point:[72]

Justification as Co-Crucifixion

Gal 2:19a	A	For I through the law died to the law	Previous Source of Justification
	B	so that I might live to God	
Gal 2:19b–20a	A'	I have been crucified with Christ	New Source of Justification
	A''	and it is no longer I who live	
	B'	but Christ who lives in me.	
	B''	And the life I now live in the flesh I live by faith[fulness] in the Son of God	

72. Gorman, *Inhabiting the Cruciform God,* 66.

Gorman therefore concludes, "In [Galatians] 2:19–20, Paul is clearly not speaking about some experience *subsequent* to justification but is speaking of justification itself, understood now as occurring by co-crucifixion instead of Law-keeping."[73]

Finally, that Paul identifies justification as co-crucifixion finds confirmation in Romans, when Paul writes, "For he who has *died* is *justified* [*dedikaiōtai*] from sin" (Rom 6:7 RSV, slightly adapted). In the preceding verses, Paul explicitly ties justification to *co-crucifixion* with Jesus: "We know that *our old self was crucified with him* so that the body of sin might be destroyed, and we might no longer be enslaved to sin" (Rom 6:6). This "new life" described by Paul is something more than mere biological life or a new earthly existence. To have life in Christ is nothing less than sharing in the life of the divine Son ("live with him"). For Paul, then, justification is not simply the result of Christ's death but also his resurrection (Rom 4:25); believers are to experience not only a death to self in Christ but also new life in him,[74] a life that operates on the basis of Christ's Spirit.

Justification and the Gift of the Spirit

Faithfulness is only possible because of the indwelling of Christ. Furthermore, it should be remembered from our discussion above that in using the language of "Christ" (*christos*), Paul emphasizes that Christ himself has "anointed us [*chrisas hēmas*], by putting his seal on us and giving us his Spirit [*pneumatos*] in our hearts as a first installment" (2 Cor 1:21–22). Not surprisingly, then, Paul implicitly links "justification" not only to union with Christ but also to *pneumatology*. Paul's treatment of justification as co-crucifixion with Christ at the end of Galatians 2 therefore immediately gives way to an account of the Spirit's activity:

> *Did you receive the Spirit by doing the works of the law or by believing what you heard?* Are you so foolish? Having started with the Spirit, are you now ending with the flesh? Did you experience so much for nothing?—if

---

73. Gorman, *Inhabiting the Cruciform God*, 67. See also Andrew K. Boakye, *Death and Life: Resurrection, Restoration, and Rectification in Paul's Letters* (Eugene, OR: Pickwick, 2017), 109.

74. See the classic study, David Michael Stanley, *Christ's Resurrection in Pauline Soteriology* (Rome: Pontificio Instituto Biblico, 1961).

it really was for nothing. Well then, does God supply you with the Spirit and work miracles among you by your doing the works of the law, or by your believing what you heard? (Gal 3:2–5)

In the overall structure of the argument, justification and the gift of the Spirit are paired together:[75]

Justification	Gift of the Spirit
not from works of the law	not from works of the law
through faith in/of Christ	from hearing with faith
cf. Gal 2:16	*cf. Gal 3:2, 5*

Given these parallels, Jean Nöel Aletti writes, "If one extends the series of correspondences that exist between Gal 2:16 and 3:2, 5, one sees that justification and the Spirit are received by the same means of faith."[76]

Justification language then explicitly resurfaces in the lines that follow. Citing Genesis 15:6, Paul states, "Just as Abraham 'believed God, and *it was reckoned to him as righteousness*'" (Gal 3:6). This, we are told, prefigures the way that God would "justify the Gentiles by faith" (Gal 3:8). Many interpreters view this passage as indicating that justification involves a juridical decree that is counterfactual to moral character. The quotation from Genesis is said to reveal that Abraham's faith merely "*counts* as his righteousness."[77] This reading is unpersuasive for two reasons. First, within the narrative of Genesis, Abram departs from his homeland in obedience to a divine commandment (cf. Gen 12:1–3) and, later, moves about the promised land as directed by God (e.g., Gen 13:17–18). Hence, by the time he makes his act of "believing" God in Genesis 15, Abraham has already been walking with God for some years. In other words, prior to God's declaration in Genesis 15, Abraham *had already been faithful.* Moreover, the Greek word used in the phrase "Abraham '*believed* God'" is *pisteuō*, the verbal form of *pistis* (Gal 3:6). Like the noun, *pisteuō* signals something beyond a simple act of intellectual agreement. That Paul has this broader meaning in mind is confirmed by the fact that he goes on in the next verse

---

75. Chart slightly adapted from Aletti, *Justification by Faith in the Letters of Saint Paul*, 62.

76. Aletti, *Justification by Faith in the Letters of Saint Paul*, 62.

77. See, e.g., Thomas Schreiner, *Faith Alone—The Doctrine of Justification: What the Reformers Taught . . . and Why It Still Matters* (Grand Rapids: Zondervan, 2015), 238.

to call the patriarch *"faithful* Abraham [*tō pistō Abraam*]" (Gal 3:9 ASV, KJV).[78] As we have seen, Paul connects *pistis*—faith/faithfulness—to obedience. To think Paul believes God's declaration that Abraham was justified includes the idea that the patriarch was morally unrighteous is to ask too much of Paul's language.

Nevertheless, Hans Dieter Betz insists that Paul intends his readers to recognize that he is using the word "righteousness" in an entirely new fashion.[79] Such a reading is unconvincing. As virtually all interpreters acknowledge, Galatians addresses a particular controversy, namely, whether gentile believers should be required to undergo circumcision (cf. Gal 5:1–12). Responding to the claims of some, the apostle is showing that in fact circumcision is not necessary for justification.[80] What Paul wants to stress is that circumcision—or, for that matter, any other work done apart from the Spirit's power—is insufficient. Paul underscores the notion that the torah cannot *cause* saving righteousness: "If a law had been given *which could make alive*, then *righteousness* would indeed be by the law" (Gal 3:21 RSV). Only through Christ is righteousness possible: through the Spirit, one is able to have life in Christ. This point is worth driving home. As F. F. Bruce, drawing on E. P. Sanders, rightly notes, "*zōopoieō* is practically synonymous with *dikaioō*. To be justified by faith is to receive life (by faith); '*dikaiosynē*,' which often means the righteousness that *leads to life*, can become simply the equivalent of 'life.'"[81] To maintain, then, that Paul's point is that God declared Abraham righteous by faith because he was not actually righteous simply reads too much into the text.

Justifying faithfulness is a gift—even for Abraham.[82] All those who are justified are unworthy of the gift of justification, which comes to them as an extreme mercy. All are under the power of sin and need forgiveness in order to be restored to right relationship. Nothing one does prior to the gift could ever merit it. At the same time, the gift enables justifying faithfulness. Moreover, it even brings something more than just

---

78. See, e.g., Fitzmyer, *Romans*, 375. It is also worth noting that Paul explains that those who are justified are "sons of Abraham" because they are "men of faith [*hoi ek pisteōs*]" (Gal 3:7 RSV). See Peter Oakes, *Galatians*, Paideia (Grand Rapids: Baker Academic, 2015), 106.

79. See Hans Dieter Betz, *Galatians*, Hermeneia (Philadelphia: Fortress, 1979), 14.

80. See, e.g., Richard B. Hays, "Galatians," 1085.

81. F. F. Bruce, *The Epistle to the Galatians*, NIGTC (Grand Rapids: Eerdmans, 1982), 180; citing E. P. Sanders, *Paul and Palestinian Judaism: A Comparison of Patterns of Religion* (Minneapolis: Fortress, 1977), 503.

82. See Campbell, *Quest for Paul's Gospel*, 195–202.

true obedience. According to Paul, justification brings "life," which is a sharing in divine life through the Spirit that is ordered to immortality or "glorification."

Justification Is Inseparable from Glorification

As we have seen, Paul views justifying faith in terms of new life: "*The life I now live* in the flesh *I live by faith[fulness] in the Son of God*" (Gal 2:20; cf. 3:21). The believer's new life of faithfulness is enabled by Christ's life in believers (i.e., grace). That justification entails a real share in the life of the divine Son through the actual indwelling of the Spirit is reinforced by the way the apostle views justification as ordered to *glorification*.[83] Think here of Paul's words in Romans: "Therefore, since we are *justified by faith*, we have peace with God through our Lord Jesus Christ, through whom we have *obtained access to this grace* in which we stand; and we boast in our *hope of sharing the glory of God*" (Rom 5:1-2). What is this "glory" (*doxa*) Paul speaks of? Ben Blackwell shows that the terminology in Paul is related to immortality (Rom 1:23; 2:7; 8:21). He concludes that, for the apostle, "glory" essentially means "participation in divine life."[84]

Though the language of the "hope of sharing the glory of God" might seem to suggest that glorification is merely a future reality, this is not the apostle's understanding. As Paul affirms elsewhere in his letters, glorification occurs in the present: "We . . . are *being changed* into his likeness from one degree of glory to another [*apo doxēs eis doxan*]" (2 Cor 3:18 RSV). Why then does Paul speak of "sharing the glory of God" as "hope"? To answer this question, it is important to understand how he defines "hope." Specifically, in Romans "hope" pertains to "what we do not see" (Rom 8:25). In Romans 8, we are also told that "glory" will only be revealed at the eschaton (Rom 8:18). This would explain why he can speak of the saints as both being glorified (i.e., in the present) and also having "hope" of it (pointing to a future expectation).

That the justified are initially glorified is also implicit in Romans 3, where Paul views "falling short of the glory [*doxa*] of God" as the precise

---

83. See Dunn, *Romans*, 2:533–34, who recognizes "glory" (*doxa*) as a major leitmotif of Romans.

84. Ben C. Blackwell, "Immortal Glory and the Problem of Death in Romans 3.23," *JSNT* 32 (2010): 304.

problem solved by "justification."[85] Paul writes, "Since *all have sinned* and *fall short of the glory of God*, they are now *justified* by his grace as a gift, through the redemption that is in Christ Jesus" (Rom 3:23–24). For Paul, then, *justification is inseparable from glorification*.[86] This raises serious problems for the view that justification simply constitutes a change in legal status. Are we to think that Paul really believes the saints are justified and so share in God's glory but that this justification is also merely a change in legal status that is counterfactual to their interior moral character? This is highly improbable. Instead, Paul's language in Romans strongly suggests that justification is "not new bookkeeping."[87]

Paul immediately goes on to speak of Jesus's role as an atoning sacrifice (Rom 3:25). That Paul speaks of glory in the same breath as Christ's sacrificial role is no accident. The sanctuary was often understood as the place where God's "glory" resides. At the end of Exodus, "*the glory of the LORD filled the tabernacle*" (Exod 40:34). Similarly, when Solomon dedicates the temple, we read, "*The glory of the LORD filled the house of the LORD*" (1 Kgs 8:11). Likewise, the psalmist declares, "So I have looked upon you *in the sanctuary, beholding your power and glory*" (Ps 63:2). The point of such passages is that God's presence is found in the temple. That Paul links "glory" and temple imagery so closely in Romans 3 should thus not be dismissed as coincidental.

What are the implications of this link between glory and the sanctuary for explicating the meaning of Pauline justification? We have noted that "grace" is nothing less than the life of the divine Son in believers. In Galatians 2, this is precisely what justifying faith involves: "It is no longer I who live, but it is Christ who lives in me" (Gal 2:20). Given Paul's identification of Jesus with the Lord of the *Shemaʿ* (1 Cor 8:6), it makes sense that he associates "justification" with "glory." Those who are justified have the life of the divine Son within them by virtue of the working of God's Spirit. This is precisely why Paul will go on in other places to identify believers as God's temple (cf. 1 Cor 3:16–17; 6:19): the justified have nothing less than the divine presence—that is, divine life—within them.

This connection between justification and glorification in Paul's thought also explains why he ties justification not only to "righteousness"

---

85. See Blackwell, "Immortal Glory and the Problem of Death," 302, for the observation that the Greek term translated "falling short" (*hystereō*) probably has the sense here of "lacking."

86. See, e.g., Blackwell, "Immortal Glory and the Problem of Death," 303.

87. Frank Stagg, *Galatians—Romans* (Atlanta: John Knox, 1980), 11.

but also to "life." For instance, in Romans 5 Paul sets up a dichotomy in which "sin," "condemnation," and "death" came through Adam, and "righteousness," "justification," and "life" are attributed to the Christ-gift.

> Therefore, just as sin came into the world through one man, and *death came through sin*, and so *death* spread to all because all have sinned . . . For if the many *died* through the one man's trespass, much more surely have the grace of God and the free gift in the grace of the one man, Jesus Christ, abounded for the many. . . . For the judgment following one trespass brought *condemnation*, but *the free gift* following many trespasses brings *justification*. If, because of the one man's *trespass*, *death* exercised dominion through that one, much more surely will those who receive the abundance of *grace* and *the free gift of righteousness* exercise dominion in *life* through the one man, Jesus Christ.
>
> Therefore just as one man's trespass led to *condemnation* for all, so one man's act of *righteousness* leads to justification and *life* for all. For just as by *the one man's disobedience the many were made sinners, so by the one man's obedience the many will be made righteous.* (Rom 5:12, 15–19)

The following chart helps to illustrate Paul's logic:

"in Adam"	"in Christ"
Sin	Grace
Condemnation	Justification
Death	Life
Trespass	Righteousness

Although some interpreters insist that Romans 5:12–21 supports a merely juridical account of imputed righteousness, such an interpretation would require Adam to be considered sinful without actually *being* sinful. The realistic nature of Paul's teaching is unavoidable. Just as the sin of Adam caused those who are in him to *become* sinful, the righteous act of Christ enables those who are in him to *become* righteous. Drawing together the various texts in Romans, Thomas Stegman puts it this way:

> Jesus' obedience, which led to his "act of righteousness" (*dikaiōma*) [Rom 5:18], to his offering himself on the cross, has brought about a new possibility, namely, "righteousness leading to life" [Rom 5:21; Stegman's

translation]. Not only will those who respond with faith to the gospel be declared "righteous" (i.e., be forgiven); they will also be empowered to *become* righteous (cf. "will be made righteous" [Rom 5:19]) after the likeness of Jesus, who is the "Righteous One" (cf. 1:17; also, Isa 53:11).[88]

Likewise, Craig Keener writes:

> Paul's understanding is not that Jesus merely reverses Adam's punishment (although his accomplishment includes that), but that Jesus came to form a new basis for humanity, enabling people to serve God fully from the heart.[89]

According to Paul, Adam and those in him are *actually* sinners. Likewise, Christ is *actually* righteous. It seems difficult to maintain, then, that those in Christ are righteous in regard to their legal standing and yet not *actually* righteous in him.

That We Might "Become the Righteousness of God"

This reading finds support in Paul's treatment of righteousness in 2 Corinthians. We saw above that Paul views justification as "cardiac righteousness" in 2 Corinthians: the ministry of the "new covenant" is a "dispensation of righteousness [*dikaiosynē*]"(RSV) precisely because it is written on "tablets of human hearts" by "the Spirit" who "gives life" (2 Cor 3:9; cf. 3:3, 6). Something similar is found in Romans 5: Paul views "justification" and "righteousness" (*dikaiosynē*) in terms of "life" (Rom 5:16–17). Here justification is truly linked to *spiritual life*. This "righteousness" is directly tied to the indwelling of Christ: as Paul says, "If Christ is in you, though the body is dead because of sin, *the Spirit is life because of righteousness*" (Rom 8:10).

This should resolve the question of whether or not justification is a change in legal status with no corresponding interior moral transformation. For Paul, *justification is juridical, but the divine decree corresponds to the reality of the believer's character, which is changed by the power of grace.* Those in Christ really do "become the righteousness of God" (2 Cor 5:21).

---

88. Thomas D. Stegman, "Romans," in Chiu et al., *The Paulist Commentary*, 1255. See also Fitzmyer, *Romans*, 421.

89. Keener, *Romans*, 77.

In support of this reading, Michael Gorman points out a parallel in the preceding context:

Text	Main Clause: Death of Christ Narrated	Purpose: Conjunction	Purpose Clause: Goal of Christ's Death Indicated
2 Cor 5:15	"And he died"	"so that" (*hina*)	"those who live might live [*zōsin*] no longer for themselves, but for him who died and was raised for them"
2 Cor 5:21	"For our sake he [God] made him to be sin who knew no sin"	"so that" (*hina*)	"in him we might become [*genōmetha*] the righteousness of God"[90]

As Christ died "so that" believers can truly have resurrection life, Christ becomes (a) sin (offering) "so that" believers can become righteous. Gorman therefore argues, "It would be textually inappropriate to interpret 2 Cor 5:21 as anything less than reference to new life in Christ."[91] This is further reinforced by what we saw in the last chapter: Christ's self-giving on the cross is ordered to enabling believers to be transformed into life-giving lovers themselves.

In sum, Pauline justification pertains both to Christ and to the Spirit: it is therefore both christological and pneumatological. In a passage we shall have more to say about below, we read, "You were washed, you were sanctified, you were justified in the name of the Lord Jesus Christ [*christos*] and in the Spirit [*pneuma*] of our God" (1 Cor 6:11). Some may wish to isolate these concepts from one another,[92] but such is not Paul's way of thinking. As Thomas Schreiner insists, one is not *first* justified and *later* sanctified: "It would be a mistake to conceive of 'sanctification' (*hagiasmos*) as subsequent to righteousness in this verse, as if Paul were attempting to chart out

90. Chart adapted from Michael Gorman, "Paul's Corporate, Cruciform, Missional *Theosis* in 2 Corinthians," in *"In Christ" in Paul: Explorations in Paul's Theology of Union and Participation*, ed. Michael J. Thate, Kevin J. Vanhoozer, and Constantine R. Campbell, WUNT 2/384 (Tübingen: Mohr Siebeck, 2014), 196.

91. Gorman, "Paul's Corporate, Cruciform, Missional *Theosis* in 2 Corinthians," in Thate, Vanhoozer, and Campbell, *"In Christ" in Paul*, 196.

92. See, e.g., K. P. Donfried, "Justification and Last Judgment in Paul," *ZNW* 67 (1976): 90–110.

the order in which these saving acts occurred."[93] Later he writes, "Sanctification and justification are all gifts given at conversion."[94] We affirm this. *But if this is the case, why must we insist that when God declares the believer "justified" this involves acknowledgement of legal standing that does not concur with the character of the believer?* Additionally, one might ask, *If righteousness is imputed here, then why is that not also true of holiness?*

Justification as Conformity to the Character of the Divine Son

As we have seen, the new life associated with justification is nothing less than life in Christ effected by the Spirit. Since Christ is the divine Son, Paul describes the "Spirit of Christ" not only as the "Spirit of God" but also as the "spirit of sonship" (RSV) or "the spirit of adoption" (NRSV):

> For *all who are led by the Spirit of God are children of God*. For you did not receive a spirit of slavery to fall back into fear, but you have received *a spirit of adoption*. When we cry, "Abba! Father!" *it is that very Spirit bearing witness with our spirit that we are children of God.* (Rom 8:14–16)

> But when the fullness of time had come, *God sent his Son*, born of a woman, born under the law, in order to redeem those who were under the law, so that we might receive *adoption as children*. And *because you are children*, God has sent *the Spirit of his Son* into our hearts, crying, "Abba! Father!" So you are no longer a slave but *a child*, and *if a child then also an heir*, through God. (Gal 4:4–7)

What is especially notable here is the way Paul identifies adoption as the ultimate *purpose* of the coming of the divine Son: "God sent his Son . . . so that we might receive adoption as children [*huiothesian*]" (Gal 4:4–5).[95] In other words, justification is connected to a real participation through

93. Schreiner, *Paul, Apostle of God's Glory in Christ*, 220–21.

94. Schreiner, *Paul, Apostle of God's Glory in Christ*, 220–21.

95. A similar idea might be contained in Rom 8:23, although here there is a textual issue: the authenticity of "adoption" is disputed. For arguments against its inclusion, see Fitzmyer, *Romans*, 510–11; Pierre Benoit, "'We Too Groan Inwardly . . .' (Romans 8:23)," in *Jesus and the Gospel*, 2 vols. (London: Darton, 1974), 2:40–50; for arguments in favor, see Bruce M. Metzger, *A Textual Commentary on the Greek New Testament* (London: UBS, 1975), 457; Jewett, *Romans*, 505.

the "spirit of adoption" or, more literally, the "spirit of sonship" (*pneuma huiothesias*) in Christ (Rom 8:15).

Nowhere is this teaching about believers' participation through the Spirit in the divine sonship of Christ given more emphasis than in Romans 8. We have already looked at how Paul links justification to glorification. In Romans 8:28–30, however, we see that this is only one aspect of God's overarching design for salvation:

> We know that all things work together for good for those who love God, who are called according to his purpose. For those whom he foreknew he also predestined *to be conformed to the image of his Son, in order that he might be the firstborn among many brethren.* And those whom he predestined he also called; and those whom he called he also justified; and those whom he justified he also glorified. (Rom 8:28–30 NRSV, slightly adapted)

For Paul, the goal of the Christ-event is familial; the divine Son became flesh so that he might become the "firstborn" of "many brethren" (Rom 8:29).[96] Paul holds that adoptive divine sonship involves a juridical dimension, namely, the legal decree of justification. Yet—and this is of vital importance—this entails being "conformed to the image of his Son [*symmorphous tēs eikonos tou huiou autou*]" (Rom 8:29). The structure of Paul's statement bears this out:

Justification = Being Conformed to Christ's Image

8:29a	A	*[God] predestined*
8:29b	B	To be conformed to the image of his Son . . .
8:30a	A′	*[God] predestined*
8:30b	B′	He also called . . . justified . . . glorified

Here Paul reveals what it means to be "conformed to the image of [God's] Son": it means to be "called," "justified [*edikaiōsen*]," and "glorified [*edoxasen*]" (Rom 8:30). Those in Christ are glorified, because without it they would not be fully "conformed to the image of his Son," who is nothing less than "the Lord of glory" (1 Cor 2:8). Justification is inseparable from glorification because the justified are to be conformed to the image of the "Lord of glory."

---

96. See Campbell, *Quest for Paul's Gospel*, 83.

For Paul, glorification is truly *theōsis* ("divinization"). Believers are "glorified" because they are "in Christ."[97] Paul tells the Corinthians, "God is faithful; by him you were *called* [*eklēthēte*] into the *communion* [*koinōnian*] *of his Son*, Jesus Christ our Lord" (1 Cor 1:9 NRSV, slightly adapted). For this reason, Ben Blackwell characterizes the apostle's teaching aptly with the term *Christōsis*, which underscores the way Pauline *theōsis* occurs through the divine Son.[98] Romans 8:29–30 reveals that such *Christōsis* includes justification. Here we are in position to see that this includes being conformed to Christ himself. It is hard to believe that Paul holds that this does not include being conformed to Christ's character. As we noted above, in antiquity the language of righteousness refers to one's moral disposition. The same is true for Paul, something that is underscored by the notion of cardiac righteousness that comes through the obedience of faith. To apply this to the passage at hand, Romans 8:29–30, when Paul states that justification includes conformity to the image of Christ, this specifically means conformity to Christ's character. This suggestion aligns well with Paul's teaching elsewhere, for he tells believers to "be clothed [*endysasthe*] with our Lord Jesus Christ" (Rom 13:14; cf. Gal 3:27).[99] The metaphor of being clothed with another person was used by ancient writers to signify putting on the person's character.[100] Anthanasios Despotis therefore correctly observes that "putting on Christ and putting on the new human being 'are semantically equivalent' for both concepts refer to unification and conformity to the resurrected Christ."[101]

Thus, for Paul, the saints are "justified by faithfulness": they are conformed to the image of the one who is faithful par excellence and, sharing in his life, they actually become like him.[102] As E. P. Sanders writes:

---

97. See Schweitzer, *The Mysticism of Paul*, 3–5.

98. See Ben C. Blackwell, *Christosis*, WUNT 2/314 (Tübingen: Mohr Siebeck, 2011).

99. Authors' translation.

100. Michael B. Thompson, *Clothed with Christ: The Example and Teaching of Jesus in Romans 12:1–15:13* (Sheffield: JSOT Press, 1991); Jung Hoon Kim, *The Significance of Clothing Imagery in the Pauline Corpus*, LNTS (London: T&T Clark, 2004).

101. Athanasios Despotis, "*Ho gar apothanōn dedikaiōtai apo tēs hamartias*: Rethinking the Application of the Verb *dikaiousthai* in Baptismal Contexts from the Perspective of Rom 6:7," in *Participation, Justification, and Conversion: Eastern Orthodox Interpretation of Paul and the Debate between "Old and New Perspectives on Paul,"* ed. Athanasios Despotis, WUNT 2/442 (Tübingen: Mohr Siebeck, 2017), 41–42 [29–57].

102. See Stegman, "Paul's Use of *dikaio*- Terminology," 520.

Fictional or *imputed righteousness* . . . is a bulwark of Protestant exegesis of Paul. Thus in this interpretation . . . *nothing happens to the person*; rather, he or she is simply declared innocent, not guilty, even though he or she continues to perform acts that make one guilty. Paul thought Christians were *changed*. . . . It would be closer to Paul's meaning to translate the passive phrase "to be righteoused by faith" as "faith in Christ" *makes a person righteous*.[103]

Faithfulness, then, necessarily means conformity to Christ, the one who is "faithful." The question, then, is how does this happen? With this we come to the third and final section of this chapter.

You Were Washed, You Were Justified

Many contemporary Christians speak of salvation in terms of a singular event (i.e., I "got saved"). In Paul's teaching, however, it is more complex than this. Salvation is described not only as a past event (e.g., Rom 8:24: "we were saved [*esōthēmen*]") but also as both present (e.g., 1 Cor 1:18: "us who are being saved [*sōzomenois*]") and future (e.g., 1 Cor 3:15: "[the believer] will be saved [*sōthēsetai*]"). Something analogous is found in his teaching about justification. As we saw at the beginning of this chapter, Paul speaks of justification as a future event in 1 Corinthians 4:4–5. Here, then, we shall discuss what specialists have called "initial" justification.[104] Specifically, it is important to point out the way that Paul links this dimension of justification to baptism.[105] As we shall see, the past, present, and future "salvation" passages in Paul refer not to different realities but to one.

---

103. Sanders, *Paul: The Apostle's Life, Letters, and Thought*, 506 (emphasis original). As noted above, adherences to the traditional Protestant view of imputation readily admit that the justified are transformed, a fact Sanders fails to acknowledge. That being said, we concur with Sanders that transformation is constitutive of justification itself.

104. See, e.g., Dunn, *New Perspective*, 75; Martyn, *Galatians*, 272 ("rectification"); Wright, *Paul and the Faithfulness of God*, 2:960, 1030–32.

105. Our treatment here is greatly indebted to Isaac Augustine Morales, OP, "Baptism and Union with Christ," in Thate, Vanhoozer, and Campbell, *"In Christ" in Paul*, 157–77.

Baptism and Justification

Paul himself ties justification to baptism. This is evident, for example, in 1 Corinthians:

> You were *washed*, you were *sanctified*, you were *justified* in the name of the Lord Jesus Christ and in the Spirit of our God. (1 Cor 6:11)

In this verse, Paul makes a direct connection between being "washed [*apolouō*]" and being "justified [*dikaioō*]" (1 Cor 6:11). Some commentators dispute a baptismal reading, insisting that the language is simply intended as a metaphor rather than an allusion to ritual immersion.[106] This is unlikely.[107] First, not only does the New Testament indicate that baptism was widely practiced in the early church,[108] we know that the ritual had an important place in the communal life at Corinth. Its significance was apparently so well established that it became the basis of quarrels that Paul felt forced to address at the very outset of this epistle (cf. 1 Cor 1:11–17). Second, the language of 1 Corinthians 6:11 uses terminology employed in other Pauline texts where baptism is in view. Believers are said to be "washed . . . *in the name* of the Lord Jesus Christ," language which evokes the baptism controversy Paul addresses in 1 Corinthians 1, which specifically swirls around the "name" into which believers have been "baptized" (1 Cor 1:13–14). In addition, the washing described in 1 Corinthians 6:11 is also associated with the "Spirit," who is identified with baptism later in the same epistle: "For in the one *Spirit* we were all *baptized* into one body" (1 Cor 12:13). As other interpreters recognize, 1 Corinthians 6 even goes on to use the language of "members" (1 Cor 6:15), anticipating the discussion of Christians as "members" of Christ's body later in the letter (cf. 1 Cor 12:14–27). Given these connections to baptismal passages, to insist that the language of washing involves a mere metaphor seems like special pleading. Finally, physical baptism is linked to spiritual washing in other texts (cf. Acts 22:16; Eph 5:26; Titus 3:5; Heb 10:22). First Corinthians 6 is thus best read as an early Pauline expression of this theology.

---

106. See, e.g., Gordon Fee, *The First Epistle to the Corinthians*, NICNT (Grand Rapids: Eerdmans, 1987), 245–47; Campbell, *Paul and Union with Christ*, 336.

107. See Fitzmyer, *First Corinthians*, 258.

108. Morales, "Baptism and Union with Christ," 164–65n22, citing Acts 2:38, 41; 8:12–13, 16, 36, 38; 9:18; 10:47–48; 16:15, 33; 18:8; 19:3–5; 22:16.

Paul also talks about baptism in other places where justification is in view. Above we noted Paul's teaching that "whoever has died is *justified* [*dedikaiōtai*] from sin" (Rom 6:7 NRSV, slightly adapted). What we did not mention is the way that this "justifying death" appears related to baptism:

> What then are we to say? Should we continue in sin in order that grace may abound? By no means! How can we who died to sin go on living in it? Do you not know that all of us who have been *baptized into Christ Jesus were baptized into his death*? Therefore we have been buried with him *by baptism into death*, so that, just as Christ was raised from the dead by the glory of the Father, so we too might walk in newness of life.
>
> For if we have been *united with him in a death like his*, we will certainly be united with him in a resurrection like his. We know that *our old self was crucified with him* so that the body of sin might be destroyed, and we might no longer be enslaved to sin. *For whoever has died is justified from sin.* (Rom 6:1–7 NRSV, slightly adapted)

This is an extremely significant passage, for it shows that baptism not only causes one to be "in Christ" but that Paul also views the sacrament in terms of co-crucifixion and justification. For Paul, baptism justifies because it is a real participation in the crucifixion, death, burial, and resurrection of Christ.[109]

Of course, in speaking of co-crucifixion one cannot also help but think of Galatians 2, which has numerous points of contact with Romans 6.[110] Due to the similarities, many have read the apostle's teaching in Galatians 2 as relating to baptism.[111] There are differences in focus. While Galatians 2 connects co-crucifixion imagery to justifying faith, Romans 6 ties it specifically to baptism. Nevertheless, as Michael Gorman explains, one should not infer that baptism is a mere "supplement" to faith or that Paul holds that faith and baptism can serve as alternatives to one another.

> Rather, it shows that for Paul faith and baptism are theologically coterminous, and faith is the essence of baptism even as baptism is the

109. Käsemann, *Romans*, 96.
110. Gorman, *Inhabiting the Cruciform God*, 76–79.
111. See Morales, "Baptism and Union with Christ," 171n43, for references.

public expression of faith. Thus what Paul predicates of faith he can also predicate of baptism, and vice versa, because together they effect . . . transfer into Christ and thus participatory justification in him.[112]

Lars Hartman therefore rightly concludes that "no tension or contradiction" exists between faith and baptism for Paul.[113]

Baptism, Justification, and Divine Sonship in Christ

The relationship between justifying faith(fulness) and baptism is also evident in Galatians 3:

> Now before faith came, we were imprisoned and guarded under the law until faith would be revealed. Therefore the law was our disciplinarian until Christ came, so that we might be *justified by faith*. But now that faith has come, we are no longer subject to a disciplinarian, for *in Christ Jesus you are all children of God through faith*. As many of you *as were baptized into Christ have clothed yourselves with Christ*. There is no longer Jew or Greek, there is no longer slave or free, there is no longer male and female; *for all of you are one in Christ Jesus*. And if you belong to Christ, then you are Abraham's offspring, *heirs* according to the promise. (Gal 3:23–29 NRSV, slightly adapted)

We have already cited this passage above to show that Paul identifies the coming of Christ with the arrival of faith(fulness). To this we can now add another observation: the apostle moves directly from talking about being "justified [*dikaiōthōmen*] by faith(fulness)" to being "baptized [*ebaptisthēte*] into Christ" (Gal 3:24, 27). The logic suggests that those who have been "clothed" with Christ and who are "children of God through faith[fulness]" are precisely those who have been baptized into Christ.[114]

As Isaac Morales argues, this connection between faith and baptism should not be overlooked. Here we find an aspect of Paul's thought often

---

112. Gorman, *Inhabiting the Cruciform God*, 79.

113. Lars Hartman, "Baptism," *ABD* 1:587.

114. See Morales, "Baptism and Union with Christ," 174n53, for further arguments in favor of the baptismal interpretation.

underdeveloped by Pauline specialists.[115] For example, in his classic study of Paul, Albert Schweitzer writes:

> The sacramental is therefore non-rational. The act and its effect are not bound together by religious logic, but laid one upon the other and nailed together. With that is connected the fact that in Paul we find the most prosaic conception imaginable of the *opus operatum*.[116]

Yet nothing suggests that "baptism" was "non-rational" or "magical" for Paul. Instead, baptism itself is always understood as a faith event. Hence, justifying faith and baptism should not be separated. James Prothro makes the following astute observation:

> In every undisputed letter in which *dikaioō* ["to justify"] occurs, it occurs in proximity to baptismal traditions (1 Cor 6:11; Gal 3:24, 27; Rom 6:3–4, 7). This connection extends beyond Paul's Law-polemic, which is not prominent in 1 Cor and is certainly not the impetus for his justification-talk there. Especially given that in these letters Paul assumes his audiences have been baptized, it is unsurprising if Paul assumed they would have been familiar with his vocabulary.[117]

To be justified is to be conformed to the image of the Son. For Paul, justification and conformity to Christ begin at baptism.

Finally, it is worth adding that by connecting justification to baptism, it becomes even clearer that it is not construed in "individualistic" terms. Paul connects faith to baptism, through which one is united not only to Christ but to all believers. The apostle insists that all are "baptized into one body" (1 Cor 12:13). As Thomas Söding observes, "For Paul, 'faith' in itself is not only personal but *ecclesial*: 'We believe' (Gal 2:16) and 'I' believe (cf. Gal 2:19–20)."[118]

---

115. See, e.g., Richard B. Hays, "What Is 'Real Participation in Christ'?," in Udoh, *Redefining First-Century Jewish and Christian Identities*, 343–45, pointing out the dearth of references to sacraments in Sanders, *Paul and Palestinian Judaism*.

116. Albert Schweitzer, *Paul and His Interpreters: A Critical History*, trans. W. Montgomery (1912; repr., Eugene, OR: Wipf & Stock, 2004), 213.

117. Prothro, "The Strange Case of Δικαιόω in the Septuagint and in Paul," 67.

118. Thomas Söding, "Justification and Participation," in *Galatians and Christian Theology: Justification, the Gospel, and Ethics in Paul's Letter*, ed. Mark W. Elliot, Scott J. Hafemann, N. T. Wright, and John Frederick (Grand Rapids: Baker Academic, 2014), 69–70.

This ecclesial dimension of justifying faith would also seem to be implied in the relationship between Paul's "righteousness" language (*dik*-terms) and his references to the concept of the "covenant." Within the context of Israel's scriptures, "righteousness" (Heb. *tsedeq*) is closely connected to the idea of right relationship, often seen in covenantal terms.[119] Scholars such as N. T. Wright have therefore argued that Paul's doctrine of justification is informed by the dynamics of covenant relations—specifically, their forensic (i.e., "legal") aspect.[120]

Without necessarily agreeing with Wright's particular take on how this should be understood, we concur that it seems unlikely that the juridical dimension of justification for Paul was unrelated to the matrix of the covenant. Paul's teaching about justification is indeed closely bound up with covenantal imagery in 2 Corinthians 3. Returning to the passage with which we began our analysis in this chapter, let us point out that the apostle explicitly identifies the "new covenant [*kainēs diathēkēs*]" with the "ministry of righteousness [*hē diakonia tēs dikaiosynēs*]" (2 Cor 3:6, 9).[121] Paul's self-identification as one of the "ministers of the new covenant" is thus hardly irrelevant to justification.

Moreover, covenants were typically seen—particularly in the biblical literature—as establishing kinship bonds.[122] The logic of the covenant is thus inexorably *familial*. If the covenant informs Paul's doctrine of justi-

---

119. See, e.g., Schreiner, *Faith Alone*, 148.

120. See Wright, *Paul and the Faithfulness of God*, 2:795–804; 925–66; 1026–32. Others have also written compelling accounts of the covenantal dimension of Paul's doctrine of justification. See, e.g., Gorman, *Inhabiting the Cruciform God*, 40–104; Bird, *Saving Righteousness*, 113–54.

121. For a thoughtful overview and critique of Wright on this point, see Prothro, *Both Judge and Justifier*, 14–19, 142–45. Although we have learned much from Wright, it remains unclear whether his view on this particular topic is not just a more "participatory" expression of old perspective forensics in which imputation is replaced by covenant membership. For an incisive critique, see Gregory Tatum, "Law and Covenant in *Paul and the Faithfulness of God*," in Heilig, Hewitt, and Bird, *God and the Faithfulness of Paul*, 311–27. See also the more conciliatory yet still critical response to Wright in Stegman, "Paul's Use of *dikaio*-Terminology," 496–524. Indeed, the covenantal dimension can easily be joined to a reading that recognizes justification also relates to moral character. In fact, Wright himself provides the very key for such a reading—namely, to view Paul's faith language as directly connected to faithfulness and as ordered to the final judgment according to works.

122. Frank Moore Cross, "Kinship and Covenant in Ancient Israel," in *From Epic to Canon: History and Literature in Ancient Israel* (Baltimore: Johns Hopkins University Press, 1998), 3–21. See the fuller treatment tracing out the implications for biblical theology in Hahn, *Kinship by Covenant*.

fication, the judge in view can be no anonymous tribunal. This is what he affirms elsewhere: the "justifier" is not simply "God" but "Father." Justification is found in God's Son—indeed, by being "in" the divine Son. This would suggest that Paul's teaching regarding justification cannot be simply reduced to legal "acquittal." In the words of Michael Gorman:

> For Paul, then, justification is not merely or even primarily juridical or judicial—the image of a divine judge pronouncing pardon or acquittal. That is part, but only part, of the significance of justification. The judicial image must be understood within a wider covenantal, relational, participatory, and transformative framework.[123]

To build on Gorman's analysis, those who are justified belong to God's covenant people—that is, the family of God. As Gorman writes, justification "is not a private act of reconciliation but one both intended by God and experienced by people in community, as a people." Going on, he observes that it is for this reason that when Paul speaks of justification in Romans 5, for example, "the subject of the verbs . . . is 'we,' not 'I.'"[124] With this we have come full circle, for those who are members of the new covenant people of God are justified—that is, they have the cardiac righteousness that comes with the grace of the new covenant, a graced righteousness that brings about conformity to the divine Son and is ordered to being declared "righteous" at the final judgment, when God will judge the hearts of all.

In Summary: The Righteousness of Divine Sonship

Paul's outlook as a new covenant Jew anticipated the fulfillment of Jeremiah's promise: God would one day solve the problem of sin, "unrighteousness [*adikia*]" (Jer 31:34). It is no wonder, then, that Paul's teaching prominently features the notion of God's action to "justify" (*dikaioō*) sinners. What does this mean for Paul? Our analysis of the new covenant nature of Pauline justification follows Paul in Romans 8:29–30 and argues that justification comes through an ontologically real divine sonship that involves three key realities: *cardiac righteousness, baptismal initiation, and conformity to Christ.*

---

123. See Gorman, *Inhabiting the Cruciform God*, 56.
124. Gorman, *Inhabiting the Cruciform God*, 55.

First, Pauline justification is defined by the *cardiac* righteousness of the new covenant, such that one could say that justification is by the cardiac righteousness of faith (2 Cor 3:9; Rom 10:10). This reading is confirmed by both the nature of Pauline faith including fidelity or obedience (Rom 1:5; 3:31; 14:23; Gal 3:23–25; 5:6; 1 Thess 1:3) and the nature of the final judgment itself. It is hard to overstate the importance of the final judgment in rightly accounting for Pauline justification; Paul holds that God will judge all according to the (new covenant) works of faith that reveal the "heart" (Rom 2:5–16; 1 Cor 4:5; 2 Cor 5:9–10). This indicates that Paul's understanding of justification in general and his manner of employing the verb "to justify" (*dikaioō*) in particular is *realistic and not counterfactual*. Paul's description of the final judgment itself shows that justification must include the cardiac righteousness requisite to be just at the eschaton.

As we noted, many exegetes conclude that Pauline justification must involve nothing more than a change in legal standing.[125] For example, Thomas Schreiner insists that the meaning of justification is constrained due to the nature of juridical authority. He points out that judges "do not 'make' a person righteous" but can only "pronounce what is in fact the case." Yet Schreiner goes on to argue that in pronouncing a decree that is counterfactual to moral character, God transcends the bounds of normal juridical authority: God's "verdict violates the normal and just procedure for a judge. . . . Judges who declare the guilty to be righteous violate the standards of justice."[126]

Paul does teach that the divine judge has a power that transcends that which is given to human judges. Nevertheless, it is also possible to argue that Paul holds that God does this in a way that does not violate justice or contradict reality. We affirm with Schreiner that God's juridical power transcends that of human judges, but we understand this in a different way. Rather than arguing that God's legal decree violates "the standards of justice," we argue that God's juridical power transcends that of human judges because through the Christ-gift he *remakes* the wicked. God's declaration can thus be seen as in accord with the reality he speaks of (cf. Isa 55:10–11).[127] When God says, "Let there be light," there is light (Gen 1:3). Likewise, in the "new creation," when God pronounces the sinner "jus-

---

125. Thomas R. Schreiner, *Galatians*, ZECNT (Grand Rapids: Zondervan, 2010), 156.

126. Schreiner, *Galatians*, 156.

127. John Henry Newman, *Lectures on the Doctrine of Justification*, 3rd ed. (New York: Longmans, Green, and Co., 1990), 81–82.

tified," he is righteous and a "new creation." In a similar way, the decree of justification could be seen as *both* forensic *and* transformative of moral character.[128] The heart is truly changed and man is thus truly "justified"— that is, he *is* righteous.

Second, this cardiac righteousness is actualized through *baptismal initiation* (Rom 6:1–11; 1 Cor 6:11; Gal 3:24–27). Nevertheless, as the close connection between baptism and justification helps to show, Pauline justification is defined by more than cardiac righteousness. It also includes a third dimension—namely, being *conformed* to the character of Christ himself. As we have highlighted above, Paul connects justification to dying and rising with Christ such that Gorman is right to suggest that justification is by co-crucifixion (Gal 2:15–21; Phil 3:7–12; cf. Rom 6:1–11). We have further argued that Paul offers in Romans 8:29–30 what is (likely) his most comprehensive account of justification, connecting together predestination, divine sonship, and justification. In short, Paul asserts that adoptive divine sonship is ordered to conformity to Christ himself, which Paul further clarifies as including justification. As a result, we have argued that justification is defined by conformity to Christ and, in particular, to conformity to the character of Christ.

By virtue of being united to the divine Son, the believer shares in new life—that is, the divine life—and is transformed by it. This union with Christ entails nothing less than being conformed to the image of God's Son (Rom 8:29), such that the believer is now empowered to live a life of *pistis*, faithfulness. Those in Christ are so truly united to him that they share in the Lord Jesus's own divine sonship, becoming adopted children of God in him, living in union with him and in conformity to his character. They do not simply *imitate* him but *participate* in his sonship. As Morna Hooker, drawing on the ancient language of Irenaeus, puts it, "Christ became as we

---

128. Interpreters sometimes make a crucial error in this regard. The consensus that *dikaioō* ("to justify") has a strong juridical dimension is sometimes said to necessarily rule out a realistic or factitive (causal) dimension to Paul's use of the term. For instance, Michael Horton makes this precise mistake when he argues against the Catholic view. See Michael S. Horton, "Traditional Reformed Response to the Roman Catholic View," in *Justification: Five Views*, ed. James K. Beilby and Paul R. Eddy (Downers Grove, IL: IVP Academic, 2011), 293. Instead, scholars across a wide theological spectrum, including a number of Protestant scholars, take *dikaioō* to signify the creation or confirmation of the righteousness that comes through faith. See, e.g., Barclay, *Paul and the Gift*, 476; David A. deSilva, *Galatians: A Handbook on the Greek Text* (Waco, TX: Baylor University Press, 2014), 42, 105; de Boer, *Galatians*, 34–35; Dunn, *The Theology of Paul the Apostle*, 344; Fitzmyer, *Romans*, 347.

are so we might become as he is."[129] Or as Michael Gorman states, "To become the righteousness/justice of God is to be transformed into the image of God, which is to become *like* Christ by being *in* Christ."[130] This begins at baptism but requires maturation, which receives its fullest expression at the end of time, when believers are justified by works—that is, the works they have been transformed to perform with and in Christ.

129. See Hooker, *From Adam to Christ*, 113; based on Irenaeus, *Against Heresies* 5.Pr.1.
130. Gorman, *Becoming the Gospel*, 32.

CHAPTER 6

The Lord's Supper and the New Creation

As the divine action in Creation and Resurrection is directed towards us as "body," so, too, is the sacramental action. . . . It is by means of our actually eating the broken bread and drinking from the cup of blessing that he makes us partakers in his crucified body and of the new [covenant] founded on his blood.

—Ernst Käsemann[1]

That Jesus' words and gestures [at the Last Supper] were symbolic is clear; but the question is whether the symbolism excludes all realism or whether they might be both symbolic and realistic.

—Joseph Fitzmyer[2]

In the previous chapter we explained that Paul teaches that the new covenant means that those who were ungodly become not only "righteous" but also sharers in Christ's divine sonship. Nevertheless, the apostle's teaching about salvation involves more than simply an individualistic account. For Paul, salvation has a particularly ecclesial shape. The controversy over justification has often contributed to the neglect of this ecclesial dimension of Pauline soteriology. According to the apostle, believers are not saved in an atomistic manner. Rather, they are united to one another in the church, the body of Christ. In 1 Corinthians we are told, "For just as the body is one and has many members, and all the members of the body, though many, are one body, so it is with Christ. For *in the one Spirit we were all baptized into one body*" (1 Cor 12:12–13).

---

1. Ernst Käsemann, *Essays on New Testament Themes*, trans. W. J. Montague (1960; repr., Philadelphia: Fortress, 1982), 135.
2. Fitzmyer, *First Corinthians*, 438.

But God's saving plan includes even more than that. Christ's work of redemption involves more than reconciling humans. According to Paul, there is a genuinely cosmic dimension to the plan of salvation realized by Christ's work. The apostle affirms the goodness of creation, which points to the Creator (Rom 1:20). The material world will also somehow share in Christ's work of redemption. In Romans 8, creation itself "waits with eager longing for the revealing of the sons of God" (Rom 8:19 RSV). Believers, therefore, entertain a hope that is truly all-encompassing of everything God has made. He tells the Corinthians, "For all things are yours, whether Paul or Apollos or Cephas or the world or life or death or the present or the future, all are yours; and you are Christ's; and Christ is God's" (1 Cor 3:21–23 RSV). At the end of time, all things will be subjected to the reign of Christ "so that God may be all in all [*hina ē ho theos panta en pasin*]" (1 Cor 15:28). Yet, as we noted briefly above and will more fully explain below, Romans 8 also indicates that the dawning of this new creation is explicitly tied to the suffering not only of Christ but of believers as well, who endure affliction not merely as individuals but together as the children of God.

In this chapter, we will explore how the ecclesial and cosmic features of Paul's view of salvation can be seen as operative in another aspect of his teaching that is also frequently given short shrift in treatments of his thought: the Lord's Supper. As we shall see, in Paul's teaching about the "cup of blessing" and "the bread" (1 Cor 10:16) we discover how both the church as body and the material world itself *participates* in Christ's work of redemption.

A Resurrection Like His

Before we can put Paul's teaching on the Lord's Supper in its proper eschatological context, it is important first to say a few words about how Paul understands the resurrection of the body and the coming of the new creation. As we will see by the end of this chapter, a firm grasp of Paul's concept of the resurrected body will play a crucial role in properly interpreting his statements about the "body" of Christ in the "Lord's Supper" (1 Cor 10:16; 11:20).

The Resurrection and the "Body" of Christ

We have already seen that Paul teaches that salvation entails being conformed to the image of God's Son, and that this involves suffering in union with him. Yet the apostle also insists that conformity to Christ also entails sharing in his resurrection:

> If we have been united with him in a death like his, we will certainly be united with him in a resurrection like his. (Rom 6:5)

In 1 Corinthians 15, Paul provides further details about what this means. There the resurrected body is identified as a "spiritual body [*sōma pneumatikon*]" (1 Cor 15:44). What does Paul mean by this expression? Is the resurrection merely a metaphor? Not in the least. While modern readers often conflate "spiritual" with "metaphorical," such tendencies fail to account for the realism of Paul's language.[3] For him the resurrection is an actual future event.

This is not to suggest that the concept of the resurrection of the dead was not controversial. First Corinthians 15 indicates that the epistle's original readers harbored doubts about it. Underscoring the realism of his teaching on the subject, Paul addresses two questions in 1 Corinthians 15:35: (1) How are the dead raised? and (2) With what kind of body do they come? The first question addresses the issue of agency—that is, what will *cause* the resurrection of the body? The answer, according to Paul, is divine power. Paul later writes, "Flesh and blood cannot inherit the kingdom of God" (1 Cor 15:50). This should not be taken as suggesting that the kingdom of God excludes a bodily dimension since, in context, Paul is affirming the very notion of the resurrection of the *body*. Rather, the apostle's point seems to be that the mortal body cannot be raised on its own power; some sort of transformation is necessary.[4] Elsewhere Paul makes clear that the resurrection is the work of the Spirit, who will enable mortal bodies to share in the work of Christ: "If the Spirit of him who raised Jesus from the dead dwells in you, he who raised Christ from the dead will give life to your mortal bodies [*thnēta sōmata*] also through his Spirit that dwells in you" (Rom 8:11).

---

3. Stanley K. Stowers, "What Is 'Pauline Participation in Christ'?," in Udoh, *Redefining First-Century Jewish and Christian Identities*, 354–57.

4. Fitzmyer, *First Corinthians*, 603; Raymond Collins, *First Corinthians*, SP 7 (Collegeville, MN: Liturgical Press, 1999), 573–80.

With this in mind, we turn to the second question Paul answers—namely, what will the resurrected body be like? Though some have attempted to argue that the resurrected body is a "spiritual body [*sōma pneumatikon*]" (1 Cor 15:44) in the sense of being composed of "spirit-stuff" (i.e., a body lacking "flesh" or anything earthly),[5] such proposals ignore certain nuances of Paul's discussion.[6] For one thing, Paul contrasts the "spiritual body" of the resurrection with the "soulish body" (*sōma psychikon*) of the present age (cf. 1 Cor 15:44). That said, it is evident that Paul does not think that the pre-resurrection body is merely composed of "soul-stuff."[7] Richard Hays thus correctly explains Paul's thinking in the following terms: "Our mortal bodies embody the *psychē* ('soul'), the animating force of our present existence, but the resurrection body will embody the divinely given *pneuma* ('spirit')."[8] For Paul, then, the resurrected body is a "spiritual body" not because it is a "metaphorical" body but rather because it is animated by the Spirit. In support of this point, Paul goes on to indicate that believers will be "changed [*allagēsometha*]" (1 Cor 15:51, 52). He is not claiming that the resurrection body will be entirely discontinuous with the present body; instead, it will be transformed. As he says in Philippians, Christ "will change [*metaschēmatisei*] our lowly body to be like his glorious body, by the power which enables him even to subject all things to himself" (Phil 3:21 RSV). In other words, the body that dies is raised—that is, what is "sown" is also in some sense "raised" (cf. 1 Cor 15:36–37, 44). This body is "changed" inasmuch as it is given supernatural qualities by the Spirit's power.[9]

The New Adam and the New Creation

As the passage from Philippians 3 quoted above also makes clear, the source of transformation is union with Christ, the new Adam.

5. E.g., Dale B. Martin, *The Corinthian Body* (New Haven: Yale University Press, 1995), 129.

6. See Volker Rabens, *The Holy Spirit and Ethics in Paul: Transformation and Empowering for Religious-Ethical Life*, 2nd ed. (Minneapolis: Fortress, 2010), 86–96; Peter Orr, *Christ Absent and Present*, WUNT 2/354 (Tübingen: Mohr Siebeck, 2014), 67–86.

7. See Rabens, *Holy Spirit and Ethics in Paul*, 95n67.

8. Richard B. Hays, *First Corinthians*, Interpretation (Louisville: John Knox, 1997), 272.

9. Rabens, *Holy Spirit and Ethics in Paul*, 96.

> Thus it is written, "The first man, Adam, became a living being"; the
> last Adam became a life-giving *spirit* [*pneuma*]. . . . The first man was
> from the earth, a man of dust; the second man is from heaven. As was
> the man of dust, so are those who are of the dust; and as is the man of
> heaven, so are those who are of heaven. Just as we have borne the image
> of the man of dust, we will also bear the image of the man of heaven.
> (1 Cor 15:45, 47–49)

In short: just as Christ was glorified, those who belong to him will also be
glorified. The resurrected body is a "spiritual body" because of the "life-
giving spirit [*pneuma*]" identified with Christ. As Joseph Fitzmyer explains,
"Christ belongs to the realm of *pneuma* ["spirit"], to which the adj[ective]
pneumatikos is related."[10]

While the apostle certainly affirms that the resurrection will involve
the individual bodies of believers (cf. Rom 8:11), the language of the eschatological vision in 1 Corinthians 15 is *ecclesial*—he does not speak of the
resurrection of "bodies" but of "the body." Christ does not simply raise
up individuals but the church as a whole. The language in 1 Corinthians 15
should not be disconnected from his teaching a few chapters earlier where
he describes the church as the "body of Christ [*sōma Christou*]" (1 Cor
12:27). The resurrection of Christ is thus understood as the "first fruits"
of the final harvest—that is, the eschatological resurrection (1 Cor 15:20).
For Paul, what happened to Christ in his personal body will finally be realized in his ecclesial body. As John A. T. Robinson writes, "The Christian,
because he is in the Church . . . is part of Christ's body so literally that all
that happened in and through that body in the flesh can be repeated in and
through him now."[11]

Finally, Paul views the resurrection as part of a hope that includes *all
of creation*. In Romans 8, we read:

> For I consider that the sufferings of this present time are not worth
> comparing with the glory to be *revealed in us. For the creation waits with
> eager longing for the revealing of the sons of God*; for the creation was sub-
> jected to futility, not of its own will but by the will of him who subjected

---

10. Fitzmyer, *First Corinthians*, 597. On the more difficult question of the distinction
between Christ and the Spirit in Paul, see Hill, *Paul and the Trinity*, 135–66.

11. John A. T. Robinson, *The Body: A Study in Pauline Theology*, SBT 5 (London: SCM,
1952), 47.

it in hope; because *the creation itself will be set free from its bondage to decay and obtain the freedom of the glory of the children of God*. For we know that the whole creation has been groaning in *birth pangs* together until now; and *not only the creation, but we ourselves*, who have the first fruits of the Spirit, groan inwardly *as we wait for adoption as sons, the redemption of our bodies*. For in this hope we were saved. (Rom 8:18–24a RSV, slightly adapted)[12]

Paul is awaiting the consummation of a new age in which all of creation will share in the glorification of the righteous that will be "revealed [*apokalyphthēnai*]" in the resurrection of the "sons of God [*tōn huiōn tou theou*]" (Rom 8:18–19). This, however, will only be realized after a period of suffering, described as "birth pangs." In using this language, the apostle seems to be drawing on Jewish eschatological expectations.

The Eschatological Suffering of the Righteous

To return to a theme introduced in chapter 1, Paul's teaching that eschatological liberation will take place following a period of affliction coheres well with other Jewish sources in which the final restoration of God's people is depicted as following a period of great tribulation.[13] Such traditions are attested in numerous texts, perhaps most prominently in Daniel. Most notably, in Daniel 7 the eschatological kingdom arrives only after a period in which the saints are persecuted (Dan 7:25–27). Commentators have detected echoes of this vision in Paul's description of the future victory of Christ and resurrection of the dead in 1 Corinthians 15.[14] Likewise, Daniel 12 envisions resurrection and transformation, but only after a period of unparalleled tribulation.

> There shall be a time of *anguish* [LXX: *thlipseōs*], such as has never occurred since nations first came into existence. *But at that time your people*

---

12. Cf. Fitzmyer, *Romans*, 506.

13. For a comprehensive treatment, see Pitre, *Jesus, the Tribulation, and the End of the Exile*. In addition, see Harry A. Hahne, *The Corruption and Redemption of Creation: Nature in Romans 8:19-22 and Jewish Apocalyptic Literature*, LNTS (London: T&T Clark, 2006); C. Marvin Pate and Douglas W. Kennard, *Deliverance Now and Not Yet: The New Testament and the Great Tribulation*, SBL 54 (New York: Peter Lang, 2003).

14. See Goodrich, "After Destroying Every Rule," 290.

shall be delivered, everyone who is found written in the book. *Many of those who sleep in the dust of the earth shall awake,* some to everlasting life, and some to shame and everlasting contempt. Those who are wise shall *shine like the brightness of the sky,* and those who lead many to righteousness, *like the stars forever and ever.* (Dan 12:1–3)

Many other sources witness to such expectations.[15]

As we have seen, Paul uses the imagery of creation undergoing "birth pangs" (Rom 8:22) in order to refer to the suffering which precedes the final resurrection. Jewish texts frequently describe the coming of the future age with the same metaphor.

> For children come through the breakers of death and the woman expectant with a boy is racked by her pangs, for through the breakers of death she gives birth to a male, and through the pangs of Sheol there emerges, from the <<crucible>> of the pregnant woman a wonderful counselor [cf. Isa 9:6–7] with his strength. (1QH³ 11:9–10)[16]

> And pain will come upon them as (upon) a woman in labor, when the child enters the mouth of the womb, and she has difficulty giving birth . . . and pain will seize them when they see that Son of Man sitting on the throne of his glory. (*1 En.* 62:4–5)

Paul's teaching in Romans 8 probably does not draw directly from either of these passages. Nevertheless, it seems to be "breathing the same air." Paul teaches that those who "belong" to the messiah (Rom 8:9) will be "glorified" (Rom 8:17), but only after sharing in the "birth pangs" (Rom 8:22).[17] The "birth pangs" of the eschatological age have been inaugurated by the messiah's coming, and those who "belong" to him can expect to share in them.[18]

---

15. See, e.g., *1 En.* 46:8–47:2; 56:5–57:3; 91:5–74; 93:1–10; 103:15; *Jub.* 23:11–31; *Sib. Or.* 3:182–95; *Pss. Sol.* 17:11–32; *T. Mos.* 9:1–7; 4Q171 ii 9–19; 4Q174 1 i 18–19; 1 ii 1–7; 4Q177 ii 8–11; 1QS 1:17–18; 3:23; 4:18–23; 8:1–3; 9:8–11; CD³ 1:4–17; 1QM 1:11–12; 15:1–3; 16:15–17:3; 17:8–9.

16. *DSSSE* 1:149. That the messiah is in view is affirmed by many. See, e.g., Novenson, *The Grammar of Messianism,* 167.

17. See, e.g., Hahne, *Corruption and Redemption of Creation,* 204.

18. Dale C. Allison Jr., *The End of the Ages Has Come: An Early Interpretation of the Passion and Resurrection of Jesus* (Eugene: Wipf and Stock, 2013), 65.

The eschaton, for Paul, involves both suffering and bodily resurrection. In Romans 8, this hope is signaled by the reference to "the redemption of our bodies" (Rom 8:23). Paul's thought seems to track with passages such as the one from Daniel 12 above where the great tribulation is followed by resurrection and glorification ("Those who are wise shall *shine like the brightness of the sky*, and those who lead many to righteousness, *like the stars* forever and ever" [Dan 12:3]). As David Burnett convincingly argues, the language likely reflects an eschatological reading of God's promise to Abraham that his descendants would be "as the stars of heaven" (Gen 22:17; Sir 44:21). Paul's teaching in 1 Corinthians 15 on the glory of the resurrected body confirms that he held to similar views.[19]

Suffering, Divine Sonship, and Sacrifice

Paul associates the suffering of the righteous with divine sonship. This also coheres with Jewish texts that describe the eschatological tribulation and speak of the suffering saints as God's children. For instance, in the passage from *1 Enoch* 62 cited above, we hear that the "Lord of the Spirits" will turn over the fallen angels to be punished, "so that they may exact retribution from them for the iniquity that they did to *his children*" (*1 En.* 62:11).[20] Similarly, in *Sibylline Oracles* 3:704 we read, "*The sons of the great God* will all live peacefully around the Temple, rejoicing in these things with the Creator."[21] In fact, the identification of the suffering righteous as God's children is broadly attested in other Jewish sources (cf. Add Esth 16:14–16; 3 Macc 6:28; 7:6; Wis 2:13–20; 5:4–5; 16:1–13). Brendan Byrne writes:

> In short, it may be said that around sonship of God there hovers the idea of immunity from death. This immunity does not preclude suffering, or even physical death; but it involves an ultimate destiny to preservation, to life with God, which human oppressors are compelled to recognize,

---

19. David A. Burnett, "'So Shall Your Seed Be': Paul's Use of Genesis 15:5 in Romans 4:18 in Light of Early Jewish Deification Traditions," *JSPL* 5, no. 2 (2015): 211–36; Burnett, "A Neglected Deuteronomic Scriptural Matrix for the Nature of the Resurrection Body in 1 Corinthians 15:39–42," in *Scripture, Texts, and Tracings in 1 Corinthians*, ed. B. J. Oropeza and Linda Belleville (Minneapolis: Fortress, forthcoming 2019).

20. From Nickelsburg and VanderKam, *1 Enoch*, 81.

21. Translation from Charlesworth, *Old Testament Pseudepigrapha*, 1:377.

and which even spiritual powers must respect. God's "sons" are those who enjoy or are destined to enjoy eternal life with him.[22]

Paul views the eschaton in terms of "the revealing of the children of God" (Rom 8:19). In short, in envisioning the future, Paul paints a picture with hues taken from Jewish eschatological traditions.

Significantly, the in-breaking of the world to come centers on the children of God who suffer ("groan") until their glorification (Rom 8:23). As Trevor Burke rightly notes, "The created order is not only dependent upon but looks to the sons of God for its future liberation."[23] Likewise, John Gager states, "The suffering of the believer now appears not as an isolated instance, but as an integral and necessary stage in the cosmic birth process whose culmination will be the glorious liberty of the children of God."[24]

In drawing these threads together, Paul is making an important point: by sharing in the sufferings of the "birth pangs," the saints are conformed to Christ and participate in his redemptive work. Of course, as we have seen, Paul maintains that Christ's death had atoning value (Rom 3:25). The notion of redemptive suffering coheres well with Paul's Jewish perspective. In 4 Maccabees the suffering of the righteous is explicitly linked to atonement language (cf. 4 Macc 17:22). Perhaps even more important given the context of Romans 8 is this: the affliction of the righteous during the eschatological tribulation is often seen as having atoning significance. In Daniel 9:24, the period of tribulation is specifically linked to the need "to atone for iniquity." In one of the Dead Sea Scrolls, 1QS 7:4, the righteous must endure suffering faithfully "in order to atone for sin by doing justice and undergoing trials."[25] Likewise, in another text from the Dead Sea, 4Q171 ii 9–12, we read about the righteous "taking upon themselves" the period of "affliction." The word translated "affliction" is the very same term used

---

22. Brendan J. Byrne, *"Sons of God"—"Seed of Abraham": A Study of the Idea of the Sonship of God of All Christians in Paul Against the Jewish Background* (Rome: Biblical Institute Press, 1979), 63.

23. Trevor J. Burke, *Adopted into God's Family: Exploring a Pauline Metaphor*, NSBT 22 (Downers Grove, IL: InterVarsity Press, 2006), 181.

24. John G. Gager, "Functional Diversity in Paul's Use of End-Time Language," *JBL* 89 (1970): 330. See also Scott Broduer, *The Holy Spirit's Agency in the Resurrection of the Dead: An Exegetico-Theological Study of 1 Corinthians 15,44b–49 and Romans 8,9–13* (Rome: Gregorian University, 1996), 251: "Believers, now redeemed in Christ, in turn become one of the means through which the Spirit renews the face of the earth."

25. *DSSSE* 1:89.

for the "Day of *Atonement*" in the Dead Sea Scrolls (cf. CDᵃ 6:19). In short, "by bearing the sufferings of this period, the righteous will engage in an act of redemption."[26] Many other texts could be cited.[27] Suffice it say, Paul's teaching that Jesus has ushered in the eschatological age by his atoning death coheres well with a Jewish outlook. *Yet it is not simply Christ's sufferings that are understood as part of the eschatological tribulation; the suffering of the saints is also cast against this backdrop.* As Craig Keener notes, "For believers living between the Messiah's first and second comings, that era of eschatological suffering was present."[28]

According to Paul, then, what Christ has done in his personal body, he now accomplishes in his ecclesial body—that is, in believers. Just as Paul links sacrificial language to Christ's work (e.g., Rom 3:25; 8:3), he also indicates that believers are to make themselves sacrifices (e.g., Rom 12:1).[29] Since Christ's sufferings redound to the benefit of others, it is unsurprising to find that Paul teaches something similar about the suffering of believers.[30] This idea flows logically from his view of believers' unity with one another in the body of Christ: "If one member suffers, all suffer together with it; if one member is honored, all rejoice together with it" (1 Cor 12:26). Thus in 2 Corinthians 1 he can write:

> If we are afflicted, it is for your comfort and salvation; and if we are comforted, it is for your comfort, which you experience when you patiently endure the same sufferings that we suffer. Our hope for you is unshaken; for we know that as you share in our sufferings, you will also share in our comfort. (2 Cor 1:6–7 RSV)

For Paul, those in Christ are not disconnected from one another but truly have communion in the one body not only with Christ but with one another. As Gorman says, "Union with Christ apart from the community is

---

26. Pitre, *Jesus, the Tribulation, and the End of the Exile*, 452.

27. See Pate and Kennard, *Deliverance Now and Not Yet*, 78–92; Craig A. Evans, *Mark 8:27–16:20*, WBC 34B (Nashville: Thomas Nelson, 2001), 387–88; Pitre, *Jesus, the Tribulation, and the End of the Exile*, 402–3, 451–54.

28. Craig S. Keener, *Romans*, NCCS (Eugene: Cascade, 2009), 107.

29. See John A. Kincaid and Michael Patrick Barber, "'Conformed to the Image of His Son': Participation in Christ as Divine Sonship in Romans 8," *Letter and Spirit* 10 (2015): 54–62.

30. Barry D. Smith, *Paul's Seven Explanations of the Suffering of the Righteous* (New York: Peter Lang, 2002), 179.

impossible."[31] The church suffers together and shares together the effects of one another's suffering. Perhaps that is why Paul tells the saints that they too must offer themselves up as a sacrifice:

> I appeal to you therefore, brethren, by the mercies of God, to *present your bodies* as *a living sacrifice*, holy and acceptable to God, which is your spiritual worship. (Rom 12:1 RSV)

Notice here Paul's ecclesial vision—the offering of the *bodies* (plural) of believers constitutes a singular "living sacrifice"—the sacrificial *bodies* are all part of the sacrifice of the *body*.[32] Given such evidence, it seems only natural that in Romans 8 the suffering of the saints plays a role in ushering in the new creation. As in other Jewish sources, for Paul the suffering of the righteous in the eschatological tribulation plays a role in *redemption*. Is this because Christ's redemptive work is somehow insufficient? Not in the least. Rather, *Christ's work involves enabling believers to participate in his redemptive work.* Those in Christ are thus fully conformed to his image, offering themselves as sacrifices in union with him. They are incapable of liberating themselves from sin; only Christ can atone for sin. Nevertheless, once in him, believers truly share in his redemptive work.[33] Robinson sums up Paul's teaching well when he says, "His whole doctrine of the Church is an extension of his Christology."[34]

How is participation in the sacrificial body of Christ realized? For Paul, the answer appears bound up with the Lord's Supper, in which the sacrificial "death" of Jesus's body is proclaimed (1 Cor 11:23–26). To this issue we now turn.

---

31. Gorman, *Becoming the Gospel*, 30.

32. See, e.g., Colin D. Miller, *The Practice of the Body of Christ: Human Agency in Pauline Theology after MacIntyre* (Cambridge: James Clark & Co., 2014), 174: "The whole church is viewed as one sacrifice." See also Scot McKnight, *A Community Called Atonement* (Nashville: Abingdon, 2007), 9: "Any theory of atonement that is not an ecclesial theory of atonement is inadequate."

33. McKnight makes the statement that humans cannot atone for themselves or for others (*Community Called Atonement*, 118) but then goes on to explain that the church truly participates in Christ's work, affirming that its missional activity in the world participates in atonement (*Community Called Atonement*, 122, 134, 141). We would say something similar. Those in Christ cannot redeem themselves. Nevertheless, once united to him, Christ truly works within them such that, by his power, their works are therefore also in some respect atoning—for their works are ultimately Christ's.

34. Robinson, *The Body*, 49.

Participation in the Body and Blood of Christ

The Lord's Supper often makes little more than cameo appearances in discussions about Paul's theology. For example, in N. T. Wright's massive work of over 1,500 pages, *Paul and the Faithfulness of God,* the only substantial treatments of the Lord's Supper are in Wright's sections on Paul's world and history rather than in his treatment of Paul's theology.[35] The lack of attention given to the Lord's Supper in Paul's teaching is especially surprising given that he identifies the "cup" and the "bread" with the notion of "participation [*koinōnia*]" (1 Cor 10:16, 17 ESV), an aspect of the apostle's thought that has attracted intense interest since the work of E. P. Sanders. Sanders himself recognizes the important link between participation and the sacraments of baptism and Eucharist in Paul, explaining, "Christians are *one person* with Christ and *participate* in him through *baptism* and the *Lord's Supper.* These two Christian rites were taking on a 'mystical' or 'sacramental' meaning."[36]

Nevertheless, despite Sanders's recognition of its importance for understanding the participatory dimension of the apostle's teaching, the Lord's Supper still often receives scant attention in Pauline scholarship, even in works that specifically focus on the role of participation in Paul's thought.[37] The frequent neglect of this topic cannot simply be attributed to the fact that it is explicitly described in only one of Paul's epistles (1 Corinthians). After all, other singularly attested aspects of Paul's message have been pored over by scholars: for example, the controversy with Peter at Antioch (cf. Gal 2:11–14), the implications of Christ as a "sacrifice of atonement [*hilastērion*]" (Rom 3:25), the notion that in Christ there is no longer "male" or "female" (Gal 3:28), and the role of civil authorities (Rom 13:1–7).

The tendency to pass over the Lord's Supper is not entirely inexplicable. Going back to the pioneers of modern biblical scholarship such as Julius Wellhausen,[38] critical exegesis has been shaped by anti-sacrificial biases. For Wellhausen, for example, it was the "priestly" tradition that represented the final stage of Judaism, understood as a decline from the

---

35. See Edith Humphrey, "Bishop Wright: Sacramentality and the Role of the Sacraments," in Heilig, Hewitt, and Bird, *God and the Faithfulness of Paul,* 662. See also Miller, *Practice of the Body of Christ,* 156; Hays, "What Is 'Real Participation in Christ'?," 343–44.

36. Sanders, *Paul: The Apostle's Life, Letters, and Thought,* 329 (emphasis original).

37. E.g., Campbell, *Quest for Paul's Gospel,* has no treatment of the Lord's Supper.

38. See especially Julius Wellhausen, *Prolegomena to the History of Ancient Israel,* trans. J. Sutherland Black and Allan Enzies (1885; repr., New York: Meridian Books, 1957).

dynamic religion of the prophets. The priestly source was seen to embody a hidebound, ritualistic Jewish faith, ripe for a "reformation" launched by Jesus.[39] As many have detailed, such thinly veiled prejudices have long translated into a lack of interest and even hostility toward the priestly and sacrificial dimension of biblical texts.[40] Thus, for instance, after speaking of the validity of Protestant concerns about "empty encrustation of ritual," Mary Douglas laments the way such attitudes have led to "a tendency to suppose that any ritual is empty form" and "that any external religion betrays true interior religion."[41] In the treatment below, we hope to show that a deeper appreciation of Paul's dependence on cultic traditions helps make greater sense of his teaching on the Lord's Supper and its relationship to both participation in Christ and the new creation.

Guilty of the Body and Blood of the Lord

Paul's most explicit account of what he calls "the Lord's Supper [*kyriakon deipnon*]" (1 Cor 11:20) appears in 1 Corinthians 11. There we learn that the Lord's Supper is celebrated as part of a larger gathering involving a communal meal. Such meals were typical in Greco-Roman societies (e.g., the *eranos*).[42] Paul's concern that "each one goes ahead with his own meal" (1 Cor 11:21 RSV) might indicate that the rich were bringing their own food and eating before the poor—who had to work longer hours—could arrive.[43] Whatever the precise nature of the problem, Paul's core message

---

39. As Michael Zank (trans. and ed., *Leo Strauss: The Early Writings [1921–1932]* [New York: State University of New York Press, 2002], 100n12) explains, "Wellhausen regarded the Jewish theocracy established by Ezra the Scribe after the Babylonian Exile as a phenomenon of degeneration, a step from the life-affirming religion of ancient Israel, and a proto-Catholic Church." See also Gary Anderson, "Sacrifice and Sacrificial Offerings (OT)," in *ABD* 5:873–75.

40. See, e.g., Jonathan Klawans, *Purity, Sacrifice, and the Temple: Symbolism and Supersessionism in the Study of Ancient Judaism* (Oxford: Oxford University Press, 2006), 6 (see also pp. 3–10). Likewise, see Crispin H. T. Fletcher-Louis, "Jesus as the High Priestly Messiah: Part 1," *JSHJ* 4, no. 2 (2006): 155–56.

41. Mary Douglas, *Purity and Danger: An Analysis of Concepts of Pollution and Taboo* (New York: Routledge, 1966), 76.

42. See Panayotis Coutsoumpos, *Paul and the Lord's Supper: A Socio-Historical Investigation*, SBL 84 (New York: Peter Lang, 2005); David E. Garland, *1 Corinthians*, BECNT (Grand Rapids: Baker Academic, 2003), 543–44.

43. Keener, *1–2 Corinthians*, 98.

is that the Corinthians are neglecting the underprivileged.[44] This is a grave problem for Paul because he maintains that the Lord's Supper is, at its core, about ecclesial communion in Christ. This is a point the apostle makes in the preceding chapter, when he writes, "Because there is one bread, we who are many are one body [*hen sōma*], for we all partake of the one bread [*henos artou*]" (1 Cor 10:17).[45] Indeed, the ecclesial significance of the Lord's Supper is obviously at the heart of Paul's message in 1 Corinthians 11. Paul's identification of the church as Christ's "body" (*sōma*) likely has its origin in the Lord's Supper.[46] By ignoring the needs of the poor, the Corinthians are thus undermining an essential meaning of the meal—namely, communion in Christ.

Highlighting this aspect of Paul's teaching, some commentators have made the case that the bread and wine at the supper are not inherently significant in the apostle's view of the meal.[47] For example, Troels Engberg-Pedersen argues that it is not the bread and wine themselves but rather the acts associated with them that matter most for Paul—that is, the *breaking* of the one bread, which is distributed to all, and the *sharing* of the one cup. These actions signify ecclesial unity, as Paul makes clear (1 Cor 10:17).[48]

The issue of divisions in the church remains in the background, then, of Paul's startling indictment of the way the Corinthians are receiving the Lord's Supper unworthily:

> Whoever, therefore, eats the bread or drinks the cup of the Lord in an unworthy manner will be guilty of the body and blood of the Lord. Let a man examine himself, and so eat of the bread and drink of the cup. For any one who eats and drinks without discerning the body eats and drinks judgment upon himself. That is why many of you are weak and ill, and some have died. (1 Cor 11:27–30 RSV, slightly adapted)

What are we to make of these words? What does Paul mean when he says that whoever "eats the bread or drinks the cup" in an "unworthy manner"

---

44. Hays, *First Corinthians*, 197; Fitzmyer, *First Corinthians*, 434–35.

45. Troels Engberg-Pedersen, "Proclaiming the Lord's Death: 1 Corinthians 11:17–34 and the Forms of Paul's Theological Argument," in *Pauline Theology*, vol. 2, *1 and 2 Corinthians*, ed. David M. Hay (Minneapolis: Fortress, 1993), 117.

46. Jostein Ådna, "The Eucharist in Paul and in Hebrews," in *Institutions of the Emerging Church*, LNTS 305 (London: Bloomsbury, 2016), 104.

47. See, e.g., Garland, *1 Corinthians*, 477–78.

48. Engberg-Pedersen, "Proclaiming the Lord's Death," 117.

will be "guilty [*enochos*] of the body [*sōmatos*] and blood [*haimatos*] of the Lord" (1 Cor 11:27)? And what does Paul mean when he indicts those who eat and drink "without discerning [*diakrinōn*] the body [*to sōma*]" (1 Cor 11:29)?

On the one hand, many interpreters take the position that when Paul speaks of judgment coming upon those who receive the bread and the cup unworthily, it is not due to a belief that the bread and wine are themselves inherently special. For example, Richard Hays remarks, "'Discerning the body' here cannot mean 'perceiving the real presence of Christ in the sacramental bread.' . . . For Paul, 'discerning the body' means recognizing the community of believers for what it really is: the one body of Christ."[49] In this view, then, some are "weak" and "ill" and "have died" (1 Cor 11:30) because Christians have neglected the poor, causing them to go "hungry" (1 Cor 11:21, 33–34). It is this behavior that contradicts the meaning of the meal.

On the other hand, while this reading rightly preserves the ecclesial dimension of Paul's teaching, the attempt to downplay the significance of the bread and wine itself minimizes the crucial fact that Paul warns against becoming "guilty of the body *and blood of the Lord*" (1 Cor 11:27). Notice here that Paul speaks not only of "the body"—which of course can be applied to the church as a whole—but also of the "blood of the Lord [*tou haimatos tou kyriou*]" (1 Cor 11:27). Nowhere in Paul's letters does the apostle ever use the *blood of Christ* as an image for the church—a point that suggests that an offense against the elements of the meal themselves is his primary meaning.[50] Hence, the view that Paul is solely concerned with offenses against other believers—that is, the "body of Christ" as the church—fails to make sense of the text as a whole. As C. K. Barrett explains, "That *body* is not to be interpreted here as equivalent to *church* is shown by the addition of *blood*. It seems necessary to interpret verse 27 in the light of verse 26."[51] Indeed, those who insist that Paul has in view only an offense against the church and see absolutely no reference here to the elements have to wrench the statement in verse 27 about being guilty of

---

49. Hays, *First Corinthians*, 200. Along similar lines, see, e.g., Günther Bornkamm, *Early Christian Experience*, trans. P. L. Hammer (New York: Harper & Row, 1969), 148–49; Käsemann, *Essays on New Testament Themes*, 130–32.

50. See, e.g., C. K. Barrett, *The First Epistle to the Corinthians*, BNTC (Peabody, MA: Hendrickson, 1968), 273.

51. Barrett, *1 Corinthians*, 273. See also Ben Witherington III, *Making a Meal of It: Rethinking the Theology of the Lord's Supper* (Waco, TX: Baylor University Press, 2007), 59–60. This is not to deny that Paul *also* finds here an offense against the community.

the body and blood of the Lord out of context and ignore verse 26: "For as often as you eat *this bread* and *drink the cup*, you proclaim the Lord's death until he comes."

Along similar lines, some also hold that the bread and wine are only significant for Paul as a symbol or reminder of the meaning of Christ's death.[52] This too offers a truncated account of the apostle's teaching. According to Paul, the bread is precisely what *actualizes* ecclesial union. He insists, "Because [*hoti*] there is one bread, we who are many are one body, for [*gar*] we all partake of the one bread" (1 Cor 10:17).[53] To suggest Paul simply means that the Lord's Supper "affirms" the message of Christ's death and/or that its proper celebration merely manifests the unity believers already have in Christ by faith fails to do justice to this verse. Paul does not write, "Because we are one body we share in the one bread," but rather, "*Because there is one bread*, we who are many are one body." Even Ernst Käsemann, who called Paul's theology "anti-cultic," correctly articulates Paul's message when he explains that the language he uses indicates that the Lord's Supper "effects incorporation into the Body of Christ."[54]

The Table of Demons versus the Table of the Lord

The realistic nature of Paul's view of the Lord's Supper can be seen in another way. Earlier in 1 Corinthians Paul compares the *participation* that believers have with Christ in the Lord's Supper to what occurs in the Jewish temple and in feasts associated with pagan gods. We will come back to the temple imagery momentarily. For now, simply focus on how Paul uses the language of "participation" for the Lord's Supper as well as for Jewish and pagan sacrifices:

> What do I imply then? That food sacrificed to idols is anything, or that an idol is anything? No, I imply that what pagans sacrifice, they sacri-

---

52. See Garland, *1 Corinthians*, 552.

53. Ådna, "The Eucharist in Paul and in Hebrews," 104–6; Otfried Hofius, "The Lord's Supper and the Lord's Supper Tradition," in *One Loaf, One Cup: Ecumenical Studies of 1 Cor 11 and Other Eucharistic Texts; The Cambridge Conference on the Eucharist, August 1988*, ed. B. F. Meyer, NGS 6 (Macon, GA: Mercer University Press, 1993), 97–98.

54. See Käsemann, *Essays on New Testament Themes*, 111. See also A. J. B. Higgins, *The Lord's Supper in the New Testament*, SBT 6 (London: SCM, 1952), 70; Hofius, "The Lord's Supper and the Lord's Supper Tradition," 97–98.

fice to demons and not to God. I do not want you to be participants [*koinōnous*] with demons. You cannot drink the cup of the Lord and the cup of demons. *You cannot partake of the table of the Lord and the table of demons.* (1 Cor 10:19–21 NRSV, slightly adapted)

Notice here that Paul's description of the believers' meal as the "Lord's Supper" parallels the terminology used in ancient sources for pagan cultic celebrations. For example, ancient invitations welcome worshipers to eat "at the table of Lord Serapis,"[55] language that indicates the god's presence as host at such banquets.[56] Moreover, Paul's concern with believers' participation in pagan feasts seems predicated on the assumption that spiritual forces were truly present in such activities. The logic here is straightforward: those who are in Christ must not participate in pagan cultic meals because participation in them renders one a "partner" (*koinōnos*) with demons (1 Cor 10:20). There is also a remarkable analogy drawn in this passage: the Eucharist is the "Lord's Supper"—that is, the meal hosted by Christ. This implies that Christ is present in the eucharistic meal in a way that is somehow similar to the presence of demons at pagan cultic celebrations.[57]

With this we come to an interpretive dilemma. On the one hand, Paul explains that idolatrous meals unite the participants to demons in a way analogous to the Lord's Supper.[58] The parallel is clearer in the Greek: the Lord's Supper involves "participation" or "communion" (*koinōnia*) with Jesus (1 Cor 10:16) just as idolatrous meals make their participants "partners" or "communicants" (*koinōnous*) with demons (1 Cor 10:20). On the other hand, while Paul believes in the existence of demons, he also agrees with statements apparently made by other early Christians that insist that idols are not real: "We know that 'no idol in the world really exists,' and that 'there is no God but one'" (1 Cor 8:4). Going on, the apostle seems to affirm the claim that idol food has no special properties: "'Food will not bring us close to God.' We are no worse off if we do not eat, and no better

55. Oxyrhynchus Papri 110, 523, 1484, and 1755.

56. See Coutsoumpos, *Paul and the Lord's Supper*, 13, 140n26.

57. On the tension of Christ both absent and present in the Lord's Supper, see Orr, *Christ Absent and Present*, 174–81, who writes, "Here Christ's presence is at its most 'dense'" (180).

58. See John Fotopoulos, "Arguments Concerning Food Offered to Idols: Corinthian Quotations and Pauline Refutations in a Rhetorical *Partitio* (1 Corinthians 8.1–9)," *CBQ* (2005): 611–31.

off if we do" (1 Cor 8:8). The same sentiment is found in Romans 14, where, once again, Paul is addressing the question of eating idol food: "For the kingdom of God is not food and drink but righteousness and peace and joy in the Holy Spirit" (Rom 14:17). At first glance (and even a second), Paul appears to make two contrary claims: (1) idol food is harmless (1 Cor 8); (2) idolatrous feasts unite persons to demons (1 Cor 10).

While some have argued that Paul is hopelessly self-contradictory or that the passage consists of composite Pauline material,[59] such conclusions are not necessary.[60] Paul's concern about "idol food" (*eidōlothyta*) in 1 Corinthians 8 refers to meat originally sacrificed to idols but later purchased outside of pagan sacrificial rites. Yet in 1 Corinthians 10 Paul addresses not "idol food" (*eidōlothyta*) but "idolatry" (*eidōlolatria*). The latter word refers to active engagement in idolatrous worship, something expressly forbidden by the Decalogue (Exod 20:1-6) and condemned by Paul elsewhere (Rom 1:21-25).[61] From this it seems that Paul teaches that since idols are nothing (cf. 1 Cor 8:4) the food offered to idols has no inherent spiritual properties; the food is simply a dead animal. Nevertheless, idolatrous feasts—that is, meals celebrated as part of pagan rites—*are* spiritually dangerous. Meat purchased in the marketplace—even if originally sacrificed to idols—has no intrinsically dangerous properties, but worshiping idols is a real problem because such worship is associated with demons.[62]

In sum: interpreters generally conclude that Paul must have held something similar to be true of the "cup of blessing" and the "bread" of the Lord's Supper (1 Cor 10:16). Paul believes that what happens in pagan worship is somehow analogous to the Lord's Supper—one is a "table of demons," the other is "the table of the Lord" (1 Cor 10:21). Just as demons

59. E.g., Stanley K. Stowers, "Elusive Coherence: Ritual and Rhetoric in 1 Corinthians 10-11," in *Reimagining Christian Origins: A Colloquium Honoring Burton L. Mack*, ed. E. A. Castelli and H. Taussig (Valley Forge, PA: Trinity Press, 1996), 68-83; Khiok-Khng Yeo, *Rhetorical Interaction in 1 Corinthians 8 and 10: A Formal Analysis with Preliminary Suggestions for a Chinese Cross-Cultural Hermeneutic* (Leiden: Brill, 1995); Johannes Weiß, *Der erste Korintherbrief* (Göttingen: Vandenhoeck & Ruprecht, 1910), 212-13, 264.

60. For a fuller critique see Garland, *1 Corinthians*, 483-85.

61. See, e.g., Stephen Richard Turley, *The Ritualized Revelation of the Messianic Age*, LNTS 544 (London: T&T Clark, 2015), 137-38; Derek Newton, *Deity and Diet: The Dilemma of Sacrificial Food at Corinth* (Sheffield: Sheffield Academic Press, 1998), 338; Bruce N. Fisk, "Eating Meat Offered to Idols: Corinthian Behavior and Pauline Response in 1 Corinthians 8-10 (A Response to Gordon Fee)," *Trinity Journal* 10 (1989): 49-70; David Horrell, "Theological Principle or Christological Praxis? Pauline Ethics in 1 Corinthians 8.1-11.1," *JSNT* 67 (1997): 99-102.

62. Newton, *Deity and Diet*, 338.

are present in idolatrous feasts, so Christ is present in the church's counterpart—the *Lord's* Supper. Due to these observations, many contend that the bread and wine of the Lord's Supper, like idol food, themselves have no intrinsic value.[63] While this reading may at first glance make sense given Paul's statements in 1 Corinthians 8, it ultimately fails because it overlooks other key aspects of his teaching regarding the Eucharist. Specifically, it fails to consider the way Paul identifies the Lord's Supper in terms drawn from the Jewish temple sacrifices.

The Lord's Supper and the Sacrificial Death of Christ

As is well known, in 1 Corinthians 11 Paul links the celebration of the Lord's Supper to Jesus's final meal. What is overlooked, however, is that Paul's account of the Last Supper is also deeply rooted in Jewish temple language and imagery. Consider the following:

> For I received from the Lord what I also handed on to you, that the Lord Jesus on the night when he was handed over took a loaf of bread, and when he had given thanks, he broke it and said, "*This is my body that is for you. Do this in remembrance of me.*" In the same way he took the cup also, after supper, saying, "*This cup is the new covenant in my blood.* Do this, as often as you drink it, *in remembrance of me.*" For as often as you eat this bread and drink the cup, you proclaim the Lord's death until he comes. (1 Cor 11:23–26 NRSV, slightly adapted)

Numerous allusions to Jewish cultic traditions can be detected in these verses.

First, the words over the cup indicate that *Christ's death was a covenant-making sacrifice.* As we have seen elsewhere in our study, covenants were typically established through ritual sacrifice: "Gather to me my faithful ones, who made a covenant with me by sacrifice!" (Ps 50:5).[64]

---

63. See, e.g., Mary Patton Baker, "Participating in the Body and Blood of Christ: Christian *Koinōnia* and the Lord's Supper," in *"In Christ" in Paul: Explorations in Paul's Theology of Union and Participation,* ed. Michael J. Thate, Kevin J. Vanhoozer, and Constantine R. Campbell, WUNT 2/384 (Tübingen: Mohr Siebeck, 2014), 520; C. K. Barrett, *Church, Ministry, and Sacraments in the New Testament* (Exeter: Paternoster, 1985), 66–67.

64. See Wiseman, "The Vassal-Treaties of Esarhaddon," 1–99; Hahn, *Kinship by Covenant,* 59.

Furthermore, as has long been acknowledged, the pairing of "blood" and "covenant" evokes the covenant ratification ceremony described in Exodus 24:[65]

> And Moses took half of *the blood* and put it in basins, and half of the blood he threw against *the altar*. Then he took the book of the covenant, and read it in the hearing of the people; and they said, "All that the LORD has spoken we will do, and we will be obedient." And Moses took the blood and threw it upon the people, and said, *"Behold the blood of the covenant* which the LORD has made with you in accordance with all these words." (Exod 24:6–8 RSV)

As commentators routinely point out, the altar is to be taken as a symbol of God.[66] Moses's act of placing the blood of the sacrifices on both the people and the altar thus symbolically demonstrates their covenant communion with God.[67] With this echo in place, Paul depicts Christ's death as the sacrificial act that establishes the "new" covenant promised in Jeremiah's famous oracle (cf. Jer 31:33).[68]

Second, *the words spoken over the bread appear to describe Christ's death as a sacrifice offered on behalf of others.* Jesus is said to have identified the bread with his body, which he explains is "for you [*hyper hymōn*]" (1 Cor 11:24). Admittedly, without the cup saying, Jesus's words over the bread lack explicit sacrificial referent. Nevertheless, in light of the sacrificial imagery associated with the cup, the phrase "for you" should be seen as having cultic resonances.[69] Parallel language even occurs later in 1 Corinthians where Paul explains that Christ died "for our sins [*hyper tōn hamartiōn*]" (1 Cor 15:3).[70] Such a reading makes sense within the context of the other letters of Paul that portray Christ's death as a sacrificial offering (e.g., Rom 3:25). In addition, "for you" may also echo Isaiah 53:10–12, which identifies the Servant as a cultic sacrifice.[71] Against this backdrop,

---

65. E.g., Fitzmyer, *First Corinthians*, 442–43.

66. Durham, *Exodus*, 343; Sarna, *Exodus*, 152.

67. Durham, *Exodus*, 343; Sarna, *Exodus*, 151.

68. Gorman, *Death of the Messiah*, 53.

69. Anthony C. Thiselton, *The First Epistle to the Corinthians*, NIGTC (Grand Rapids: Eerdmans, 2000), 876–78; Garland, *1 Corinthians*, 546–48.

70. Gathercole, *Defending Substitution*, 55–79.

71. See, e.g., Garland, *1 Corinthians*, 547; Ben Meyer, "The Expiation Motif in the Eucharistic Words," in Meyer, *One Loaf, One Cup*, 19; Fee, *First Epistle to the Corinthians*, 551.

Richard Hays makes the case that Jesus's being "handed over" (*paredideto*) in 1 Cor 11:23 is best "heard as echoes of the Septuagint's rendering of Isa 53:6 ('And the Lord *gave him up* [*paredōken*] for our sins') and 53:12b ('And he bore the sins of many, and on account of their iniquities he *was handed over* [*paredothē*]')."[72]

The Lord's Supper as a Sacrificial Meal

The cultic and sacrificial dimensions of the Lord's Supper in Paul are also evident from his teaching to the Corinthians. Paul explicitly links his participatory view of the Lord's Supper to what he seems to assume his readers know about Jewish views of Israel's temple cult:

> The cup of blessing that we bless, is it not a *participation* [*koinōnia*] in the blood of Christ? The bread that we break, is it not a *participation* [*koinōnia*] in the body of Christ? Because there is one bread, we who are many are one body, for we all partake of the one bread. *Consider the people of Israel; are not those who eat the sacrifices participants* [*koinōnoi*] *in the altar?* (1 Cor 10:16–18 NRSV, slightly adapted)

It is important to highlight the significance of that last line: according to Paul, in Israel's cult "eating the sacrifices" (*tas thysias*) makes the Jews into "partners" or "communicants" (*koinōnoi*) in "the altar" (*thysiastērion*). There is good reason to think that this represents more than just a general allusion. The language evokes the covenant-making ceremony at Sinai described in Exodus 24, a passage that we have already recognized in the background of the Last Supper narrative in 1 Corinthians 11. There, as we saw above, Moses places the blood of the sacrifices on both Israel and *the altar*: "Moses took half of the blood and put it in basins"—later thrown on the people—"and half of the blood he dashed against *the altar*" (Exod 24:6). Since the altar symbolized God himself, this action symbolically depicts Israel's covenantal communion with God. While we cannot go into detail here, there is an overwhelming amount of evidence indicating

---

72. Hays, *First Corinthians*, 198. See also Otfried Hofius, "The Fourth Servant Song in the New Testament Letters," in *The Suffering Servant: Isaiah 53 in Jewish and Christian Sources*, ed. Bernd Janowski and Peter Stuhlmacher (Grand Rapids: Eerdmans, 2004), 176n54.

that *ancient Jews recognized a participatory dimension of the cult,* suggesting that Paul's treatment here relied on well-established Jewish traditions.[73]

Nonetheless, Paul does not merely appeal to the Last Supper tradition to speak of Jesus's death in cultic terms; in his presentation, the Lord's Supper *itself* has cultic significance. Paul specifically links the participatory aspect of the meal to Israel's cult (1 Cor 10:18). The words associated with the celebration of the Lord's Supper in 1 Corinthians 11 reinforce such a connection. For instance, Jesus's instruction that the meal be celebrated in "remembrance" (*anamnēsis*) of him (1 Cor 11:24, 25) uses a term frequently used in reference to Israel's cultic worship.[74] Such a cultic allusion is further suggested by other considerations. Twice we hear Christ's command, "*Do* [*poieite*] this in remembrance of me" (1 Cor 11:24, 25). We also learn that in the celebration believers "proclaim" (*katangellete*) the Lord's death (1 Cor 11:26). The words translated "do" and "proclaim" were also prominent in Israel's sacrificial worship.[75] The convergence of such terminology here should not be dismissed as coincidental.

In addition, Paul's description of the eucharistic table as the "table of the Lord [*trapezēs kyriou*]" (1 Cor 10:21) mirrors the language the prophet Malachi uses for the sacrificial altar of Israel's cult.

> Oh, that someone among you would shut the temple doors, so that you would not kindle fire on my altar in vain! I have no pleasure in you, says the LORD of hosts, and I will not accept an offering from your hands. For from the rising of the sun to its setting my name is great among the nations, and *in every place* incense is offered *to my name,* and a pure offering; for my name is great among the nations, says the LORD of hosts. But you profane it when you say that *the table of the Lord* is polluted, and the food for it may be despised. (Mal 1:10–12 NRSV, slightly adapted)

For Malachi, the "table of the Lord" is the place where pure worship should be made but is not. This prophecy seems to stand in the background of

---

73. See Barber and Kincaid, "Cultic Theosis in Paul and Second Temple Judaism," 237–56.

74. See, e.g., Num 10:10, where the cultic offers are said to "serve you for *remembrance* [LXX: *anamnēsis*] before your God" (RSV). See also Garland, *1 Corinthians,* 548; Daniel Harrington, *First Corinthians,* SP 7 (Collegeville, MN: Liturgical Press, 1999), 428.

75. See Fitzmyer, *First Corinthians,* 444; I. Howard Marshall, *Commentary on Luke: A Commentary on the Greek Text* (Exeter: Paternoster, 1978), 804; Hofius, "The Lord's Supper and the Lord's Supper Tradition," 101, 106–11; Joachim Jeremias, *The Eucharistic Words of Jesus,* trans. Norman Perrin (London: SCM, 1966), 249–50.

Paul's eucharistic theology. In the Greek version of the Old Testament, the phrase rendered in English as "the table of the Lord" is *trapeza kyriou*—the same term Paul applies to the eucharistic table. E. P. Sanders notes the allusion when he writes:

> In 1 Cor. 10:21, [Paul] turns to Malachi and Isaiah to contrast the "table of the Lord" (Mal. 1:7, 12) and "the table of demons" (Isa. 65:11). The verses in Malachi deal with the "pollution" or "defilement" of *the altar* ("the table of the Lord") by *sacrificing* maimed animals.[76]

In warning the Corinthians not to pollute the "altar" of their eucharistic sacrifice, the apostle turns to Malachi's description. A number of considerations support this reading.

First, as we have seen, Paul has already *explicitly* compared the eucharistic table to the altar of Israel's sanctuary (cf. 1 Cor 10:18). Second, Paul specifically alludes to this oracle at the beginning of the book. In 1 Corinthians 1:2, Paul refers to "those who in every place call on the name of our Lord Jesus Christ." Paul's words line up so well with Malachi 1 that it is hard to avoid drawing the conclusion that he is deliberately evoking his prophecy:[77]

Malachi 1:11	1 Corinthians 1:2
in every place [LXX: *en panti topō*] incense is offered to *my name* [LXX: *tō onomati mou*]	those who *in every place* [*en panti topō*] call on the *name* [*to onoma*] of our Lord Jesus Christ

Third, the "pure" worship offered "in every place" could easily accommodate an eschatological reading.[78] Given that Paul sees the Lord's Supper

76. Sanders, *Paul: The Apostle's Life, Letters, and Thought*, 326 (emphasis added).

77. Roy E. Ciampa and Brian S. Rosner, *The First Letter to the Corinthians*, PNTC (Grand Rapids: Eerdmans, 2010), 57–58; Ciampa and Rosner, "1 Corinthians," in *Commentary on the New Testament Use of the Old Testament*, ed. D. A. Carson and G. K. Beale (Grand Rapids: Baker Academic, 2007), 696.

78. Admittedly, Mal 1:11 is a difficult passage to interpret. That an eschatological view is likely present is suggested by the similarity of language to the eschatological visions of other prophets contained in the collection of the "Book of the Twelve." For example, Malachi's vision shares certain points of contact with Zephaniah: "Yea, at that time I will change the speech of the peoples to a pure speech, that all of them may call on the name of the LORD and serve him with one accord. From beyond the rivers of Ethiopia my suppliants, the daughter of my dispersed ones, shall bring my offering" (Zeph 3:9–10

as the table of the new covenant, the passage fits a eucharistic reading particularly well. Paul thus applies Malachi's vision of ideal, pure worship to the church's devotion to Christ. It is perfectly natural then—particularly in a section dealing with cultic issues in which the Lord's Supper is linked to Israel's worship—to draw from Malachi's oracle. The eucharistic table, then, is thus identified as Israel's "altar" par excellence.

The significance of this connection should not be underappreciated. Paul gets his description of "the Lord's Supper" as "the table of the Lord" from the *biblical* name for the *altar of sacrifice in the Jewish temple*. There is only one explanation for Paul's use of "the table of the Lord" (Mal 1:7–12) as a name for the eucharistic celebration: he thought of the Lord's Supper as a *sacrifice*. This impression is further reinforced when one notes that Paul bases his notion of participation in the Lord's Supper on an understanding of what occurs in the Jewish temple—the worshipers there are made "partakers [*koinōnoi*] of the altar" (1 Cor 10:18 NRSV, modified), a point that we will return to below.

Finally, it is also worth noting that Mary Douglas finds in Paul's language something more than a general allusion to Israel's cultic worship. Specifically, she highlights the coordination of the terms "remembrance" (*anamnēsis*) and "covenant" in close connection with bread and wine. This, she argues, likely signals an allusion to the *bread of the Presence*, a sacrificial offering that was not only linked with both the motifs of "remembrance" and "covenant" but that also was associated with drink offerings:[79]

> You shall make its plates and dishes for incense, and *its flagons and bowls* with which to pour *drink offerings*; you shall make them of pure gold. And you shall set *the bread of the Presence* on the table before me always. (Exod 25:29–30)

RSV). The Malachi passage also seems similar to Mic 4:1–2. Moreover, the use of the "all-peoples" motif—a theme present in other eschatological visions (cf., e.g., Isa 25:6; 56:7; Dan 7:14)—would also fit well with such a reading. See the discussion in Donald K. Berry, "Malachi's Dual Design: The Close of the Canon and What Comes Afterward," in *Forming Prophetic Literature: Essays on Isaiah and the Twelve in Honor of D. W. Watts*, ed. J. W. Watts, J. D. W. Watts, and P. R. House (Sheffield: Sheffield Academic Press, 1996), 277–78; Peter Verhoef, *The Books of Haggai and Malachi*, NICOT (Grand Rapids: Eerdmans, 1987), 228.

79. On the "sacrificial" nature of this offering, see Brant Pitre, *Jesus and the Last Supper* (Grand Rapids: Eerdmans, 2015), 127–28.

And he made the vessels of pure gold that were to be on *the table* [of the bread of the Presence], its plates and dishes for incense, and its bowls and flagons with which to pour *drink offerings.* (Exod 37:16)

This sacrificial bread (and wine) of the presence was celebrated as a constant reminder of God's everlasting covenant with Israel (Lev 24:1-9).[80] According to Douglas, Paul's account of the Last Supper suggests that the Lord's Supper serves a similar role in relation to the new covenant.[81]

The suggestion made by Douglas would dovetail nicely with Paul's identification of the eucharistic table with the "table of the Lord" reference in Malachi 1. The sacrifice there is said to be made from the "rising of the sun to its setting," evoking imagery of the daily *Tamid*, a sacrificial ritual that was performed every evening and morning. The imagery of the "pure *offering* [*minha*]" in Malachi 1 thus seems related to this rite. What is more, descriptions of the bread of the Presence often occur within contexts relating the *Tamid.*[82] It makes perfect sense, then, that Paul would understand the Lord's Supper against the backdrop of *both* the bread of the Presence *and* Malachi's vision of idealized worship.[83]

Sharing in the Sacrificial Offering of Christ

By identifying Jesus's body as food, Paul's account of the Last Supper casts Christ in the role of sacrificial victim. This is particularly intriguing when we recall that, in context, Paul's teaching regarding idol food is, in part, dealing with the precise question of whether believers can consume the meat of the sacrificial victims of pagan cultic rites (cf. 1 Cor 8:1-6). Paul simply assumes that his readers know that the food of cultic meals came

80. See P. V. M. Flesher, "Bread of the Presence," *ABD* 1:780-81.

81. Mary Douglas, "The Eucharist: Its Continuity with the Bread Sacrifice of Leviticus," *Modern Theology* 15, no. 2 (1999): 209-24. See also Pitre, *Jesus and the Last Supper*, 126-29, citing Michael Patrick Barber, "The Historical Jesus and Cultic Restoration Eschatology: The New Temple, the New Priesthood, and the New Cult" (PhD diss., Fuller Theological Seminary, 2010), 209-24.

82. See Exod 29:38-42; Num 28:3-8; *m. Tamid* 3:9; 6:1-3; *m. Yoma* 5:1.

83. Paul's language may be seen as the origin of such associations in the patristic tradition, which occur rather early. For example, as for the Malachi connection, see, e.g., *Didache* 14:1-2; Justin Martyr, *Dialogue* 31.3; Irenaeus, *Against Heresies* 4.17.5; Tertullian, *Against Marcion* 3.22; Eusebius, *Proof of the Gospel* 1.10. For eucharistic interpretations of the bread of the Presence, see Origen, *On Leviticus* 13; Cyril of Jerusalem, *Mystagogic Catechesis* 5-6, 9.

from the meat of sacrificial offerings. He writes, "Do you not know that those who are employed in the temple service get their food from the temple, and those who serve at the altar share in the sacrificial offerings?" (1 Cor 9:13 RSV).

Given Paul's explicit statement affirming that sacrificial victims were consumed in 1 Corinthians 9, we would do well to consider a feature of Paul's report about the Last Supper that frequently gets overlooked. In particular, it seems significant that the apostle's account of Jesus's institution of the Lord's Supper specifically alludes to a context in which the meat of sacrificial victims was consumed by Israel. As we have already seen, Jesus's words over the cup evoke the account of the covenant ratification ceremony at Mount Sinai (Exod 24). We should not fail to note what Paul knew about this passage: namely, that there the covenant is explicitly established through the sacrifice of "peace offerings"—that is, sacrificial offerings that are to be consumed by the worshiper (cf. Lev 7:15–18; 19:5–8).[84] These peace offerings in fact play a vital role in the covenant-making ceremony. After the sacrificial offerings are made (Exod 24:3–8), the scene immediately gives way to a remarkable depiction of the elders of Israel eating in God's presence:

> Then Moses and Aaron, Nadab, and Abihu, and seventy of the elders of Israel went up, and *they saw the God of Israel*. Under his feet there was something like a pavement of sapphire stone, like the very heaven for clearness. God did not lay his hand on the chief men of the people of Israel; also *they beheld God, and they ate and drank*. (Exod 24:9–11)

The reader of the narrative is expected to know that the sacral meal consists of the meat taken from the peace offerings sacrificed as part of the covenant ceremony.[85] The meal is thus of one piece with the covenant sacrificial offering. That Paul's account of the Last Supper specifically echoes this passage is noteworthy and should not be overlooked. It also bears noting that this meal in the divine presence at Sinai appears as the prototype for the very rite that Mary Douglas finds an allusion to in the words of institution, the bread of the Presence, which was eaten by the priests in the sanctuary (cf. Lev 24:1–9).[86]

---

84. Anderson, "Sacrifice and Sacrificial Offerings (OT)," 5:879.
85. Sarna, *Exodus*, 151.
86. Pitre, *Jesus and the Last Supper*, 127.

What is more, Paul's depiction of Christ as a sacrificial victim whose flesh can be eaten finds important corroboration in the fact that earlier in the epistle Paul identifies Christ as the Passover lamb:

> Clean out the old yeast so that you may be a new batch, as you really are unleavened. *For our paschal lamb, Christ, has been sacrificed.* Therefore, let us celebrate the feast, not with the old yeast, the yeast of malice and evil, but with the unleavened bread of sincerity and truth. (1 Cor 5:7–8 NRSV, slightly adapted)

In Paul's day the cultic character of the Passover meal was unmistakable since it was a *sacrificial* animal that was consumed.[87] The Passover meal was inextricably bound up with the sacrifice of the lamb. Because of this, a growing number of scholars recognize that when Paul speaks of the "feast [*heortē*]" (1 Cor 5:8) kept by believers, he is referring to the Lord's Supper—which, naturally enough, depicts Christ as both sacrificial victim and cultic food.[88] In this, Paul's account of the Last Supper seems to be an early witness to the church's memory, also attested in the canonical Gospels, that Jesus's final meal took place within the context of the Jewish Passover (cf., e.g., Matt 26:2, 17–30; Mark 14:1–2, 12–26; Luke 22:1, 7–23; John 13:1, 29; 18:28; etc.).[89] For one thing, Paul's assertion that this event occurred "at night [*en tē nukti*]" (1 Cor 11:23) probably shows an awareness of the Passover context, since meals were not typically eaten at nighttime—the Passover meal is the premier exception (cf. Exod 12:8; Deut 16:4–8; Josephus, *Jewish Antiquities* 18.29; 11Q19 17:6–9).[90] As others have noted, the additional themes of "remembrance," covenant imagery, and sacrificial death are also concepts closely linked to Passover traditions: (1) Passover is identified as a "remembrance" (cf. Exod 12:14), (2) covenant

---

87. See Scot McKnight, *Jesus and His Death: Historiography, the Historical Jesus, and Atonement Theory* (Waco, TX: Baylor University Press, 2005), 246–53; Sanders, *Judaism: Practice and Belief*, 132–38.

88. See Jane Lancaster Patterson, *Keeping the Feast: Metaphors of Sacrifice in 1 Corinthians and Philippians* (Atlanta: SBL Press, 2015), 149–54; Albert L. A. Hogeterp, *Paul and God's Temple*, BTS 2 (Leuven: Peeters, 2006), 335–36; Pitre, *Jesus, the Tribulation, and the End of the Exile*, 441n176. Although Fredriksen (*Paul*, 245) maintains the non-sacrificial nature of 1 Cor 5, she can only do so by isolating this passage from Paul's account of the Last Supper in 1 Cor 11. Similarly, see Hays, *First Corinthians*, 86, who thinks Paul's allusion to the Lord's Supper is "possible" but "hardly certain."

89. See Pitre, *Jesus and the Last Supper*, 251–443.

90. Patterson, *Keeping the Feast*, 151; Pitre, *Jesus and the Last Supper*, 387.

renewal often occurred within the context of paschal celebrations (cf. Josh 3:7–5:12; 2 Kgs 23:21–23; 2 Chr 29; 34:29–35:19), and (3) the Passover involved cultic sacrifice.[91] Furthermore, one of the present authors has demonstrated that the terminology of "body" reflects the way that the sacrificial lamb was spoken of in Jewish Passover traditions.[92] It is difficult to believe that all of these connections are merely coincidental.[93] Given the larger context of the epistle, Paul's point seems to be that since Christ the *Passover* Lamb has been slain, it is now necessary to consume the Passover *sacrifice*. Only with difficulty can such imagery be detached from the Lord's Supper, and there seems little exegetical basis for sundering the two.

The Eating of the Temple Sacrifices

Finally, we return to a type of sacrifice we have already seen Paul link to Christ's death elsewhere—namely, the sin offering (Rom 8:3; 2 Cor 5:21). It is necessary to recall that the torah often stipulates that sacrificial victims are to be eaten. For example, according to the torah, the peace offering had to be eaten in the correct time frame, or else the one who offered the sacrifice would not be accepted and would even be forced to bear iniquity (Lev 7:18; 19:6–8). Likewise, the Levitical code also stipulates that the thank offering must be eaten within a day, or else it also would not be acceptable (cf. Lev 22:30).[94] Though the priest's ritual consumption of sacrifices is attested in connection with other offerings,[95] it had especially important significance in the case of the sin offering. Leviticus indicates that *the sacred meal of the priests was meant to play a crucial and integral part of the atoning process.* In one chapter, Moses asks the priests:

91. Barber, "Historical Jesus," 665–68.

92. Pitre, *Jesus and the Last Supper*, 407–9.

93. Patterson, *Keeping the Feast*, 149–54.

94. The consumption of the sacrificial victim was broadly related to other sacrifices.

95. Eating the sacrificial animal and bread is linked with the ordination of the priests (Exod 29:31–34; Lev 8:31–36). The holy things to be eaten also include the bread of the Presence (cf. Lev 21:22; 24:9; cf. the extensive list in Num 18:13–20, 25–31). The priests also eat of the cereal offerings (cf. Lev 6:16) and the sin offerings (cf. Lev 6:24–26, 29; 7:6–10; 10:12–13, 17–18). Hosea mentions the practice while condemning the wicked priests (Hos 8:13; 9:4). Conversely, Ezekiel describes how the priests in the eschatological age will eat of the sacrifices in holiness (cf. Ezek 42:13; 44:29).

Why have you not eaten the sin offering in the place of the sanctuary, since it is a thing most holy and has been given to you that you may bear the iniquity of the congregation, *to make atonement* for them before the LORD? (Lev 10:17 RSV)

As both ancient Jewish tradition and modern pentateuchal specialists recognize, the logic of this passage is inescapable: if the priests fail to properly consume the sin offering, they cannot bear the sins of the people and make atonement for them.[96]

In summary: in his letters, Paul not only draws an analogy between participation in Israel's cult and the bread and cup of the Lord's Supper (1 Cor 10:18), but his specific depiction of Christ's death as a covenant sacrifice, a paschal lamb, and sin offering would reinforce the notion that Christ's sacrifice would involve *a cultic meal*. The elements of bread and wine, then, appear as part of an overall *temple paradigm* that shapes Paul's understanding of both Christ's death and the Lord's Supper. This is particularly fitting, for it is in 1 Corinthians that Paul unambiguously states that the church is the temple of God (1 Cor 3:16–17; 6:19).

All of this is important background for interpreting Paul's words about partaking of the Lord's Supper unworthily. Paul's warning that one can be guilty of "the body and blood" (1 Cor 11:27) is likely more than just a rebuke against offenses committed against the community. Paul's language indicates that one can in some way sin against the *elements* of the meal themselves. As further support of this, recall that Paul's warning is consistent with Israel's cultic traditions regarding the dangers of eating *temple sacrifices* in an unworthy manner. Consuming sacred food—which was among the "holy things" (e.g., Lev 21:22; 22:4, 6; etc.)—was no minor issue. One had to be properly disposed to eat of it. The Torah explicitly warns:

> Out of all the gifts to you, you shall present every offering due to the LORD. . . . And *you may eat it* in any place, you and your households;

---

96. See Baruch A. Levine, *Leviticus*, JPSTC (Philadelphia: The Jewish Publication Society, 1989), 62; Gane, *Cult and Character*, 96; Milgrom, *Leviticus*, 1:638. Such a view is well attested in rabbinic tradition: "The priests eat [of the sin offering] and *the owner is atoned for*" (*Sipra*, Shemini 2:4; taken from Jacob Neusner, *Sifra: An Analytical Translation*, 2 vols., BJS 139 [Atlanta: Scholars Press, 1988], 2:148). See also *b. Pesaḥ.* 59b; *b. Yoma* 68b; *b. Yebam.* 40a, 90a. The context makes clear why the priests did not consume the sin offering in Leviticus 10. The guilt being atoned for was in part due to them, and they were not permitted to eat of the sacrifices that addressed their own sins. See Sklar, *Leviticus*, 161.

for it is your reward in return for your service in the tent of meeting. . . .
And you shall not profane the holy things of the people of Israel, lest you
die. (Num 18:29, 31–32 RSV)

Commenting on this passage, Jacob Milgrom explains, "It is lethal to eat
it [the sacrifice] or touch it if one is in a state of impurity—even to tamper
with it in a state of purity. That the punishment is death by God is expressly
stated at the end of the verse."[97] With this biblical background in mind, it is
no wonder that Paul makes the (otherwise baffling) statement that some of
the Corinthians who have eaten and drunk in an "unworthy manner" have
suffered physical effects: "For this reason many of you are weak and ill,
and *some have died*" (1 Cor 11:30). Given these features of his discussion of
the Lord's Supper, Paul's warning about improper reception makes sense:
the reason the penalty is so serious is precisely because the elements *are*
significant.[98] Interpretations that insist that Paul is only concerned with
improper behavior toward other members of the community fail to take
seriously both his Jewish identity and the cultic background of his language.

The Lord's Supper and the Sacrifice of the Ecclesial Body

Paul's understanding of salvation involves sharing in Christ's sacrificial sufferings. Furthermore, as we highlighted at the beginning of this chapter,
this sacrificial offering is made not simply individually but *corporately*—that
is, in the body. Colin Miller thus writes, "The whole church is viewed as
one sacrifice."[99] This comports well with what the Last Supper teaches
about Christ's body—it is "for you"—that is, it is offered as a sacrificial
offering. In the words of E. P. Sanders:

> Paul creates an entire soteriology that is based on the idea of partici-
> pation. The word itself comes from his discussion of the Lord's Supper
> and meat offered to idols. I have sometimes guessed that sharing Christ's
> body and blood in the Eucharist all by itself might have led to something
> like Paul's ideal of Christians being one with Christ.[100]

---

97. Jacob Milgrom, *Numbers*, JPSTC (Philadelphia: Jewish Publication Society, 1990), 157.
98. See Fitzmyer, *First Corinthians*, 446–47.
99. Miller, *Practice of the Body of Christ*, 174.
100. See Sanders, *Paul: The Apostle's Life, Letters, and Thought*, 720–21; see also p. 239.

Along similar lines, Miller goes on to make the case that Paul's account of the Last Supper sheds light on his words in Romans 12:1: "I appeal to you therefore, brethren, by the mercies of God, to present your bodies as a living sacrifice, holy and acceptable to God, which is your *spiritual* [*logikēn*] worship" (RSV). Miller makes the case that the terminology of *logikē* in Greek thought had the connotation of what "fits" or "meshes" with nature. "As such, to live 'logically' is to live 'according to nature.'"[101] For the church to offer itself as a sacrificial body is "logical" worship, because in doing so the church realizes its identity. Miller explains:

> The church worships by embodying that which it is, Christ, who was himself a pleasing sacrifice to God (cf. Rom 3:25, Eph 5:25). . . . If the church is only the church *as* the body of Christ, it follows that *if* the church is going to be glorified with Christ it will also be sacrificed as Christ was (Rom 8:17).[102]

According to Paul, the community is the one body of Christ because of the Lord's Supper (1 Cor 10:17). It is not the case, then, that the church's spiritual worship simply coheres with partaking of the table of the Lord. A careful reading of Paul indicates that it is actually by participating in the Lord's Supper that members are united to the body and, becoming members of it, are so empowered to participate in this eschatological reality. In other words, by receiving the body of Christ, believers are united to Christ *and* to one another. By virtue of this, their sufferings are united with those of not only the Savior but also other "members." In this way, the whole church is taken up into the sacrifice of Christ.

Spiritual Food and Spiritual Drink

The Lord's Supper as "Spiritual Food" and "Spiritual Drink"

Finally, no treatment of Paul's view of the Lord's Supper can ignore what he says in the opening verses of 1 Corinthians 10:

---

101. Miller, *Practice of the Body of Christ*, 175.
102. Miller, *Practice of the Body of Christ*, 175.

> I do not want you to be unaware, brothers and sisters, that our ancestors were all under the cloud, and all passed through the sea, and all were baptized into Moses in the cloud and in the sea, and all ate the same *spiritual food*, and all drank the same *spiritual drink*. For they drank from the *spiritual rock* that followed them, and the rock was Christ. Nevertheless, God was not pleased with most of them, and they were struck down in the wilderness. Now *these things occurred as examples for us*, so that we might not desire evil as they did. (1 Cor 10:1–6)

This retelling of the story of Israel's exodus and wilderness experience is obviously shaped by the church's praxis. There is no evidence that anyone before Paul described the event of Israel's miraculous deliverance through the waters (cf. Exod 14:19–22) in terms of baptism.[103] Paul is recasting what happened to Israel in terms of the community's cultic rites. Hays writes, "The expression 'baptized into Moses' is nowhere to be found in Jewish sources; Paul has coined the phrase on the basis of Christian language."[104] For Paul these things are "examples" or "types" (*typoi*) of what would come in the new covenant.

Moreover, alongside the reference to baptism, interpreters detect an allusion to the Lord's Supper in the language of "spiritual food [*pneumatikon brōma*]" and "spiritual drink [*pneumatikon poma*]" (1 Cor 10:3–4). Although these expressions are allusions to the gifts of the manna (cf. Exod 16:1–36; Num 11:4–35) and the miraculous drink from a rock in the wilderness (cf. Exod 17:6; Num 20:7–13), it is widely recognized that Paul uses these images in connection with the Lord's Supper, which he goes on to mention explicitly in both this chapter and the next (1 Cor 10:16; 11:23–25). Again, to quote Richard Hays, "Just as the Corinthians receive spiritual food and drink at the Lord's Supper (cf. *Didache* 10.3), so also the Israelites were given spiritual food and drink in the wilderness."[105]

All of this raises the difficult question of what Paul means by speaking of "spiritual" (*pneumatikos*) food and drink. In some cases, Paul does use such terminology to refer to realities that are not "physical" or "fleshly" (*sarkikos*) (cf. Rom 15:27; 1 Cor 9:11; Eph 6:12).[106] On the other hand, that which is

---

103. See Thiselton, *First Epistle to the Corinthians*, 722.

104. See Hays, *First Corinthians*, 160.

105. See Hays, *First Corinthians*, 160. See also Käsemann, *Essays on New Testament Themes*, 113–14.

106. While affirming this, many reduce the ancient perspective to that of the Stoics, who viewed *pneuma* as a material reality. As Rabens observes, this is an overly determined reading. A substance need not be "material" to be conceived as "real," and caution should

"spiritual" is not *necessarily* "immaterial." For example, though believers obviously have material bodies, they are nonetheless identified by the apostle as "spiritual" (*pneumatikos*) (1 Cor 14:37). Furthermore, the word "spiritual" in the Pauline epistles often has the connotation of something that is linked to the Spirit (*pneuma*). For instance, Paul speaks of "spiritual gifts" (1 Cor 12:1) such as "healing" and "tongues," which are gifts associated with the working of the Spirit.[107] Those things invested with the power of the Spirit can therefore be seen as "spiritual"—that is, "*pneumatic* realities."[108] For Paul, the bread and wine of the Lord's Supper can be placed in this category.

The Pneumatic Bread and Cup: A Foretaste of the New Creation

In support of this point, it is important to notice that Paul uses the language of "spiritual food" and "spiritual drink" not only in 1 Corinthians 10, but just a couple of chapters later, he also speaks of how believers "drink of one Spirit":

> For just as the body is one and has many members, and all the members of the body, though many, are one body, so it is with Christ. For in the one Spirit we were all baptized into one body—Jews or Greeks, slaves or free—and *we were all made to drink of one Spirit*. (1 Cor 12:12–13)

What exactly does Paul mean when he speaks of "drinking of one Spirit" (1 Cor 12:13) and "baptism"? Some have argued that the imagery should be taken as merely metaphorical.[109] Yet as we argued in the previous chapter, given the numerous references to baptism as a rite of initiation (especially within 1 Corinthians—e.g., 1:13–17; 10:2) and Paul's teaching elsewhere linking ritual baptism to union with Christ, it "beggars belief to suggest that this baptism is a metaphorical one."[110]

---

be used in making literal statements that could be intended as metaphorical. See Rabens, *Holy Spirit and Ethics in Paul*, 25–79; Orr, *Christ Absent and Present*, 72–81.

107. Other passages where the "spiritual" is explicitly linked to the Spirit include, e.g., 1 Cor 2:13–15; 14:1–2; Gal 5:25–6:1.

108. See, e.g., Miller, *Practice of the Body of Christ*, 147–56.

109. See, e.g., James D. G. Dunn, *Baptism in the Holy Spirit: A Re-examination of the New Testament Teaching on the Gift of the Spirit in Relation to Pentecostalism Today* (Philadelphia: Westminster, 1970), 130; Fee, *First Epistle to the Corinthians*, 604–6.

110. Morales, "Baptism and Union with Christ," 170.

That said, commentators are divided as to whether "to drink of one Spirit" is a reference to baptism or the Lord's Supper. Several points support a baptismal interpretation. First, since ritual baptism is most probably in view in the first part of the verse, the drinking imagery is often thought to be read as "merely a literary parallel"—that is, a further baptismal allusion.[111] Second, the appearance of the aorist tense (*epotisthēmen*: "we were made to drink"; 1 Cor 12:13) is said to better reflect a baptismal reading since participation in the Lord's Supper is repeated but baptism was likely received only once.[112] Third, the aorist tense often carries the meaning not of "drinking" but of being "watered" (e.g., 1 Cor 3:6: "Apollos watered"), an image that fits well with baptism.[113] Fourth, though "drinking" is obviously linked to the Lord's Supper, to "drink the Spirit" is not an expression used elsewhere for it. If Paul wanted to signal an allusion to the Lord's Supper, it is said, he would have spoken of drinking of the "blood" of Christ or even of imbibing Christ himself.[114]

Nevertheless, there are important reasons for finding the baptismal interpretation of "drink of one Spirit" unpersuasive. First, there is no reason to assume that "drink of one Spirit" is necessarily intended as a literary parallel. Second, Paul's use of the aorist in 1 Corinthians 12:13 is explicable on stylistic grounds and is not necessarily incompatible with a reference to the Lord's Supper.[115] Most obviously, Paul's reference to the Israelites who "drank [*epion*] the same spiritual drink" also uses an aorist (1 Cor 10:4). Third, while *potizein* can carry the sense of "water" when used in reference to nonhuman subjects (animals, plants, etc.), "drink" would be the expected meaning where it is applied to humans.[116] Fourth, Paul identifies Christ as a "life-giving spirit [*pneuma*]" (1 Cor 15:45). If Paul can speak

111. Fitzmyer, *First Corinthians*, 479. See, e.g., Hays, *First Corinthians*, 214. John Chrysostom also rejected a eucharistic reference here (*Homilies on 1 Corinthians* 30.2; PG 61.251).

112. This would make the most sense out of the controversy described in 1 Corinthians, which entails divisions based on the identity of one's baptizer (1 Cor 1:13-17). This might also be suggested in Eph 4:5, which speaks of "one baptism," though the language could be interpreted in different ways.

113. E. R. Rogers, "*Epotisthēmen* Again," *NTS* 29 (1983): 139-42.

114. Rabens, *Holy Spirit and Ethics in Paul*, 116; Garland, *1 Corinthians*, 591.

115. Hans-Josef Klauck, *Herrenmahl und hellenistischer Kult: Eine religionsgeschichtliche Untersuchung zum ersten Korintherbrief* (Münster: Aschendorff, 1986), 334-35.

116. Klauck, *Herrenmahl und hellenistischer Kult*, 334-35; Friedrich W. Horn, *Das Angeld des Geistes: Studien zur paulinischen Pneumatologie*, FRLANT 154 (Göttingen: Vandenhoeck & Ruprecht, 1992), 174.

of Christ as a life-giving spirit, there is no reason to think he would not have spoken of drinking of the Spirit in connection with communion with Christ in the Lord's Supper.

Indeed, the wider context suggests that the Lord's Supper is more likely in view than baptism.[117] First and foremost, *there is no evidence that Christian baptism involved ingesting water.* Hence, the language of "drinking" would seem an odd way to describe the practice.[118] Second, while it would be strange to describe baptism with the image of "drinking"[119] (1 Cor 12:13), such terminology would be perfectly consistent with the command of Jesus to "drink" in remembrance of him (1 Cor 11:26; cf. 1 Cor 10:4). Third, as we have seen, in speaking of the manna and the water from the rock, Paul has already introduced the concept of "spiritual food" and "spiritual drink" (1 Cor 10:3–4). The phrase "drink of one Spirit" is simply too close to this passage to dismiss a connection. Fourth, in 1 Corinthians 10:1–3 Paul combines imagery of baptism (Israel's deliverance through the waters) and the Lord's Supper (spiritual food and drink). Reading 1 Corinthians 12:13 as a combination of baptismal and eucharistic references would fit this pattern. Finally, given that Paul spent so much time treating the Lord's Supper in 1 Corinthians 11, it seems highly unlikely that the eucharistic connections are merely coincidental in 1 Corinthians 12. The best reading of 1 Corinthians 12:13, therefore, is that it refers to the Eucharist. Miller seems on target when he states:

> The Eucharistic meal consists of pneumatic bread and pneumatic cup, because Christ's resurrected body is pneumatic and the meal is for consumption of and communion [*koinōnia*] with Christ himself ["This is my body"]. In a physical sense then, the church materially participates [*metechomen*] (1 Cor 12:13) in Christ's pneumatic body through the Lord's Supper (cf. 1 Cor 6:17 ["But anyone united to the Lord becomes one spirit with him"]).[120]

---

117. See, e.g., Baker, "Participating," 523.

118. See Klauck, *Herrenmahl und hellenistischer Kult*, 335.

119. As noted above, translating the verb with "watered" would be strange given the subject.

120. Miller, *Practice of the Body of Christ*, 150. See also A. J. M. Wedderburn, *Baptism and Resurrection: Studies in Pauline Theology against Its Graeco-Roman Background*, WUNT 44 (Tübingen: Mohr Siebeck, 1987), 246; Käsemann, *Essays on New Testament Themes*, 113. We part with such writers, however, in that we do not think Paul's logic depends on a "material-spirit" conception. Attempts to attribute to Paul a strict allegiance to the Stoic

According to Paul, participation in the elements of the Lord's Supper is a participation in the body and blood of Christ (1 Cor 10:16–17), which is effected through the Spirit (1 Cor 12:13; 6:17).[121] In other words, through the working of the Spirit, the bread and the wine become "spiritual food" and "spiritual drink" (1 Cor 10:3–4), uniting believers to the body and blood of the risen Lord. *In the Lord's Supper, then, participants have a foretaste of the resurrected body and the life of the world to come.*

As we have seen, the resurrection is part and parcel of Paul's teaching about the new creation. The apostle holds that God's salvific plan fulfilled in Christ is cosmic in scope. The material world points to its Creator (Rom 1:20); shares in the corruption that enters the world due to sin and is made subject to decay (Rom 8:21); and is described as "groaning" as it awaits the eschaton (Rom 8:22). Specifically, this is tied in Romans 8 to the resurrection—that is, the glorification of the saints. Likewise, in 1 Corinthians 15 we read that the terrestrial body will be "changed":

> Listen, I will tell you a mystery! We will not all die, but we will all be *changed*, in a moment, in the twinkling of an eye, at the last trumpet. For the trumpet will sound, and *the dead will be raised imperishable*, and *we will be changed*. For *this perishable body must put on imperishability*, and *this mortal body must put on immortality*. (1 Cor 15:51–53)

This glorification (1 Cor 15:43) marks the climax of a process that has already begun in this life in the believer (2 Cor 3:18). The arrival of the "spiritual [*pneumatikon*] body" (1 Cor 15:44) thus marks the event that all of creation has been longing to share in.

Against this backdrop, Paul's use of "spiritual [*pneumatikon*] food" and "spiritual [*pneumatikon*] drink" (1 Cor 10:3–4) appears especially significant. As Paul has read baptism into the exodus story, here too he views

---

perspective of spirit as material are overstated. See Rabens, *Holy Spirit and Ethics in Paul*, 86–120; C. Kavin Rowe, *One True Life: The Stoics and Early Christians and Rival Traditions* (New Haven: Yale University Press, 2016). Paul seems to believe that through the Spirit we have a material participation in the body of Christ. Nevertheless, this does not require him to hold a "material-spirit" pneumatology.

121. See Käsemann, *Essays on New Testament Themes*, 113: "The Lord's Supper dispenses *pneumatikon brōma* ["spiritual food"] and *poma* ["drink"] from the spiritual rock which is Christ. Therefore the sacrament effects the transformation of man. . . . The sacrament mediates the new existence by giving me the new Lord, the one true *Kyrios*. . . . And therefore we are entitled at this point to speak at last of incorporation into the Body of Christ."

the manna and water Israel drank from the rock as images of the Lord's Supper. At the same time, in light of 1 Corinthians 15, Paul's choice of wording indicates that he is not simply looking backward but also forward. The elements of the meal are described in terms associated with the resurrected body. In fact, as the "first fruits" of the resurrection (1 Cor 15:23), Christ's risen body—which Paul identifies with the bread—is already a spiritual body (1 Cor 15:44). Taking Paul's identification of the bread with Jesus's risen body seriously explains why he sees it as "spiritual food." Miller is correct: the Lord's Supper entails "pneumatic bread" and "pneumatic cup" because Christ's risen body is "pneumatic."[122] Believers, therefore, are given a foretaste of the new creation in the Lord's Supper.

In fact, given that the resurrected body is a "spiritual body" because it has in some way been "changed," it would seem right to suggest that *something similar happens* to the "spiritual food" and "spiritual drink" of the Lord's Supper. While Paul does not (of course) use the language of "real presence" or "transubstantiation," to insist that "spiritual" is merely a metaphor resists the *eschatological and christological realism* of Paul's language. It also involves downplaying his teaching concerning the role of the created world in Christ's saving work as well as the way he affirms that the future age has already broken into the present. The "spiritual" food and drink of the table of the Lord *effect* communion with the body (1 Cor 10:17). In other words, this is no mundane food and no mundane drink.

In Summary: Cosmic Redemption and the Table of the Lord's Body

In a response to Edith Humphrey, who critiques him for failing to fully account for the sacraments' place in Paul's theology, N. T. Wright acknowledges:

> It is not difficult, again joining up dots which Paul himself leaves in the realm of implication, to suppose that with the vision of the new creation in Rom 8 Paul would say that, since one day God will be "all in all" (1 Cor 15:28), the sacraments are advance signs of that filling, that suffusing with the divine presence, power and love of the creation which will yet remain other than the creator.[123]

---

122. Miller, *Practice of the Body of Christ*, 150.

123. Wright, "The Challenge of Dialogue," in Heilig, Hewitt, and Bird, *God and the Faithfulness of Paul*, 760.

Yet while Wright would seem to push the connection between the sacraments and the new creation into the realm of the "implications" of the apostle's thought, this underplays the language of Paul's actual teaching. The bread and wine of the Lord's Supper are not inconsequential aspects of the church's celebration for Paul.

For one thing, as we have seen above, there can be no question that Paul explicitly connects participation in Christ with the cultic celebration of the Lord's Supper. The apostle explicitly teaches that "participation" (*koinōnia*) involves a cultic dimension: Paul roots his understanding of what happens in drinking the "cup" and eating "the bread" in the Jewish temple "sacrifices [*thysias*]" (1 Cor 10:18). As Israel partook of the sacrificial offerings, Christ identifies the food of the new covenant meal with that which is sacrificed to secure it—namely, his body and blood. The Lord's Supper is therefore *itself* a cultic meal because, as with many of the cultic offerings of the old covenant, those in the new in some way consume the sacrificial victim. Paul writes that the Passover lamb has been killed, "therefore let us keep the feast" (1 Cor 5:8 NAB, slightly modified). The feast he most likely has in view is in fact the Lord's Supper.

Moreover, while many have downplayed importance of the eucharistic elements in Paul's teaching, the cultic logic in play undermines such attempts: Christ, the sacrificial offering, is somehow to be consumed.[124] To interpret Paul's identification of the bread and wine as Christ's "body" and "blood" as mere metaphors fails to do justice to his teaching. After all, Paul identifies the church as the body of Christ: "We who are many are one body" (1 Cor 10:17); and he tells the Corinthians, "Now you are the body of Christ" (1 Cor 12:27). But it would be wrong to insist that Paul thinks believers merely "symbolize" the body of Christ to the world. Paul holds that believers share *a real union* in the risen Lord through the Spirit so that Christ is *actually* present in them: "Do you not realize that Jesus Christ is in you?" (2 Cor 13:5). Similarly, downplaying the bread and wine of the Lord's Table as merely representational fails to account for Paul's teaching that they are "spiritual food" and "spiritual drink" (1 Cor 10:1–21). The same Spirit who raised Jesus's body from the dead now effects participation with Christ through the "cup of blessing" and the broken "bread" (1 Cor 10:16).

---

124. See Coutsoumpos, *Paul and the Lord's Supper*, 15: "Apparently Paul's view is that there are more than mere symbols involved in the Lord's Supper. There seems to be some sort of real spiritual communion with Christ. To participate at the table for the Christian meal was to have fellowship in Christ and his body (10:16–17)."

Believers thus "drink of the one Spirit" of Christ, the one who became "a life-giving spirit" by virtue of his glorious resurrection, when they drink of "the cup of the Lord" (1 Cor 10:21). For Paul, partaking of "the Lord's table" therefore does not merely symbolize ecclesial communion in Christ; it *actualizes* it in some way, as he clearly indicates when he declares, *"Because there is one bread, we who are many are one body"* (1 Cor 10:17).

Seen in this light, the bread and wine of the Lord's Supper are far from inconsequential for Paul's view of eucharistic participation. As in Israel's cult, Christians share in a sacred meal consisting of the sacrificial offering of the new covenant. Although in context he seems to downplay its significance, Otfried Hofius rightly draws on the language of Justin Martyr when he states, "Neither are the eucharistic gifts for Paul—to borrow a formulation from Justin [Martyr]—*koinos artos* (ordinary bread) and *koinon poma* (ordinary drink). Rather, they are, as the Apostle himself explains in 1 Cor 10:3–4, *pneumatikon brōma* ["spiritual food"] and *pneumatikon poma* ["spiritual drink"], i.e., gifts of a supraterrestrial, heavenly origin and nature."[125] In other words, the meal is the "Lord's" Supper because, among other things, he is present in the sacrificial food to be consumed.[126] Through the Spirit, his body and blood are made present. As Ernst Käsemann writes, in an ancient mind-set, "the representing dimension does actually bring about the presence of what is represented. . . . Thus, whatever objections may be raised against the term 'Real Presence,' it expresses exactly what Paul wants to say."[127]

To be sure though, while the Lord's Supper is a pneumatic event for Paul, it is not "magical"—that is, it does not effect participation apart from genuine faith.[128] Those who receive the Lord's Supper unworthily—for example, having neglected the poor or the hungry, undermining church unity, and so on—eat and drink judgment upon themselves (1 Cor 11:27–29). Such behavior contradicts the meaning of the meal, and Paul's admonition once again underscores the special significance of the eucharistic elements.[129] In context, Paul's warning is inextricably linked to the Lord's Supper's cultic associations. In the previous chapter, 1 Corinthians 10,

---

125. Hofius, "The Lord's Supper and the Lord's Supper Tradition," 100–101, citing Justin, *Apology* 1.66.2.

126. Fee, *First Epistle to the Corinthians*, 539–40; Hofius, "The Lord's Supper and the Lord's Supper Tradition," 78.

127. Käsemann, *Essays on New Testament Themes*, 128.

128. See Morales, "Baptism and Union with Christ," 158n4.

129. Leander E. Keck, *Paul and His Letters* (Philadelphia: Fortress, 1982), 62.

Paul warns that participation in pagan cultic meals is dangerous due to the spiritual powers at work in them. Yet Christ's sacrificial death ushers in a sacrificial celebration of even greater spiritual power. Believers have participation in the body and blood of Christ precisely because he offered himself as the sacrifice of the "new covenant" (1 Cor 11:25), an offering ordered to the cultic meal par excellence—a meal that brings one into communion with the "man from heaven" (1 Cor 15:47).

Through participating in the Lord's Supper, then, the community becomes what is consumed—the body of Christ. Since the body of Christ was sacrificed, believers are taken up into this offering. By uniting its sacrifice with his, patiently enduring the sufferings of the tribulation that will precede the resurrection, the church participates in ushering in the new creation itself, of which the "spiritual food" and "spiritual drink" are but a foretaste. Or, as Albert Schweitzer once put it, "Baptism and the Lord's Supper effect an initiation of the believer of the 'last times,' which entitles him to participate in the glories of the Messianic Kingdom."[130]

130. Schweitzer, *The Mysticism of Paul*, 21.

Paul's Gospel of Divine Sonship

In this volume we have attempted to offer an analysis of Paul's theology in light of contemporary scholarship. In particular, we have argued that Paul's view is informed by a conviction that the apocalyptic new covenant has arrived in Jesus, the one Paul recognizes as the messiah of Israel. Specifically, Paul views himself as one of the "ministers of the new covenant" (2 Cor 3:6), a notion shaped by Jeremiah 31. This specific feature of the apostle's thought illuminates various aspects of his theology and helps to reinforce the explicitly Jewish shape of his message. Paul is *both* an apostle to the gentiles and yet *also* concerned with the salvation of "all Israel" (Rom 11:26). He views hopes for the restoration of Israel as fulfilled in the inclusion of the nations in the one new covenant people of God. Consistent with his new covenant ministry, he claims that the law is "spiritual" (Rom 7:14) while also holding that it brought "death" (Rom 7:10) because it was unable of itself to produce obedience of itself. In this, Paul's message was shaped by the scriptures of Israel, which recognized that divine heart surgery and the pouring out of the Spirit would be necessary for the law to be fulfilled in obedience (cf., e.g., Ezek 36:26–27). As Jeremiah announced, the law would need to be written on the people's hearts (Jer 31:33). This power had arrived in Christ's gift (grace) and was poured out in believers' hearts through the Spirit.

At the center of Paul's theology is his view of Jesus. For Paul, Jesus is the messiah, the "Christ," the Son of David (cf. Rom 1:3). In addition, Paul's Christology is informed by Jewish apocalyptic traditions, which looked forward to the revelation of a heavenly deliverer. Moreover, faithful to common Jewish expectations, Paul believes that the restoration of God's people would occur only through a period of tribulation. In keeping with other Jewish perspectives, the suffering of the righteous could even be seen to effect atonement for sin in a way analogous to Israel's sacrificial worship.

251

Yet it would be wrong to insist that Paul's theology was merely predetermined by preconceived expectations he held before coming to faith in Christ. For Paul, the coming of Christ not only fulfilled Jewish hopes but it did so in ways that confounded expectations. For one thing, Paul tells us that the notion of a crucified messiah represented a stumbling block to Jews (1 Cor 1:23). Despite the fact that Jewish thought often linked the restoration of Israel to a period of tribulation, the revelation of the cross constituted a scandal to Jewish audiences. Nevertheless, for the apostle Christ's act of giving himself in love was not only to be accepted, it also represented a new revelation about the very identity of God himself. Paul's Christology was not simply predetermined by his first-century Judaism. Rather, he believed the revelation of God in Christ was so momentous that it even shed new light on the mystery of YHWH's identity as the one Lord. For Paul, Christ is Lord and therefore "Son of God" in an utterly unique way.

Given this identity, Jesus's act of self-offering involved a sacrifice that went beyond anything that could have been made in the Jerusalem temple. Because of his righteous act of obedience, the dominion of sin and death established with Adam has ended, and all can live through the gift of grace (Rom 5:12–21). This grace is inseparably connected to Christ's gift of self and, indeed, involves nothing less than a sharing in the life of the divine Son, which empowers believers to act in faithful obedience as he did (e.g., Phil 2:8, 12–13). In dying, Christ creates the conditions of possibility for the in-breaking of a new age, the new creation, which dawns with his resurrection from the dead. Through his risen life Christ draws the members of the new covenant into his very life of divine sonship.

Moreover, through the work of his Spirit, the risen Lord conforms the members of the new covenant people of God to himself, in particular in justification, bringing about the cardiac righteousness of the new covenant. As Jeremiah announced, in the new covenant God solves the problem of unrighteousness (*adikia*) (Jer 31:34 [LXX Jer 38:34]). God reveals his faithfulness and righteousness in causing his people to act faithfully and righteously by his Spirit, through which he writes his law on human hearts. Furthermore, this cardiac righteousness is realized through baptism, wherein believers die and rise with Christ and are thereby conformed to his death and resurrection (Rom 6:1–4), such that justification can be rightly defined as conformity to the character of Christ (cf. Rom 8:29). Furthermore, it is through the "table of the Lord" (1 Cor 10:21) that both Jew and gentile are united and drawn into a real participation with Christ as members of his body. Through participating in the sacrifice of the new covenant, the eucharistic table of the Lord conforms the members of the new covenant to his heavenly life by conforming them to himself.

What can we conclude from all of this? We would suggest that Paul was a minister of the new covenant and his gospel is best understood as the gospel of divine sonship. This serves not only to bring together the various dimensions of Paul's message into a coherent whole but also makes perfect sense given the ancient understanding of the nature of covenants. As we explained above, according to that view, covenant-making was viewed as creating kinship bonds. The message that Paul proclaims is that in the new covenant both Jews and gentiles are invited to become the sons and daughters of God in Christ.

Still, we have to be very clear about the proper order of the gospel of divine sonship. First and foremost, Paul's gospel of divine sonship is about Christ the Lord, the Son of God in an utterly unique way. It is this gospel that he proclaims to the nations—namely, that Jesus Christ is the risen Lord of heaven and earth, of this world and the world to come. Yet in and through the divine Son, both Jew and Greek are united to the body of Christ and given the grace of adoption in him. At the very core of this message is the proclamation of what the Catholic tradition has long called the *admirabile commercium* (the "great exchange"): he became as we are so that we may become as he is. From the time of Irenaeus, this has been recognized as the heart of Christian soteriology, and, as our treatment shows, it is a notion derived from Paul. Or, as he put it in his own words, "Though he was rich, yet for your sakes he became poor, so that by his poverty you might become rich" (2 Cor 8:9).

BIBLIOGRAPHY

Adams, Edward. *The Stars Will Fall from Heaven: Cosmic Catastrophe in the New Testament and Its World.* LNTS 347. London: T&T Clark, 2007.

Adeyẹmi, Fẹmi. *The New Covenant Torah in Jeremiah and the Law of Christ in Paul.* SBL 94. New York: Peter Lang, 2006.

Ådna, Jostein. "The Eucharist in Paul and in Hebrews." In *Institutions of the Emerging Church*, 93–111. LNTS 305. London: Bloomsbury, 2016.

Aletti, Jean-Noël. *Justification by Faith in the Letters of Saint Paul: Keys to Interpretation.* Translated by Peggy Manning Meyer. AnBib 5. Rome: Gregorian & Biblical Press, 2015.

Allison, Dale C., Jr. *The End of the Ages Has Come: An Early Interpretation of the Passion and Resurrection of Jesus.* Eugene: Wipf & Stock, 2013.

Ambrose, Kimberly. *Jew among Jews: Rehabilitating Paul.* Eugene, OR: Wipf & Stock, 2015.

Anderson, Gary. "From Israel's Burden to Israel's Debt: Towards a Theology of Sin in Biblical and Early Second Temple Sources." In *Reworking the Bible: Apocryphal and Related Texts at Qumran*, edited by E. G. Chazon, D. Dimant, and R. Clements, 1–30. Leiden: Brill, 2005.

———. *Sin: A History.* New Haven: Yale University Press, 2009.

Aquinas, Thomas. *Commentary on the Letter of Saint Paul to the Romans.* Translated by Fabian R. Larcher, OP. Lander, WY: Aquinas Institute, 2012.

———. *Commentary on the Letters of Saint Paul to the Corinthians.* Translated by Fabian R. Larcher, OP, Beth Mortensen, and Daniel Keating. Lander, WY: Aquinas Institute, 2012.

———. *Commentary on the Letters of Saint Paul to the Galatians and Ephesians.* Translated by Fabian R. Larcher, OP, and Matthew L. Lamb. Lander, WY: Aquinas Institute, 2012.

———. *Commentary on the Letters of Saint Paul to the Philippians, Colossians, Thessalonians, Timothy, Titus, and Philemon.* Translated by Fabian R. Larcher, OP. Lander, WY: Aquinas Institute, 2012.

Arnold, Clinton E. *Powers of Darkness: Principalities and Powers in Paul's Letters.* Downers Grove, IL: InterVarsity Press, 1992.

Attridge, Harold. "How the Scrolls Impacted Scholarship on Hebrews." In *The Bible and the Dead Sea Scrolls*, edited by James H. Charlesworth, 331–55. 3 vols. Waco, TX: Baylor University Press, 2006.

Augustine, *The Spirit and the Letter.* In *Answer to the Pelagians I.* Works of Saint Augustine 1. Translated by Roland Teske, SJ. Hyde Park, NY: New City Press, 1997.

Aune, David E. *Prophecy, Apocalypticism, and Magic in Early Christianity.* WUNT 199. Tübingen: Mohr Siebeck, 2006.

———, ed. *Rereading Paul Together: Protestant and Catholic Perspectives on Justification.* Grand Rapids: Baker Academic, 2006.

———, with Eric Stewart. "From the Idealized Past to the Imaginary Future: Eschatological Restoration in Jewish Apocalyptic Literature." In *Restoration: Old Testament, Jewish, and Christian Perspectives*, edited by James M. Scott, 147–78. Leiden: Brill, 2001.

Baker, Mary Patton. "Participating in the Body and Blood of Christ: Christian *Koinōnia* and the Lord's Supper." In *"In Christ" in Paul: Explorations in Paul's Theology of Union and Participation*, edited by Michael J. Thate, Kevin J. Vanhoozer, and Constantine R. Campbell, 503–28. WUNT 2/384. Tübingen: Mohr Siebeck, 2014.

Barber, Michael P. "The Historical Jesus and Cultic Restoration Eschatology: The New Temple, the New Priesthood, and the New Cult." PhD diss., Fuller Theological Seminary, 2010.

Barber, Michael P., and John A. Kincaid. "Cultic Theosis in Paul and Second Temple Judaism." *JSPL* 5, no. 2 (2015): 237–56.

Barclay, John M. G. "Apocalyptic Allegiance and Disinvestment in the World." In *Paul and the Apocalyptic Imagination*, edited by Ben C. Blackwell, John K. Goodrich, and Jason Maston, 257–74. Minneapolis: Fortress, 2016.

———. "Believers and the 'Last Judgment' in Paul: Rethinking Grace and Recompense." In *Eschatologie—Eschatology: The Sixth Durham-Tübingen Research Symposium; Eschatology in Old Testament, Ancient Judaism and Early Christianity*, edited by Hans-Joachim Eckstein, Christof Landmesser, and Hermann Lichtenberger, 195–208. Tübingen: Mohr Siebeck, 2009.

———. "'By the Grace of God I Am What I Am': Grace and Agency in Philo and Paul." In *Divine and Human Agency in Paul and His Cultural*

Environment, edited by John M. G. Barclay and Simon J. Gathercole, 140–57. London: T&T Clark, 2006.

———. "Grace and the Countercultural Reckoning of Worth: Community Construction in Galatians 5–6." In *Galatians and Christian Theology: Justification, the Gospel, and Ethics in Paul's Letter*, edited by Mark W. Elliot, Scott J. Hafemann, N. T. Wright, and John Frederick, 306–17. Grand Rapids: Baker Academic, 2014.

———. "Grace and the Transformation of Agency in Christ." In *Redefining First-Century Jewish and Christian Identities: Essays in Honor of Ed Parish Sanders*, edited by Fabian E. Udoh, 372–89. Notre Dame, IN: University of Notre Dame Press, 2008.

———. "Manna and the Circulation of Grace: A Study of 2 Corinthians 8:1–15." In *The Word Leaps the Gap: Essays on Scripture and Theology in Honor of Richard B. Hays*, edited by J. Ross Wagner, C. Kavin Rowe, and A. Katherine Grieb, 409–26. Grand Rapids: Eerdmans, 2008.

———. *Obeying the Truth: A Study in Paul's Ethics in Galatians*. Edinburgh: T&T Clark, 1998.

———. *Paul and the Gift*. Grand Rapids: Eerdmans, 2015.

———. "Under Grace: The Christ-Gift and the Construction of a Christian Habitus." In *Apocalyptic Paul: Cosmos and Anthropos in Romans 5–8*, edited by Beverly Roberts Gaventa, 59–76. Waco, TX: Baylor University Press, 2013.

Barker, P. A. "Jubilee." In *Dictionary of the Pentateuch*, 695–707. Downers Grove, IL: IVP Academic, 2003.

Barrett, C. K. *Church, Ministry, and Sacraments in the New Testament*. Exeter: Paternoster, 1985.

———. *The First Epistle to the Corinthians*. BNTC. Peabody, MA: Hendrickson, 1968.

Barrier, Jeremy. *The Acts of Paul and Thecla: A Critical Edition and Commentary*. WUNT 2/27. Tübingen: Mohr Siebeck, 2009.

Bates, Matthew. "A Christology of Incarnation and Enthronement: Romans 1:3–4 as Unified, Nonadoptionist, and Nonconciliatory." *CBQ* 77 (2015): 107–27.

———. *Salvation by Allegiance Alone*. Grand Rapids: Baker Academic, 2017.

Bauckham, Richard. "Biblical Theology and the Problems of Monotheism." In *Out of Egypt: Biblical Theology and Biblical Interpretation*, edited by Craig Bartholomew, Mary Healy, Karl Möller, and Robin Perry, 188–96. Scripture and Hermeneutics 5. Grand Rapids: Zondervan, 2004.

————. *God Crucified: Monotheism and Christology in the New Testament.* Grand Rapids: Eerdmans, 1999.

————. *Jesus and the God of Israel: God Crucified and Other Studies on the New Testament's Christology of Divine Identity.* Grand Rapids: Eerdmans, 2008.

Baur, F. C. *Paul the Apostle: His Life and Works, Epistles and Teachings.* Translated by Allan Menzies. 2 vols. 1873–1875. Repr., Peabody, MA: Hendrickson, 2003.

Beale, G. K. *A New Testament Biblical Theology: The Unfolding of the Old Testament in the New.* Grand Rapids: Baker Academic, 2011.

Benedict XVI (Joseph Ratzinger). *Saint Paul.* Translation by *L'Observatore Romano.* San Francisco: Ignatius Press, 2009.

Benoit, Pierre. "'We Too Groan Inwardly . . .' (Romans 8:23)." In *Jesus and the Gospel,* 40–50. 2 vols. London: Darton, 1974.

Bentley, Roland Thomas. "'Worship God Alone': The Emerging Christian Tradition of *Latreia.*" PhD diss., University of Virginia, 2009.

Bergsma, John S. *The Jubilee from Leviticus to Qumran: A History of Interpretation.* VTSup 115. Leiden: Brill, 2007.

————. "Qumran Self-Identity: 'Israel' or 'Judah'?" *DSD* 15 (2008): 172–89.

Berry, Donald K. "Malachi's Dual Design: The Close of the Canon and What Comes Afterward." In *Forming Prophetic Literature: Essays on Isaiah and the Twelve in Honor of D. W. Watts,* edited by J. W. Watts, J. D. W. Watts, and P. R. House, 269–302. Sheffield: Sheffield Academic Press, 1996.

Betz, Hans Dieter. *Galatians.* Hermeneia. Philadelphia: Fortress, 1979.

Bird, Michael F. *An Anomalous Jew: Paul among Jews, Greeks, and Romans.* Grand Rapids: Eerdmans, 2016.

————. *The Saving Righteousness of God: Studies on Paul, Justification, and the New Perspective.* Paternoster Biblical Monographs. Eugene, OR: Wipf & Stock, 2007.

Bird, Michael F., and Joseph Dodson, eds. *Paul and the Second Century.* LNTS 412. London: T&T Clark, 2012.

Black, Matthew. *An Aramaic Approach to the Gospels and Acts.* Oxford: Clarendon Press, 1967.

Blackwell, Ben C. *Christosis.* WUNT 2/314. Tübingen: Mohr Siebeck, 2011.

————. *Christosis: Engaging Paul's Soteriology with His Patristic Interpreters.* Grand Rapids: Eerdmans, 2016.

————. "Immortal Glory and the Problem of Death in Romans 3.23." *JSNT* 32 (2010): 285–308.

Blackwell, Ben C., John K. Goodrich, and Jason Maston. "Paul and the

Apocalyptic Imagination: An Introduction." In *Paul and the Apocalyptic Imagination*, edited by Ben C. Blackwell, John K. Goodrich, and Jason Maston, 3–21. Minneapolis: Fortress, 2016.

———, eds. *Paul and the Apocalyptic Imagination*. Minneapolis: Fortress, 2016.

Boakye, Andrew K. *Death and Life: Resurrection, Restoration, and Rectification in Paul's Letters*. Eugene, OR: Pickwick, 2017.

Boccacini, Gabriele, and Carlos A. Segovia, eds. *Paul the Jew: Rereading the Apostle as a Figure of Second Temple Judaism*. Minneapolis: Fortress, 2016.

Bockmuehl, Markus. "Did Paul Go to Heaven When He Died?" In *Jesus, Paul, and the People of God: A Theological Dialogue with N. T. Wright*, edited by Nicholas Perrin and Richard Hays, 211–30. Downers Grove, IL: IVP Academic, 2011.

Bornkamm, Günther. *Early Christian Experience*. Translated P. L. Hammer. New York: Harper & Row, 1969.

———. *Paul*. Translated by D. M. G. Stalker. 1969. Repr., Minneapolis: Fortress, 1995.

Bousset, William. *Kyrios Christos: A History of the Belief in Christ from the Beginnings of Christianity to Irenaeus*. Translated by John E. Steeley. 1913. Repr., Waco, TX: Baylor University Press, 2013.

Broduer, Scott. *The Holy Spirit's Agency in the Resurrection of the Dead: An Exegetico-Theological Study of 1 Corinthians 15,44b–49 and Romans 8,9–13*. Rome: Gregorian University, 1996.

Bruce, F. F. *The Epistle to the Galatians*. NIGTC. Grand Rapids: Eerdmans, 1982.

Bultmann, Rudolf. *Theology of the New Testament*. Translated by Kendrick Grobel. New York: Charles Scribner's Sons, 1951, 1955.

Burke, Trevor J. *Adopted into God's Family: Exploring a Pauline Metaphor*. NSBT 22. Downers Grove, IL: InterVarsity Press, 2006.

Burkert, Walter. *Greek Religion: Archaic and Classical*. Cambridge: Harvard University Press, 1985.

Burnett, David. "A Neglected Deuteronomic Scriptural Matrix for the Nature of the Resurrection Body in 1 Corinthians 15:39–42." In *Scripture, Texts, and Tracings in 1 Corinthians*, edited by B. J. Oropeza and Linda Belleville. Minneapolis: Fortress, forthcoming 2019.

———. "'So Shall Your Seed Be': Paul's Use of Genesis 15:5 in Romans 4:18 in Light of Early Jewish Deification Traditions." *JSPL* 5, no. 2 (2015): 211–36.

Byrne, Brendan J. *"Sons of God"—"Seed of Abraham": A Study of the Idea of the Sonship of God of All Christians in Paul Against the Jewish Background.* Rome: Biblical Institute Press, 1979.

Caird, G. B. *Principalities and Powers: A Study in Pauline Theology.* Oxford: Oxford University Press, 1956.

Campbell, Constantine R. *Paul and Union with Christ: An Exegetical and Theological Study.* Grand Rapids: Zondervan, 2012.

Campbell, Douglas. "Apocalyptic Epistemology: The *Sine Qua Non* of Valid Pauline Interpretation." In *Paul and the Apocalyptic Imagination*, edited by Ben C. Blackwell, John K. Goodrich, and Jason Maston, 65–86. Minneapolis: Fortress, 2016.

———. *The Deliverance of God: An Apocalyptic Rereading of Justification in Paul.* Grand Rapids: Eerdmans, 2009.

———. Foreword to *Paul's Divine Christology*, by Chris Tilling, x–xix. Grand Rapids: Eerdmans, 2015.

———. *Framing Paul: An Epistolary Biography.* Grand Rapids: Eerdmans, 2014.

———. *The Quest for Paul's Gospel: A Suggested Strategy.* London: T&T Clark, 2005.

Capes, David. *The Divine Christ: Paul, the Lord Jesus, and the Scriptures of Israel.* Grand Rapids: Baker Academic, 2018.

———. *Old Testament Yahweh Texts in Paul's Christology.* WUNT 2/267. Tübingen: Mohr Siebeck, 1992.

———. "YHWH Texts and Monotheism in Paul's Christology." In *Early Jewish and Christian Monotheism*, edited by Loren T. Stuckenbruck and Wendy E. S. North, 120–37. JSNTSup 263. London: T&T Clark, 2004.

Carson, D. A. "Atonement in Romans 3:21–26: 'God Presented Him as a Propitiation.'" In *The Glory of the Atonement*, edited by C. E. Hill and F. A. James III, 119–39. Downers Grove, IL: InterVarsity Press, 2004.

———. "The Vindication of Imputation: On Fields of Discourse and Semantic Fields." In *Justification: What's at Stake in the Current Debates?*, edited by Mark Husbands and Daniel J. Treier, 46–78. Downers Grove, IL: InterVarsity Press, 2004.

Chancey, Mark. Foreword to *Paul and Palestinian Judaism: A Comparison of Patterns of Religion*, by E. P. Sanders, xx–xxiii. 40th anniversary ed. Minneapolis: Fortress, 2017.

Charlesworth, James H., ed. *The Old Testament Pseudepigrapha.* 2 vols. ABRL. New York: Doubleday, 1983, 1985.

Chester, Andrew. *Messiah and Exaltation: Jewish Messianic and Visionary*

Traditions and New Testament Christology. WUNT 207. Tübingen: Mohr Siebeck, 2007.

Chester, Stephen J. *Reading Paul with the Reformers: Reconciling Old and New Perspectives.* Grand Rapids: Eerdmans, 2017.

Ciampa, Roy E., and Brian S. Rosner. "1 Corinthians." In *Commentary on the New Testament Use of the Old Testament,* edited by D. A. Carson and G. K. Beale, 695–752. Grand Rapids: Baker Academic, 2007.

———. *The First Letter to the Corinthians.* PNTC. Grand Rapids: Eerdmans, 2010.

Cohen, Shaye J. D. "Galatians." In *The Jewish Annotated New Testament,* edited by Amy-Jill Levine and Marc Zvi Brettler, 373–87. 2nd ed. Oxford: Oxford University Press, 2017.

Collins, Adela Yarbro, and John J. Collins. *King and Messiah as Son of God: Divine, Human, and Angelic Messianic Figures in Biblical and Related Literature.* Grand Rapids: Eerdmans, 2008.

Collins, John J. *Apocalypse, Prophecy, and Pseudepigraphy: On Jewish Apocalyptic Literature.* Grand Rapids: Eerdmans, 2015.

———. *The Apocalyptic Imagination: An Introduction to Jewish Apocalyptic Literature.* 3rd ed. Grand Rapids: Eerdmans, 2016.

———. *Daniel.* Hermeneia. Minneapolis: Fortress, 1993.

———. *The Scepter and the Star: Messianism in Light of the Dead Sea Scrolls.* 2nd ed. Grand Rapids: Eerdmans, 2010.

Collins, Raymond. *First Corinthians.* SP 7. Collegeville, MN: Liturgical Press, 1999.

Coutsoumpos, Panayotis. *Paul and the Lord's Supper: A Socio-Historical Investigation.* SBL 84. New York: Peter Lang, 2005.

Cranfield, C. E. B. *A Critical Exegetical Commentary on the Epistle to the Romans.* 2 vols. ICC. Edinburgh: T&T Clark, 1975.

Cross, Frank Moore. *From Epic to Canon: History and Literature in Ancient Israel.* Baltimore: Johns Hopkins University Press, 1998.

Danker, Frederick William. *Benefactor: Epigraphic Study of a Graeco-Roman Semantic Field.* St. Louis: Clayton, 1982.

———, ed. *A Greek-English Lexicon of the New Testament and Other Early Christian Literature.* 3rd ed. Chicago: University of Chicago Press, 2000.

Das, A. Andrew. *Paul and the Stories of Israel: Grand Thematic Narratives in Galatians.* Minneapolis: Fortress, 2016.

Davies, John A. *A Royal Priesthood: Literary and Intertextual Perspectives on an Image of Israel in Exodus 19:6.* JSOTSup 395. London: T&T Clark, 2004.

Davies, J. P. *Paul among the Apocalypses? An Evaluation of the "Apocalyptic Paul" in the Context of Jewish and Christian Apocalyptic Literature.* LNTS 562. London: Bloomsbury T&T Clark, 2016.

Davies, W. D. *Jewish and Pauline Studies.* Philadelphia: Fortress, 1984.

———. *Paul and Rabbinic Judaism.* 5th ed. 1948. Repr., Mifflintown, PA: Sigler, 1998.

de Boer, Martinus C. "Apocalyptic as God's Eschatological Activity." In *Paul and the Apocalyptic Imagination,* edited by Ben C. Blackwell, John K. Goodrich, and Jason Maston, 45–63. Minneapolis: Fortress, 2016.

———. *The Defeat of Death: Apocalyptic Eschatology in 1 Corinthians 15 and Romans 5.* LNTS. Sheffield: Sheffield Academic Press, 1988.

———. *Galatians: A Commentary.* NTL. Louisville: Westminster John Knox, 2011.

Deidun, T. J., IC. *New Covenant Morality in Paul.* AnBib 89. Rome: Editrice Pontificio Instituto Biblico, 1981.

Deissmann, Adolf. *Paul: A Study in Social and Religious History.* Translated by W. E. Wilson. New York: Harper Torchbooks, 1957.

———. *Paulus. Eine Kultur- und Religionsgeschichtliche Skizze.* Tübingen: J. C. B. Mohr, 1911.

deSilva, David A. *Galatians: A Handbook on the Greek Text.* Waco: Baylor University Press, 2014.

———. *Transformation: The Heart of Paul's Gospel.* Bellingham, WA: Lexham, 2014.

Despotis, Athanasios. "*Ho gar apothanōn dedikaiōtai apo tēs hamartias:* Rethinking the Application of the Verb *dikaiousthai* in Baptismal Contexts from the Perspective of Rom 6:7." In *Participation, Justification, and Conversion: Eastern Orthodox Interpretation of Paul and the Debate between "Old and New Perspectives on Paul,"* edited by Athanasios Despotis, 29–57. WUNT 2/442. Tübingen: Mohr Siebeck, 2017.

DiTomasso, Lorenzo. "Jerusalem, New." In *The Eerdmans Dictionary of Early Judaism,* edited by John J. Collins and Daniel C. Harlow, 797–99. Grand Rapids: Eerdmans, 2010.

Dodd, C. H. "*ΙΛΑΣΚΕΣΘΑΙ,* Its Cognates, Derivatives, and Synonyms in the Septuagint." *JTS* 32 (1930–31): 352–60.

Donfried, J. P. "Justification and Last Judgment in Paul." *ZNW* 67 (1976): 90–110.

Douglas, Mary. "The Eucharist: Its Continuity with the Bread Sacrifice of Leviticus." *Modern Theology* 15, no. 2 (1999): 209–24.

————. *Purity and Danger: An Analysis of Concepts of Pollution and Taboo.* New York: Routledge, 1966.

Duling, Dennis C. "The Testament of Solomon." In vol. 1 of *Old Testament Pseudepigrapha*, edited by James H. Charlesworth, 935–59. 2 vols. New York: Doubleday, 1983, 1985.

Dunn, James D. G. *Baptism in the Holy Spirit: A Re-examination of the New Testament Teaching on the Gift of the Spirit in Relation to Pentecostalism Today.* Philadelphia: Westminster, 1970.

————. *Beginning from Jerusalem.* Christianity in the Making 2. Grand Rapids: Eerdmans, 2009.

————. *Christology in the Making: A New Testament Inquiry.* Grand Rapids: Eerdmans, 1980.

————. *Did the First Christians Worship Jesus? The New Testament Evidence.* London: SPCK, 2010.

————. *The Epistle to the Galatians.* Black's New Testament Commentary. 1993. Repr., Grand Rapids: Baker Academic, 2011.

————. *Jesus, Paul, and the Gospels.* Grand Rapids: Eerdmans, 2011.

————. "The Justice of God: A Renewed Perspective on Justification by Faith." *JTS* 43 (1992): 1–21.

————. *Neither Jew nor Greek: A Contested Identity.* Christianity in the Making 3. Grand Rapids: Eerdmans, 2015.

————. *The New Perspective on Paul.* Rev. ed. Grand Rapids: Eerdmans, 2008.

————. *The Parting of the Ways: Between Christianity and Judaism and Their Significance for the Character of Christianity.* 2nd ed. London: SCM, 2006.

————. *Romans.* 2 vols. WBC 38A–B. Nashville: Thomas Nelson, 1988.

————. *The Theology of Paul the Apostle.* Grand Rapids: Eerdmans, 1998.

Durham, John. *Exodus.* WBC 3. Waco, TX: Word, 1987.

Ehrhardt, A. A. T. "Jesus Christ and Alexander the Great." *JTS* 46 (1945): 45–51.

Ehrman, Bart. *How Jesus Became God: The Exaltation of a Jewish Preacher from Galilee.* San Francisco: HarperOne, 2014.

Eisenbaum, Pamela. *Paul Was Not a Christian: The Original Message of a Misunderstood Apostle.* San Francisco: HarperOne, 2009.

Elliot, J. K. *The Apocryphal New Testament: A Collection of Apocryphal Christian Literature in an English Translation.* Oxford: Oxford University Press, 1993.

Engberg-Pedersen, Troels. "Proclaiming the Lord's Death: 1 Corinthians

11:17–34 and the Forms of Paul's Theological Argument." In *Pauline Theology*, vol. 2, *1 and 2 Corinthians*, edited by David M. Hay, 103–32. Minneapolis: Fortress, 1993.

Eubank, Nathan. *Wages of Cross-Bearing and Debt of Sin: The Economy of Heaven in Matthew's Gospel*. BZNW 196. Berlin: De Gruyter, 2013.

Evans, Craig A. *Mark 8:27–16:20*. WBC 34B. Nashville: Thomas Nelson, 2001.

Fee, Gordon. *The First Epistle to the Corinthians*. NICNT. Grand Rapids: Eerdmans, 1987.

———. *Pauline Christology*. Grand Rapids: Baker Academic, 2007.

Finlan, Stephen. *The Background and Content of Paul's Cultic Metaphors*. AcBib 19. Atlanta: Society of Biblical Literature, 2004.

Fisk, Bruce N. "Eating Meat Offered to Idols: Corinthian Behavior and Pauline Response in 1 Corinthians 8–10 (A Response to Gordon Fee)." *Trinity Journal* 10 (1989): 49–70.

Fitzmyer, Joseph A., SJ. *First Corinthians*. AYB 32. New Haven: Yale University Press, 2008.

———. *The One Who Is to Come*. Grand Rapids: Eerdmans, 2007.

———. *Paul and His Theology: A Brief Sketch*. Englewood Cliffs, NJ: Prentice Hall, 1987.

———. "Pauline Theology." In *The New Jerome Biblical Commentary*, edited by Raymond E. Brown, SS, Joseph A. Fitzmyer, SJ, and Roland E. Murphy, OCarm, 1382–1416. Upper Saddle River, NJ: Prentice Hall, 1990.

———. *Romans*. AYB 33. New Haven: Yale University Press, 1993.

Fletcher-Louis, Crispin H. T. "Jesus as the High Priestly Messiah: Part 1." *JSHJ* 4, no. 2 (2006): 155–75.

Fotopoulos, John. "Arguments Concerning Food Offered to Idols: Corinthian Quotations and Pauline Refutations in a Rhetorical *Partitio* (1 Corinthians 8.1–9)." *CBQ* (2005): 611–31.

Fredriksen, Paula. *Paul: The Pagan's Apostle*. New Haven: Yale University Press, 2017.

Gadenz, Pablo T. *Called from the Jews and from the Gentiles: Pauline Ecclesiology in Romans 9–11*. WUNT 2/267. Tübingen: Mohr Siebeck, 2009.

Gager, John G. "Functional Diversity in Paul's Use of End-Time Language." *JBL* 89 (1970): 325–37.

———. *Reinventing Paul*. Oxford: Oxford University Press, 2000.

Gane, Roy. *Cult and Character: Purification Offerings, Day of Atonement and Theodicy*. Winona Lake, IN: Eisenbrauns, 2005.

———. "Privative Preposition *min* in Purification Offering Pericopes and the Changing Face of 'Dorian Gray.'" *JBL* 127, no. 2 (2008): 209–22.

García Martínez, Florentino, and Eibert J. C. Tigchelaar. *The Dead Sea Scrolls Study Edition.* 2 vols. Leiden: Brill, 1997/1998.

Garland, David E. *1 Corinthians.* BECNT. Grand Rapids: Baker Academic, 2003.

Garlington, Don. *Studies in the New Perspective on Paul: Essays and Reviews.* Eugene, OR: Wipf & Stock, 2008.

Gaston, Lloyd. *Paul and the Torah.* Vancouver: University of British Columbia Press, 1987.

Gathercole, Simon. *Defending Substitution: An Essay on Atonement in Paul.* Grand Rapids: Baker Academic, 2015.

Gaventa, Beverly Roberts, ed. *Apocalyptic Paul: Cosmos and Anthropos in Romans 5–8.* Waco, TX: Baylor University Press, 2013.

———. *Our Mother Saint Paul.* Louisville: Westminster John Knox, 2007.

Goff, Matthew. "The Mystery of God's Wisdom, the Parousia of a Messiah, and Visions of Heavenly Paradise: 1 and 2 Corinthians in the Context of Jewish Apocalypticism." In *The Jewish Apocalyptic Tradition and the Shaping of New Testament Thought*, edited by Benjamin E. Reynolds and Loren T. Stuckenbruck, 188–92. Minneapolis: Fortress, 2017.

Goldingay, John. *Israel's Gospel.* OTT 1. Downers Grove, IL: InterVarsity Press, 2003.

Gooder, Paula R. *Only the Third Heaven? 2 Corinthians 12.1–10 and Heavenly Ascent.* LNTS 313. London: Bloomsbury T&T Clark, 2006.

Goodrich, John K. "After Destroying Every Rule, Authority, and Power: Paul, Apocalyptic, and Politics in 1 Corinthians." In *Paul and the Apocalyptic Imagination*, edited by Ben C. Blackwell, John K. Goodrich, and Jason Maston, 279–85. Minneapolis: Fortress, 2016.

Gorman, Michael J. "The Apocalyptic New Covenant and the Shape of Life in the Spirit according to Galatians." In *Paul and the Apocalyptic Imagination*, edited by Ben C. Blackwell, John K. Goodrich, and Jason Maston, 317–37. Minneapolis: Fortress, 2016.

———. *Apostle of the Crucified Lord: A Theological Introduction to Paul and His Letters.* 2nd ed. Grand Rapids: Eerdmans, 2016.

———. *Becoming the Gospel: Paul, Participation, and Mission.* Grand Rapids: Eerdmans, 2015.

———. *Cruciformity: Paul's Narrative Spirituality of the Cross.* Grand Rapids: Eerdmans, 2001.

———. *The Death of the Messiah and the Birth of the New Covenant.* Eugene, OR: Cascade, 2014.

———. *Inhabiting the Cruciform God: Kenosis, Justification, and Theosis in Paul's Narrative Soteriology.* Grand Rapids: Eerdmans, 2009.

———. "Paul's Corporate, Cruciform, Missional *Theosis* in 2 Corinthians." In *"In Christ" in Paul: Explorations in Paul's Theology of Union and Participation,* edited by Michael J. Thate, Kevin J. Vanhoozer, and Constantine R. Campbell, 181–208. WUNT 2/384. Tübingen: Mohr Siebeck, 2014.

Gratry, Alphonse. *Commentaires sur l'Evangile selon Saint Matthieu.* Paris: Téqui, 1909.

Greenwood, David C. "On the Jewish Hope for a Restored Northern Kingdom." *ZAW* 88 (1976): 376–85.

Grieb, A. Katherine. "'So That in Him We Might Become the Righteousness of God' (2 Cor 5:21): Some Theological Reflections on the Church Becoming Justice." *Ex Auditu* 22 (2006): 58–80.

Gupta, Nijay. *Worship That Makes Sense to Paul: A New Approach to the Theology and Ethics of Paul's Cultic Metaphors.* BNZW 175. Berlin: De Gruyter, 2010.

Hafemann, Scott J. *Paul, Moses, and the History of Israel: The Letter/Spirit Contrast and the Argument from Scripture in 2 Corinthians 3.* Tübingen: Mohr Siebeck, 1995.

Hahn, Scott W. "'All Israel Will Be Saved': The Restoration of the Twelve Tribes in Romans 9–11." *Letter and Spirit* 10 (2015): 63–104.

———. *Kinship by Covenant: A Canonical Approach to the Fulfillment of God's Saving Promises.* AYBRL. New Haven: Yale University Press, 2009.

Hahne, Harry A. *The Corruption and Redemption of Creation: Nature in Romans 8:19–22 and Jewish Apocalyptic Literature.* LNTS. London: T&T Clark, 2006.

Hamilton, Victor P. *Exodus: An Exegetical Commentary.* Grand Rapids: Baker Academic, 2011.

Hamm, Dennis, SJ. *Philippians, Colossians, Philemon.* CCSS. Grand Rapids: Baker Academic, 2013.

Harkins, Angela Kim, Kelley Coblentz Bautch, and John C. Endres, SJ, eds. *The Watchers in Jewish and Christian Tradition.* Minneapolis: Fortress, 2014.

Harlow, Daniel C. "Ascent to Heaven." In *The Eerdmans Dictionary of Early Judaism,* edited by John J. Collins and Daniel C. Harlow, 387–90. Grand Rapids: Eerdmans, 2010.

Harrington, Daniel. *First Corinthians.* SP 7. Collegeville, MN: Liturgical Press, 1999.

Harrison, James R. *Paul's Language of Grace in Its Graeco-Roman Context.* WUNT 2/172. Tübingen: Mohr Siebeck, 2003.

Hawthorne, Gerald F. "In the Form of God." In *Where Christology Began: Essays on Philippians 2*, edited by R. P. Martin and B. J. Dodd, 96–110. London: Westminster John Knox, 1998.

———. *Philippians.* WBC 43. Waco, TX: Word, 1983.

Hays, Richard B. *The Conversion of the Imagination: Paul as an Interpreter of Israel's Scripture.* Grand Rapids: Eerdmans, 2005.

———. *Echoes of Scripture in the Letters of Paul.* New Haven: Yale University Press, 1989.

———. *The Faith of Jesus Christ: The Narrative Substructure of Galatians 3:1–4:11.* Grand Rapids: Eerdmans, 2002.

———. *First Corinthians.* Interpretation. Louisville: John Knox, 1997.

———. "The Letter to the Galatians." In *New Interpreter's Bible.* 12 vols. Edited by L. E. Keck. 11:183–348. Nashville: Abingdon, 2000.

———. *Moral Vision of the New Testament: A Contemporary Introduction to New Testament Ethics.* San Francisco: HarperSanFrancisco, 1996.

———. "What Is 'Real Participation in Christ'?" In *Redefining First-Century Jewish and Christian Identities*, edited by Fabian E. Udoh, 336–51. Notre Dame, IN: University of Notre Dame Press, 2008.

Hellerman, Joseph H. *Reconstructing Honor in Roman Philippi:* Carmen Christi *as* Cursus Pudorum. SNTSMS 132. Cambridge: Cambridge University Press, 2005.

Hengel, Martin. *Judaism and Hellenism: Studies in Their Encounter in Palestine during the Early Hellenistic Period.* 2 vols. Philadelphia: Fortress, 1974.

———. *Studies in Early Christology.* Edinburgh: T&T Clark, 1995.

Higgins, A. J. B. *The Lord's Supper in the New Testament.* SBT 6. London: SCM, 1952.

Hill, Charles E., and Frank A. James III, eds. *The Glory of the Atonement.* Downers Grove, IL: InterVarsity Press, 2004.

Hill, David. *Greek Words and Hebrew Meaning: Studies in the Semantics of Soteriological Terms.* Cambridge: Cambridge University Press, 1967.

Hill, Wesley. "The God of Israel—Crucified?" In *The Crucified Apostle*, edited by Todd A. Wilson and Paul R. House, 261–75. WUNT 2/450. Tübingen: Mohr Siebeck, 2017.

————. *Paul and the Trinity: Persons, Relations, and the Pauline Letters.* Grand Rapids: Eerdmans, 2015.

Himmelfarb, Martha. *Ascent to Heaven in Jewish and Christian Apocalypses.* Oxford: Oxford University Press, 1993.

Hoffman, Norbert. "Atonement and the Ontological Coherence between the Trinity and the Cross." In *Towards a Civilization of Love*, translated by E. Leiva-Merikakis, 213–66. San Francisco: Ignatius Press, 1985.

Hofius, Otfried. "The Fourth Servant Song in the New Testament Letters." In *The Suffering Servant: Isaiah 53 in Jewish and Christian Sources*, edited by Bernd Janowski and Peter Stuhlmacher, 163–88. Grand Rapids: Eerdmans, 2004.

————. "The Lord's Supper and the Lord's Supper Tradition." In *One Loaf, One Cup: Ecumenical Studies of 1 Cor 11 and Other Eucharistic Texts: The Cambridge Conference on the Eucharist, August 1988*, edited by B. F. Meyer, 75–115. NGS 6. Macon, GA: Mercer University Press, 1993.

Hogan, Karina Martin. "The Apocalyptic Eschatology of Romans: Creation, Judgment, Resurrection, and Glory." In *The Jewish Apocalyptic Tradition and the Shaping of New Testament Thought*, edited by Benjamin E. Reynolds and Loren T. Stuckenbruck, 155–74. Minneapolis: Fortress, 2017.

Hogeterp, Albert L. A. *Paul and God's Temple.* BTS 2. Leuven: Peeters, 2006.

Hooker, Morna D. *From Adam to Christ: Essays on Paul.* Cambridge: Cambridge University Press, 1990.

Hoover, Roy W. "The Harpagmos Enigma: A Philological Solution." *HTR* 64 (1971): 95–119.

Horn, Friedrich W. *Das Angeld des Geistes: Studien zur paulinischen Pneumatologie.* FRLANT 154. Göttingen: Vandenhoeck & Ruprecht, 1992.

Horrell, David. "Theological Principle or Christological Praxis? Pauline Ethics in 1 Corinthians 8.1–11.1." *JSNT* 67 (1997): 99–102.

Horsley, Richard. *1 Corinthians.* ANTC. Nashville: Abingdon, 1988.

Horton, Michael S. "Traditional Reformed Response to the Roman Catholic View." In *Justification: Five Views*, edited by James K. Beilby and Paul R. Eddy, 83–112. Downers Grove, IL: IVP Academic, 2011.

Hugenberger, Gordon P. *Marriage as Covenant: A Study of Biblical Law and Ethics Governing Marriage, Developed from the Perspective of Malachi.* VTSup 52. Leiden: Brill, 1994.

Humphrey, Edith M. "Apocalyptic as Theoria in the Letters of Paul." In *Paul and the Apocalyptic Imagination*, edited by Ben C. Blackwell, John K. Goodrich, and Jason Maston, 87–110. Minneapolis: Fortress, 2016.

————. "Bishop Wright: Sacramentality and the Role of the Sacraments." In

God and the Faithfulness of Paul, edited by Christoph Heilig, J. Thomas Hewitt, and Michael F. Bird, 661–81. Minneapolis: Fortress, 2017.

Hurtado, Larry. *How on Earth Did Jesus Become a God? Historical Questions about Earliest Devotion to Jesus*. Grand Rapids: Eerdmans, 2005.

———. *Lord Jesus Christ: Devotion to Jesus in Early Christianity*. Grand Rapids: Eerdmans, 2003.

———. *One God, One Lord: Early Christian Devotion and Ancient Jewish Monotheism*. Philadelphia: Fortress, 1988.

Jacob, Benno. *Das Buch Exodus*. Stuttgart: Calver Verlag, 1997.

Jeremias, Joachim. *The Eucharistic Words of Jesus*. Translated by Norman Perrin. London: SCM, 1966.

———. *New Testament Theology*. Translated by John Bowden. New York: Charles Scribner's Sons, 1971.

Jewett, Robert. *Romans*. Hermeneia. Minneapolis: Fortress, 2007.

Jipp, Joshua. *Christ Is King: Paul's Royal Ideology*. Minneapolis: Fortress, 2015.

Johnson, E. Elizabeth. *The Function of Apocalyptic and Wisdom Traditions in Rom 9–11*. SBLDS. Atlanta: Scholars Press, 1989.

Johnson, Luke Timothy. *The First and Second Letters to Timothy*. AB 35A. New York: Doubleday, 2001.

———. "The Paul of the Letters: A Catholic Perspective." In *Four Views on the Apostle Paul*, edited by Michael F. Bird, 159–93. Grand Rapids: Zondervan, 2012.

Josephus. *Josephus*. Translated by Henry St. J. Thackeray et al. 10 vols. LCL. Cambridge: Harvard University Press, 1926–1965.

Kalluveettil, Paul. *Declaration and Covenant*. AnBib 88. Rome: Pontifical Biblical Institute, 1982.

Käsemann, Ernst. *Commentary on Romans*. Translated by G. W. Bromiley. Grand Rapids: Eerdmans, 1980.

———. *Essays on New Testament Themes*. Translated by W. J. Montague. 1960. Repr., Philadelphia: Fortress, 1982.

———. *New Testament Questions of Today*. Translated by W. J. Montague and Wilfred F. Bunge. Philadelphia: Fortress, 1969.

———. *Perspectives on Paul*. Translated by Margaret Kohl. 1969. Repr., London: SCM, 1971.

Keck, Leander E. *Paul and His Letters*. Philadelphia: Fortress, 1982.

———. *Romans*. ANTC. Nashville: Abingdon, 2005.

Keener, Craig S. *Galatians*. Cambridge: Cambridge University Press, 2018.

————. *1–2 Corinthians*. NCBC. Cambridge: Cambridge University Press, 2005.

————. *Romans*. NCCS. Eugene: Cascade, 2009.

Kim, Jung Hoon. *The Significance of Clothing Imagery in the Pauline Corpus*. LNTS. London: T&T Clark, 2004.

Kim, Seyoon. *Paul and the New Perspective: Rethinking the Origin of Paul's Gospel*. Grand Rapids: Eerdmans, 2001.

Kincaid, John A. "New Covenant Justification by Cardiac Righteousness: An Augustinian Perspective on Pauline Justification." *Letter and Spirit* 12 (2017): 37–58.

Kincaid, John A., and Michael Patrick Barber. "'Conformed to the Image of His Son': Participation in Christ as Divine Sonship in Romans 8." *Letter and Spirit* 10 (2015): 35–62.

Kittel, Gerhard, and Gerhard Friedrich, eds. *Theological Dictionary of the New Testament*. Translated by Geoffrey W. Bromiley. 10 vols. Grand Rapids: Eerdmans, 1964–1976.

Klauck, Hans-Josef. *Herrenmahl und hellenistischer Kult: Eine religionsgeschichtliche Untersuchung zum ersten Korintherbrief*. Münster: Aschendorff, 1986.

Klawans, Jonathan. *Impurity and Sin in Ancient Judaism*. Oxford: Oxford University Press, 2000.

————. *Purity, Sacrifice, and the Temple: Symbolism and Supersessionism in the Study of Ancient Judaism*. Oxford: Oxford University Press, 2006.

Kruse, Colin G. *Paul's Letter to the Romans*. Pillar New Testament Commentary. Grand Rapids: Eerdmans, 2012.

Lapide, Pinchas, and Peter Stuhlmacher. *Paul: Rabbi and Apostle*. Minneapolis: Fortress, 1984.

Lapsley, Jacqueline E. *Can These Bones Live? The Problem of the Moral Self in the Book of Ezekiel*. Berlin: Walter de Gruyter, 2000.

Lebarq, J., ed. *Œuvres oratoires de Bossuet*. 6 vols. Lille: Desclée de Brouwen, 1891.

Lee, Aquila H. I. *From Messiah to Preexistent Son: Jesus' Self-Consciousness and Early Exegesis of Messianic Psalms*. WUNT 2/192. Tübingen: Mohr Siebeck, 2005.

————. "Messianism and Messiah in Paul." In *God and the Faithfulness of Paul*, edited by Christoph Heilig, J. Thomas Hewitt, and Michael F. Bird, 375–92. Minneapolis: Fortress, 2017.

Levenson, Jon D. *The Death and Resurrection of the Beloved Son*. New Haven: Yale University Press, 1993.

———. *Sinai and Zion: An Entry into the Jewish Bible.* San Francisco: Harper & Row, 1985.

Levering, Matthew. *Paul in the Summa Theologiae.* Washington, DC: Catholic University of America Press, 2014.

Levine, Baruch. *In the Presence of the Lord: A Study of Cult and Some Cultic Terms in Ancient Israel.* SJLA 5. Leiden: Brill, 1974.

———. *Leviticus.* JPSTC. Philadelphia: The Jewish Publication Society, 1989.

Lewis, Bryan E. *Jew and Gentile Reconciled: An Exploration of the Ten Tribes in Pauline Literature.* Wilmore, KY: Glossa House, 2016.

Liddell, Henry George, Robert Scott, and Henry Stuart Jones. *A Greek-English Lexicon.* 9th ed. with revised supplement. Oxford: Clarendon, 1996.

Lincoln, Andrew T. *Paradise Now and Not Yet: Studies in the Role of the Heavenly Dimension in Paul's Thought with Special Reference to His Eschatology.* SNTSMS 43. Cambridge: Cambridge University Press, 1981.

Lindemann, Andreas. *Der Erste Korintherbrief.* HNT 9/1. Tübingen: Mohr Siebeck, 2000.

Linebaugh, Jonathan A. *God, Grace, and Righteousness in Wisdom of Solomon and Paul's Letter to the Romans: Texts in Conversation.* NovTSup 152. Leiden: Brill, 2013.

Litwa, M. David. *Iesus Deus: The Early Christian Depiction of Jesus as a Mediterranean God.* Minneapolis: Fortress, 2014.

———. *We Are Being Transformed: Deification in Paul's Soteriology.* BZNW 187. Berlin: De Gruyter, 2012.

Loke, Andrew Ter Ern. *The Origin of Divine Christology.* SNTSMS 169. Cambridge: Cambridge University Press, 2017.

Lundbom, Jack R. *Jeremiah.* 3 vols. AB 21A–C. New York: Doubleday, 1999, 2004.

Lust, Johan, Erik Eynikel, and Katrin Hauspie, eds. *Greek-English Lexicon of the Septuagint.* Rev. ed. Stuttgart: Deutsche Bibelgesellschaft, 2003.

MacDonald, Nathan. *Deuteronomy and the Meaning of "Monotheism."* 2nd ed. FAT 2/1. Tübingen: Mohr Siebeck, 2012.

———. "The Origin of 'Monotheism.'" In *Early Jewish and Christian Monotheism*, edited by Loren T. Stuckenbruck and Wendy E. S. North, 204–15. JSNTSup 263. London: T&T Clark, 2004.

Marcus, Joel. *The Way of the Lord: Christological Exegesis of the Old Testament in the Gospel of Mark.* London: T&T Clark, 1992.

Marshall, I. Howard. *Commentary on Luke: A Commentary on the Greek Text.* Exeter: Paternoster, 1978.

Martin, Dale B. *The Corinthian Body.* New Haven: Yale University Press, 1995.

Martin, Ralph P. *2 Corinthians.* 2nd ed. WBC 40. Grand Rapids: Zondervan, 2014.

Martyn, J. Louis. *Galatians.* AB 33A. New York: Doubleday, 1997.

———. *Theological Issues in the Letters of Paul.* Edinburgh: T&T Clark, 1997.

Matera, Frank J. *Galatians.* SP 9. Collegeville, MN: Liturgical Press, 1992.

———. *God's Saving Grace: A Pauline Theology.* Grand Rapids: Eerdmans, 2012.

———. *New Testament Christology.* Louisville: Westminster John Knox, 1999.

———. "Philippians." In *The Paulist Commentary,* edited by José Enrique Aguilar Chiu, Richard J. Clifford, SJ, Carol J. Dempsey, OP, Eileen M. Schuller, OSU, Thomas D. Stegman, SJ, and Ronald D. Witherup, PSS, 1419–28. New York: Paulist Press, 2018.

———. *Romans.* Paideia. Grand Rapids: Baker Academic, 2010.

———. *II Corinthians: A Commentary.* NTL. Louisville: Westminster John Knox, 2003.

Matlock, R. B. *Unveiling the Apocalyptic Paul: Paul's Interpreters and the Rhetoric of Criticism.* Sheffield: Sheffield Academic Press, 1996.

Mauss, Marcel. *The Gift.* Translated by W. D. Halls. London: Routledge, 1990.

McCarthy, Dennis J. "Covenant and Law in Chronicles-Nehemiah." *CBQ* 44 (1982): 25–44.

———. *Treaty and Covenant.* Rome: Biblical Institute Press, 1981.

———. "Twenty-Five Years of Pentateuchal Study." In *The Biblical Heritage in Modern Catholic Scholarship,* edited by J. J. Collins and J. D. Crossan, 34–57. Wilmington, DE: Michael Glazier, 1986.

McCormack, Bruce L., ed. *Justification in Perspective: Historical Developments and Contemporary Challenges.* Grand Rapids: Baker Academic, 2006.

McCready, Wayne O., and Adele Reinhartz, eds. *Common Judaism: Explorations in Second Temple Judaism.* Minneapolis: Fortress, 2008.

McGrath, Alister E. *Iustitia Dei: A History of the Christian Doctrine of Justification.* 3rd ed. Cambridge: Cambridge University Press, 2007.

McGrath, James F. *The Only True God: Early Christian Monotheism in Its Jewish Context.* Urbana: University of Illinois Press, 2009.

McKnight, Scot. *Colossians*. NICOT. Grand Rapids: Eerdmans, 2017.

———. *A Community Called Atonement*. Nashville: Abingdon, 2007.

———. *Jesus and His Death: Historiography, the Historical Jesus, and Atonement Theory*. Waco: Baylor University Press, 2005.

McNamara, Martin. *Targum and Testament*. Grand Rapids: Eerdmans, 1972.

Meier, John P. *A Marginal Jew: Rethinking the Historical Jesus*. 5 vols. AYBRL. New Haven: Yale University Press, 1991–2016.

Melvin, David P. *The Interpreting Angel Motif in Prophetic and Apocalyptic Literature*. Minneapolis: Fortress, 2013.

Metzger, Bruce M. *A Textual Commentary on the Greek New Testament*. London: UBS, 1975.

Meyer, Ben F. "The Expiation Motif in the Eucharistic Words." In *One Loaf, One Cup: Ecumenical Studies of 1 Cor 11 and Other Eucharistic Texts: The Cambridge Conference on the Eucharist, August 1988*, edited by B. F. Meyer, 11–33. NGS 6. Macon, GA: Mercer University Press, 1993.

Milgrom, Jacob. *Leviticus*. 3 vols. AB 3–3B. New York: Doubleday, 1991, 2000, 2001.

———. *Numbers*. JPSTC. Philadelphia: Jewish Publication Society, 1990.

———. "The Preposition *min* in the *ḥaṭṭā't* Pericopes." *JBL* 126 (2007): 161–63.

Miller, Colin D. *The Practice of the Body of Christ: Human Agency in Pauline Theology after MacIntyre*. Cambridge: James Clark & Co., 2014.

Mitchell, Margaret. *The Heavenly Trumpet: John Chrysostom and the Art of Pauline Interpretation*. Louisville: Westminster John Knox, 2002.

Moo, Douglas J. *The Epistle to the Romans*. NICNT. Grand Rapids: Eerdmans, 1996.

Morales, Rodrigo J. "Baptism and Union with Christ." In *"In Christ" in Paul: Explorations in Paul's Theology of Union and Participation*, edited by Michael J. Thate, Kevin J. Vanhoozer, and Constantine R. Campbell, 157–79. WUNT 2/384. Tübingen: Mohr Siebeck, 2014.

———. *The Spirit and the Restoration of Israel: New Exodus and New Creation Motifs in Galatians*. WUNT 2/282. Tübingen: Mohr Siebeck, 2010.

Morgan, Teresa. *Roman Faith and Christian Faith: Pistis and Fides in the Early Roman Empire and Early Churches*. Oxford: Oxford University Press, 2015.

Morris, Leon L. *The Apostolic Preaching of the Cross*. London: Tyndale, 1955.

———. "The Meaning of *hilastērion* in Romans 3:25." *NTS* 2 (1955–56): 33–43.

Moses, Robert Ewusie. *Practices of Power: Revisiting the Principalities and Powers in the Pauline Letters.* Minneapolis: Fortress, 2014.

Mowinckel, Sigmund. "The Hidden Messiah." In *He That Cometh: The Messiah Concept in the Old Testament and Later Judaism,* translated by G. W. Anderson, 304–8. 1954. Repr., Grand Rapids: Eerdmans, 2005.

Mullin, Robert Bruce. *A Short World History of Christianity.* Rev. ed. Louisville: Westminster John Knox, 2014.

Murphy-O'Connor, Jerome. *Paul: A Critical Life.* Oxford: Oxford University Press, 1996.

Murphy-O'Connor, Jerome, and James H. Charlesworth, eds. *Paul and the Dead Sea Scrolls.* New York: Crossroad, 1990.

Nanos, Mark D. "How Could Paul Accuse Peter of 'Living *Ethné*-ishly' in Antioch (Gal 2:11–21) If Peter Was Eating according to Jewish Dietary Norms?" *Journal for the Study of Paul and His Letters* 6.2 (2016): 199–223.

———. "A Jewish View." In *Four Views on the Apostle Paul,* edited by Michael F. Bird, 159–93. Grand Rapids: Zondervan, 2012.

———. *The Mystery of Romans: The Jewish Context of Paul's Letter.* Minneapolis: Fortress, 1996.

———. "Paul's Relationship to Torah in Light of His Strategy 'to Become Everything to Everyone' (1 Corinthians 9.19–23)." In *Paul and Judaism: Crosscurrents in Pauline Exegesis and the Study of Jewish-Christian Relations,* edited by R. Bieringer and D. Pollefeyt, 106–40. LNTS 463. London: T&T Clark, 2012.

———. "Reading the Antioch Incident (Gal 2:11–21) as a Subversive Banquet Narrative." *Journal for the Study of Paul and His Letters* 7.1–2 (2017): 26–52.

———. "Was Paul a 'Liar' for the Gospel? The Case for a New Interpretation of Paul's 'Becoming Everything to Everyone' in 1 Corinthians 9:19–23." *Review and Expositor* 110 (2013): 591–608.

———. "What Was at Stake in Peter's 'Eating with Gentiles' at Antioch?" In *The Galatians Debate: Contemporary Issues in Rhetorical and Historical Interpretation,* edited by Mark D. Nanos, 282–317. Peabody, MA: Hendrickson, 2002.

Nanos, Mark D., and Magnus Zetterholm, eds. *Paul within Judaism: Restoring the First-Century Context to the Apostle.* Minneapolis: Fortress, 2015.

Neusner, Jacob. *Sifra: An Analytical Translation.* 2 vols. BJS 139. Atlanta: Scholars Press, 1988.

Newman, John Henry. *Apologia Pro Vita Sua.* New York: D. Appleton and Company, 1865.

———. *Lectures on the Doctrine of Justification.* 3rd ed. New York: Longmans, Green, and Co., 1990.

Newton, Derek. *Deity and Diet: The Dilemma of Sacrificial Food at Corinth.* Sheffield: Sheffield Academic Press, 1998.

Nickelsburg, George W. E. *1 Enoch 1.* Hermeneia. Minneapolis: Fortress, 2001.

Nickelsburg, George W. E., and James C. VanderKam. *1 Enoch: The Hermeneia Translation.* Minneapolis: Fortress, 2012.

Nolland, John. "Grace as Power." *NovT* 28, no. 1 (1986): 26–31.

North, J. Lionel. "Jesus and Worship, God and Sacrifice." In *Early Jewish and Christian Monotheism*, edited by Loren T. Stuckenbruck and Wendy E. S. North, 186–202. JSNTSup 263. London: T&T Clark, 2004.

Novenson, Matthew V. *Christ among the Messiahs: Christ Language in Paul and Messiah Language in Ancient Judaism.* Oxford: Oxford University Press, 2012.

———. *The Grammar of Messianism: An Ancient Jewish Political Idiom and Its Users.* New York: Oxford University Press, 2017.

Oakes, Peter. *Galatians.* Paideia. Grand Rapids: Baker Academic, 2015.

O'Brien, Peter Thomas. *The Epistle to the Philippians: A Commentary on the Greek Text.* NIGTC. Grand Rapids: Eerdmans, 1991.

O'Collins, Gerald, and Mario J. Farrugia. *The Story of Catholic Christianity.* 2nd ed. Oxford: Oxford University Press, 2015.

Oegema, Gerbern S. *The Anointed and His People: Messianic Expectations from the Maccabees to Bar Kochba.* JSPSS 27. Sheffield: Sheffield Academic Press, 1998.

Oliver, Isaac W. "Baptism and Eucharist." In *The Jewish Annotated New Testament*, edited by Amy-Jill Levine and Marc Zvi Brettler, 674–77. 2nd ed. Oxford: Oxford University Press, 2017.

Olson, Robert C. *The Gospel as the Revelation of God's Righteousness: Paul's Use of Isaiah in Romans 1:1–3:26.* WUNT 2/428. Tübingen: Mohr Siebeck, 2016.

Oropeza, B. J. *Paul and Apostasy: Eschatology, Perseverance, and Falling Away in the Corinthian Congregation.* WUNT 2/115. Tübingen: Mohr Siebeck, 2000.

Orr, Peter. *Christ Absent and Present.* WUNT 2/354. Tübingen: Mohr Siebeck, 2014.

Pate, C. Marvin, and Douglas W. Kennard. *Deliverance Now and Not Yet: The New Testament and the Great Tribulation.* SBL 54. New York: Peter Lang, 2003.

Patterson, Jane Lancaster. *Keeping the Feast: Metaphors of Sacrifice in 1 Corinthians and Philippians*. Atlanta: SBL Press, 2015.

Pietersma, Albert, and Benjamin G. Wright. *A New English Translation of the Septuagint*. Oxford: Oxford University Press, 2007.

Piper, John. *Counted Righteous in Christ: Should We Abandon the Imputation of Christ's Righteousness?* Wheaton, IL: Crossway, 2002.

Pitre, Brant. "Apocalypticism, Apocalyptic Teaching." In *Dictionary of Jesus and the Gospels*, edited by Joel B. Green, Jeannine K. Brown, and Nicholas Perrin, 23–33. Downers Grove, IL: IVP Academic, 2014.

———. *Jesus and the Last Supper*. Grand Rapids: Eerdmans, 2015.

———. *Jesus, the Tribulation and the End of the Exile*. WUNT 2/205. Tübingen: Mohr Siebeck, 2005.

Pitta, Antonio. "Second Corinthians." In *The Paulist Commentary*, edited by José Enrique Aguilar Chiu, Richard J. Clifford, SJ, Carol J. Dempsey, OP, Eileen M. Schuller, OSU, Thomas D. Stegman, SJ, and Ronald D. Witherup, PSS, 1341–79. New York: Paulist Press, 2018.

Polak, F. H. "The Covenant at Mount Sinai in the Light of Texts from Mari." In *Sefer Moshe: The Moshe Weinfeld Jubilee Volume*, edited by C. Cohen, A. Hurvitz, and S. M. Paul, 119–34. Winona Lake, IN: Eisenbrauns, 2004.

Powers, Daniel G. *Salvation through Participation: An Examination of the Notion of the Believers' Corporate Unity with Christ in Early Christian Soteriology*. Leuven: Peeters, 2001.

Prat, Ferdinand. *The Theology of St. Paul*. Translated by John L. Stoddard. 2 vols. Westminster, MD: The Newman Press, 1950.

Prothro, James B. *Both Judge and Justifier: Biblical Legal Language and the Act of Justifying in Paul*. WUNT 2/461. Tübingen: Mohr Siebeck, 2018.

———. "The Strange Case of Δικαιόω in the Septuagint and in Paul: The Origins and Oddity of Paul's Talk of Justification." *ZNW* 107 (2016): 48–69.

Rabens, Volker. *The Holy Spirit and Ethics in Paul: Transformation and Empowering for Religious-Ethical Life*. 2nd ed. Minneapolis: Fortress, 2010.

Rad, Gerhard von. *Old Testament Theology*. 2 vols. New York: Harper & Row, 1965.

Reasoner, Mark. *Romans in Full Circle: A History of Interpretation*. Louisville: Westminster John Knox, 2005.

Renaud, Bernard. *L'alliance un mystère de miséricorde: une lecture de Exode 32–34*. Paris: Cerf, 1998.

Reumann, John. *Philippians*. AYB 33B. New Haven: Yale University Press, 2008.

Rey, Jean Sébastien, ed. *The Dead Sea Scrolls and Pauline Literature.* Leiden: Brill, 2014.

Reynolds, Benjamin E., and Loren T. Stuckenbruck, eds. *The Jewish Apocalyptic Tradition and the Shaping of New Testament Thought.* Minneapolis: Fortress, 2017.

Ricks, Stephen D. "The Prophetic Literality of Tribal Reconstruction." In *Israel's Apostasy and Restoration*, edited by Avraham Gileadi, 273–81. Grand Rapids: Baker, 1988.

Robertson, O. P. "Genesis 15:6: New Covenant Exposition of an Old Covenant Text." *WTJ* 42 (1980): 265–66.

Robinson, John A. T. *The Body: A Study in Pauline Theology.* SBT 5. London: SCM, 1952.

Rogers, E. R. "*Epotisthēmen* Again." *NTS* 29 (1983): 139–42.

Rowe, C. Kavin. *One True Life: The Stoics and Early Christians and Rival Traditions.* New Haven: Yale University Press, 2016.

Rowland, Christopher. *The Open Heaven: A Study of Apocalyptic in Judaism and Early Christianity.* New York: Crossroad, 1982.

Rudolph, David J. *A Jew to the Jews: Jewish Contours of Pauline Flexibility in 1 Corinthians 9:19–23.* WUNT 2/304. Tübingen: Mohr Siebeck, 2011.

Russell, D. S. *The Method and Message of Jewish Apocalyptic.* Philadelphia: Westminster, 1964.

Sanders, E. P. *Comparing Judaism and Christianity: Common Judaism, Paul, and the Inner and the Outer in Ancient Religion.* Minneapolis: Fortress, 2016.

———. *Jesus and Judaism.* Minneapolis: Fortress, 1985.

———. *Judaism: Practice and Belief 63 BC–66 CE.* London: SCM, 1992.

———. *Paul: The Apostle's Life, Letters, and Thought.* Minneapolis: Fortress, 2015.

———. *Paul and Palestinian Judaism: A Comparison of Patterns of Religion.* Minneapolis: Fortress, 1977.

———. *Paul and Palestinian Judaism: A Comparison of Patterns of Religion.* 40th anniversary ed. Minneapolis: Fortress, 2017.

———. "Paul's Jewishness." In *Paul's Jewish Matrix*, edited by Thomas G. Casey and Justin Taylor, 51–73. Rome: Gregorian and Biblical Press, 2011.

———. *Paul, the Law, and the Jewish People.* Minneapolis: Fortress, 1983.

Sarna, Nahum M. *Exodus.* JPSTC. Philadelphia: The Jewish Publication Society, 1991.

Schauf, Scott. "Galatians 2:20 in Context." *NTS* 52 (2006): 86–101.

Scheck, Thomas P. *Origen and the History of Justification: The Legacy of Origen's Commentary on Romans.* Notre Dame, IN: University of Notre Dame Press, 2008.

Schmid, Konrad, and Odil Hannes Steck. "Restoration Expectations in the Prophetic Tradition of the Old Testament." In *Restoration: Old Testament, Jewish and Christian Perspectives,* edited by J. M. Scott, 41–82. Leiden: Brill, 2001.

Schreiner, Thomas R. *Faith Alone—The Doctrine of Justification: What the Reformers Taught... and Why It Still Matters.* Grand Rapids: Zondervan, 2015.

———. *Galatians.* ZECNT. Grand Rapids: Zondervan, 2010.

———. *Paul, Apostle of God's Glory in Christ: A Pauline Theology.* Downers Grove, IL: IVP Academic, 2001.

———. *Romans.* BECNT. Grand Rapids: Baker, 1998.

Schürer, Emil. *The History of the Jewish People in the Age of Jesus Christ (175 B.C.–A.D. 135).* Rev. and ed. Geza Vermes et al. 3 vols. Edinburgh: T&T Clark, 1973, 1979, 1986, 1987.

Schweitzer, Albert. *The Mysticism of Paul the Apostle.* Translated by William Montgomery. London: Black, 1931.

———. *Paul and His Interpreters: A Critical History.* Translated by W. Montgomery. 1912. Repr., Eugene, OR: Wipf & Stock, 2004.

Scott, James M. "And Then All Israel Will Be Saved." In *Restoration: Old Testament, Jewish, and Christian Perspectives,* edited by James M. Scott, 500–515. Leiden: Brill, 2001.

Sechrest, Love L. *A Former Jew: Paul and the Dialectics of Race.* LNTS 410. London: T&T Clark, 2009.

Seifrid, Mark. *Christ, Our Righteousness: Paul's Theology of Justification.* New SBT 9. Downers Grove, IL: InterVarsity Press, 2000.

———. "Righteousness Language in the Hebrew Scriptures and Early Judaism." In *Justification and Variegated Nomism,* vol. 1, *The Complexities of Second Temple Judaism,* edited by D. A. Carson, Peter T. O'Brien, and Mark A. Seifried, 415–42. Tübingen: Mohr Siebeck, 2001.

Silva, Moisés. *Philippians.* 2nd ed. BECNT. Grand Rapids: Baker Academic, 2005.

Sklar, Jay. *Leviticus.* TOTC 3. Downers Grove, IL: IVP Academic, 2014.

———. "Sin and Impurity: Atoned or Purified? Yes!" In *Perspectives on Purity and Purification in the Bible,* edited by Baruch J. Schwartz et al., 18–31. London: T&T Clark, 2008.

———. *Sin, Impurity, Sacrifice, and Atonement: The Priestly Conception.* Hebrew Bible Monographs 2. Sheffield: Sheffield Phoenix Press, 2005.

Smith, Barry D. *Paul's Seven Explanations of the Suffering of the Righteous.* New York: Peter Lang, 2002.

———. "'Spirit of Holiness' as Eschatological Principle of Obedience." In *Christian Beginnings and the Dead Sea Scrolls*, edited by John J. Collins and Craig A. Evans, 75–99. Grand Rapids: Baker Academic, 2006.

Soards, Marion L., and Darrell J. Pursiful. *Galatians.* Macon, GA: Smyth and Helwys, 2015.

Söding, Thomas. "Justification and Participation." In *Galatians and Christian Theology: Justification, the Gospel, and Ethics in Paul's Letter*, edited by Mark W. Elliot, Scott J. Hafemann, N. T. Wright, and John Frederick, 62–81. Grand Rapids: Baker Academic, 2014.

Sprinkle, Preston M. *Paul and Judaism Revisited: A Study in Divine and Human Agency in Salvation.* Downers Grove, IL: IVP Academic, 2013.

Stagg, Frank. *Galatians—Romans.* Atlanta: John Knox, 1980.

Stanley, David Michael. *Christ's Resurrection in Pauline Soteriology.* Rome: Pontificio Instituto Biblico, 1961.

Staples, Jason A. "Reconstructing Israel: Restoration Eschatology in Early Judaism and Paul's Gentile Mission." PhD diss., University of North Carolina–Chapel Hill, 2016.

———. "What Do the Gentiles Have to Do with 'All Israel'? A Fresh Look at Romans 11:25–27." *JBL* 130, no. 2 (2011): 371–90.

Stegman, Thomas D., SJ. "Paul's Use of *dikaio-* Terminology: Moving beyond N. T. Wright's Forensic Interpretation." *TS* 72 (2011): 496–524.

———. "Romans." In *The Paulist Commentary*, edited by José Enrique Aguilar Chiu, Richard J. Clifford, SJ, Carol J. Dempsey, OP, Eileen M. Schuller, OSU, Thomas D. Stegman, SJ, and Ronald D. Witherup, PSS, 1234–88. New York: Paulist Press, 2018.

———. *Second Corinthians.* CCSS. Grand Rapids: Baker Academic, 2009.

Stendahl, Krister. *Final Account: Paul's Letter to the Romans.* Minneapolis: Fortress, 1995.

———. *Paul among Jews and Gentiles.* Philadelphia: Fortress, 1976.

Stökl Ben Ezra, Daniel. *The Impact of Yom Kippur on Early Christianity: The Day of Atonement from Second Temple Judaism to the Fifth Century.* WUNT 163. Tübingen: Mohr Siebeck, 2003.

Stone, Michael E. *4 Ezra.* Hermeneia. Minneapolis: Fortress, 1990.

Stowers, Stanley K. "Elusive Coherence: Ritual and Rhetoric in 1 Corinthians 10–11." In *Reimagining Christian Origins: A Colloquium Honoring Burton L. Mack*, edited by E. A. Castelli and H. Taussig, 68–93. Valley Forge, PA: Trinity Press, 1996.

———. "What Is 'Pauline Participation in Christ'?" In *Redefining First-Century Jewish and Christian Identities*, edited by Fabian E. Udoh, 336–71. Notre Dame, IN: University of Notre Dame Press, 2008.

Stuckenbruck, Loren. "'Angels' and 'God': Exploring the Limits of Early Jewish Monotheism." In *Early Jewish and Christian Monotheism*, edited by Loren T. Stuckenbruck and Wendy E. S. North, 45–70. JSNTSup 263. London: T&T Clark, 2004.

Stuhlmacher, Peter. *Revisiting Paul's Doctrine of Justification: A Challenge to the New Perspective*. Downers Grove, IL: IVP Academic, 2001.

Sullivan, Kevin P. *Wrestling with Angels: A Study of the Relationship between Angels and Humans in Ancient Jewish Literature and the New Testament*. AGJU 55. Leiden: Brill, 2004.

Tanner, Norman P., SJ. *Decrees of the Ecumenical Councils*. 2 vols. Washington, DC: Georgetown University Press, 1990.

Tatum, Gregory, OP. "Law and Covenant in *Paul and the Faithfulness of God*." In *God and the Faithfulness of Paul*, edited by Christoph Heilig, J. Thomas Hewitt, and Michael F. Bird, 311–27. Minneapolis: Fortress, 2017.

———. *New Chapters in a Life of Paul: A Relative Chronology of His Letters*. CBQMS 41. Washington, DC: Catholic Biblical Association of America, 2006.

Thiselton, Anthony C. *The First Epistle to the Corinthians*. NIGTC. Grand Rapids: Eerdmans, 2000.

Thomas, Matthew J. *Paul's "Works of the Law" in the Perspective of Second Century Reception*. WUNT 2/468. Tübingen: Mohr Siebeck, 2018.

Thompson, Michael B. *Clothed with Christ: The Example and Teaching of Jesus in Romans 12:1–15:13*. Sheffield: JSOT Press, 1991.

Thrall, Margaret. *The Second Epistle to the Corinthians*. 2 vols. ICC. London: T&T Clark, 1994, 2000.

Tilling, Chris. *Paul's Divine Christology*. Grand Rapids: Eerdmans, 2015.

Torrance, Isabelle C. "Ways to Give Oaths Extra Sanctity." In *Oaths and Swearing in Ancient Greece*, 132–55. Berlin: Walter de Gruyter, 2014.

Trinité, Philippe de la. *What Is Redemption?* Translated by Anthony Armstrong. New York: Hawthorn Books, 1961.

Tucker, G. M. "Covenant Forms and Contract Forms." *VT* 15 (1965): 487–503.

Turley, Stephen Richard. *The Ritualized Revelation of the Messianic Age*. LNTS 544. London: T&T Clark, 2015.

VanderKam, James C. "Covenant." In *Encyclopedia of the Dead Sea Scrolls*, edited by Lawrence H. Schiffman and James C. VanderKam, 151–55. Oxford: Oxford University Press, 2000.

———. "The Righteous One, Messiah, Chosen One, and the Son of Man in 1 Enoch 37–71." In *The Messiah: Developments in Earliest Judaism and Christianity*, edited by James H. Charlesworth, 169–91. Minneapolis: Fortress, 1992.

Verhoef, Peter. *The Books of Haggai and Malachi*. NICOT. Grand Rapids: Eerdmans, 1987.

Vermes, Geza. *Jesus the Jew*. Philadelphia: Fortress, 1973.

Watson, Francis. *Paul and the Hermeneutics of Faith*. 2nd ed. London: Bloomsbury T&T Clark, 2016.

———. *Paul, Judaism, and the Gentiles: Beyond the New Perspective*. Grand Rapids: Eerdmans, 2007.

Wedderburn, A. J. M. *Baptism and Resurrection: Studies in Pauline Theology against Its Graeco-Roman Background*. WUNT 44. Tübingen: Mohr Siebeck, 1987.

Weiß, Johannes. *Der erste Korintherbrief*. Göttingen: Vandenhoeck & Ruprecht, 1910.

Wellhausen, Julius. *Prolegomena to the History of Ancient Israel*. Translated by J. Sutherland Black and Allan Enzies. 1885. Repr., New York: Meridian Books, 1957.

Wells, Kyle B. *Grace and Agency in Paul and Second Temple Judaism: Interpreting the Transformation of the Heart*. NovTSup 157. Leiden: Brill, 2014.

Westerholm, Stephen. *Justification Reconsidered: Rethinking a Pauline Theme*. Grand Rapids: Eerdmans, 2013.

———. "Paul and the Law in Romans 9–11." In *Paul and the Mosaic Law*, edited by James D. G. Dunn, 215–37. Grand Rapids: Eerdmans, 2001.

———. *Perspectives Old and New on Paul: The Lutheran Paul and His Critics*. Grand Rapids: Eerdmans, 2003.

———. "Righteousness, Cosmic and Microcosmic." In *Apocalyptic Paul: Cosmos and Anthropos in Romans 5–8*, edited by Beverly Roberts Gaventa, 21–38. Waco, TX: Baylor University Press, 2013.

Widmer, Michael. *Moses, God, and the Dynamics of Intercessory Prayer: A Study of Exodus 32–34 and Numbers 13–14*. FAT 2/8. Tübingen: Mohr Siebeck, 2004.

Williams, Guy. *The Spirit World in the Letters of Paul the Apostle: A Critical Examination of the Role of Spiritual Beings in the Authentic Pauline Epistles*. FRLANT 231. Göttingen: Vandenhoeck & Ruprecht, 2009.

Williams, Jarvis. *Maccabean Martyr Traditions in Paul's Theology of Atonement: Did Martyr Theology Shape Paul's Conception of Jesus' Death?* Eugene, OR: Wipf & Stock, 2010.

————. *One New Man: The Cross and Racial Reconciliation in Pauline Theology*. Nashville: B&H Academic, 2010.

Williams, S. K. "The 'Righteousness of God' in Romans." *JBL* 99 (1980): 241–90.

Wiseman, D. J. "The Vassal-Treaties of Esarhaddon." *Iraq* 20 (1958): 1–99.

Witherington, Ben, III. *Making a Meal of It: Rethinking the Theology of the Lord's Supper*. Waco: Baylor University Press, 2007.

Wright, Archie T. "Angels." In *The Eerdmans Dictionary of Early Judaism*, edited by John J. Collins and Daniel C. Harlow, 328–31. Grand Rapids: Eerdmans, 2010.

Wright, N. T. "The Challenge of Dialogue." In *God and the Faithfulness of Paul*, edited by Christoph Heilig, J. Thomas Hewitt, and Michael F. Bird, 711–68. Minneapolis: Fortress, 2017.

————. *The Climax of the Covenant: Christ and the Law in Pauline Theology*. Minneapolis: Fortress, 1992.

————. "God Put Jesus Forth: Reflections on Romans 3:24–26." In *In the Fullness of Time: Essays on Christology, Creation, and Eschatology*, edited by Daniel M. Gurtner, Grant Macaskill, and Jonathan Pennington, 135–61. Grand Rapids: Eerdmans, 2016.

————. *Justification: God's Plan and Paul's Vision*. Downers Grove, IL: IVP Academic, 2009.

————. "The Letter to the Romans." In *New Interpreter's Bible*. 12 vols. Edited by L. E. Keck, 10:395–770. Nashville: Abingdon, 2002.

————. *Paul and His Recent Interpreters*. Minneapolis: Fortress, 2015.

————. *Paul and the Faithfulness of God*. 2 vols. COQG 4. Minneapolis: Fortress, 2013.

————. *The Paul Debate: Critical Questions for Understanding the Apostle*. Waco, TX: Baylor University Press, 2015.

————. *Paul in Fresh Perspective*. Minneapolis: Fortress, 2009.

Yeo, Khiok-Khng. *Rhetorical Interaction in 1 Corinthians 8 and 10: A Formal Analysis with Preliminary Suggestions for a Chinese Cross-Cultural Hermeneutic*. Leiden: Brill, 1995.

Zank, Michael, trans. and ed. *Leo Strauss: The Early Writings (1921–1932)*. New York: State University of New York Press, 2002.

Zetterholm, Magnus. "Paul within Judaism: The State of the Questions." In *Paul within Judaism: Restoring the First-Century Context to the Apostle*, edited by Mark D. Nanos and Magnus Zetterholm, 31–51. Minneapolis: Fortress, 2015.

Ziesler, J. A. *The Meaning of Righteousness in Paul: A Linguistic and Theological Inquiry*. SNTSMS 20. Cambridge: Cambridge University Press, 1972.

INDEX OF AUTHORS

Adams, Edward, 67–68
Adeyẹmi, Fẹmi, 14, 57, 166, 170
Ådna, Jostein, 224, 226
Aletti, Jean-Noël, 180, 191
Allison, Dale C., Jr., 217
Ambrose, Kimberly, 31
Anderson, G. W., 89
Anderson, Gary, 147, 223, 236
Aquinas, Thomas, 1, 3
Armstrong, Anthony, 130
Arnold, Clinton E., 79
Attridge, Harold, 155
Augustine, 18, 44
Aune, David E., 3, 56, 68, 83

Baker, Mary Patton, 229, 245
Barber, Michael P., ix–xi, 107, 110, 220, 232, 235, 238
Barclay, John M. G., 43–44, 70, 71, 134–35, 140, 152, 153, 167–69, 209
Barker, P. A., 148
Barrett, C. K., 225, 229
Barrier, Jeremy, 2
Barth, Karl, 38
Bartholomew, Craig, 113
Bates, Matthew W., 98, 99, 101, 105, 185
Bauckham, Richard, 95, 109, 112, 113, 116, 117, 119, 125
Baur, F. C., 97, 99
Bautch, Kelley Coblentz, 73
Beale, G. K., 233
Behm, Johannes, 170
Beilby, James K., 209
Belleville, Linda, 218

Benoit, Pierre, 198
Bentley, Roland Thomas, 114
Bergsma, John S., 56, 100, 148
Berry, Donald K., 234
Betz, Hans Dieter, 192
Bieringer, Reimund, 48
Bird, Michael F., 6, 9, 12, 14, 16, 39, 46, 99, 158, 175, 206, 222, 247
Black, J. Sutherland, 222
Black, Matthew, 146, 151
Blackwell, Benjamin C., 6, 51, 65–66, 69–70, 84, 93, 193, 194, 200
Boakye, Andrew K., 190
Boccaccini, Gabriele, 11
Bockmuehl, Markus, 84
Bornkamm, Günther, 182, 225
Bousset, Wilhelm, 109
Bowden, John, 146
Brettler, Marc Zvi, 87, 133
Broduer, Scott, 219
Bromiley, Geoffrey W., 13
Brown, Jeannine K., 66
Brown, Raymond E., SS, 7
Bruce, F. F., 192
Bultmann, Rudolf, 13, 15–16, 17–18
Bunge, Wilfred F., 13
Burke, Trevor J., 219
Burkert, Walter, 142
Burnett, David A., 218
Byrne, Brendan J., 219

Caird, G. B., 79
Campbell, Constantine R., 163, 164, 178, 197, 201, 229

Campbell, Douglas A., 6, 12, 53, 64–65, 95, 129, 136, 150, 156–58, 185, 188, 192, 199, 202, 222

Capes, David B., 111, 119

Carson, D. A., 158, 163, 181, 233

Casey, Thomas G., 20

Castelli, E. A., 228

Chancey, Mark, 4

Charlesworth, James H., 48, 69, 74, 75, 76, 90, 155, 218

Chazon, E. G., 147

Chester, Andrew, 98, 107

Chester, Stephen J., 3, 4

Chiu, José Enrique Aguilar, 39, 46, 106, 196

Ciampa, Roy E., 233

Clements, R., 147

Cohen, Chaim, 143

Cohen, Shaye J. D., 86–87

Collins, Adela Yarbro, 93, 96, 104–5, 106, 120

Collins, John J., 44, 67, 68, 69, 74, 82, 83, 90–91, 93, 96, 97–98, 104–5, 106, 120, 142

Collins, Raymond, 213

Coutsoumpos, Panayotis, 223, 227, 248

Cranfield, C. E. B., 57, 151, 157

Cross, Frank Moore, 206

Crossan, J. D., 142

Danker, Frederick William, 15, 67, 135

Das, A. Andrew, 57, 59, 133

Davies, John A., 143

Davies, J. P., 64, 65, 66–67, 68, 89

Davies, W. D., 20, 23, 25, 27, 29

de Boer, Martinus C., 65, 69, 71, 72, 79, 92, 209

Deidun, T. J., IC, 94, 172

Deissmann, Adolf, 188

deSilva, David A., 179, 209

Despotis, Athanasios, 200

Dimant, D., 147

DiTomasso, Lorenzo, 83, 84

Dodd, B. J., 106

Dodd, C. H., 149

Dodson, Joseph, 6

Donfried, K. P., 197

Douglas, Mary, 223, 234–35, 236

Duling, Dennis C., 76

Dunn, James D. G., x, 2, 3, 4, 19, 20–21, 22, 23, 25, 27, 34, 52–53, 73, 86, 87, 95, 102–3, 105–6, 118, 120–21, 133, 138, 151, 156, 157, 193, 201, 209, 243

Durham, John, 144, 230

Eckstein, Hans Joachim, 43

Eddy, Paul R., 209

Ehrhardt, A. A. T., 105

Ehrman, Bart, 93, 105, 106, 108, 109, 121–22, 125, 127

Eisenbaum, Pamela, 12, 31–33, 35–38

Elliot, Mark W., 43, 205

Elliott, J. K., 2

Endres, John C., SJ, 73

Engberg-Pedersen, Troels, 224

Enzies, Allan, 222

Eubank, Nathan, 147

Evans, Craig A., 44, 220

Farrugia, Mario J., 9

Fee, Gordon, 93, 95, 103, 117, 202, 230, 243, 249

Finlan, Stephen, 150, 152

Fisk, Bruce N., 228

Fitzmyer, Joseph A., SJ, x, 7, 39, 47, 60, 61, 91, 93, 95, 96, 101, 119, 122, 132, 133, 136–37, 149, 157, 185, 192, 196, 198, 202, 209, 211, 213, 215, 216, 224, 230, 232, 240, 244

Flesher, P. V. M., 235

Fletcher-Louis, Crispin H. T., 223

Fotopoulos, John, 227

Frederick, John, 43, 205

Fredriksen, Paula, 31, 60–61, 97, 98, 100, 151, 237

Gadenz, Pablo T., 18, 55

Gager, John G., 30–31, 32, 33, 35–36, 37, 219

Gane, Roy E., 145, 239

Garland, David E., 223, 224, 226, 228, 230, 232

Garlington, Don, 4
Gaston, Lloyd, 30–31, 33, 37, 166
Gathercole, Simon J., 44, 130, 230
Gaventa, Beverly Roberts, 43, 65, 134, 174
Goff, Matthew, 85
Goldingay, John, 171
Gooder, Paula R., 85
Goodrich, John K., 51, 65–66, 69–70, 84, 93, 216
Gorman, Michael J., ix–xi, 5, 38–39, 41–42, 46, 47, 51, 66, 81, 94, 103–4, 133, 137–38, 165, 183, 188–90, 197, 203–4, 206, 207, 210, 220–21, 230
Gratry, Alphonse, 131
Green, Joel B., 66
Greenwood, David C., 56
Grieb, A. Katherine, 43, 183
Grobel, Kendrick, 13
Gupta, Nijay, 152
Gurtner, Daniel M., 129, 155

Hafemann, Scott J., 43, 46, 205
Hahn, Scott W., x, 39, 49–50, 52, 55, 58, 132, 143, 153, 156, 206, 229
Hahne, Harry A., 216, 217
Halls, W. D., 135
Hamilton, Victor P., 144
Hamm, Dennis, SJ, 118
Hammer, P. L., 225
Harkins, Angela Kim, 73
Harlow, Daniel C., 74, 83
Harrington, Daniel, 232
Harrison, James R., 135
Hartman, Lars, 204
Hawthorne, Gerald F., 103, 106, 107
Hay, David M., 224
Hays, Richard B., x, 38–39, 40, 41, 45, 46, 51, 66, 68, 79–80, 84, 153, 156, 158, 173, 182, 183, 185, 187–88, 192, 205, 214, 222, 224, 225, 231, 237, 242, 244
Healy, Mary, 113
Heilig, Christoph, 99, 206, 222, 247
Hellerman, Joseph, 137–38
Hengel, Martin, 100, 110–11

Hewitt, J. Thomas, 99, 206, 222, 247
Higgins, A. J. B., 226
Hill, Charles E., 130, 158
Hill, David, 147
Hill, Wesley, 118, 127–28, 215
Himmelfarb, Martha, 80
Hofius, Otfried, 226, 231, 232, 249
Hogan, Karina Martin, 64, 69, 71
Hogeterp, Albert L. A., 237
Hooker, Morna D., 188, 209–10
Hoover, Roy W., 107
Horn, Friedrich W., 244
Horrell, David, 228
Horsley, Richard, 133
Horton, Michael S., 209
House, Paul R., 118, 234
Hugenberger, Gordon P., 142
Humphrey, Edith M., 84, 86, 88, 222, 247–48
Hurtado, Larry, 95, 109, 116
Hurvitz, Avi M., 143
Husbands, Mark, 163, 181

Jacob, Benno, 144
James, Frank A., III, 130, 158
Janowski, Bernd, 231
Jeremias, Joachim, 146, 232
Jewett, Robert, 76, 133, 149, 152, 156, 157, 198
Jipp, Joshua, 158
Johnson, E. Elizabeth, 58
Johnson, Luke Timothy, 6, 9
Josephus, 78, 106, 111, 112, 122, 145, 156

Kalluveettil, Paul, 143
Käsemann, Ernst, 13, 15–17, 19–20, 64–65, 94, 151, 158, 167, 203, 211, 225, 226, 242, 245, 246, 249
Keating, Daniel, 3
Keck, L. E., 38, 151, 249
Keener, Craig S., 87, 166, 182, 196, 220, 223
Kennard, Douglas W., 216, 220
Kim, Jung Hoon, 200
Kim, Seyoon, 4

Kincaid, John A., ix–xi, 107, 110, 168, 172, 186, 220, 232
Klauck, Hans-Josef, 244, 245
Klawans, Jonathan, 145, 223
Kohl, Margaret, 13
Kruse, Colin G., 151

Lamb, Matthew L., 3
Landmesser, Christof, 43
Lapide, Pinchas, 33
Lapsley, Jacqueline E., 171
Larcher, Fabian R., OP, 1, 3
Lee, Aquila H. I., 99, 101, 105–6, 107
Leiva-Merikakis, E., 138
Levenson, Jon D., 143, 155
Levering, Matthew, 6
Levine, Amy-Jill, 87, 133
Levine, Baruch A., 145, 239
Lewis, Bryan E., 55
Lichtenberger, Hermann, 43
Lincoln, Andrew T., 50, 84, 86
Lindemann, Andreas, 119
Linebaugh, Jonathan A., 163
Litwa, M. David, 109, 110–14
Loke, Andrew Ter Ern, 103, 107, 108, 112, 116, 120, 121
Lundbom, Jack R., 141

Macaskill, Grant, 129, 155
MacDonald, Nathan, 110, 113–14
Marcus, Joel, 131
Marcus, Ralph, 78
Marshall, I. Howard, 232
Martin, Dale B., 214
Martin, Ralph P., 42, 85, 106, 172
Martyn, J. Louis, 64–66, 72, 78, 80, 92, 136, 201
Maston, Jason, 51, 65–66, 69–70, 84, 93
Matera, Frank J., x, 39, 40, 46, 47, 49–50, 60, 95, 98, 101, 103–4, 106, 133, 139, 155, 177
Mauss, Marcel, 135
McCarthy, Dennis J., 142, 143
McCormack, Bruce L., 18
McGrath, Alister E., 18
McGrath, James F., 117, 119

McKnight, Scot, 6, 221, 237
McNamara, Martin, 146
Meier, John P., 11
Melvin, David P., 74
Menzies, Allan, 97
Metzger, Bruce M., 198
Meyer, Ben F., 226, 230
Meyer, Peggy Manning, 180
Milgrom, Jacob, 142, 145–46, 148, 239, 240
Miller, Colin D., 221, 222, 240–41, 243, 245, 247
Mitchell, Margaret, 6
Möller, Karl, 113
Montague, W. J., 13, 211
Montgomery, William, 1, 20, 205
Moo, Douglas J., 184
Morales, Isaac Augustine, OP, 201, 202, 203, 204–5
Morales, Rodrigo J., 44, 153, 243, 249
More, Henry, 110
Morgan, Teresa, 184
Morris, Leon L., 149
Mortensen, Beth, 3
Moses, Robert Ewusie, 78, 79
Mowinckel, Sigmund, 88
Mullin, Robert Bruce, 3
Murphy, Roland E., OCarm, 7
Murphy-O'Connor, Jerome, 5, 48

Nanos, Mark D., 13, 30–31, 33, 35–36, 37, 48, 54
Neusner, Jacob, 239
Newman, John Henry, 8, 208
Newton, Derek, 228
Nickelsburg, George W. E., 68, 74, 82, 88, 90–91, 218
Noffman, Norbert, 138
Nolland, John, 167
North, J. Lionel, 114
North, Wendy E. S., 110, 114, 115
Novenson, Matthew V., 96, 97, 98, 99, 100, 217

Oakes, Peter, 192
O'Brien, Peter T., 158, 180

O'Collins, Gerald, 9
O'Cready, Wayne O., 15
Oegema, Gerbern S., 96
Oliver, Isaac W., 133
Olson, Robert C., 171
Oropeza, B. J., 123, 218
Orr, Peter, 214, 227, 243

Pate, C. Marvin, 216, 220
Patterson, Jane Lancaster, 237, 238
Paul, Shalom M., 143
Pennington, Jonathan, 129, 155
Perrin, Nicholas, 66, 84, 232
Perry, Robin, 113
Pietersma, Albert, 150, 185
Piper, John, 180
Pitre, Brant, ix–xi, 56, 57, 66, 149, 216, 220, 234, 235, 236, 237, 238
Pitta, Antonio, 46
Polak, F. H., 143
Pollefeyt, Didier, 48
Powers, Daniel G., 182
Prat, Ferdinand, 187
Prothro, James B., 184, 186, 205, 206
Pursifal, Darrell J., 188

Rabens, Volker, 214, 242–43, 244, 246
Rad, Gerhard von, 141
Reasoner, Mark, 53
Reinhartz, Adele, 15
Renaud, Bernard, 144
Reumann, John, 103
Rey, Jean Sébastien, 48
Reynolds, Benjamin E., 64, 67, 69, 85
Ricks, Stephen D., 56
Robertson, O. P., 184
Robinson, John A. T., 215, 221
Rogers, E. R., 244
Rosner, Brian S., 233
Rowe, C. Kavin, 43, 246
Rowland, Christopher, 73, 82, 83
Rudolph, David J., 54
Russell, D. S., 73, 83, 84, 89, 91

Sanders, E. P., x, 3–4, 5, 7, 11, 15, 20, 22–25, 27, 30, 34, 43, 46, 78–79, 103,
105, 117, 162, 166, 180, 192, 200–201, 222, 233, 237, 240–41
Sarna, Nahum M., 142, 236
Schauf, Scott, 188–89
Scheck, Thomas P., 18, 53
Schiffman, Lawrence H., 48
Schmid, Konrad, 56
Schreiner, Thomas R., 57, 151, 163, 185, 191, 197–98, 206, 208
Schürer, Emil, 68
Schwartz, Baruch J., 146
Schweitzer, Albert, 1, 20–21, 25, 26–27, 29–30, 72, 78, 79–80, 200, 205, 250
Scott, James M., 56
Sechrest, Love L., 13, 15–16
Segovia, Carlos A., 11
Seifrid, Mark, 158, 162
Silva, Moisés, 103
Sklar, Jay, 144, 145, 146, 239
Smith, Barry D., 44, 63, 220
Soards, Marion L., 188
Söding, Thomas, 205
Sprinkle, Preston M., 44, 170
Stagg, Frank, 194
Stalker, D. M. G., 182
Stanley, David Michael, 190
Staples, Jason A., 55–56, 58–60
Steck, Odil Hannes, 56
Steeley, John E., 109
Stegman, Thomas D., SJ, x, 139, 180–81, 182, 183, 195–96, 200, 206
Stendahl, Krister, 30–31, 32, 35, 37–38
Stewart, Eric, 56
Stoddard, John L., 187
Stökl Ben Ezra, Daniel, 150
Stone, Michael, 68, 90
Stowers, Stanley K., 213, 228
Stuckenbruck, Loren T., 64, 67, 69, 85, 110, 114, 115
Stuhlmacher, Peter, 4, 33, 231
Sullivan, K. P., 73

Tanner, Norman P., 162
Tatum, Gregory, OP, 5, 206
Taussig, H., 228
Taylor, Justin, 20

Thate, Michael J., 197, 201, 229
Thiselton, Anthony C., 230, 242
Thomas, Matthew J., 53
Thompson, Michael B., 200
Thrall, Margaret, 138, 152
Tilling, Chris, 93, 95, 113, 122–26
Torrance, Isabelle C., 142
Treier, Daniel J., 163, 181
Trinité, Philippe de la, 130, 131
Tucker, G. M., 142
Turley, Stephen Richard, 228

Udoh, Fabian E., 43, 134, 205

VanderKam, James C., 48, 68, 88, 90–91, 218
Vanhoozer, Kevin J., 197, 201, 229
Verhoef, Peter, 234
Vermes, Geza, 68, 88–89, 99

Wagner, J. Ross, 43
Watson, Francis, 4, 156
Watts, J. D. W., 234
Watts, J. W., 234
Wedderburn, A. J. M., 245
Weiß, Johannes, 228

Wellhausen, Julius, 222–23
Wells, Kyle B., 44, 45, 94, 170, 171, 172
Westerholm, Stephen, 4, 13, 15, 17, 19, 174
Widmer, Michael, 144
Wikgren, Allen, 78
Williams, Guy, 79
Williams, Jarvis, 144, 151
Williams, S. K., 157
Wilson, Todd A., 118
Wiseman, D. J., 131, 142, 229
Witherington, Ben, III, 225
Wright, Archie T., 74, 79
Wright, Benjamin G., 150, 185
Wright, N. T., x, 4, 6, 38–39, 43, 46, 57, 58, 61, 62, 64–66, 69, 72, 73, 78, 80, 86, 87, 95, 97, 106, 117, 129, 136, 139, 151, 154, 155, 164, 178, 181, 182, 201, 205, 206, 222, 247–48

Yeo, Khiok-Khng, 228

Zank, Michael, 223
Zetterholm, Magnus, 30–31, 33, 37
Ziesler, J. A., 164

INDEX OF SUBJECTS

Abraham, 16, 23, 50, 130, 218; believers in Christ as Abraham's offspring, 52; blessing of, 155; faithfulness of as obedience, 191–92; faithfulness of as righteousness, 183–84, 185–86; God's oath given to, 156; God's reckoning of Abraham as righteous apart from circumcision, 152–53

Acts of Paul and Thecla, 2

Adam: the new Adam and the new creation, 214–16; sin of, 195–96, 252

angelology, 73, 127; angels as elemental spirits (*stoicheia*), 75–76, 77, 78, 79–80; angels as invisibly governing worldly kingdoms, 74–75; and deliverance from angelic bondage, 80; divergences of Paul from typical Jewish thought concerning, 77–78; early Jewish angelology, 74–76; heavenly bodies as identified with angels, 79; honorific and worship language ascribed to angelic beings, 115; on the law as ordained through angels, 78; Pauline angelology, 76–82

apocalypses, Jewish, 67, 71–73; and early Jewish cosmology, 82–84

atonement (*kipper*), in Jewish scripture, 145–46; connection of to forgiveness, 145; cultic atonement as presented in the Torah, 149, 150; as delivering the guilty sinner from death, 146; as purification/cleansing, 145, 149; "ransom" connotation of, 145–46, 152; and the "sacrifice of atonement,"

149–50; the "sin offering" and Christ, 150–52, 182, 197, 238–40. *See also* cross, the, and atonement

baptism, 80, 211, 250; baptism imagery Paul used in describing "drinking of one Spirit" at the Lord's Supper, 243–45; identification of with spiritual washing, 202; of Jews, 52; and justification, 202–4; and justification and divine sonship, 204–7; and justifying faithfulness, 204; salvation for both Jew and Greek through faith and baptism, 19; union of with Christ through baptism and the Lord's Supper, 22, 222. *See also* Corinth: place of baptism in the communal life of

Caligula, Gaius, 109

Cephas. *See* Peter (Cephas)

Christianity, 11, 20, 32; Paul on conversion of Israel to Christianity, 37; Paul as representative of a "Torah-free gentile Christianity," 16

Christians, 15, 23, 201, 240; divisions among concerning interpretations of Paul's thought, 3; early Christians, 2, 227; Galatian Christians, 88; Jewish Christians, 37; as "members" of Christ's body, 202; necessity of faith in Jesus to, 188; non-Jewish Christians, 34; sharing of in the Lord's Supper, 249; term "Christians" not available to Paul, 31, 32; union of with Christ through baptism and the Lord's Supper, 22, 222

Christology: early Jewish, 89–91; "incarnational Christology," 105. *See also* Christology, Pauline

Christology, Pauline, 95–96, 252; on Christ devotion and the language of God-relation, 122–25; "divine Christology" of, 122–23; on the identity of Jesus as the "Son of God" (*huiou theou*), 99–100, 121; on the Messiah descended from David, 96–101, 108, 110, 126, 251; on the messianic identity of Jesus as associated with Jesus's resurrection, 100–101; Pauline apocalyptic Christology, 91–93, 128; repetitive usage by Paul of Jesus as "Christ" (*christos*), 97–98; supposed angel Christology of Paul, 121–22, 127. *See also* Christology, Pauline, on equality with God

Christology, Pauline, on equality with God, 1–2; on Christ in the "form of God" (*morphē theou*), 102, 103–5, 106, 108, 127, 137–39, 140, 160; equality of Christ with God before Christ's birth, 105–7; on exaltation of Christ, 73, 94, 107–8, 139; on God sending his Son in the "likeness of sinful flesh," 102–3. *See also* Jesus Christ, as one God and Lord

circumcision, 17, 22, 24–25, 50, 51, 52, 53, 54, 71; Abraham as righteous apart from circumcision, 152–53; the "circumcision faction," 34; of the heart, 170, 177; Paul's opposition to, 35, 80; requirement for in the Torah, 81–82, 87–88; as unnecessary for justification, 192. *See also* soteriology: Pauline new covenant soteriology concerning circumcision

Corinth: celebration of the Lord's Supper in, 47, 224–25; place of baptism in the communal life of, 202

cosmology: Jewish, 82–84; Pauline (spatial axis), 84–88; on YHWH as the Sovereign Ruler of the cosmos, 113

Council of Trent (1545–1563), statement of on justification, 162

covenant, new. *See* new covenant

"covenantal nomism," 24; structure of, 24

covenants, ancient, ratification of by sacrifice, 142–43

Creator-creature debate, 119–21, 127

cross, the, and atonement, 129–31, 140–41; as apocalyptic revelation, 160–61; atonement and the idea of a vengeful God, 131; on Christ becoming poor although he was rich, 139–40; Christ's willing/voluntary sacrifice of himself for our sins (new covenant sacrifice), 131–34, 139; Christ's willing/voluntary sacrifice of himself reflected in the Last Supper, 132; covenantal logic as crucial to understanding Paul's discussion of the cross, 130; the cross as an apocalyptic revelation of Jesus's divinity, 137–39; the cross as a divine gratuity/gift (*charis*) expressing God's love (*agapē*) for humanity, 129, 134–37, 140; the cross as means by which salvation is accomplished, 130; the cross as revelation of God's justice and mercy, 156; the cross as revelation of God's righteousness, 155, 156–60; the cross as "sacrifice of atonement" (*hilastērion*), 130, 149, 150, 151, 222; difficulty in understanding Paul's discussion concerning, 129; inseparability of the cross from the concept of grace, 134–37; and Moses, 143–44. *See also* atonement (*kipper*), in Jewish scripture

culture, Greco-Roman, 111, 223

David, 53, 184–85; anointing of by Samuel, 101; on Israel paying homage to both God and king, 114–15; Jesus (the Messiah) as direct descendent of, 96–101, 108, 110, 126, 251

Davidic king, 97, 110

Davidic kingdom, 56, 97

Day of Atonement, 148, 160, 220; liturgy of, 150

Dead Sea Community, 155

Dead Sea Scrolls, 4, 44–45, 111, 220

divinity: in the ancient context of Paul's time, 109, 111; in Christian theology as always referring to the Trinity, 109; of God, 140; Jesus's actions as a human an expression of what he does in his divinity, 138–39; terms associated with, 110; and the truth of Jesus's divinity (his "being in the form of God"), 138. *See also* sonship, divine

Ephraim, 59

eschatology, Jewish, 20, 22; dawning of eschatological age, 45; and distinction between "two ages" and "two worlds," 20–21, 22, 67–69; and final age/the end (*eschaton*), 20, 23, 193, 208, 218, 219, 246; influence of Jewish apocalypses on, 67, 68–69; Jewish belief in eschatological tribulation, 57–58, 252. *See also* eschatology, Pauline

eschatology, Pauline: difference of from the eschatology of Jewish apocalypses, 71–73; on the eschatological suffering of the righteous, 216–18; sharing by Paul of the Jewish eschatological concept of "two ages" and "two worlds," 69, 70–71; of "two worlds" (temporal axis), 69–73; use of the language of revelation in, 70

faith (*pistis*), 52, 78, 80; of Abraham, 191–92; as believing in the gift of forgiveness, 17; justification by faith and not by works of the law, 16–18, 25, 33–35, 54, 167, 186, 188–89; righteousness by faith, 180; the term "faith" (*pistis*) in ancient Greek

writers, 184–85; those having faith no longer "under the torah," 80. *See also* Israel: salvation of as possible only through explicit faith in Christ

forgiveness, 17, 130, 146, 148, 154, 163; connection of to atonement, 145; need for, 192; as provided by through the new covenant, 61, 141

Gabriel, 74

gentiles: and the blessing of Abraham, 155; as incorporated into the righteous remnant of Israel, 59–60; Paul as apostle to the, 23, 35; redemption of, 59

gift-giving: expectations in ancient times for the receiver of a gift, 135, 136; "pure altruism" as the motivation for, 135. *See also* grace: as a gift (*charis*)

glorification, 246; as inseparable from justification, 193–96; as *theōsis* ("divinization"), 200

God: as Creator God, 112–13; divine love of, 136–37; as the divine surgeon, 171; divinity of, 140; gift of the Holy Spirit given by, 44; glory of, 193–94; judgment of, 175–79; juridical power of, 208–9; kindness of, 175; relationship of with Israel, 122–23; response of to "un-righteousness" (*adikia*), 163; transforming of human agency by, 169; as "Wisdom personified," 120–21. *See also* Creator-creature debate; God, righteousness of; new covenant righteousness; YHWH (the tetragrammaton)

God, righteousness of, 14, 176, 180, 183; becoming the righteousness of God through Christ, 196–98; and the "blessing" of God, 155–56; meaning of, 157–58; new covenant justification through, 178–79; relation of to the new covenant, 159–60; revelation of through the cross, 155, 156–60

grace: as the cause of obedience, 168;

connection of to God's glory, 193–94; connection of to righteousness, 167; as divine empowerment, 168; as empowerment for self-giving, 140; as a gift (*charis*), 129, 134–37, 140, 167; ineffectiveness of the Torah versus the grace of Christ, 166–69; inseparability of Christ's sacrifice on the cross from the concept of grace, 134–37, 252; and the new covenant, 43–44; powerful effect of on Paul and his ministry, 167–68; shown in God's covenant with Israel, 24

Greco-Roman culture, 111, 223

Hagar, 49, 50, 85–86
Hellenization, 110
historiography, "sympathetic," 111–12
Holy Spirit, 228; action of in establishing a "covenant of peace" and an "everlasting covenant," 171–72; anointing by, 100; first fruits of, 25, 70, 216; as a giver of life, 40, 42; as God's gift, 44; justification and the gift of, 190–93; as life/life-giving power, 45, 196; promise of true obedience given through, 45; role of in our bodily resurrection, 214
hope, 70, 89, 99, 212, 215–16, 218; of a Jewish community for future spiritual renewal and restoration of the twelve tribes, 44–45, 56–58, 60, 97; for a new covenant, 155; of sharing the glory of God, 193

idolatry, 123, 228; commission of by Israel, 142, 143
imputation: imputed redemption, 181; imputed righteousness, 182, 185, 195, 198, 201; imputed sanctification, 181; imputed wisdom, 181
interpretive movement. *See* "New Perspective on Paul"
Irenaeus, 209, 253
Isaac, "binding" of, 156
Israel, 41; exile of in Assyria, 56, 58;

idolatry committed by, 142, 143; Jewish hope for the restoration of, 56; northern tribes of ("the house of Israel"), 56, 57–59; Paul on the conversion of Israel to Christianity, 37; Paul on the salvation of, 28–30; paying homage to both God and king, 114–15; prohibitions against for worshiping other gods, 114–15; relationship of with God, 122–23; retelling by Paul of Israel's exodus and wilderness experience, 242; sacrificial cult of, 150, 234–35, 237–38, 239; salvation of as possible only through explicit faith in Christ, 18–20; southern tribes of ("the house of Judah"), 57; twelve-tribe structure of, 56–57

Jacob, 36, 59
Jeremiah: on iniquity as "injustices," 159; olive tree image of, 59; prophecy of concerning the new covenant, 40–42, 55, 56–57, 60–61, 141, 149
Jerusalem, as the heavenly Jerusalem, 82, 84, 86–88, 94; those in Christ already belong to the heavenly Jerusalem, 86–87; those in Christ are free from the earthly Jerusalem and the torah, 87–88. *See also* cosmology: Jewish; cosmology: Pauline (spatial axis)
Jesus Christ, 65, 70; actions of in human form as a reflection of actions in his divinity, 138–39; believers in as Abraham's offspring, 52; as the climax of the covenants between God and Israel, 66; compared to Adam, 105–6; as completely human, 126; core/divine identity of, 160, 162; as the Davidic king, 60, 126; death/crucifixion of, 17, 38, 73, 94, 154; death of as a covenant-making sacrifice, 229–31; divine love of God revealed through Jesus's act of giving himself for sinners, 137; as divine Son, 126–28; as "Divine Wisdom,"

121; exaltation of, 73, 94, 107–8, 139; form of before becoming human, 127; humbleness of, 102, 108, 137; as a Jew, 11; lordship of, 20, 116–19; as the Messiah descended from David (the royal Messiah), 96–101, 108, 110; obedience of, 138, 188, 195, 252; passion of, 73, 94; relationship of with believers, 122–23; resurrection of, 23, 38, 73, 94, 100–101, 215, 247; revelation of, 5, 92; role of as an "atoning sacrifice," 129, 131, 150, 152, 181–82, 194, 219–20; sin offering of, 150–52, 182, 197, 238–40; as the Son of God, 101–2, 121, 139, 252, 253; as the Son of Man, 89–90, 217; union with, 220–21. *See also* cross, the, and atonement; Jesus Christ, as one God and Lord

Jesus Christ, as one God and Lord, 108–9; and the exclusive worship of one God, 113–16; identification of Jesus by Paul as being on the "Creator" side of the "Creator-creature" debate, 119–21; identification of Jesus by Paul as an "incarnate divine being," 109; influence of Isaiah on Paul's conception of Jesus, 117–18; and Jewish monotheism, 109–11; as the "one God" of Israel (YHWH), 111–13, 118–19, 123, 127, 128; Paul's identification of Christ as the "one Lord" of the *Shema*ʻ, 116–19

Jubilee Year, 148

Judah, 40–41, 57

Judaism, 14, 20, 27, 157; conceptions of divinity in first-century Jewish sources, 110–11; first-century ("Second Temple") era of, 11, 15, 24, 55–56, 67; non-monolithic nature of in Paul's day, 4; priestly tradition in the final stage of, 222–23. *See also* Judaism, *Shema*ʻ ("Hear") prayer of; monotheism, Jewish; Paul, as a Jew

Judaism, *Shema*ʻ ("Hear") prayer of, 109–10, 111, 123, 128; Paul's identification of Christ as the "one Lord"

of the *Shema*ʻ, 116–19; significance of as representing the relationship between YHWH and Israel, 113–14

justification, doctrine of, 26–27, 194–95; as conformity to the character of divine sonship (the "spirit of sonship"), 198–201, 204–10; as directed against Jewish legalism, 16, 17; and the dynamics of covenant relations, 206–7; and the gift of the Holy Spirit, 190–93; "initial justification," 201; as inseparable from glorification, 193–96; juridical dimension of, 196, 199, 206, 207, 208; justification as "co-crucifixion," 188–90, 203; justification by Christ-empowered faithfulness, 186–88; justification by faith versus works-righteousness (the works of the law), 16–18, 25, 33–35, 54, 167, 175, 186, 188–89, 193, 200–201; on justification creating a change in a believer's legal status, 163–64, 183, 194; new covenant justification through divine sonship, 162–64, 198–201; new covenant justification through God's righteousness, 178–79, 182–83; proselyte conversion as the contextual contrast to, 35–36. *See also* baptism: and justification

Justin Martyr, 249

Last Supper, the, 141–42, 231, 232, 235, 237; Jesus's words and actions during, 132

legalism: Jewish, 16, 17, 23–24, 34; pagan, 18

Lord's Prayer, the, expression of sin as a "debt" in, 147

Lord's Supper, the, 222–23; and the actualization of ecclesial union, 226; allusions by Paul to Israel's cultic worship in the celebration of, 234–35, 237–38, 239, 248–49; baptism imagery of Paul used in describing "drinking of one Spirit" at the Lord's Supper, 243–45; and being guilty of the body and blood of the Lord, 223–26; as a communal meal, 223–24; cosmic redemption provided through, 247–50; description and importance of the eucharistic table/altar to, 232–34; and the eating of temple sacrifices, 238–40; identification of Jesus's body and blood as food and drink, 235–36, 248; and "idol food," 227–29, 235; as "participation" (*koinōnia*) in the "blood" of the new covenant, 47–48, 250, 253; Paul's criticism of the Corinthian manner of celebrating, 47, 224–25, 240; and the sacrifice of the ecclesial body, 240–41; and the sacrificial death of Christ, 229–31, 237; as a sacrificial meal (cultic and sacrificial dimensions of), 231–35; sharing of the sacrificial offering of Christ during, 235–38; as spiritual (*pneumatikos*) food and drink, 241–43, 248–50; spiritual (*pneumatikos*) food and drink as a foretaste of the new creation, 243–48; the table of demons versus the table of the Lord, 226–29; themes of linked to Passover traditions, 237–38; warnings concerning partaking of the Lord's Supper unworthily, 239–40

Luther, Martin, 134

Messiah: early Jewish Christology concerning, 89–91; the hidden, 88–89; messianic identity of Jesus as associated with his resurrection, 100–101. *See also* Christology, Pauline: on the Messiah descended from David

Michael, 74

monotheism, Jewish, 113, 116, 127; concern of that God alone carried out the work of creation, 120; and the question of divinity, 109–11

Moses, 33, 50, 112, 171; and blood sacrifice, 230; pleading of with the Lord for atonement regarding Israel's sins of idolatry, 143–45; and the sacred

meal of the priests, 238–39; smashing of the Ten Commandments by, 142. *See also* old covenant (Mosaic covenant at Mount Sinai); Torah (the Mosaic Torah)

new covenant, 5, 10, 126–27, 156, 169, 242, 250; apocalyptic new covenant, 94, 130; as bringing about a change in Israel's heart, 170–72; and Christ's willing/voluntary sacrifice of himself for our sins (the new covenant sacrifice), 131–34; competence of believers to be ministers of, 40; as a "covenant of peace" and an "everlasting covenant," 171–72; establishment of by the righteous of the messianic era, 155; and the freedom of new covenant Jerusalem, 48–54; and grace, 43–44; Jeremiah's prophecy concerning, 40–42, 55, 56–57, 60–61, 141, 149; new covenant approach to the reading of Paul within Judaism, 62–63; the new covenant as written on the heart by the Holy Spirit, 42; "participation" (*koinōnia*) in the Lord's Supper as participating in the "blood" of the new covenant, 47–48, 250, 253; Paul as a minister of the new covenant, 39–48; promise of related to the old "broken" covenant, 141–42; salvation for all Israel through, 55–62. *See also* new covenant righteousness; soteriology: Pauline new covenant soteriology concerning circumcision

new covenant righteousness, 164–66, 196; "cardiac righteousness" of, 172–74, 196, 209, 252; Christ as the believer's source of righteousness, 181; as merely extrinsic righteousness, 179–86; new covenant justification through God's righteousness, 178–79, 182–83; origin of in Christ, 179–80; relation of God's righteousness to, 159–60, 180 new creation, 27, 67, 80, 209, 246, 252; all believers in Christ as part of the new creation, 72, 73; and the new Adam, 214–16. *See also* Lord's Supper, the: spiritual (*pneumatikos*) food and drink as a foretaste of the new creation

"New Perspective on Paul," 3–4, 25, 34; "Radical New Perspective on Paul," 30, 34n86, 36

obedience, 98, 166, 188, 208, 251, 252; of Abraham, 191–92; eschatological principle of, 63; genuine faith as obedience, 17, 191–92, 200; grace as the cause of, 168; the heart (*kardia*) as the source of, 170; role of the Holy Spirit in, 44, 45, 63, 171. *See also* Jesus Christ: obedience of; old covenant (Mosaic covenant at Mount Sinai): role of obedience in

offerings: peace offering, 238; the "sin offering" and Christ, 150–52, 182, 197, 238–40; thank offering, 238

old covenant (Mosaic covenant at Mount Sinai), 38, 49–50, 130, 132–33, 156; breaking of the covenant by Israel's commission of idolatry, 142, 143; consequences of the broken covenant, 141–45; identification of the old "broken" covenant with Sinai, 141–42; ratification of the covenant, 236; role of obedience in, 24, 44; the Ten Commandments as a symbol of, 142

Paul, 1–4; apocryphal story of his meeting with Onesiphorus, 2; as apostle to the gentiles, 23, 35; as "an apostle to Israel," 23; baptism of, 81; conversion of, 11–12, 14–16, 21–23, 39–48; declaration of that he is not himself "under the law," 14–15; description of his own identity and that of other apostles, 45–46; effect of the revelation of Jesus Christ on, 5; as an

enigma or paradox, 1, 2; as a "minister of Christianity," 62; prominence of as a theologian, 2–3. *See also* Paul, as a Christian; Paul, epistles of; Paul, as a Jew; Paul, as a minister of the new covenant; theology, Pauline

Paul, as a Christian, 31–33; the Christ-event in Paul's life as reconfiguring his understanding of God, 127–28

Paul, epistles of: Peter's view that they are "hard to understand," 2; Peter's view that they are part of the "scriptures," 2; undisputed Pauline epistles, 6; as written exclusively to gentile audiences, 33–34

Paul, as a Jew, 11–13, 65, 66, 252; conversion of from Judaism to Christianity, 14–16, 30, 32; debates over Paul's relationship with Judaism, 12, 51; discontinuity between Paul and Jewish contemporaries of, 21; discontinuity between Paul the Christian apostle and Saul the Jewish Pharisee, 13; major aspects of his relationship with Judaism, 13; new covenant approach to the reading of Paul within Judaism, 62–63; relationship with Judaism after his conversion from persecutor to apostle, 11–12, 46; self-reference of Paul to his Jewish heritage, 11, 15. *See also* Paul, as a Jew, categories of; Paul, as a "Torah-observant Jew"

Paul, as a Jew, categories of: as the "eschatological Jew," 12, 20–24, 25–26, 29, 39, 62; as the "former Jew," 12, 13–15, 16, 39, 62; as a "new covenant Jew," 12, 38–39, 48–50, 62–63, 66–67, 126. *See also* Paul, as a minister of the new covenant

Paul, as a minister of the new covenant, 39–48, 172–74, 251; allusion of Paul to Jeremiah's oracle of the "new covenant," 40–42, 55, 56–57, 60–61; on becoming a child of the new covenant, 51–52; ecclesial nature of Paul's theology concerning, 59–60;

on eschatological tribulation, 57–58, 252; on hope and the new covenant, 44–45; how Paul exercised his new covenant ministry, 47–48; on the law (Mosaic Torah) and the freedom of new covenant Jerusalem, 48–54; Paul's olive tree metaphor concerning, 59; on the reality of "two covenants" (matriarchal covenants), 48–51, 85–86; on salvation of "all Israel" through the new covenant, 55–62; use of "heart" language by Paul in describing the new covenant, 42

Paul, as a "Torah-observant Jew," 12, 16–18, 23–28, 30–31, 52, 62; and Torah observance for Jews but not gentiles, 33–36; as a Torah-observant Jew and not a convert to Christianity, 31–33

Pelagius, 18

Peter (Cephas), 34, 35; Peter's view of Paul's epistles as "hard to understand," 2; Peter's view of Paul's epistles as part of the "scriptures," 2

Pharisees, tensions of with the Sadducees, 4

Philo of Alexandria, 107, 111; on the divine Word as a "second God," 116

pneumatology, 6, 190

Protestants, 18

reconciliation, 28, 207; due to the death and resurrection of Christ, 38

redemption, 148–49, 152, 156, 181, 220, 221; through "being in Christ," 27; Christ's death on the cross as an act of redemption, 130, 140, 194, 212; cosmic redemption and the table of the Lord's body, 247–50; and the "covenant curse," 152–55; economic imagery of, 147; of gentiles, 59; of Israel, 37; new covenant redemption, 160; of our bodies, 216, 218; ransom/ redemption imagery, 130, 147, 149, 152, 154; redemption for the "debt" of sin, 146–49, 152

resurrection, of the body, 212, 246; animation of our bodies by the Holy Spirit, 214; and the "body" of Christ, 213–14; the resurrected body as a "spiritual body," 214, 215, 247; as resurrection of the ecclesial body, 215. See also Jesus Christ: resurrection of

righteousness, 16, 17, 19, 228; Christian, 162; connection of to grace, 167; of divine kingship, 158; by faith, 180; imputed righteousness, 201; juridical dimension of, 164, 166, 172, 173–74, 180, 182, 191, 195; under the new covenant, 164–66. See also God, righteousness of; new covenant righteousness

Roman Catholicism/Roman Catholics, 7–9, 18

Sabbath, observance of, 17, 25, 50

Sadducees, tensions of with the Pharisees, 4

salvation, 24, 160, 201; for "all Israel" through the new covenant, 55–62; for both Jew and Greek through faith and baptism, 19; in Christ, 61–62; as a gift (charis), 129, 134; history of, 36–37; of Israel, 18–20; "two ways" of, 19; as underscoring God's righteousness, 156. See also theology, Pauline: on the "two ways" of salvation law

sanctification (hagiasmos), 197–98; angels of, 75; Christ as the source of, 181; "imputed sanctification," 181

Sarah, 49–50; the "Sarah" covenant of "freedom," 50

Satan, 76

Saul, 13

scholarship, Pauline, 12–13; contemporary Pauline exegesis, 6–7; major developments of in the last fifty years, 3; on Paul's relationship to Judaism,

3–4, 12; Roman Catholic tradition
and legacy concerning, 7–9
Shema' ("Hear") prayer. *See* Judaism,
Shema' ("Hear") prayer of
sin, 26, 151, 203, 207, 219; and the consequences of the broken covenant,
141–45; as covenant infraction, 144;
death as the penalty for, 72, 73, 144–
45, 147; economic connotation of (as
a "debt") in Jewish tradition, 146–49;
as impurity, 145; knowledge of, 53; as
offense against both God and Christ,
123; power and gravity of, 160–61,
192; as preventing God's people from
truly "knowing" the Lord, 141. *See
also* Adam: sin of; Jesus Christ: sin
offering of
Sinai, Mount, 85–86. *See also* old
covenant (Mosaic covenant at Mount
Sinai)
Solomon, 75, 194
sonship, divine, 94, 96, 100–101,
218–21; and baptism and justification, 204–7; and Christ in "the
form of God" (preexistent divine
sonship), 102, 103–5; justification as
conformity to the character of divine
sonship (the "spirit of sonship"),
198–201, 204–10; new covenant
justification through divine sonship,
162–64, 198–201; summary of Paul's
gospel of, 251–53
soteriology, 148; the Catholic tradition
of *admirabile commercium* (the "great
exchange") at the heart of Christian
soteriology, 253; neglect of the ecclesial dimension of, 211; Pauline, 25, 211,
240; Pauline new covenant soteriology concerning circumcision, 81–82
suffering, of the righteous, 218–21

Ten Commandments, 17; smashing of
by Moses, 142; as a symbol of the old
covenant, 142
tetragrammaton. *See* YHWH (the
tetragrammaton)

theology, Pauline, 5–6, 251–53; on the
baptism of Jews, 52; on being "in
Christ" versus being "under the Law,"
21–22, 23–28; centrality of Paul's faith
in Jesus as the Son of God to, 135,
167, 169, 189, 193; on condemnation,
172–73; on conversion to Christ,
39–40; on the day of fulfillment of
God's promises, 45; elements of
both continuity and discontinuity
with Judaism in, 39; on the final
judgment, 175–79; God-relation
and Christ-relation in, 124–25; on
good works, 34–35; identification of
Christ as "Divine Wisdom" and the
divine Son of God in, 121, 126–28;
influence of Hosea's prophecy on,
58; linking of the crucifixion with
union to Christ through baptism,
22; nonsystematic nature of, 6–7;
occasional self-conscious language
used by Paul in, 168–69; portrayal
of Jesus as human in, 126; rejection
of works (*erga*) in, 17; remnant theology of, 55, 60; as targeting Jewish
works-righteousness, 25; on the "two
ways" of salvation law, 36–38; use of
the language of salvation in, 61–62;
view of Christ as the climax of the
covenants between God and Israel,
66; on works of the law, 16–17, 18,
23–24, 25, 33–35, 52–53, 54, 63, 153,
167, 176, 186, 188–89, 190–91. *See
also* angelology: Pauline angelology;
Christology, Pauline; cross, the, and
atonement; justification, doctrine of;
Lord's Supper, the; new covenant;
soteriology: Pauline; theology, Pauline, as apocalyptic
theology, Pauline, as apocalyptic,
64–67, 126, 251; debates concerning
the meaning of Paul's theology as
"apocalyptic," 65–67; "Eschatological Invasion" approach to, 65; key
themes of, 66; summary of, 93–94;
"Unveiled Fulfillment" approach

to, 66. *See also* angelology: Pauline
angelology; cosmology: Pauline
(spatial axis); eschatology, Pauline
Torah (the Mosaic Torah), 15, 16–18,
38; curse imagery in, 154; faith frees
us from being "under the torah,"
80; and the freedom of new covenant Jerusalem, 48–54; inability of
to bring about obedience, 166–67;
ineffectiveness of versus the grace
of Christ, 166–69; as a "ministry of
condemnation," 173; as one of the
"divine" gifts, 166; presentation of
cultic atonement in, 149; warnings
in concerning presenting offerings

in a profane manner, 239–40; works
(ritual, ceremonial, moral) required
by, 17

universalism, 38
Uriel, 74, 76

YHWH (the tetragrammaton), 111,
252; Jesus as the "one God" of Israel
(YHWH), 111–13, 118–19, 123, 127,
128; the power of YHWH to create,
112–13; relationship between YHWH
and Israel, 113–14; as the Sovereign
Ruler of the cosmos, 113

INDEX OF SCRIPTURE AND OTHER ANCIENT TEXTS

OLD TESTAMENT

Genesis

1:3	208
1:26	112, 120
1:26–27	105
6:9	174
12:1–3	191
12:3	153
13:17–18	191
15	191
15:4	50
15:6	152, 183, 191
16:1–7	50
17	53
17:9–14	81
17:18–21	50
18:9–15	50
18:19	174
18:25	174
20:5 LXX	174
21:1–7	50
21:23	174
22	156
22:1–19	155
22:9	155
22:17	218
22:18	153
22:18a	156
24:27	174
30:33	174
32:4	122
32:7	122
32:11	174
48:19	59
49	174

Exodus

6:6	149
7:1	110
12:8	237
12:14	237
14:19–22	242
15:11	110
16:1–36	242
17:6	242
20:1–4	115
20:1–6	228
23:7	184
24	236
24:3–8	141, 236
24:4–6	143
24:6	231
24:6–8	133, 230
24:7	143
24:8	143
24:9–11	143, 236
25:21	150
25:21–22	150
25:22 LXX	150
25:29–30	234
29:31–34	238
29:38–42	235
30:12	146
30:16	145, 146
32:10	144
32:19	142
32:30–34	143–44

32:34	144
34:1–4	41
34:28–29	41
37:16	235
40:34	194

Leviticus

4:1–3	151
4:3 LXX	151
4:3 MT	151
4:26	145
4:31	145
4:33 LXX	182
4:35	145
5:5	145
5:8	151
5:10	145
5:13	145
5:16	145
6:16	238
6:24–26	238
6:29	238
7:6–10	238
7:15–18	236
7:18	238
8:31–36	238
10:12–13	238
10:17	239
10:17–18	238
12:8	145
14:31	151
14:52	145
16:30	145, 148
18:5	153

19:5–8	236	27–30	153	29	238
19:6–8	238	27:23	154	29:10	126
20:17–21	145	27:26	153	34:29–35:19	238
21:22	238, 239	30:1	153	34:31–32	126
22:4	239	30:3–4	56		
22:6	239	30:6	171	**Nehemiah**	
22:30	238	30:8	171	1:9	56
24:1–9	235, 236	32:8	74	9:6	112
24:9	238	32:17	110		
24:15–16	145	32:39	113	**Job**	
25	148	33:2 LXX	78	1:6	121
25:8–10	148	33:26	110	12:4	174
25:10	148			22:19	174
25:13	148	**Joshua**		34:11	43
25:39–43	148	3:7–5:12	238		
		24:14	174	**Psalms**	
Numbers				1:6	174
5:19	145	**1 Samuel**		2:7	99
6:10 LXX	151	2:10 LXX	174	7:9	174
9:13	145	16:1–23	99	10:7	174
10:10	232	16:13	100	14:2	174
11:4–35	242	26:23	184–85	16:1	174
18:13–20	238			16:15	174
18:25–31	238	**2 Samuel**		17:21	174
18:29	240	7:13–16	97	17:25	174
18:31–32	240	7:14	99	22	131
20:7–13	242	15:4	184	22:3	174
25:15	154	22:21 LXX	174	22:19–31	131
28:3–8	235	22:25 LXX	174	32:1–2	53
31:50	145			32:11	174
35:31	146	**1 Kings**		33:6	113
35:31–33	145–46	3:6 LXX	174	37:21	174
35:33	146	8:11	194	50:5	132, 142, 229
		12	56	51:5	174
Deuteronomy				57:2	174
6:4	109, 111, 127	**2 Kings**		62:12 [61:13 LXX]	43
6:4–5	110, 117, 121, 170	23:21–23	126	63:2	194
6:4–6	117, 123	23:21–24	238	64:10 [MT 64:11]	174
6:5	127			68:4	110
9:5	174	**1 Chronicles**		68:17 LXX	78
10:12	170	17:11–14	97	82:1	110
10:14	112	29:20	114	82:6	110
10:16	170	29:20–22	114	82:8	113
16:4–8	237			86:4–5 LXX	86
25:1	184	**2 Chronicles**		87	86
27	153	10	56	89:3–4	97

89:6–7	110
89:27	99
89:35–37	97
94:21	174
95:5	113
97:7	110
97:11	174
104:3	110
104:24	113
110:4	97
132:11	97

Proverbs

3:19	113
8:22–31	120
8:30	113

Isaiah

2	87
2:1–5	83
9:1–9	56, 60
9:6	110
9:6–7	217
9:7	97
10:22	57
10:23	57
11:1	56, 60, 97
11:10–16	56
11:11–13	60
11:13	56
14:1–2	56
16:5	97
25:6	234
27:2–13	56
27:9	57, 60
28:16	111
30:15	111
40–66	58
40:26	112
40:28	112
42:5	112
43:1	149
43:4–6	56
44:24	112, 120
45:12	112
45:18	112

45:22–24	118
46:6–7	115
48:13	112
49:1–3	90
49:2	90
49:5–6	56
49:7	91
49:16	83
51:16	90, 112
52:1	83
52:3	149
52:13–16	91
53:6	231
53:10–12	152, 230
53:11	196
53:12b	231
54:1	86
54:1–55:5	50
54:11–12	83
55:3	126
55:10–11	208
56	87
56:7	234
59:18	43
59:20	57
59:20–21	60
60:10–11	83
61:1	100
64–66	23, 69
65:15	111
65:17	21–22, 71, 83
66:18–21	56
66:18–24	58
66:22	21–22, 71, 83

Jeremiah

3:11	56
3:18	56
10:12	113
11:16–17	59
16:14–15	56
17:10	43
23:5	97
23:5–6	56, 60
23:5–8	56
30:1–11	56, 60

30:9	97, 126
31	56, 57, 59, 251
31:7–14	56
31:11	149
31:31	57, 61, 126, 133
31:31–32	5
31:31–33	40–41, 160
31:31–34	39, 160, 165
31:32	41, 42
31:32–34	141
31:33	41, 57, 170, 230, 251
31:33–34	42, 61
31:34	57, 149, 159, 163, 207
31:34 [LXX 38:34]	252
32:37	56
33:15–26	126
33:25	97
34:18	143
38:11	149
38:34 LXX	163, 252
51:15	113

Ezekiel

1:28	110
11:17	56
11:19	42
11:19–20	171
20:1–44	56
34:11–16	56
34:23–24	97
34:23–25	126
34:23–31	56, 60
34:25	172
36	45
36:24	56
36:26–27	42, 165, 171, 251
36:27	44, 45
37	45
37:11–14	56
37:15–19	56, 60
37:15–28	56
37:24	97
37:25–27	126

37:26	172
40–48	83
42:13	238
44:29	238
47:13	56
47:21–23	56
48:1–29	56
48:30–35	56

Daniel

2:47	113
7	110
7:1–27	74
7:13–14	91
7:14	82, 234
7:25–27	216
8:1–27	74
9:24	148, 219
10:13	74
12:1–3	216–17
12:1–4	67
12:3	218

Hosea

1:9	58
1:10	57
1:11	56
2:23	57
8:13	238
9:4	238
11:10–11	56
12:2	43
13:4 LXX	112

Amos

9:11	97
9:11–15	56

Micah

4–5	87
4:1–2	234

Habakkuk

2:4	153

Zephaniah

3:9–10	233

Zechariah

2:5–9	83
2:10	56
8–10	87
8:13	56
9:1	56
9:9–11	126

Malachi

1	235
1:7	233
1:7–12	234
1:10–12	232
1:11	233
1:12	233

NEW TESTAMENT

Matthew

6:12	147
16:27	43
25:34–46	43
26:2	237
26:17–30	237

Mark

14:1–2	237
14:12–26	237

Luke

7:27	122
22:1	237
22:7–23	237

John

5:29	43
13:1	237
13:29	237
18:28	237

Acts

2:38	202
2:41	202
7:38	78
7:53	78
8:12–13	202

8:16	202
8:36	202
8:38	202
9:18	202
10:47–48	202
11:26	31
16:15	202
16:33	202
18:8	202
19:3–5	202
20:7	47
22:16	202
23:6–10	4
26:28	31

Romans

1:1	46
1:1–7	98
1:3	60, 102, 105, 126, 158, 251
1:3–4	99
1:4	99, 100
1:5	185, 188, 208
1:7	163
1:9	125
1:17	125, 157, 158, 196
1:18	124
1:20	212, 246
1:21–25	228
1:23	193
1:24	176
1:25	119
2:1	178
2:1–16	43, 176
2:3–13	175
2:5–6	176
2:5–16	208
2:6	175
2:7	193
2:13	175, 176, 178, 184
2:14–16	177
2:15	178
2:17	125
2:25–29	177
2:28–29	178
3:3	185, 188

3:9	61	5:21	134, 195–96	8:29b	199
3:9–20	61	6–8	72	8:30	199
3:19	26	6:1–4	252	8:30a	199
3:20	53, 175	6:1–7	203	8:30b	199
3:21	157	6:1–11	209	8:32	101, 156
3:21–26	157, 159	6:3	22	8:38	76, 77
3:22	187	6:3–4	81, 205	9–11	18, 29, 55, 57, 133
3:23–24	194	6:5	213	9:3–4	31, 32
3:23–25	149	6:6	22, 190	9:4	133, 166
3:24	130	6:7	190, 203, 205	9:5	98
3:24–26	184	6:11	23, 26, 125	9:6	29
3:24–4:5	25	6:11–14	26	9:6–8	28
3:25	130, 149, 151, 160,	6:14	26, 48	9:6–10:21	61
	194, 219, 220,	6:23	138, 147	9:11–12	134
	222, 230, 241	7:6–8:4	45	9:25	57, 58
3:26	186	7:7	53, 166	9:26	57
3:28	16, 17	7:10	251	9:27	28, 29, 57, 118
3:31	185, 208	7:12	48, 166	9:27–29	60
4:1–5	183	7:12–13	81	9:29	118
4:2–5	16	7:14	166, 251	9:30–32	19
4:3	183	8	57	10:1	19, 61, 124
4:3–5	164	8:1	172	10:1–4	16, 19
4:5	183–84, 185–86	8:3	102, 103, 104, 151,	10:9–13	19
4:6	53		160, 220, 238	10:10	61, 178, 208
4:7–8	118	8:8	125	10:10–13	188
4:10–11	153	8:9	124, 217	10:13	119
4:17	125	8:10	124, 196	11:1–5	29
4:25	101, 152, 190	8:11	213, 215	11:2–3	59
5:1	25, 186	8:14–16	198	11:6	162
5:1–2	193	8:15	199	11:13–14	19
5:6–8	137	8:17	217, 241	11:13–15	28
5:6–10	136	8:18	71, 193	11:14	29
5:8	129	8:18–19	71, 216	11:24	59, 60
5:10	101, 136, 137	8:18–23	70	11:25	59, 61
5:12	195	8:18–24a	215–16	11:25–26	28
5:12–13	166	8:19	212, 219	11:25–27	55, 60
5:12–19	105	8:21	193, 246	11:25–29	37
5:12–21	195, 252	8:22	58, 217, 246	11:26	10, 19–20, 28,
5:15	134	8:23	198, 218, 219		29–30, 36–37,
5:15–19	195	8:24	201		55, 60–61, 251
5:16	134, 172	8:25	193	11:26–27	57, 59, 60
5:16–17	196	8:27	163	11:27	57, 61
5:17	134	8:28–30	199	11:29	5, 37, 133, 166
5:19	196	8:29	163, 199, 209, 252	11:32	125
5:20	166	8:29–30	200, 207, 209	11:33	120
5:20–21	167	8:29a	199	11:34	118

11:36	120, 121	2:6–10	92	9:20	14–15, 48, 51, 54	
12:1	220, 221, 241	2:8	93, 126, 199	9:22	61	
12:13	163	2:9	5	10:1–3	245	
13:1–7	222	2:10	93	10:1–6	242	
13:14	200	2:13–15	243	10:1–21	248	
14	54	2:16	119	10:2	243	
14:8	125	3:6	244	10:3–4	242, 245,	
14:17	228	3:15	201		246, 249	
14:23	185, 208	3:16	124	10:4	244, 245	
15:9	118	3:16–17	194, 239	10:9	123	
15:11	118	3:20	118	10:14–16	47	
15:12	60, 99, 158	3:21–23	212	10:14–22	125	
15:13	124	3:23	108	10:16	212, 222, 227,	
15:15–18	168	4:3	178		228, 242, 248	
15:17–18	169	4:3–5	177–78	10:16–17	246	
15:18–19	124	4:4	178	10:16–18	231	
15:25	163	4:4–5	122, 201	10:17	119, 222, 224,	
15:25–26	87	4:5	178, 184, 208		226, 241, 247,	
15:26	163	4:15–16	46		248–49	
15:27	242	5:7–8	237	10:18	232, 233, 234,	
15:31	163	5:8	237, 248		239, 248	
16:2	163	6	202	10:19–21	227	
16:15	163	6:1	163	10:20	76, 227	
16:18	125	6:2	163	10:21	228, 232–33,	
22:12	156	6:2–3	122		249, 252	
22:16	156	6:3	80	11	132, 159, 231–32	
		6:11	197, 202, 205, 209	11:3	108	
1 Corinthians		6:15	202	11:10	76	
1–2	72	6:17	246	11:20	212, 223	
1:1	46	6:19	194, 239	11:21	223, 225	
1:2	233	6:20	136	11:23	231, 237	
1:7–8	70	7:23	147	11:23–24	140, 160	
1:8	71	7:25	125	11:23–25	242	
1:9	200	7:31	70	11:23–26	47, 132, 152,	
1:11–17	202	7:32	125		221, 229	
1:13–14	202	8	119–21	11:24	132, 230, 232	
1:13–17	243, 244	8–10	123	11:25	132, 133, 141,	
1:17	47	8:1–6	235		159, 232, 250	
1:18	201	8:4	109, 227, 228	11:26	225–26, 232, 245	
1:20–25	129	8:5–6	116, 123	11:27	225–26, 239	
1:23	252	8:6	96, 117, 119, 120,	11:27–29	249	
1:24	120, 127		123, 127, 128, 194	11:27–30	224	
1:28–29	124	8:8	228	11:29	225	
1:30	125, 130, 181	8:12	123	11:30	225, 240	
1:31	119, 125	9:11	242	11:32	122	
2:2	125	9:13	236	11:33–34	225	

12:1	243	3:2–16	40	**Galatians**	
12:2	85	3:3	40, 41, 165, 170,	1:1	46
12:12–13	211, 243		173, 196	1:1–5	135
12:13	81, 202, 205,	3:6	5, 38, 39, 41, 42, 46,	1:3	135
	243, 244,		49, 62, 165, 170, 196,	1:3–5	71
	245, 246		206, 251	1:4	72
12:14–27	202	3:7	41, 165, 172–73	1:8	77
12:26	220	3:7–11	172	1:11–17	92
12:27	215, 248	3:9	41, 159, 165,	1:12	92, 187
14:1–2	243		166, 172–73,	1:13	15, 65
14:33	163		196, 206, 208	1:13–14	14
14:37	243	3:10–11	41, 165, 173	1:14	15
15	216, 218	3:11	41, 42, 165, 172	1:15–16	187
15:3	129, 140, 230	3:14	46, 47	1:16	127
15:20	215	3:14–16	5	1:17	152
15:22	105	3:16	39, 46	2	203
15:23	100, 247	3:18	193, 246	2:11–14	222
15:24	77	4:1–6	47	2:11–16	34
15:24–28	108	4:3–4	46	2:11–21	35
15:28	212, 247	4:6	124	2:12	35
15:35	213	5:9–10	43, 208	2:14	35
15:36–37	214	5:10	176	2:15	11, 31, 32
15:43	246	5:11	125	2:15–16	54
15:44	213–14, 246, 247	5:15	197	2:15–18	189
15:45	215, 244	5:16–17	22, 71	2:15–21	184, 209
15:45–49	105	5:17	22, 72, 182	2:16	17, 35, 54,
15:47	250	5:21	152, 181–82,		125, 176, 186–87,
15:47–49	215		196, 197, 238		189, 191, 205
15:50	213	5:21b	182	2:16–17	25
15:51	214	6:1	168	2:16–21	189
15:51–53	246	6:18	118	2:19–20	80, 135,
15:52	214	7:1	125		189–90, 205
16:1	163	7:3	172	2:20	125, 136, 169,
16:2	47	8:4	163		193, 194
16:3	87	8:9	139, 253	2:20–21	167
16:15	163	9:1	163	2:21	167, 189
16:17	245	9:12	163	3:1–5:1	42
		11:14	76	3:2	191
2 Corinthians		12:1	85	3:2–5	191
1:1	46, 163	12:1–5	85	3:5	191
1:6–7	220	12:4	85	3:6	183, 191
1:21	100	12:8–9	124	3:6–9	153, 183
1:21–22	190	12:9	168	3:8	140, 191
2:10	124	13:5	248	3:9	192
3	41–46, 165–66	13:12	163	3:10	176
3:1–9	164, 165, 169			3:10–12	153

3:13	152	5:4	25, 167	3:10	180
3:13–14	154, 155	5:6	54, 185, 208	3:18–20	86
3:14a	156	5:16	136	3:20	51, 86
3:19	78, 80, 87,	5:24	136	3:21	214
	121, 127	5:25–6:1	243	4:21	163
3:19–20	78	6:2	63	4:22	163
3:21	192, 193	6:8	156		
3:23	187	6:14	22, 72	**1 Thessalonians**	
3:23–25	42, 188, 208	6:14–15	22, 71, 80	1:3	169, 185, 208
3:23–26	184, 185, 187	6:15	54, 67, 72, 80, 81	1:4	125
3:23–28	26	20:21	185	1:8–10	185
3:23–29	52, 78, 204			1:9	116
3:24	204–5	**Ephesians**		1:10	124
3:24–27	209	4:5	244	3:2–10	185
3:26	80	5:25	241	3:10	169
3:26–27	80	5:26	202	3:13	43, 163, 176
3:27	200, 204–5	6:12	242	4:5	125
3:28	222			4:10	169
4:1–7	52	**Philippians**		5:8	185
4:1–11	78	1:1	46, 163	5:23	43, 176
4:3	77, 78, 80	1:10	43, 176	5:23–24	169
4:4	103, 104, 105, 126	2	93, 118		
4:4–5	102, 198	2:5–8	93, 122	**Titus**	
4:4–7	198	2:5–11	102, 137	3:5	202
4:8	80	2:6	103, 105–7, 127,		
4:9	77, 78, 80, 87		138, 140, 160	**Philemon**	
4:9–10	80	2:6–11	105	5	163
4:14	121	2:7	104, 105, 106,		
4:21	50, 51		126, 138	**Hebrews**	
4:21–25	86	2:8	188, 252	2:2	78
4:21–5:1	60, 121	2:9	107, 108, 139	2:10	120
4:21–5:2	49	2:9–11	117	10:22	202
4:22	51, 87	2:10	126		
4:23	51	2:10–11	107	**1 Peter**	
4:24	48, 49, 51	2:12	103	1:17	43
4:24–26	86	2:12–13	168, 252	4:16	31
4:25	50	2:13	140		
4:26	50, 51, 86, 87, 94	3:4–6	32	**2 Peter**	
4:28	87	3:4–9	14, 15	3:15–16	1
4:29	51, 87	3:4–11	27		
4:31	50, 87	3:5	15, 32	**Revelation**	
5–6	72	3:7–12	209	2:23	43
5:1	51, 87	3:8	15, 179	20:12	43
5:1–3	87	3:8–9	180	22:12	43
5:1–12	81, 192	3:8–11	26, 179		
5:2	35, 51	3:9	179–80		

DEUTEROCANONICAL WORKS

Tobit

1:3	174
2:14	174
4:5	174
4:7	174
12:8	174
12:9	174
13:1	113
13:5	56
13:7	174
13:13	56
14:6–7	56
14:7	174
14:11	174

Judith

1:11	122
3:1	122
8:26	156

Additions to Esther

16:14–16	218

Wisdom of Solomon

2:13–20	218
5:4–5	218
7:22	113
8:4–6	113
9:1	113
9:1–2	120
9:2	113
13:1–5	115
16:1–13	218

Sirach/Ecclesiasticus

16:12–14	43
18:1	113
24:3	113
36:10–13	56
42:15	113
43:33	112
44–50	125
44:21	218

48:10	56
50:7	110

Baruch

4:37	56
5:5	56

Bel and the Dragon

5	112

1 Maccabees

1:44	122
2:52	174
7:10	122
14:35	185

2 Maccabees

1:24	112
1:25	113
1:27–29	56
2:7	56
2:17–18	56

3 Maccabees

6:28	218
7:6	218

4 Maccabees

1:4	174
1:6	174
1:18	174
2:6	174
5:24	174
7:12–14	156
13:12	156
16:20	156
17:21–22	150
17:22	219

OLD TESTAMENT PSEUDEPIGRAPHA

Apocalypse of Abraham

7:10	112
10:9	79
18:11–14	79

2 Baruch

4:2–3	50, 84
14:17	113
21:4	113
29:3	91
30:1	91
32:6	72
44:12	69
48:9	113
51:8	69
78:1–7	56

1 Enoch

1:7	68
8	74
10	74
14:1–22	82
14:19–23	79
21:1–4	75
21:10	75
22:14	126
24:1–25:7	82
25:3	126
27:3	126
27:5	126
37–71	125
40:1–7	79
40:3	126
46:8–47:2	217
48:2–3	91
48:2–7	89
48:6	90, 91
48:10	90
52:4	90
56:5–57:3	217
57:13	56
60:2–6	79
60:7	82
60:23	82
61:9–13	79
61:12	82
62:3–7	91
62:4–5	217
62:5–7	89
62:7	90, 91
62:7–9	91

70:1–4	82
71:15	68
72–82	75–76
72:1	72
72:4	72
82:7	76
82:8	76
82:9–11	76
82:10–20	76
89:59	74
90:33	56
91:5–74	217
93:1–10	217
103:15	217

2 Enoch

8:1	83
8:3	83
33:4	112
47:3–4	112
66:4	112

4 Ezra

3–12	74
3:4	112
6:38	113
7:12–13	68
7:26	50
7:26–27	83
7:28–29	91
7:50	69
7:75	72
8:21–22	79
8:52	50, 83
12:31–32	97
13:1–52	91
13:12–13	56
13:25–26	90
13:26	91
13:32	90, 91
13:32–36	84
13:32–50	56
13:36	50
13:37	91
13:51	90
13:51–52	90

13:52	91
14:9	91

Joseph and Aseneth

12:1–2	112

Jubilees

1:15–17	56
1:27–29	78
1:28	56
4:26	72
12:3–5	112
12:4	113
15:31	74
23:11–31	217

Sibylline Oracles

frag. 1:5–6	112
2:170–73	56
frag. 3	112
3:20	113
3:20–35	112
3:182–95	217
3:704	218
8:375–76	112

Psalms of Solomon

8:28	56
11:1–9	56
17:4–10	97
17:11–32	217
17:21	97
17:26–37	56
17:31	56, 60

Testament of Abraham A

9:6	113

Testament of Abraham B

8:2–16	83

Testament of Benjamin

9:2	56
10:11	56

Testament of Job

2:4	112

Testament of Joseph

19:3–8 [Arm.]	56

Testament of Levi

17:10–11	148
18:9	148

Testament of Moses

9:1–7	217
10:7	113

Testament of Solomon

8:1–2	75
8:4	75

RABBINIC LITERATURE

Amidah

10th benediction	56

Gen. Rab.

98:2	56

m. Sanh.

10:1	30
10:3	56

m. Sotah

7:5–6	111

m. Tamid

3:9	235
6:1–3	235

m. Yoma

5:1	235

b. Pesaḥ

59b	239

b. Yebam.

40a	239

90a   239

b. Yoma
68b   239

DEAD SEA SCROLLS

CD
6:19   48
8:21   48
19:33–34   48
20:10–12   48

CDᵃ
1:4–17   217
6:19   220
7:18–21   97

1QpHab
2:4–6   48

1Q22
3:1–12   148

1QS
1:17–18   217
3:6–10   45
3:23   217
4:18–23   217
7:4   219
8:1–3   217
9:8–11   217
9:20–22   45

1Q28a
2:11–12   99

1Q33
1:2–3   56
2:7–8   56
3:3–14   56
5:1–2   56

1QHᵃ
9:7   113
9:14   113

9:19–20   113
11:9–10   217

1QM
1:11–12   217
15:1–3   217
16:15–17:3   217
17:8–9   217

4Q169
3–4 i 8   154

4Q171
ii 9–12   219
ii 9–19   217

4Q174
1 i 18–19   217
1 i 21   97, 99
1 ii 1–7   217

4Q177
ii 8–11   217

4Q252
5:1–5   97
5:3–4   99

4Q285
5:2–3   97

4Q369   99

4Q373
1:6–20   56

4Q448
B 3–6   56

4Q504
1–2 vi 10–13   56

4Q544
1 i 13–25   56

4QDeutj   74

4QMMT   52

11Q13
2:4–6   148
2:6–8   154
2:18   155
2:24   155

11Q19
17:6–9   237
18:14–16   56
39:12–13   56
40:11–14   56
41:1–11   56
57:5–6   56

JOSEPHUS AND PHILO

Josephus

Against Apion
2.192   112

Jewish Antiquities
1.232   156
2.275–76   111
3.240   145
14.451   122
15.136   78
18.29   237

Jewish War
5.218   120

Philo

Allegorical Interpretation
3.207–8   110

Life of Adam and Eve
1   78

Moses
2.114   111

On Dreams
1.140–44   78

1.229–30	110
2.231–32	107

On Rewards and Punishments

164–72	56

On the Cherubim

127	120

On the Confusion of Tongues

179	112

On the Creation of the World

72–75	112

On the Decalogue

65	116

On the Special Laws

3.151–52	154

Questions and Answers on Genesis

2.62	110

PAPYRI

Oxyrhynchus Papyri

110	227
523	227
1484	227
1755	227

APOSTOLIC FATHERS

Acts of Paul and Thecla

3:3	2

CLASSICAL AND ANCIENT CHRISTIAN WRITINGS

Aristotle

Nicomachean Ethics

5.1.3	174

Augustine

On the Spirit and the Letter

8.14	44

Cyril of Jerusalem

Mystagogic Catechesis

5–6	235
9	235

Dio Cassius

Roman History

59.28.8	109
59.30.1	109

Eusebius

Proof of the Gospel

1.10	235

Irenaeus

Against Heresies

4.17.5	235
5.Pr.1	210

John Chrysostom

Homilies on 1 Corinthians

30.2	244

Justin Martyr

Apology

1.66.2	249

Dialogue

31.3	235

Origen

On Leviticus

13	235

Plato

Republic

Book IV	174

Seneca

De beneficiis	135

Tertullian

Against Marcion

3.22	235